PUBLICATIONS

OF THE

NAVY RECORDS SOCIETY

VOL. 132

THE BEATTY PAPERS
Selections from the Private and Official
Correspondence and Papers
of Admiral of the Fleet Earl Beatty

Volume II
1916–1927

THE BEATTY PAPERS

Selections from the Private and Official
Correspondence and Papers
of Admiral of the Fleet Earl Beatty

Volume II
1916–1927

edited by

B. McL. RANFT M.A. D.Phil. F.R.Hist.S.

*Formerly Professor of History, Royal Naval College,
Greenwich
Visiting Professor and Senior Research Fellow
Department of War Studies, King's College, London*

PUBLISHED BY SCOLAR PRESS
FOR THE NAVY RECORDS SOCIETY
1993

Published by
SCOLAR PRESS
Gower House
Croft Road
Aldershot
Hants GU11 3HR
England

Ashgate Publishing Company
Old Post Road
Brookfield
Vermont 05036
USA

British Library CIP data is available

Library of Congress Cataloging-in-Publication Data

Beatty, David Beatty, Earl, 1871–1936.
 The Beatty papers.

 (Publications of the Navy Records Society; vol. 132)
 Includes indexes.
 Contents: v. 1. 1902–1918—v. 2. 1916–1927.
 1. Beatty, David Beatty, Earl, 1871–1936—
Correspondence. 2. Great Britain. Royal Navy—Biography.
3. Admirals—Great Britain—Correspondence. 4. Great
Britain—History, Navy—20th century. I. Ranft, Bryan.
II. Title. III. Series.
DA70.A1 vol. 128. etc.   359′.00941 s   88–24517
[DA89.1.B4]   941.082′092

ISBN 0–85967–964–0

Phototypeset by Intype, London
Printed and bound in Great Britain by
the University Press Cambridge

THE COUNCIL
OF THE
NAVY RECORDS SOCIETY
1993

CONTENTS

MAPS AND ILLUSTRATIONS

Frontispiece

'The Day of Surrender': Admiral Beatty acknowledging the cheers of the men of the Grand Fleet, 21 November, 1918 (by courtesy of Hodder & Stoughton Ltd and New English Library Ltd).

Maps and Diagrams

PREFACE

The first volume of Lord Beatty's papers published by the Society in 1989 concentrated on his sea career, particularly during the Great War of 1914–1918, and consists, with relatively few exceptions, of selections from his own papers preserved in the National Maritime Museum at Greenwich. This, its successor, is concerned with his time as First Sea Lord, 1919–1927, when his most important role was on the national and international political stage. Therefore, although his own papers, including his letters to his wife, predominate numerically, there is far greater resort to other archives, in particular to the papers of the Admiralty, the Cabinet and the Chiefs of Staff in the Public Record Office, and to the papers and diaries of those politicians with whom he was most closely concerned. Similarly, because the Jutland controversy figured so largely in Beatty's life, papers of Lord Jellicoe, Admiral Sir Hugh Evan-Thomas, Vice-Admiral J. E. T. Harper and Viscount Long, in the British Library have been included. The other principal archive used is that of Churchill College Cambridge, concentrating on the Shane Leslie/Godfrey-Fausset Papers and those collected by Captain Stephen Roskill, whose own outstanding publications, *Admiral of the Fleet, Earl Beatty; The Last Naval Hero; An Intimate Biography* (1981) and *Naval Policy Between the Wars, Vol I (1919–1929)* (1968) have proved trustworthy pilots through the mass of relevant documents. Similarly, Professor A. Temple-Patterson's *The Jellicoe Papers, Vol II* (NRS 1968) with its Appendix of the Harper Papers, has provided a sure foundation for the section on the Jutland Controversy.

The guiding editorial principle has been to reproduce the documents as accurately as possible. The only alterations have been to Beatty's extraordinary punctuation and over-use of capitals. When omissions of insignificant material have been made, longer passages are indicated by * * * * and those of a few words by . . . . Where handwriting has made interpretation difficult, doubtful words are marked [?] and completely illegible ones [–] according to the number of missing words. Dates are printed as

Beatty and his correspondents wrote them, and shown in parentheses when approximated by the interpretation of postmarks on envelopes or internal evidence. His wife's addresses have been included whenever ascertainable as illustrative of her activities and way of life. Salutations have been included only when they illuminate the personal relationship between correspondents. All editorial material is in brackets and the numerals in the Section Introductions are designed to draw attention to the more significant of the succeeding documents.

ACKNOWLEDGEMENTS

My gratitude is due to the following owners and custodians of documents for access to their archives and for permission to print selected papers. I am also grateful to the staffs of these archives for their courtesy and helpfulness during my visits.

> The gracious permission of Her Majesty the Queen to publish letters from the Royal Archives
> The Right Honourable Lord Amery of Lustleigh
> The Clerk of the Records Office House of Lords, and the Trustees of the Beaverbrook Foundation
> The Director and Trustees of the National Maritime Museum
> The Keeper of the Public Records
> The Librarian and Syndics of the University Library, Cambridge
> The Manuscripts Librarian of the British Library
> The Master, Fellows and Scholars of Churchill College in the University of Cambridge.*

Many friends and colleagues have generously helped me with their time and knowledge, particularly Tony Bennell and Sebastian Cox of the Air Historical Branch, Ministry of Defence; Hugh l'Étang, with medical advice; David French, with his wide-ranging knowledge of the political and social background to Beatty's career; Andrew Lambert and Eric Grove with their expertise in the history of the nineteenth and twentieth century Royal Navy; David Lyon of the National Maritime Museum with his unique knowledge of maritime technological development; and Peter Howard for reproducing the plans of Singapore.

Sylvia Smither has interpreted my increasingly untidy drafts with daring and perspicacity. Tony Ryan, the Society's Honorary General Editor has been constantly encouraging during an overlong period of gestation, and my wife has accepted a second overflow of papers into our home with exemplary patience and support.

---

* For details of the collections consulted and used, see page 480 below.

The Navy Records Society and myself are most grateful to the Leverhulme Trust for the award of an Emeritus Fellowship which has covered a substantial part of the editorial expenses of this volume, after having totally met those of its predecessor.

Finally I wish to put on record all that I owe to my parents, Allan and Wilhelmina Ranft for encouraging me to become a historian; to Bob Bunn, Vivian Galbraith, Richard Southern and Humphrey Sumner, who set me high standards of research and writing; and to Michael Lewis and Christopher Lloyd whose outstanding work aroused my interest in naval history.

GLOSSARY OF ABBREVIATIONS

AA	Anti-aircraft
ACNS	Assistant Chief of Naval Staff
AFO	Admiralty Fleet Order
AG	Accountant General
BCF	Battle Cruiser Fleet
BCS	Battle Cruiser Squadron
BS	Battle Squadron
CAS	Chief of Air Staff
CID	Committee of Imperial Defence
CIGS	Chief of Imperial General Staff
C-in-C	Commander-in-Chief
CMB	Coastal Motor Boat
CNS	Chief of Naval Staff
COS	Chief(s) of Staff
DCNS	Deputy Chief of Naval Staff
DD	Deputy Director
DNC	Director Naval Construction
DNI	Director Naval Intelligence
DNO	Director Naval Ordnance
DNOT	Director Naval Ordnance and Torpedoes
DOCD	Director Communications Division
DOD	Director Operations Division
DOGD	Director Gunnery Division
DTSD	Director of Training and Staff Duties
E-in-C	Engineer-in-Chief
ERA	Engine Room Artificer
FAA	Fleet Air Arm
GCB	Knight Grand Cross of the Order of the Bath
GF	Grand Fleet
HM	His Majesty's (ship)
HS	High Seas (Fleet)
ID	Intelligence Division of Naval Staff
ISL	First Sea Lord
KG	Knight of the Garter

(N)	Navigation Specialist
NMM	National Maritime Museum
NRS	Navy Records Society
OM	Order of Merit
PAS	Principal Assistant Secretary
PM	Prime Minister
PZ	Flag Signal for Tactical Exercises and applied to Exercises themselves
RA	Rear-Admiral
RAF	Royal Air Force
RE	Royal Engineers
RFC	Royal Flying Corps
RM	Royal Marines
RN	Royal Navy
RNAS	Royal Naval Air Service
RNR	Royal Naval Reserve
RNVR	Royal Naval Volunteer Reserve
(S)	Supply or Submarine
SL	Sea Lord
S/L	Searchlight
SM	Submarine
SNO	Senior Naval Officer
USN	United States Navy
VABCF	Vice-Admiral Battle-Cruiser Force
WT	Wireless Telegraphy

THE NAVAL CAREER OF ADMIRAL OF THE FLEET EARL BEATTY, 1884–1927

The following is extracted from the Official Record of his Services and Appendix II of W. S. Chalmers, *The Life and Letters of David Beatty, Admiral of the Fleet* (London, 1951)

Ship	Rank	[Period of service] From	To
Britannia	Cadet	15 Jan. 1884	14 Jan. 1886
Alexandra	Cadet	15 Jan. 1886	14 May 1886
Alexandra	Midshipman	15 May 1886	20 July 1888
Cruiser	Midshipman	21 July 1888	20 Oct. 1888
Alexandra	Midshipman	21 Oct. 1888	19 Mar. 1889
Duke of Wellington	Midshipman	20 Mar. 1889	14 Sep. 1889
Ruby	Midshipman	15 Sep. 1889	13 May 1890
Ruby	Sub-Lieutenant	14 May 1890	15 May 1890
Duke of Wellington	Sub-Lieutenant	16 May 1890	10 June 1890
Ruby	Sub-Lieutenant	11 June 1890	31 Aug. 1890
Duke of Wellington	Sub-Lieutenant	1 Sep. 1890	1 Sep. 1890
Excellent	Sub-Lieutenant	2 Sep. 1890	13 Jan. 1892
Victory II	Sub-Lieutenant	14 Jan. 1892	4 Feb. 1892
Nile	Sub-Lieutenant	5 Feb. 1892	6 July 1892
Victoria and Albert	Sub-Lieutenant	7 July 1892	30 Aug. 1892

Ruby	Lieutenant (Seny. 25 Aug. 1892)	31 Aug. 1892	30 Sep. 1893
Camperdown	Lieutenant	1 Oct. 1893	2 Oct. 1895
Trafalgar	Lieutenant	3 Oct. 1895	18 May 1896
Victory I	Lieutenant	19 May 1896	2 June 1896
Egyptian government	Lieutenant	3 June 1896	19 Nov. 1896
Ranger (in command)	Lieutenant	9 Jan. 1897	30 June 1897
Egyptian government	Lieutenant	1 July 1897	24 Oct. 1898
	Commander	15 Nov. 1898	
Barfleur	Commander	20 Apr. 1899	12 Sep. 1900
Duke of Wellington	Commander	13 Sep. 1900	30 Sep. 1900
	Captain	9 Nov. 1900	
Juno	Captain	2 June 1902	17 Dec. 1902
Arrogant	Captain	3 Nov. 1903	29 Sep. 1904
Diana	Captain	30 Sep. 1904	11 Oct. 1904
Mars	Captain	12 Oct. 1904	24 Oct. 1904
Suffolk	Captain	25 Oct. 1904	19 Sep. 1905
Victory I	Captain	20 Sep 1905	14 Oct. 1905
Naval Adviser, Army Council	Captain	21 Dec. 1906	14 Dec. 1908
Queen	Captain	15 Dec. 1908	3 Jan. 1910
	Rear-Admiral	1 Jan. 1910	
Naval Secretary to First Lord	Rear-Admiral	8 Jan. 1912	1 July 1912
Aboukir	Rear-Admiral	2 July 1912	27 July 1912
Naval Secretary to First Lord	Rear-Admiral	28 July 1912	8 Jan. 1913
Lion	Rear-Admiral	1 Mar. 1913	2 Aug. 1914
Lion	Act Vice-Admiral	2 Aug. 1914	28 Jan. 1915
Princess Royal	Act Vice-Admiral	29 Jan. 1915	8 Apr. 1915

Lion	Act Vice-Admiral	9 Apr. 1915	8 Aug. 1915
Lion	Vice-Admiral	9 Aug. 1915	27 Nov. 1916
	Act Admiral	27 Nov. 1916	
Iron Duke	Act Admiral	28 Nov. 1916	15 Feb. 1917
Queen Elizabeth	Act Admiral	16 Feb. 1917	31 Dec. 1918
Queen Elizabeth	Admiral	1 Jan. 1919	2 Apr. 1919
Queen Elizabeth	Admiral of the Fleet	3 Apr. 1919	7 Apr. 1919
President	Admiral of the Fleet	8 Apr. 1919	31 Oct. 1919
First Sea Lord	Admiral of the Fleet	1 Nov. 1919	29 July 1927

GENERAL INTRODUCTION

Volume I of *The Beatty Papers* ended with the Commander-in-Chief receiving the surrender of the German Fleet at Scapa Flow and his rising anxiety about the terms of the naval armistice. This second volume covers the final phase of his career, in which he exchanged *Queen Elizabeth's* bridge for the First Sea Lord's office and the North Sea for the political jungle of Whitehall. Beyond the jungle was a world radically transformed from that of 1914. Yet there was marked continuity in Beatty's cares and concern. Behind the worry about the terms of the naval armistice was the theme which was to dominate his term of office, the maintenance of Britain's world-wide naval supremacy. The very fact that the High Seas Fleet was there at all in such material fighting strength because of the failure to destroy it at Jutland, was to haunt his mind and affect his conduct for the remainder of his life. The scuttling of the German ships in June 1919 was to end both his hope that the best of them might be acquired by Britain, and his apprehension that instead, they might be allocated to some of her wartime Allies and thus make the task of maintaining capital ship superiority more difficult. It was, in the event, to prove impossible. In the face of Britain's economic weakness and the determination of the United States not to agree to naval inferiority he had to accept the numerical equality of the Washington Treaty and to struggle hard to prevent its extension from capital ships to cruisers, which, he was to argue, took no account of the two countries' different strategic requirements. It was not that Beatty saw war with America as a realistic possibility, despite the anti-British rhetoric of many American naval authorities, but that he clearly understood the vulnerability of an Empire, held together by sea communications, to naval challenges in distant waters. As can be seen from the documents, he very soon began to identify Japan, with her growing naval strength and her clear intentions of taking advantage of China's internal weakness, as the most immediate threat to British interests. In case of war he was rightly sceptical of America's support, and apprehensive that the existence of a superior United States Navy might hamper Britain's freedom of strategic and political action. Moreover he fully appreciated that ability to operate successfully in the Far East depended not only on fleet strength but equally upon the existence of a fully equipped secure base, hence his prolonged struggle with successive governments over Singapore.

Beatty saw his central responsibility as First Sea Lord as one of persuading governments of the correctness of his strategic principles and of the necessity of providing the resources to put them into practice. This was essentially a political task and depended on his ability to maintain continuously good working relationships with ministers, beginning with his own political chief, the First Lord of the Admiralty, of whom there were five during his term of office. If they did not back him in Cabinet and in interdepartmental negotiations, especially with the Treasury and its political head, the Chancellor of the Exchequer, his plans for the Navy would fail. Walter Long, having overcome his original dislike of Beatty's conduct before becoming First Sea Lord, proved, as far as his poor health allowed, a strong supporter, as did Leopold Amery, Lord Chelmsford and William Bridgeman. All of them accepted his views as professionally authoritative, respected his powers of argument and persuasion, and outside formal Cabinet meetings, were content to leave the presentation of the Navy's case to him. Amery, the strongest political figure among them, did however restrain him when he appeared to be threatening unconstitutional behaviour during the controversy on naval aviation. The one exception to these generally productive relationships was with Lord Lee of Fareham who led the British naval delegation at Washington. Their mutual dislike and distrust were not ameliorated by the publicly expressed views of their respective wives.

The Treasury and the Chancellor were inevitable critics and here Beatty encountered two very different opponents, Philip Snowden and Winston Churchill. Snowden, in the first Labour government of 1924, obsessed by the need to reduce national expenditure, and sharing with many of his colleagues an instinctive dislike of militarism and imperialism, was bound to be a resolute opponent. Churchill's attitude was much more complex. As Secretary for War and Air in Lloyd George's Coalition government (1919–22), he gave Beatty strong support. But when he returned to the Conservative Party and became Chancellor in 1924, he was one of the strongest Cabinet critics of the cruiser programme, dismissed Beatty's apprehension of Japan, and rejected his pleas for granting a marriage allowance to naval officers. Beatty's potentially strained relations with the Labour government were made easier by the appointment of the politically neutral Lord Chelmsford as First Lord, and Beatty made his own contribution by winning the co-operation of the Trade Union MPs who occupied the junior political appointments in the Admiralty. Even Ramsay MacDonald who, as Prime Minister and Foreign Secretary, took the decision not to proceed with the Singapore base, made it clear that he did so on the wider political aim of encouraging disarmament and the peaceful resolution of international disputes, two of his party's highest ambitions, rather than on any rejection of Beatty's strategic arguments. Eventually he gave his support to the cruiser programme despite opposition within his party. On one issue of political persuasion, however, Beatty did definitely fail. Three Conservative administrations between 1922 and 1927 refused to accept his case for the revival of a Fleet Air Arm totally under Admiralty control.

In one respect Beatty's professional views were strongly conservative. He remained convinced that all the experiences of the war and the prospects of technological development over the next ten years at least, left the capital ship as the determinant of sea warfare. Neither the submarine nor the aircraft could supplant it. The former could be countered by the development of location systems and appropriate weapons, while the latter was important, but as an adjunct to the surface fleet. All his attempts to regain Admiralty control over maritime air power were based on the argument that the tasks required were specifically naval, essential to enable the battle fleet to fulfil its decisive role. Therefore it had to be manned by navally trained airmen, and tactically and strategically deployed and controlled by naval commanders. The documents printed in this volume contain no evidence that Beatty took any direct part in influencing the design and development of aircraft and their equipment for this maritime role. It may well be that Professor Geoffrey Till's forthcoming volume of *Documents on the Naval Air Service* will cast light on this.

On other professional matters Beatty was more progressive. His experience of the inadequacy of Admiralty staff work during the war had already convinced him of the necessity of a fully effective Naval Staff. The heavy demands made on himself and the Admiralty by the Cabinet and Committee of Imperial Defence for papers and oral evidence for committees and enquiries led him to pay continuous attention to the strength and organisation of the Staff, and to defend it against the demands for economy which threatened to weaken it. Much of the success of his own performance, orally and on paper, stemmed from the Staff's preparation of relevant arguments and information.

Beyond the Navy itself, in the wider field of defence as a whole, and despite the bitterness of his disputes with Trenchard, the Chief of Air Staff, Beatty showed increasing awareness of the need for inter-service co-operation in strategic planning. The fact that his seniority and reputation made him the most obvious choice as Chairman of the newly instituted Chiefs of Staff Committee, no doubt reassured him that this could be achieved without impinging on the Admiralty's central role and responsibilities in Imperial Defence. He was even prepared, at least informally, to envisage the creation of a Ministry of Defence, provided that the existing three single service Ministers' posts were abolished, and that the Chiefs of Staff were made responsible directly to a new Secretary of State. More practically, and strongly encouraged by Hankey, Beatty took the lead in instituting the practice of the Chiefs of Staff producing a formal annual report on the state of imperial defence for the CID, and in recommending the foundation of what was to become the Imperial Defence College.

Beatty's involvement in the Jutland controversy can only be understood in the overall context of the nature of the battle itself. In the circumstances in which it was fought, the nature of the North Sea and its weather, and the strategic imperatives of the two naval commanders-in-chief and their political masters, there was high probability that any fleet action would be indecisive. Neither Jellicoe nor Scheer was likely to take the risks of incurring heavy losses which would impair their ability to discharge the wider strategic role for which their fleets existed. Both fought the battle under directives from their Admiralties which circumscribed their freedom of action, directives to which they both subscribed. Furthermore, the nature of the fighting, the ships and equipment available and the weather conditions of the day, made it literally impossible for any participant, including the commanders-in-chief and their subordinate flag officers, to know what was going on outside their close vicinity. It was therefore inevitable that their recollections of the battle differed widely and that any future attempts to produce an accurate account were bound to produce substantial disagreements. Add to this the fact that when the various British official narratives and analyses were being compiled under the direction of a Naval Staff whose senior members were predominantly drawn from the Battle-Cruiser Force, the clash with those who had experienced the battle from other points of view was inevitable. Jellicoe's remarks in Document 244 below are compelling on this point. Jellicoe was the first to enter the field with *The Grand Fleet* (1919) and was largely supported by Julian Corbett's *Naval Operations Vol. III* (1923). It was natural for Beatty and his associates to put their point of view. The documents in Part V below provide a basis for judging the merits of the methods they used. They also reveal how intemperate Jellicoe's supporters became.

Although no longer kept apart by service afloat, Beatty and his wife were still divided by her continuing and worsening mental instability and by the frequent trips abroad in which she sought diversion from her depression and unsuccessfully sought for medical help. Beatty wrote to her virtually daily while she was abroad, trying to cheer her and hoping to interest her in his own burdens and difficulties. His relationship with Eugénie Godfrey-Faussett continued and he was even able to prevail on her to accompany his wife on at least one of her foreign visits. In making any judgement on Beatty's character it must always be remembered that despite all the grief his wife caused him, he gave her his personal care until her death in 1932. His own came four years later.

PART I

FROM GRAND FLEET TO ADMIRALTY
October 1918–October 1919

INTRODUCTION[1]

Due largely to his own conduct Beatty's passage from *Queen Elizabeth* to the Admiralty was stormy. His ungraciousness to his predecessor, Wemyss,[2] resentment of the delay in confirming his appointment, and of what he saw as lack of consideration of his views on future policy and appointments, all combined to bring out the arrogance and inability to appreciate the position of others which he had shown in the closing stages of the war. These characteristics were deeply rooted in his combat experience. In addition to the inevitable heavy strain of over four years of continuous sea command, he had suffered sharper pangs of disappointment over his inability to bring the German fleet to decisive action. These rapidly became more bitter as his conviction grew that the failure at Jutland had been disgraceful and avoidable. As the fighting drew to a close he became gloomily apprehensive that the terms of the Armistice and the subsequent Peace Treaty would not reflect the Navy's vital contribution to victory, and that the Allies' political leaders, backed by their Army commanders, and unchallenged by a weak British Admiralty, would make significant concessions to the defeated enemy. These would not only obscure the Navy's triumph but in the longer term, would also threaten the maintenance of Britain's naval supremacy which was at the centre of Beatty's aspirations [1–3, 5, 14]. His immediate aim was to demonstrate to the world Germany's complete defeat by the visible ending of her naval strength. Looking further ahead, he was determined that any distribution of Germany's capital ships

[1]For the background to this section see *The Beatty Papers*, vol. I Part VI, pp. 378, 523–574, Navy Records Society (subsequently cited as *Beatty Papers I*); and Arthur J. Marder (1970), *From the Dreadnought to Scapa Flow*, vol 5, Chapters VII, XI, London and New York, (subsequently cited as Marder *From the Dreadnought*).

[2]Later Admiral of the Fleet Lord Wester Wemyss (1864–1933): entered RN 1877; first Captain of Osborne Cadet College 1900; Rear-Admiral 1911; 2nd Battle Squadron Home Fleet; 1st and 2nd Cruiser Squadrons 1914; Governor of Lemnos during Gallipoli campaign and Vice-Admiral 1915; C-in-C East Indies 1916; designated C-in-C Mediterranean but selected to be Deputy 1st Sea Lord 1917; Admiral and 1st Sea Lord December 1917; resigned and Admiral of the Fleet 1919.

among the Allies should not impair the supremacy of the British fleet. The prospect of the United States achieving their declared ambition of having a navy second to none, seemed to him a totally unacceptable outcome to the Royal Navy's years of struggle and loss.

The delay in the announcement of Beatty's appointment as First Sea Lord was due to a complexity of causes. Most immediate was the resignation on 11 December 1918 of Eric Geddes, the First Lord of the Admiralty,[1] who had given Beatty the impression that the move was imminent. His successor, Walter Long,[2] was not nominated until 16 January 1919, and his approval had to be gained. A further complication was the failure of a proposal to make Wemyss Governor of Malta, as well as Commander-in-Chief Mediterranean, to compensate for his removal from the Admiralty to make way for Beatty. This made Wemyss reluctant to go and Long, impressed by his tact and skill in the peace negotiations in Paris, was unwilling to press him. Those politicians who knew Beatty would have realised that he would be far less flexible in moderating Britain's naval demands in order to maintain Allied unity. Winston Churchill,[3] now Secretary for War, who knew Beatty best of all, had even stronger arguments in favour of delay. In a strong letter to the Prime Minister, Lloyd George,[4] he urged that Beatty should not be appointed until the government had finalised its policy for the heavy naval retrenchment which the general economic situation demanded, and had it accepted by the Admiralty. Beatty's possible opposition to such reductions would have been a political embarrassment [18]. Churchill was not unprepared for the long struggles over the Naval Estimates,

[1]Sir Eric Geddes (1875–1937): business man and specialist in railway management; made Controller of the Navy, a Board member and Honorary Vice-Admiral by Lloyd George, May 1917, and 1st Lord September 1917; Minister of Transport January 1919; Chairman of Cabinet Committee on National Expenditure 1922, which recommended drastic cuts in expenditure, including naval personnel, the 'Geddes Axe'.

[2]Walter, later Viscount Long (1854–1924): Conservative politician; Colonial Secretary 1916; 1st Lord of Admiralty 1919; resigned due to ill health 1921.

[3]Later Sir Winston Churchill (1874–1965): MP since 1900; joined Liberals from Conservatives 1904; Under-Secretary for Colonies 1905; President Board of Trade 1908; Home Secretary 1910; 1st Lord of Admiralty 1911; resigned after Gallipoli failure 1915; Minister of Munitions 1917–18; Secretary for War and Air 1918–21; for Colonies 1921–2; rejoined Conservatives 1924; Chancellor of Exchequer 1924–9; 1st Lord of Admiralty 1939; Prime Minister and Minister of Defence 1940–45; Prime Minister 1951–4.

[4]David Lloyd George, later 1st Earl (1863–1945): Liberal MP 1890–1945; Chancellor of Exchequer 1908–15; Minister of Munitions 1915–16; Secretary of War 1916–22; Prime Minister 1916–22; leader of Liberal Party 1926–31.

which as Chancellor of the Exchequer he was to have with Beatty in the 1920s.

Nor did Beatty help his own cause with the government. His claim that he should become Commander-in-Chief of the Navy as well as First Sea Lord, added to the clamour of the Northcliffe[1] press for his appointment, a clamour which he was rightly believed to have encouraged, must have aroused resentment [4, 7–9, 12–13, 17–20, 22–23].

However, when Beatty was formally offered the appointment on 24 September 1919, he accepted it on the customary terms and recognised the inevitability of reduced naval expenditure [26, 27]. Promotion to Admiral of the Fleet and Long's repeated and flattering assurances of their future close co-operation may have soothed his sense of grievance. In any event his sense of realism would have prevented his maintaining an attitude which could have endangered gaining the position to which he rightly felt he was entitled. But it would have been totally out of character for him to express any doubts about his conduct during the preceding months. Wemyss was of more sensitive stuff [30].

The final terms of the Naval Armistice and its consequences must also have reassured Beatty. Apart from the occupation of Heligoland, his major demands had been met. Although the High Seas Fleet did not formally surrender, it was interned under his custody, thus demonstrating, in Beatty's words, 'a great passive victory which has swept the enemy from the seas' [1–3, 14]. Its scuttling on 21 June 1919, after he had relinquished his command of the Grand Fleet, solved the problem of the disposal of its ships, but the underlying question of the future relative strength of the victorious naval powers remained.

Although he was not to assume his appointment until November 1919, Beatty had been preoccupied since the end of hostilities with the central question of Britain's place in the post-war world and the strength of the sea power upon which it depended. Superficially, his conduct was paradoxical. On the one hand he complained strongly that he was not being consulted by the Admiralty on the vital problems of naval policy, but at the same time refused

[1]Alfred Harmsworth, later Lord Northcliffe (1865–1922): after early career as a journalist in 1896, with his brother Harold, later Viscount Rothermere, acquired the *Daily Mail* and opened a new era in British popular journalism; in 1908 became chief proprietor of *The Times*; a prominent public figure during the war his newspapers noted for their critical attitude to political and military leaders; in 1917 Lloyd George made him Head of the British War Mission to the USA, and, in 1918, Director of Propaganda.

Long's invitation to come to the Admiralty, with his staff, to give advice or chair an enquiry. But this can also be seen as justifiable caution in not becoming involved until he could be confident of access to all available information and had the formal status to ensure that his views would be respected [10–11, 17, 19, 22, 28].

Beatty was certainly not ignored as far as documentary information was concerned. Papers sent to him provided clear outlines of the Admiralty's thinking on post-war problems. On one level it was concerned with attempts to digest and interpret the experience of the war, especially relating to the significance of submarines and aircraft [21]. On wider matters of national policy and strategy attention was focused on the new European situation in which there was no considerable naval challenge, and then turned further afield to consider future relations with the United States and Japan. The former had already clearly indicated that it was no longer prepared to accept British global naval dominance, and the latter was developing an attitude and potential to challenge Britain's political and economic interests in the Far East [25, 28–29].

Thus Beatty was not to come to the Admiralty without considered views on the fundamental problems which were to face him as First Sea Lord. His own thinking was generally in harmony with the positions the Admiralty had already taken. The question that remained was whether he would be able to muster the political and persuasive skills needed to convince governments, dominated by the need for national economy, to produce the necessary funding. He was very soon to face this issue in what he saw as the essential requirement to build new capital ships. As early as December 1918 he was uneasy about the Admiralty's proposals for post-war fleet strength and dispositions. In particular he was convinced of the revived centrality of the Mediterranean in national strategy, arising from Britain's increased responsibilities in the Middle East because of the collapse of the Turkish Empire. The destruction of Germany's naval power now made it possible to re-establish the Mediterranean Fleet as the pivot of Britain's global strategy. To be effective it had to consist of the most modern capital ships the government could be persuaded to build. He expressed no doubts about the heavy gun remaining the dominant naval weapon and although conscious of the new significance of maritime air power, he shared the views of the exceptionally air-minded Richard Phillimore, that its main function was as an auxiliary to battleship gun fire [5, 6].

1. Beatty: Notes on the Naval Armistice

[Holograph]

[BTY/7/11/2]   21 October 1918

The views of the Commander-in-Chief Grand Fleet, as expressed at the War Cabinet Meeting on Monday 21st October. To the Cabinet as a whole and to individual members of the Cabinet on the subject of:–

The Naval Terms of an Armistice

1. I assumed that the object of the War was 'The Destruction of German Militarism' —
From the Naval point of view 'The Destruction of German Sea Power'.

2. I asked whether the general circumstances of the war from the Military point of view made it necessary or desirable that we should have an Armistice? If the answer was in the affirmative I recognized that the Naval Terms proposed would most certainly prevent it at this juncture.

But if the enemy condition was such as would cause them to accept the Military Terms as outlined by the Field Marshals then it was possible that they would accept also the Naval Terms —

The military successes have been great and the Military Terms are commensurate with their achievements. The Navy made them possible and therefore shares in them.

The Navy also, has won a great passive victory, has swept the enemy from the seas, and rendered secure the vast lines of communications with our Allies, and permitted the trade of this country necessary for existence to continue.

Because our victory is a passive victory it is no reason why the Navy also should not reap the fruits of that victory.

We have built up a great military organization. But the British nation still exists upon sea power.

Although a platitude it is one which will bear constant repetition, that we may gain many victories on land but one defeat at sea and the Allies cause is lost. And inversely we may be defeated on land, but if we maintain our supremacy at sea the Empire will weather the storm.

Therefore in framing the Naval Terms, since our existence depends on our sea power, we must ensure that no enemy Fleet in being is left which can threaten our supremacy.

No compromise on this vital point is possible.

If there is to be elasticity in the Terms of the Armistice, it must be on the military side and not on the naval side.

It must be our particular case to safeguard the naval side of any Armistice with the enemy.

Our allies as land powers may be expected to safeguard the military side.

3. The question as to what approximation the Terms of the Armistice should have to the Terms of Peace —

It was apparently the opinion of the Cabinet that the time between arriving at an Armistice and signing the Terms of Peace would be long, even possibly as much as 12 months. It was also accepted that after living under conditions of an Armistice for so long, the possibility of returning to war conditions was highly improbable.

During the Armistice and in arranging the Terms of Peace (details), assuming the best will in the world, friction was bound to arise between the Allies, which would be intensified by the action of Germany who would devote every effort to sowing dissension. These factors make it very desirable that the Terms of the Armistice should be as nearly as possible the Terms of Peace. Therefore the Naval terms of the Armistice must be stiff and such that will achieve one of the objects for which we are fighting, 'The Destruction of German Sea Power' —

4. To achieve 'The Destruction of German Sea Power' and reduce Germany to 'The Status of a Second Rate Naval Power' it is necessary to lay down in the Naval Terms of the Armistice conditions which would be commensurate with the result of a naval action, i.e. the result of the Armistice to be what we expect would be the result of a naval action as regards the relative strength of the two forces. The question had been asked 'Would it not be sufficient for the enemy to surrender the whole of their submarines without humiliating them to the extent that would be entailed by surrendering the ships laid down in the Naval Terms?' I attach more importance to the surrender of the surface units of the High Sea Fleet than even to the whole of the Submarine Fleet. —

The power behind the submarine warfare of the enemy was the High Sea Fleet. Remove that power and the submarine menace would completely collapse. The removal of the High Sea Fleet would allow of the whole of the forces of the Grand Fleet being set free to tackle the submarine menace at its source, i.e. the enemy bases.

The bases could be ringed in by mine barriers, obstructions, and nets, which could be guarded by comparatively light patrols which could be continuous & of sufficient strength as the circumstances required.

The removal therefore of the High Sea Fleet means the removal of the one naval menace — the Submarine —. On the other hand if we insist on the handing over of enemy submarines and leave the High Sea Fleet intact, then the position of affairs so far as his relative strength (naval) is concerned is precisely the same as that which obtained at the commencement of hostilities. During four years of war the enemy built up a huge submarine fleet.

In four years of peace he can do all and more than this, and with the High Sea Fleet in being, and assuredly stronger than ever, Germany will again menace the sea power of Great Britain. As a consequence, sea power being vital to our existence, excessive expenditure on armament will be entailed at a time when the economic effect of such expenditure is likely to be serious.

Remove the power of the High Sea Fleet now, and definitely reduce the continental nation of Germany to that of a second rate Naval Power, corresponding to her geographical position and requirements, and *our* position at sea is at once secured. The threat of the submarine disappears and Great Britain in the future will be spared a race with Germany for sea supremacy. In stating that Germany should be reduced to the status of a second class Naval Power corresponding to her requirements, it was assumed that there was no intention of returning to Germany her lost Colonies. It is known [?] that in the exchange of notes between President Wilson[1] and the enemy the naval side of the matter had not been referred to.

Doubtless President Wilson in using the term 'Military' intended it to include Naval, Army and Air questions.

This however was not clear, and Germany will certainly, and in fact has, kept the discussion to the land side only.

It is very essential that the naval side should be kept clearly before them and dealt with separately and apart from the military side.

I would add that before coming to the decisions as formulated in

[1]Woodrow Wilson (1856–1924): 28th President of the USA, 1912–19.

the draft of the Naval Terms regarding the vessels which should be surrendered I have previously discussed the question with my Second-in-Command[1] and the Senior Flag Officers of the Battle Squadrons, and the naval opinion of the Grand Fleet as repre- sented by the knowledge and experience of these Flag Officers was emphatic and unanimous that these terms should be enforced. I had then discussed the matter with the Chief of the Naval Staff who was in entire agreement.

The questions such as the Baltic situation, the Russia [sic] Baltic Fleet and its possible employment by the enemy, the occupation of Heligoland and minor questions referred to in the Draft Terms of the Armistice, all of which affect the Naval Command in the North Sea were not touched upon and I presume are left over to a further discussion as stated by the Prime Minister.

2.   From Admiral Sir Rosslyn Wemyss

[Holograph]

[BTY/13/40/20]   French G.H.Q.

Sunday Morning Nov 10th [1918]

My dear David,

I received your letter of 7th Nov late last night, and read it with a great deal of regret.

You are surely under a misapprehension as to the general state of affairs, and certainly so as to my not taking you fully into my confidence. It is true that events have occurred so rapidly during these last few days that it has been impossible for me to talk to you, and letters and telegrams are, I am well aware, very inade- quate under such circumstances as now obtain. I had hoped how- ever that Fisher's[2] visit to you would have to a great extent eased the difficulty.

---

[1]Later Admiral of the Fleet Sir Charles Madden (1862–1935): entered RN 1875; Rear-Admiral 1911; 1st Division Home Fleet 1912; 3rd and later 2nd Cruiser Squadron 1913; COS to Jellicoe August 1914–November 1916; Vice-Admiral 1915; 1st Battle Squadron and 2nd in command Grand Fleet 1916–19; Admiral 1919; C-in-C Grand Fleet and, later, Atlantic Fleet 1919–22; succeeded Beatty as 1st Sea Lord 1927.
[2]Later Admiral Sir W. W. Fisher (1875–1937): entered RN 1880; succeeded Duff as Director of Anti-Submarine Division, Naval Staff 1917; COS Mediter- ranean 1919; Rear-Admiral and 1st Battle Squadron 1922; DNI 1926; 4th Sea Lord 1927; DCNS and Vice-Admiral 1928; 1st Battle Squadron and 2nd in Command Mediterranean 1930; Admiral and C-in-C Mediterranean 1932; C-in-C Portsmouth 1936; died in office.

As regards Heligoland. I am and have been quite aware of your views. Unfortunately the Prime Minister, in spite of his original dictum that the terms of Armistice should approach as nearly as possible the terms of Peace was, as I told you anxious to cut down the naval terms. We had a great fight about the number of ships and about the difference between surrender and internment and the Prime Minister as you know, gave me an assurance that none of the ships to be interned would be given back to Germany. Heligoland however he objected to strongly, and when speaking on the subject I was obliged to tell him, in reply to a question, that I considered that if in the terms of Armistice we got all the ships, the holding of Heligoland was not of such vital importance *now*, though eventually Germany would have to give it up — and this like the question of the colonies – will be a matter for the peace conference.

Naturally I should have liked to have obtained in full all that was asked for, but under the political and existing circumstances this was impossible.

The abdication of the Emperor, the mutiny in the H.S. Fleet, the change of government & now, today, the uncertainty whether Prince Max[1] is Chancellor or not, have all combined to entirely alter the atmosphere, and I don't feel at all sure that the German plenipotentiaries who are now here are empowered to act, or if they are, whether their signatures will carry any authority. They arrived without any cyphers — a courier has gone back — & that is all for the present. If there is any difficulty about handing over the ships I shall reserve the right to occupy Heligoland in order that you may take such steps as you deem necessary to enforce their delivery. I hope to be in Paris tomorrow evening, but what my movements will be after that I am quite unable to say now.

---

[1]Prince Maximillian of Baden (1867–1929): Chancellor of German Empire October–November 1918.

3. From Wemyss

[Holograph]

[BTY/13/40/22]   Admiralty
                                                      [12 or 13 Nov. 1918]

Since seeing Brock[1] yesterday and writing to you, I have had a little time to think about matters, and believe that it is worth while writing again and giving you an idea of the general atmosphere as it presents itself to my view.

There can be no naval officer who does not see the end of this war without a feeling of incompleteness & with the knowledge that that incompleteness does not arise from any sense of failure. We all feel it — deeply – at the Admiralty & realise how much more this must be the case with you in the Grand Fleet. The Navy has won a victory even more complete in its effects than Trafalgar, but less spectacular, and, because of this lack of display, one feels that the unthinking do not fully realise what the nation — indeed what the whole world, owes to the British Navy. The way in which this fact is being ignored, (I will not say studiedly ignored), the way in which Foch[2] and his part is being exalted by the Press and the politicians, is a matter not so much of resentment on our part, as of real national danger. It is impossible to protest — you & I are in the same boat in that way and any action on our part would only be attributed to personal motives.

For the last month I have been fighting with all my strength the battle of the Navy v. the politicians, not against Geddes, he has always been on our side — and a hard struggle it has been. The politicians wanted to cut down and cut about the terms of Armistice, and it was with the very greatest reluctance that they eventually consented to them as they stand today. Lloyd George helped to make the matter more difficult by originally saying that terms of Armistice should contain as nearly as possible terms of Peace, and then hedging — being in fact as shifty as is the nature of politicians in general.

[1]Later Admiral of the Fleet Sir Osmond de Brock (1869–1947): entered RN 1882; Captain of newly commissioned *Princess Royal* July 1913; Rear-Admiral 1st Battle-Cruiser Squadron 1915; COS to Beatty as C-in-C Grand Fleet November 1916; Vice-Admiral and DCNS when Beatty made 1st Sea Lord 1919; C-in-C Mediterranean 1922–5; Admiral 1924; C-in-C Portsmouth 1926; Admiral of the Fleet 1929.

[2]Foch, Ferdinand (1851–1929): Marshal of France; appointed to overall command of French and British armies March 1918 to combat Germany's last major offensive.

As for consulting you — well, I seem to have lived for the last 3 weeks in trains and motor cars, and much of my business has actually been conducted in the latter between Versailles & Paris. Conditions were perpetually, even hourly changing, & it was physically impossible to keep you more au courant than I did. I know that you had the feeling that you were originally short-circuited, but I think I explained all this to you on Oct 21st, and again to Brock yesterday, and believe that you will readily understand that nothing was further from my thoughts & intentions than ignoring the C-in-C, Grand Fleet. I think I may claim that the whole of my attitude ever since I have been at Admiralty will bear me out in this.

I have been having a hard and difficult time lately and am quite as irritated as you are with those who call themselves our masters. We both of us have the interests of the country & of the service at heart, and I believe that we have worked too loyally and closely together during the last 12 months to allow of any shadow of misunderstanding coming between us. Whatever happens do not let us allow *that* to happen. This fine old country of ours will want all honest men to stick together in the future, and on my part at any rate, I feel that my friendship for you and my sympathy for you in these trying times, is too great for anything of that sort.

I fear that the presence of these infernal soldiers & workmen on board *Köningsberg*[1] is not making your task more easy, but I know that you will deal with them as is fit & proper.

PS A smiling face does not always mean [?] a light heart.

---

[1] *Köningsberg*: German light cruiser bringing Rear-Admiral H. Meurer to receive Beatty's terms for internment of German fleet: see *Beatty Papers I* pp. 572–4 for Beatty's description of the occasion; the three delegates of the Sailors and Workmen's Council whom Beatty refused to meet were there as a result of the High Seas Fleet mutiny.

4. *Beatty: Memorandum to Admiralty*

[Copy]

[BTY/7/10/15]   [December] 1918

ARRANGEMENTS NECESSARY ON DISPERSAL OF THE GRAND FLEET, TO SECURE CONTINUITY AND UNIFIED DIRECTION OF POLICY IN MATTERS RELATING TO THE FIGHTING EFFICIENCY OF THE FLEET

1.   The German menace led to the concentration of the greater part of the British Navy in Home Waters.

The strategical situation during the war led to the evolution of the Grand Fleet.

2.   These conditions were highly advantageous to Naval progress and fostered the efficiency of the Fleet as a weapon of warfare. In all such matters as Fleet tactics, the employment of armaments and the rapid improvement of wireless communication, the concentration of the fleet and of the command of the Fleet greatly facilitated and fostered advancement.

3.   On a return to peace conditions the concentration of the Fleet is no longer possible, nor would it be advantageous to aim at any such concentration.

On the other hand, in so far as concerns the DIRECTION of professional effort towards solving the problems of Naval warfare, the improvement of weapons, and the training of the personnel, it is highly desirable that the successful organisation which has been evolved in the Grand Fleet, and the lessons which have been learnt during the war, should not be dissipated and lost.

4.   It should be remembered that concentration of command in the Grand Fleet has been accomplished side by side with devolution of responsibility for administration.

The Commander-in-Chief has kept to himself an absolute command over the disposition of ships, the duties on which they have been employed, and the time and opportunities allowed for exercises and training. The Commander-in-Chief has further directed the general policy and lines on which practices were to be carried out. Subject to these considerations, Senior Officers of Squadrons and Flotillas have been given the widest possible measure of freedom and have been entirely responsible for the command of their Squadron or Flotilla.

5.   One of the advantages of this organisation has been the possibility of rapid decision and execution, and in this respect it may fairly be claimed that the organisation of the Fleet has attained to a high standard of excellence.

6.   To ensure that the advantages of the Grand Fleet organisation are not lost at the present critical phase in world politics, it is considered that the 1st Sea Lord should be appointed as 1st Sea Lord and *Commander-in-Chief of His Majesty's Fleets* instead of 1st Sea Lord and *Chief of the Naval Staff*.

7.   It is understood that at the present time the 1st Sea Lord, in his capacity as CNS, has authority to issue, over his own signature, orders with regard to movements, operations etc of the Fleet. The proposal, therefore, to substitute the title of C-in-C for CNS does not involve any fundamental change in his relations with the Fleet or with the Board of Admiralty.

8.   The essence of this proposal is that the 1st Sea Lord should exercise in practice the functions laid down in theory in the Admiralty patent; the title of C-in-C will enable him to do so with an authority understood throughout the Service.

9.   In the Naval Service the title Chief of the Naval Staff does not convey any indication of authority which would justify the issue of orders to a Commander-in-Chief afloat, particularly when the latter is his senior in rank.

10.   Under the Naval System, Staff Officers have no executive authority of their own, and it would be a fundamental alteration in our tried and accepted system to allow such authority to any Chief of Staff.

11.   Alteration of the 2nd title of the 1st Sea Lord from CNS to C-in-C would establish beyond question his right to exercise the functions which he is understood already to possess. It postulates that he should be senior in rank to all other C-in-C's afloat, to affect which acting rank may become necessary.

12.   Possession of the title of CNS involves no such postulate, and the non-exercise of the powers which it was intended that the CNS should wield, is evidence that this disability was recognised. The title of CNS was a mis-nomer [*sic*].

13.   The allocation of these special functions to the 1st Sea Lord was intended to meet certain obvious requirements of war. The peculiar conditions which now exist render not only the possession of these functions, but their active exercise, very necessary.

14.   The international horizon may be clear at present, but

until the terms of peace have been agreed to and goodwill between the Nations is an established fact, the British Navy should be ready to reassume its war-time role at the shortest notice. This cannot be secured if divergent views and methods are allowed to establish themselves as a result of the dispersal of the Grand Fleet.

15. At a future date when the international situation has settled down, and the peace of the world is assured, it may be considered desirable to relieve the 1st Sea Lord of these functions, and leave him, as formerly, merely the Senior Naval Member of the Board.

16. The functions which the 1st Sea Lord would undertake by virtue of his authority as C-in-C of the Fleets are merely an extension of those now vested in the CNS, and would be exercised with the object of co-ordinating and directing strategy and tactics, the training of the Fleets, and their readiness for immediate concentration.

If concentration should become necessary at any time it would be equally necessary that the Squadrons involved should be so organised and trained as to admit of their being welded once more into a force possessing the striking power and efficiency of the Grand Fleet. This can be achieved only by unity of direction coupled with wide decentralisation for administration.

17. It also would ensure that the many important lessons which have been learnt during 4½ years of war as stated in paragraph 3 will not be lost.

18. It would be essential that all should have been trained on identical lines.

19. Great developments were still in progress in the Fleet on the cessation of hostilities, and their continuance after dispersal of the Fleet can only be assured by unity of direction.

20. It is presumed that the desirability of maintaining this process of development at the present time will not be questioned.

5. Beatty to Admiralty

[Copy]

[BTY/7/10/16] SECRET [December 1918]

Be pleased to lay before the Admiralty the following remarks in regard to the composition and strength of the post-war Fleets with special reference to the Mediterranean.

2. In examining the Admiralty draft proposals put forward for post-war fleets it is observed that circumstances are expected to permit of the manning of 23 battleships and 5 battle-cruisers on a First and Second Fleet basis. It is further observed that this number of capital ships has been arrived at on the assumption that the composition and strength of the Royal Navy in the immediate future must depend upon the total number of men which Parliament will authorise the Admiralty to maintain in the ensuing financial year; and that as a basis on which to work in determining the future strength of the Navy it is assumed that this number of men will probably be approximately 20 per cent less than the pre-war establishment.

3. It may be that the basis on which the calculations as to post-war strength have been made will provide a sufficient number of men to meet our requirements. But it is suggested that to start on the assumption that only a certain number of men will be provided, and from this basis determining the British naval strength, is wrong in principle. Rather should we first formulate the naval requirements to meet our national commitments, and from these requirements deduce the number of men which Parliament should be asked by the Admiralty to provide for manning purposes.

4. In determining the general policy as to the strength and distribution of HM Ships and vessels the governing principle may be thus stated:–

The strength and distribution should be such as adequately represents the national commitments and duties, including the maintenance and protection of the highways of the sea, the upkeep of communications with our colonial Empire and distant possessions, and the shewing of the Empire's flag in outlying waters.

Further, the distribution must be such that forces of sufficient strength are so placed that they can be concentrated with despatch, to deal with situations as they arise, and by their immediate presence uphold our prestige.

No other consideration should be permitted to weigh against this principle in determining our naval strength.

5. The traditional sea-policy of the past, in conforming to the principle above stated, has been to maintain British naval prestige at a high standard in the Mediterranean seas [sic], and prior to the German naval menace strong British squadrons were always

stationed in those waters. This policy was based on the fact that the Mediterranean is of immense trade importance, and the highway to our colonial Empire and possessions in the East. The sea is surrounded by multifarious nations, constantly in conflict, whose condition and reliance on British assistance in their political development make it of the first importance that our prestige should be maintained by a powerful naval force, and one commensurate with our responsibilities as compared with those of other Mediterranean nations.

6. The traditional policy was, it is true, departed from in 1912, with reluctance, and against opposition on the part of Field-Marshal Lord Kitchener,[1] who represented correctly that weakening of our naval force in those waters would have a far-reaching effect in the Near and even Far East. What the effect would have been on the general situation in 1914 if Lord Kitchener's views had been accepted it is unnecessary at this juncture to argue. Withdrawal of our outlying naval forces and concentration in Home Waters was decided upon and carried out in view of the rapid growth of the German Navy.

7. The German naval menace no longer exists. It is assumed the naval power of Germany will be destroyed by the Peace Terms, and that the necessity for Home concentration of our naval force will no longer obtain.

Therefore an orientation of our policy, in the direction of reverting to the maintenance of strong naval force in the Mediterranean, and adherence to the governing principle of distribution of naval force in foreign waters, should be immediately undertaken.

The extension of our responsibilities, consequent on the war, especially in Palestine, Syria, Arabia, Mesopotamia and East Africa, makes this matter, in the interest of world development, of even greater importance than it was prior to the war.

8. It is noted that in the preliminary Admiralty proposals there is no provision referred to for the stationing of capital ships in the Mediterranean. Indeed nothing larger than a flotilla leader is shewn under the heading 'Mediterranean'.

It may be urged in this connection that it would be sufficient to divert naval force from Home Waters for periodical visits to the Mediterranean, and as occasion demanded. Such a policy

---

[1] Field Marshal and 1st Earl Kitchener (1850–1916): commissioned in Royal Engineers 1871; British representative and virtual ruler of Egypt 1911–14; Secretary of State for War 1914–16; drowned in sinking of HMS *Hampshire* June 1916 when on mission to Russia.

would, in my opinion, in no way meet requirements, or be adequate to our duties. Critical situations arise with great rapidity. Our prestige and responsibilities demand that these should be dealt with by strong British naval force with equal rapidity, and without the delay and disorganisation inseparable from the dispatch of special squadrons from Home Waters.

9.   In my view, a force of six battleships and six light cruisers in addition to the vessels shewn in the Admiralty list should be appropriated to the Mediterranean.

10.   I have dealt in the foregoing only with the general strategic requirements necessitating British strength in the Mediterranean, and have not touched on the following important points —

(*a*)   value to the personnel and contentment resulting from a proportion of foreign service;

(*b*)   the excellent naval training ground the Mediterranean affords.

Both these factors are important and are additional arguments for departing from Home concentration and increasing our strength in the Mediterranean.

6.   *From Rear-Admiral R. F. Phillimore*[1]

[BTY/13/30/2]   *Furious*
                                                          25th January 1919

My dear Commander in Chief,

I doubt if it is generally realised by the Admiralty how great is the need for immediate action being taken as regards the Air Force in its relations to the Navy.

On the 1st December last, the strength of the RAF attached to the Grand Fleet (embarked and in Shore Stations) was slightly over 2000: of these not one single Officer has a permanent Commission and all the men are only entered for the War.

The Royal Navy has its demobilisation difficulties, but they are

---

[1]Later Admiral Sir Richard Phillimore (1864–1940): entered RN 1878; Captain of battle-cruiser *Inflexible* at Falklands battle and Dardanelles; Rear-Admiral and head of naval mission to Russia 1915; commanded 1st Battle-Cruiser Squadron 1916; Admiral Commanding Aircraft Carriers, a new post created by Beatty, March 1918; Chairman of Post War Questions Committee (which recommended the building of large fast carriers but still saw battleships as core of fleet) 1919–20; Vice-Admiral 1920; commanded Reserve Fleet 1920–22; C-in-C Plymouth 1923–5; retired 1929.

nothing in comparison with those of the Royal Air Force, which possesses, as yet, none of the 'esprit de corps' of the older Services.

This is not to be wondered at, when its 'pivotal man' 'par excellence', the Master General of Personnel[1] (one of the only three Officers in the whole Air Force with a permanent Commission) has accepted a position in a private firm, after having been given a KCB in the New Year's Honours and having been advanced from Major to Major-General during the War.

His example is naturally, and excusably, being widely followed by smaller fry, who have not got permanent Commissions but who have been informed in the most recent Air Ministry Weekly Order that 'it is not at present possible to state what rates of pay, pensions and allowances will attach to permanent Commissions in the Royal Air Force, but these will not necessarily be as good as the scales now in force'.

The bulk of the RAF Officers are keen and gallant young fellows and, if they feel compelled to search elsewhere for a livelihood, it is not surprising that the rank and file, many of them 'trench-dodgers', who joined for an easy, safe, job, are still more anxious to leave, and that strikes and other forms of discontent are the order of the day.

The newspapers have made good 'copy' of the unrest in the different RAF Stations, thereby of course increasing it. As at a neighbouring station the Commandant has been killed flying, (rumour states that circumstances pointed to his aeroplane having been tampered with), the Officer in Command of one of the Grand Fleet Stations now allows no single-seater to be flown and only two-seaters when a suspected ringleader of the malcontents is in the Observer's seat.

Yet the Grand Fleet is at present directly dependent on this unstable Force for part of its fighting efficiency, as, though the Air can do without the Navy, we in the Senior Service cannot now do without the Air, either for Reconnaissance or Gunnery. For the latter it is essential for spotting long-range shooting, for circumventing smoke screens and for indirect fire.

---

[1] The Master-General of Personnel was Major-General (later Air Vice-Marshal) Sir William Sefton Brancker (1870–1930): retired from RAF in order to develop civil aviation 1919; returned to Air Ministry as Director of Civil Aviation 1922; killed in loss of airship R 101, 1930. The other two officers with regular commissions mentioned were, Sir Hugh Sykes (1877–1954), a later Chief of the Air Staff, and Commodore Godfrey Paine (1871–1932), 5th Sea Lord 1917–18. Along with Rear-Admiral Mark Kerr he was a member of the Air Council from its establishment in 1918; retired 1920.

It has been found necessary to order the ships quitting the Grand Fleet for Foreign Stations to leave their machines behind — not that the said machines will not be required — but because there will shortly be no Air Mechanics to look after them!

The Air Force is dissolving under our eyes and taking with it part of our gunnery efficiency. The Navy can supply Officers and men for Air work, but if this is to be done, it should be done quickly. I have no hesitation in saying that there will be no lack of volunteers from the Officers of the former RNAS and the Navy could count on drawing on a certain number of our own ERAs, electricians and carpenter's crews, who could be specially trained.

Perhaps the Admiralty may have suffered from lack of imagination in the past, but very little of that quality is now required to foresee the development of the Flying Boat of to-day into the Flying Ship (heavier-than-air) of to-morrow, — Flying Ships that will moor in harbour alongside surface vessels and that will be the 'Eyes of the Fleet' when at sea.

One cannot imagine the khaki-clad Officer of a Shore Service standing in the shoes of Nelson's Frigate Captains!

'Command of the Seas' has been defined as control of sea communications: are the Admiralty prepared to delegate part of this duty to another service, and will the country allow them to do so, when they discover what is going on?

Now is the time — when the Royal Air Force is melting away — to step in and take the matter into our own hands.

Lastly, may I say — with all diffidence — that we in the Grand Fleet have first hand knowledge of these matters and are more competent to advise Their Lordships than anyone now serving at the Admiralty.

Yours sincerely,
(Signed) RICHARD F. PHILLIMORE

7. *Walter Long [1st Lord of Admiralty] to Beatty*

[Holograph]

[BTY/13/28/1]   Admiralty
                                                              25 Feb 1919

My Dear Sir David,

I have now been able to make myself thoroughly acquainted with the position as regards your coming here as First Sea Lord.

As I told you when I was on board your flagship I had heard

no dates definitely mentioned, but I believed it was contemplated that the changes would probably take place in June or July. I find this was also due to the belief that a post would fall vacant about this time which would be offered to the First Sea Lord & be acceptable to him. It turns out, however, that this was a mistake, & so far as I am able to judge no appointment which he could accept is likely to be open for some time to come. In these circumstances he will of course remain here for the present. I am very sorry there should have been any misunderstanding & still more sorry for any annoyance it has caused you.

I hope however that when the time comes you will consent to come here as First Sea Lord & give the Empire & the Navy the immense benefit of your great abilities & invaluable experience. Meantime I trust you will be willing to pay the contemplated State Visit to the USA: it will make all the difference in the world if you are in command.

I very much regret to learn that you are dissatisfied about the appointment of Flag Officers.

I can find no authority here for the contention that the Commander-in-Chief's opinion has always been asked on these appointments. On the contrary the First Lord has more than once made it clear that he takes full responsibility for them. No doubt during the war there were departures from the rule, but now the sea-war is over, &, alas!, the Grand Fleet is rapidly demobilising, & we must, in fairness to the Navy as a whole, & in the interest of well established Admiralty practice return to the old rule.

I shall be delighted to see you tomorrow.

Sincerely yours
WALTER LONG

8. *From Wemyss*

[Holograph]

[BTY/13/40/29]   Admiralty
                                                Friday, Feb 28th [1919]

My dear Commander-in-Chief,

The First Lord has told me of his interview with you on Wednesday last, and it is with great regret that I gather that you are displeased at the general state of affairs existing between the Admiralty and yourself — the Admiralty in this case probably meaning me!

I gather that you feel that you have three principal causes of complaint — 1. That you have been, and are being, generally ignored — 2. That you are not coming to relieve me immediately, — 3. That in the matter of appointments you have not been treated with the courtesy to which you are entitled.

As regards 1. I honestly am unable to convict myself of ignoring you or your opinions, much less of having any desire to do so.

As regards 2. you will remember the conversation that we had at Hanover Lodge. I came to talk to you on that occasion with the idea of finding out what you wished to do now that hostilities had ceased, and it was then for the first time that I realized that your desire was to come and relieve me. I then told you of what was at that time just a possibility, namely, that I might go out as Governor of Malta and Naval Commander-in-Chief; but I am afraid you must have inferred from our conversation something much more definite than I intended to convey. As I have since told you, I looked upon that friendly conversation as purely speculative. The possibility of my going to Malta has, for various reasons, fallen through. The situation, therefore, has quite altered since that day; and I am quite sure you do not desire to appear to be trying to push me out.

3. The question of appointments: on this I hold the view that they are matters for the Admiralty and not for the Commander-in-Chief. It is a principle on which I am sorry that we differ – but there is no reason, so far as I can see, why, because we differ on a principle that the difference should take a personal turn. With reference to lack of courtesy, it is an unfortunate accident that you should have heard, quite by chance through Keyes[1] himself of his contemplated appointment. You have been informed of the contemplated changes directly they were officially settled, which they had not been when you saw Keyes. He had only been approached privately on the subject. I need hardly assure you that no discourtesy was intended — and given the fact that you, as C-

---

[1]Later Admiral of the Fleet Lord Keyes (1872–1945): entered RN 1885; Commodore Submarine Service 1912; COS to Admirals Carden and de Robeck in Dardanelles 1915; commanded HMS *Centurion* in Grand Fleet 1916–17; Rear-Admiral commanding 4th Battle Squadron 1917; Director of Plans Admiralty October 1917; Vice-Admiral Dover Patrol 1918; attacks on Ostend and Zeebrugge April 1918; commanding Battle-Cruiser Force March 1919 [the appointment in question here]; DCNS 1921; C-in-C Mediterranean 1925–8; Admiral 1928; C-in-C Portsmouth 1929–31; Admiral of the Fleet 1930; retired list 1935; Conservative MP for Portsmouth 1934; Director of Combined Operations 1940–41; peerage 1943; Three volumes of *The Keyes Papers*, Paul G. Halpern (ed.), (London 1972, 1979, 1981) are published by the Navy Records Society.

in-C, were not to be consulted as to the appointments (a principle on which I know you differ from me) I trust you will realize that the procedure adopted, or about to be adopted, was correct.

I suppose it is more than can be humanly expected that two men, placed as you and I are, should see actually eye to eye on every subject that may arise, but that does not seem to be a reason for any personal feeling to be brought into the matter, and so far as I am concerned let me assure you that there is none.

Nobody realises better than I do the immensity of the work which you have done during the war, and nobody appreciates better than I do how the services that you have rendered entitle you to every consideration that can be shown; but I do feel that no consideration has been lacking on my part.

However, we are I hope too old and firm friends to quarrel about anything, much less a comparatively minor question, and I am certain you are as determined as I am that the Service shall not suffer as it must do if the C-in-C Grand Fleet and 1st Sea Lord are known to be at loggerheads. I can't believe that you wish to embarrass yourself when you eventually come to Admiralty. Won't you come & see me & talk matters over?

9. *To Wemyss*

[Holograph Draft]

[BTY/13/40/30]

Grand Fleet
1.3.19

Your letter of yesterday.

As to (1) 'That I have been and am being generally ignored.' This is a statement of fact which can be substantiated & therefore need not be enlarged upon in this letter.

As to (2), 'That I am not coming to relieve you immediately', my interpretation being, not for many months. My recollection of what has passed is in entire disagreement with yours. I was informed by the late 1st Lord[1] that *you wished to leave* the Admiralty, and I was asked if I would come as 1st Sea Lord, the date of my advent being the signing of the preliminary Peace. If this seemed likely to be delayed, his intention was to ask me to come in the first place in an additional capacity in order to avoid delays in reconstruction problems. The last 1st Lord was unable at the

[1]Sir Eric Geddes.

moment to ratify the appointment owing to the uncertainty of his remaining 1st Lord, but he said he would inform his successor of his intention should he leave, as his successor's concurrence would be necessary before the appointment could be confirmed. The last 1st Lord said other things to emphasise the importance of my accepting the appointment which it is unnecessary to enter into here. The same afternoon you visited me at Hanover Lodge and informed me point blank that you wished to leave the Admiralty, that the work would not be congenial to you and expressed a wish that I should come to relieve you and the opinion that I was the most suitable person for the appointment. This confirmed what I had learned from the 1st Lord, *i.e.* that the invitation to me to come to the Admiralty was not putting your nose out of joint. There was therefore nothing speculative about it, the only thing which might alter it was the possible advent of a new 1st Lord who disagreed.

The next step was the appointment of Mr Long, who, at my first interview informed me that he understood that I was coming to relieve you and that he looked upon it as a 'fait accompli'. On the occasion of the 1st Lord [*sic*] visit to me in *Queen Elizabeth*, he confirmed again that I should relieve you, the date being dependent upon the signature of Peace, as it was necessary that you should remain until then. Thus we have two First Lords inviting me to be 1st Sea Lord and the existing 1st Sea Lord informing me that he did not wish to remain. Again I will say that there was nothing speculative about it, which was moreover confirmed by the fact that you yourself informed others of the intended change, including Browning[1] who looked upon it as settled, just as I did. I would wish you to ask him as to the accuracy of this.

The fact that you were off with the old love before you were on with the new does not alter the situation, and I think that some consideration is due to an officer of my position, and that I should not be kept 'backing and filling' indefinitely, to suit your convenience, not to speak of the unfortunate effect that it would

---

[1]Browning, Admiral Sir Montague Edward (1863–1947): entered RN 1876; Captain 1902; COS to Lord Charles Berisford C-in-C Channel 1907; Inspector of Target Practice 1910–13; Rear-Admiral 1911; commanded 3rd Battle Squadron 1913; 3rd Cruiser Squadron 1915; C-in-C North America and West Indies 1916; Vice-Admiral 1916; 4th Battle Squadron Grand Fleet 1918; President of Allied Naval Armistice Commission 1918; 2nd Sea Lord March 1919; Admiral November 1919; C-in-C Devonport 1920–23; retired list 1926.

have upon the Service, a large number of which were acquainted with the contemplated change.

As regards (3), appointments, you state that the question of appointments is a matter for the Admiralty and not for the C-in-C. I would point out that you are wrong. It is not a matter for the Admiralty or the C-in-C but for the 1st Lord alone. You say that it is a principle upon which we differ. It is not however a question of principle but a question of fact. The fact being that before the 1st Lord makes an appointment, provided time permits, he consults those whom the appointment affects. In pre-war days this was invariably done, and has also been done during the war. During the latter period however, the views of those who were affected by the appointment were given far greater consideration than in pre-war days.

I would remind you that as I was Naval Secretary for a year, I know what I am talking about. It was a matter of common sense and common courtesy.

You state that in the incident of Keyes 'I should have been informed of the changes directly they were officially settled, which they had not been.' Obviously it would have [sic] futile to consult me after they had been officially settled, but even here there is inaccuracy, because Pakenham[1] had been informed that he would be relieved by Keyes before I even [?] saw Keyes!!!

My complaint of lack of consideration and courtesy is therefore well-founded. I, of course, accept your assurance that there is nothing personal in the matter, which makes my treatment appear all the more remarkable. As matters obviously cannot be left as they are, I will come to see you as you propose if you will give me some alternative times that are convenient.

10.　*Long to Beatty*

[BTY/13/28/3]　　　　　　　　　　　　　　　　　　　　Admiralty
13th March 1919

I enclose for your information a draft of the Reference which I propose for the enquiry which I suggested to you.

[1]Later Admiral Sir William Pakenham (1861–1933): entered RN 1874; present as observer at the battle of Tsushima 1904; 4th Sea Lord 1911; Rear-Admiral commanding 3rd Cruiser Squadron Home Fleet 1913; 2nd Battle Cruiser Squadron 1915; succeeded Beatty in command of Battle Cruiser Force and Vice-Admiral 1917; Admiral President RN College Greenwich 1919; C-in-C North America and West Indies 1920; Admiral 1922; retired at own request 1926.

My proposal is that you should preside over this enquiry, and that you should bring here, in order to conduct it, such members of your Staff as you think would be of assistance to you. This would, I think, meet the wishes you expressed in your last letter; and it would do more than this — it would enable me to feel that the Board of Admiralty are securing the benefit of the experience of officers fresh from their commands, and that therefore we should be in a position later on to come to definite conclusions as to the immediate policy of the Board.

Perhaps you will be so good as to let me know at your convenience, whether you would be willing to undertake this investigation; and if so, whether you have any suggestions you wish to make as to the Terms of Reference or form of the enquiry?

[Draft Reference]

To consider, in the light of the experience of the war, the military uses and values of the different types of war vessels, and to advise as to the main naval requirements to be kept in view in dealing with future designs and building programmes.

In so doing, to investigate thoroughly and report upon the naval and tactical considerations arising out of —

(a) the greatly increased efficacy of projectiles and torpedoes relatively to hull and deck protection:
(b) the part likely to be taken in the future by aircraft, both in attack and defence.

(In connection with (a), certain secret papers will be referred to the Committee.)

11. *Beatty to Long*

[Holograph Draft]

[BTY/13/28/4]   Brooksby Hall
                                                          Leicester
                                    Saturday [15 March 1919]

My Dear First Lord,
I received your letter with draft of reference [*sic*] last night.

My view is that the subjects you wish enquired into are not such as require immediate consideration in view of the restrictions on our immediate building programme, and can well wait until such time as I can come to the Admiralty in the capacity of First Sea Lord.

I gathered from our conversation that this will not be unduly prolonged, presumably the date will not be later than some time in June.

If I am correct in this assumption, I would prefer to let these matters stand over until I come to the Admiralty, when I can give effect to the decisions arrived at.

I am very sensible of your desire to make use of my knowledge and experience, but feel that it would be better to wait until I am in a position of responsibility rather than in one of a purely advisory capacity. And I think this would prevent any possibility of friction.

I shall be in London on Friday, and if you wish, will be at your disposal, and could at the same time discuss with you and the 1st Sea Lord the questions referred to in Admiral Madden's paper of the 7th March, with which I entirely concur; also his letter to me of 5th March, of which you have a copy.

12. *Long to Beatty*

[BTY/13/28/6]   Admiralty
                                                         21st March 1919

I have to thank you for your letter of the 18th, which for some reason only reached me to-day.

I think it is desirable that the papers in question should be made official, as apparently there is a good deal of misunderstanding which can be, and ought to be, removed.

Yes, it is quite true that I told Sir Charles Madden what I had already told you, namely, that when the Grand Fleet comes to an end, I am in hopes that he will take over the command of the Home and Atlantic Fleets — always of course assuming that, on the termination of the existence of the Grand Fleet, you decide to haul down your Flag. He most fully understood that everything would depend, and must depend, upon your decision; and he told me that if it would in any way facilitate matters, he would be quite ready to continue as Second-in-Command.

I was intending to write to you to make the following suggestions for your consideration:–

(*1*)   That I should write to you semi-officially, informing you that it is intended to bring the existence of the Grand Fleet to an end somewhere about the middle of April.

(2)   That I would submit your name to His Majesty[1] to be made an Admiral of the Fleet; and that this would be gazetted at least a week before the date selected for the termination of the existence of the Grand Fleet, which would enable you to hoist your Flag as Admiral of the Fleet.

(3)   I suggest that on your leaving the Grand Fleet, the reception in London should follow with as little delay as possible, namely, that you should be received in London by a representative of the Government (whether the Prime Minister will be here or not of course I do not know): should be received by His Majesty at Buckingham Palace: and that there should be a march through London of, say, 1,000 bluejackets – you and your officers taking such part in it as you think fit: and that you and your officers should be entertained by the Lord Mayor – the men being similarly entertained.

This is of course put in very general and rough terms; and I am writing in order to ascertain what your views are. I have really only delayed because I had hoped that the Prime Minister would have been free from the exacting calls upon his time and labours in Paris, and would have been over here, so that we could have talked this and other matters over. But there seems to be no prospect of his being able to come — and therefore I shall be very glad to have any views you may care to express.

[PS]   Since writing I have seen the Lord Mayor, who thinks they could not provide for more than 600 Bluejackets.

13.   *Beatty to Long*

[Copy]

[BTY/13/28/7]   March 25th 1919

Thank you for your letter of the 21st which reached me only today, having been sent to Hanover Lodge in error.

I appreciate your courtesy in asking my wishes in regard to hauling down my Flag, but feel that it is not a matter in which it would be proper to defer to my wishes.

[1]King George V (1865–1936) had succeeded Edward VII in 1910.

My services are at the disposal of the State in any suitable capacity, and I shall be glad to know as soon as possible what is desired of me, in order that I may arrange my affairs accordingly.

If it is desired that I should haul down my Flag, I suggest 7th April as a suitable date, and that the Grand Fleet should cease to exist on the same day. There seems no good reason for delaying the formation of the Atlantic and Home Fleets beyond that date, and it would be an advantage to all concerned to make the change as soon as possible.

I thank you for the intimation that you intend to submit my name to His Majesty for promotion to Admiral of the Fleet, and I need hardly say this honour will gratify me very much.

If it is decided that my Flag should be struck on the 7th April, perhaps it would be possible for my Flag to fly in my new rank from the 3rd April.

As regards the official reception which you kindly suggest, I am not clear whether you intend to include other Flag Officers of the Grand Fleet. My feeling is that as many of us have been in London during the past three months, and many have left their appointments, such a reception at this stage would perhaps be inopportune.

As regards the proposal to march 1000 Bluejackets through London, I feel that the Fleet would be more gratified if a very much larger number could do the march at a convenient date later on. Squadrons could be moved to Southend to facilitate transport. Citizens of London could be afforded opportunity of seeing ships of the Fleet during the same visit.

14. *Beatty to Admiralty*

[Copy]

[BTY/13/29/17]   [*Queen Elizabeth*]
                                                      4 April 1919

Former [References]; Admiral Second in Command, PW 129/1280
                                                  of 20 March, 1919
Admiral Second in Command, PW 151/1280 of 28 March, 1919

SECRET
DISPOSAL OF SURRENDERED GERMAN SHIPS

With reference to the communications of the Admiral, Second in Command, quoted above relative to the disposal of the German ships, I desire to inform the Board of my complete concurrence with the views expressed therein.

2. When considering originally the disposal of the German ships, it was contemplated that the relative naval strengths of the Allied Powers would remain as during the war, and that in view of the services rendered to the Allied cause by British sea-power, no attempt would be made by any one of our Allies to dispute the maintenance of our naval supremacy.

3. It is evident, however, from the memorandum prepared by the American Naval Staff in Paris under the direction of Admiral Benson,[1] USN, and quoted in the *Times* of 24th March, 1919, that the Americans do not at the moment concur in such sea supremacy by Great Britain, believing as they do that with their present building resources they can in a few years place themselves in the position of the first naval power. They are further encouraged in their view by the admittedly more exhausted state of Great Britain after four and a half years of war.

4. If we, therefore, in the immediate future are to avoid a large building programme, and at the same time counter the American effort, it is necessary to press for the division of German vessels on the basis of Naval losses sustained by the Allies. Such a division should enable us to tide over the next few years, whilst concentrating thought on the training of personnel and the development of new types.

5. Sea supremacy, vital as it is to our existence, must be maintained at all costs, even over an admittedly friendly power such as America. To ease the burden of maintaining such supremacy for the next few years must be our utmost endeavour, and this, in the event of America refusing to modify her proposed programme, can best be achieved by insisting on the distribution referred to above. It must be remembered in this connection that during the war, so far as the Navy is concerned, we have given to the Americans our most secret intelligence and instructions. We can, therefore, at the moment no longer rely on superior strategical and tactical thought, and it becomes of the greater importance to insist now on material superiority, and at the same time to organise and ensure for the future not only material superiority but for the highest efficiency in the training of our personnel for command in war.

[1] Admiral W. S. Benson USN (1855–1932): Chief of Naval Operations USN 1915–19; represented USA in negotiations for naval terms of Armistice and later naval adviser to US delegation at Peace Conference.

6. In forwarding this submission to Their Lordships, I would urge that the most earnest consideration may be given to the views expressed herein, and in the communications of the Admiral, Second in Command. The decisions reached will certainly be of paramount importance to the welfare and safety of the Empire.

7. It may be that these matters have already received attention and that decisions have been arrived at on the lines indicated. In this case this letter is unnecessary. Of such decision I am not however aware. I have received no official information and have not been kept in touch regarding the progress of the vital naval discussions taking place in Paris. Such information as I have, has been gained from the public press; information which leaves me perturbed that a determined effort is being made, and apparently with some measure of success, to tamper with the doctrine of British Naval Supremacy.

15.   *Beatty to Grand Fleet*

[Copy]

[BTY/7/10/20]

Queen Elizabeth
5 April 1919

GENERAL ORDER TO THE GRAND FLEET

In bidding good-bye to the Grand Fleet I desire to express to officers and men the deep regret which I feel on leaving those who have shared so loyally and devotedly the stress of the past years of war.

In success, in disappointment and in monotony the spirit of the Fleet has been beyond praise, and the highest traditions of our great service have been upheld.

I leave in full confidence that the spirit of the Grand Fleet will remain, that the lessons learnt in the War will be laid to heart, and that the mutual respect and understanding which exists between officers and men will be maintained and fostered for the safety and honour of King and Empire.

DAVID BEATTY
Admiral of the Fleet

16.   *Secretary of Admiralty to Beatty*[1]

[BTY/7/10/22]   Admiralty
                                                 5th April 1919

Sir,

On the termination of your appointment as Commander in Chief, Grand Fleet, I am commanded by My Lords Commissioners of the Admiralty to place on record their high appreciation of the eminent services which you have rendered to the British Empire during the War.

2.   My Lords desire to pay their tribute to those qualities of resolute leadership, unerring insight and quick decision which were early revealed by your achievements in battle and which throughout the War have been a source of admiration and confidence to your countrymen.

3.   They also desire to record their satisfaction with your administration and organisation of the Grand Fleet. Few beside the Board of Admiralty and your own Staff can fully realise what provision, judgment, enthusiasm and unremitting industry have been required in the Officer upon whom it has ultimately rested to keep a Force of this size, with so many complex parts, continuously and under all conditions at the necessary pitch of efficiency and preparation for immediate action. In the successful performance of this duty you have, as Their Lordships are aware, been greatly assisted by your Staff and by the various Flag Officers and their Staffs, whose services you have brought to the notice of the Board.

4.   In the midst of all these heavy responsibilities you have shewn a constant solicitude for the welfare of the Officers and Men serving under you which is in accordance with the finest traditions of the Service and has made you a beloved as well as a trusted leader.

5.   The hauling down of your Flag marks the close of one of the greatest chapters in the history of the Royal Navy, and it is a chapter that Posterity will always associate with your name.

[1]Sir Oswyn Murray (1873–1936): Admiralty civil servant from 1897; Assistant Secretary 1911; Permanent Secretary in succession to Graham Green 1917; died in office July 1936.

17.   *To Eugénie Godfrey-Faussett*[1]
(Copy)

[CCC.SLGF/14/1/B]   Brooksby Hall
                                               Leicester.
                                               Saturday 19.4.19

My Golden Comrade,
I enclose you a few typewritten facts that you might keep to
yourself as to their origin and at the same time place before
Dudley Ward[2] in your own language as pertinent queries which
give food for thought. After thinking about them it struck me that
the General Public would be likely to be disturbed if they knew
the actual facts

> 1st   That up to the Cessation of Hostilities the C.-in-C. G.F.
>   was consulted upon, and actually governed every oper-
>   ation against the Enemy.
> 2nd   That immediately hostilities ceased He ceased to be con-
>   sulted or to have anything to do with the decisions arrd.
>   at, which in reality became more vital but less dangerous
>   than when the war was on.

That the advisers to the P.M. are not those who actually conducted the War and who have not the experience to enable them
to give the best advice.
Even if they had the experience or were the best advisers is it
reasonable to suppose that those who bore the actual responsibility under war conditions should not be capable of giving valuable assistance in solving some of the many problems which have
to be decided under peace conditions.
I feel at times we are living on the brink of a precipice & ask
myself am I doing the right thing in doing no more than I have
What have I done?
I have presented my views unasked to the Admlty. & have
received no answer?! Whether they give any attention to them I
do not know. I fancy *YES* but they would not wish to say so.

---

[1]Eugénie Godfrey-Faussett (née Dudley Ward): wife of Captain Bryan Godfrey-
Faussett RN, equerry and friend to King George V.
[2]Roskill identifies him as Eugénie's younger brother Charles, who had already
given publicity to Beatty's merits; see Stephen Roskill (1981) *Admiral of the
Fleet Earl Beatty; The Last Naval Hero*, London and New York, pp. 289–91
(subsequently cited as Roskill, *Beatty*).

But how much, or if any I have not the slightest idea.
It is exactly like fighting a feather bed.
Do you get me as the Yankee says.
Tomorrow 20th we return to London and are off on our pilgrimage
to France at cockcrow Monday 21st.
I pray that all will go well & my small family will get through
alright.
Weather has been lovely warm and still, I wish you had been here
with us. I shall not see you again until June it seems a long way
off but much might happen between this and then.
Bless you dear friend
  Heaps of love
   Ever yours
    David.

18.   *Winston Churchill to David Lloyd George*

[Ll.G./F/8/3/46]   War Office
               1 May 1919

My Dear Prime Minister,
  Austen Chamberlain[1] yesterday mentioned to the House the
figure of 110 millions as being the total he contemplated spending
on the three Forces in the first normal year. Without in any way
pre-judging such a matter I should like to point out to you that a
large reduction in naval expenditure is essential to any satisfactory
solution of the combined problem.

      *   *   *   *

  I have been addressing my mind to the problem as a whole,
and I do not think it impossible to find a satisfactory solution.
But this depends entirely upon a saving from the Navy, which
should to a large extent counterbalance some of the increases I
have mentioned as inevitable. I do not see why there should not
be a great saving from the Navy, at any rate until some entirely
new competition develops. For this purpose it is absolutely vital
to persuade President Wilson not to start building new big ships.
If he wants to increase the American Navy, let him take some of
the best German ships and fit them up. We could afford to give

[1]Sir Austen Chamberlain (1863–1937): son of Joseph Chamberlain and half-
brother of Neville; Conservative MP; Secretary of State for India 1915–17; Member
of War Cabinet 1918; Chancellor of Exchequer 1919–21; 1st Lord of Admiralty
1931.

these ships to the United States Navy to a reasonable extent without adding at all to our own battleship and battle-cruiser strength. It would be a mark of great confidence and trust and would do more to lay naval competition to rest than anything else. On the other hand, if he starts building vessels of a superior type, we cannot fall behind in quality, and though we might wait for a year or two to see how things went on we should soon have to start designing superior craft to match the Americans. Therefore it is really vital that he should understand that a mere increase in the size of the American Navy would not light anew the fires of competition but that naval developments in the direction of greater power, speed, armament, etc, would, after a few years, revive that competition in the most painful and embarrassing form. The old ships are quite good enough to maintain the balance of sea power throughout the world unless better ones are built which make them obsolete. It would be criminal to start this again, and I am sure that, with the great hold you must now have over President Wilson, and the great measure of his confidence which you have won for yourself, and for this country during these negotiations, you should be able to arrive at a good agreement on this point. What spectacle could be more foolish than for Britain and America to begin by sinking all these fine German ships and then starting to waste material and money on building new ones? It is fit for a madhouse.

If you are able to arrive at a satisfactory arrangement on these lines, there ought to be no need for naval new construction, except of a minor character, for many years to come. The dockyards are choked with war vessels and I cannot conceive that any new construction is required. In the year before the war my new construction vote was over 20 millions, which at present day prices is considerably over 30 millions. It is from this source alone that in the present circumstances a saving can be made which will enable us to reconcile Imperial Defence and national economy.

Again, the Air Service is a newcomer. She is most expensive . . . I do not think however that the Air Service should be a net addition to the two older Services. It must be made to discharge a portion of the work hitherto done by the Army in the garrisoning of our Eastern possessions. It must also be made to take the place of naval expenditure on cruisers built or maintained in commission, and in the arrangements for watching and patrolling the coasts. Here is the second field on which, as I see the problem, a compensatory saving can be made. But both these two depend upon the Navy which is our absolute master . . .

If you wish to bring your expenditure on defence within reasonable limits it is imperative that the Admiralty should be willing to make a really great contribution towards solving the problem, and all your authority will be necessary for that.

*   *   *   *

Another point of the highest practical importance is this, and I am sure you will permit me to write frankly but in the greatest secrecy to you about it. Wemyss is a very good First Sea Lord and I think, although I did not agree with it at the time, that your choice has been very largely justified. At the same time, he is in a weak position in his own profession and far over-shadowed by Beatty. Beatty is very anxious to become First Sea Lord, and was, I believe, encouraged by Eric Geddes to believe that his appointment was imminent. At any rate it seems to me that sooner or later Beatty will have to replace Wemyss, and in a reasonable time. I think this would be the right thing to do. On the other hand you must remember that once Beatty is enthroned he will be in a position to champion the particularist [sic] interest of the Admiralty to an extent which it would be quite impossible for Wemyss to do. It is therefore extremely important that no change should take place at the present time, that the main finance of the three Services should be discussed and adjusted, and that any newcomer should be invited to come in on the basis that he accepts in principle the decisions arrived at.

You will not mind me putting these matters to you, I am sure, although they travel outside my sphere they affect all the problems with which I have myself to deal.

yours always
WINSTON.

19.   *Long to Lloyd George*

MEMORANDUM

[Ll.G./F/33/2/54]   5.5.19

When I became First Lord, but before I had taken over, Sir Eric Geddes was good enough to come to see me, and told me generally what he had intended to do if he had remained at the Admiralty.

Among other things, he said that it was his intention to make

Sir David Beatty First Sea Lord and Commander-in-Chief of the Navy, upon the vacation of office of Admiral Sir R. Wemyss; that this latter event would take place before very long, as Sir R. Wemyss was to become Commander-in-Chief of the Mediterranean and Governor of Malta.

I, of course, made no comment at that time. I took two things for granted, which perhaps I ought more closely to have examined at the time; first, that the change in the office of First Sea Lord had the approval of the Prime Minister; secondly, that the appointment of Sir R. Wemyss had been conceded by the War Office.

When Sir David Beatty came to see me at the Admiralty after I had taken office, he told me that he had been informed by my predecessor as I have described above; and he asked me whether I was in agreement. I told him that I was, and that when the vacancy occurred, it was my intention to ask him to come as First Sea Lord. He then replied that he would only come on certain conditions, the first of which was that he became also Commander-in-Chief and was given power to issue his own orders to the Navy under his own signature independent of the Board — in other words, that he was to hold two distinct offices, First Sea Lord and Commander-in-Chief.

. I told him at once that I could not assent to his proposal as regards the creation of the post of Commander-in-Chief. I said that to make so drastic a change in the administration of the Admiralty within a year of my taking office, and before he had any opportunity of ascertaining from personal experience what the powers of the First Sea Lord are, would, in my judgment, be impossible. He did not assent or definitely dissent; and I do not know now what his views on this are.

Subsequently, I paid him a visit on his flagship, and in answer to an interrogation from him, I repeated what I had said in regard to the appointment of First Sea Lord and my views in reference to the creation of the new post. Sir David Beatty told me that the First Sea Lord had paid him a visit at Hanover Lodge and told him that when the war was over and peace finally settled, he proposed to leave the Admiralty and hoped that he would succeed him.

On my return to the Admiralty, I saw the First Sea Lord on the subject, and asked him whether the Mediterranean appointment had been finally settled. He told me he knew nothing about it, and hoped that I would make enquiries. I at once got into communication with the Secretary of State for War,[1] in whose gift the Governorship of Malta is. He was good enough to come and see me, and he told me that it would be almost impossible for him to give the Governorship of Malta to a sailor. I was not surprised at his decision, because I felt, with the large number of distinguished general officers for whom provision had to be made, that it would be difficult, if not impossible; and that in my judgment, it would be clearly an injustice to transfer one of the few appointments in the gift of the War Office, to the Admiralty. The Secretary of State was good enough to add that, if I was prepared to affirm that the interests of the State demanded that the appointment should be made, that he would consider it; but he begged me not to make the request if I could avoid it — and of course I have not made it.

I thereupon wrote a private and confidential letter to Sir David Beatty, telling him that there had been some misunderstanding, as there was no appointment at present available for Sir R. Wemyss, and that consequently it was impossible at this moment to accede to his (Sir David's) request and mention a definite date; but that otherwise things remained as they were.

This, so far as I know, is a complete statement of the case so far as the Admiralty is concerned.

Later, however, I became aware of the fact that there was general knowledge in the Grand Fleet — and, indeed, in the whole Navy — of what had passed between Sir Eric Geddes and Sir David Beatty, only it was believed that a definite offer of the appointment had been made and accepted; consequently we were threatened with a campaign in the Press, directed against me, on the assumption that I had cancelled Sir Eric Geddes' offer. I therefore wrote to the Prime Minister, telling him what had passed, and asking if he approved of the new appointment, and if he were prepared to offer Sir R. Wemyss a suitable appointment, as there was nothing for him in the Navy, Sir R. Wemyss not being prepared to go to the Mediterranean without the Governorship. I learned from the Prime Minister that he knew nothing of the proposed change, and that he was not prepared to discuss it until he was free from his duties in Paris. I told or wrote to Sir David Beatty, I am not sure which, telling him that it was customary for the First Lord to consult and receive the approval of the Prime Minister before making any change, and that in face

[1] Winston Churchill.

of the heavy demands upon the Prime Minister's time and thoughts, I could not carry the matter further at present.

It is also to be remembered that when I found that the vacancy in the office of First Sea Lord would not be likely to occur for some little time, I invited Sir David Beatty to come to the Admiralty, bring his whole Staff with him, and embark upon a series of inquiries which would enable him to advise the Admiralty as to the most important questions requiring treatment in the light of his war experiences. This offer he declined. He pointed out that he had been 4½ years at sea, had had a very strenuous time, that his boy was unhappily seriously ill, and that he wished to take him to the Riviera, which would mean his absence from England for some time. I pointed out that this would be in no way inconsistent with the work I offered him, as he could divide the questions under various heads, apportion them among his staff, and leave them to work them out in his absence, Sir David reviewing their findings on his return – but he adhered to his refusal. I then offered Admiral Brock, his Chief of the Staff, work of a similar character at the Admiralty. He asked to be excused on the ground that he was badly in need of rest.

20. *To Eugénie Godfrey-Faussett*

[SLGF/15/2]   Athens[1]
                                                       22.5.19

*   *   *   *

Picked up some English newspapers which have not [*sic*] had time to digest, except Mr Long's statement as to me [*sic*] which, needless to say, is one uninterrupted lie from end to end. Voilà.
1. It is not the case that Sir D. B. was offered the post of 1st SL.
[*Answer*] It was offered and accepted!!!
2. Sir D. B. was told unofficially by my predecessor that he hoped he would come as 1st S.L. when the post became vacant. (This obviously contradicts 1. He was hardly likely to express the hope if it was not going to become vacant.)
Answer. I was asked by late 1st Lord to come as 1st S.L. and told that the present 1st SL was leaving; *ie* was told that the post

---

[1]The Beattys were on a two month cruise in the Mediterranean and the Corinth canal on their steam yacht *Sheelah*; Long's statement was made in answer to a Parliamentary Question by Commander Carlyon Bellairs MP, a Beatty supporter, see Roskill, *Beatty*, pp. 287–8.

was about to be vacant. The present 1st Lord informed me that the late 1st Lord had informed as above [*sic*] and that he looked upon my coming as a 'fait accompli'.

3.   On no occasion has any date been mentioned or any definite official offer made.

Answer. A date was mentioned, *ie* the date of the signing of the preliminary Peace Terms. Do not understand what 'definite official offer' means.

4.   He has been consulted in Naval Policy [*sic*] since the Armistice.

[*Answer*] This is entirely inaccurate.

5.   He was invited to preside over an Enquiry, etc, but for personal reasons asked to be excused.

[*Answer*] Entirely inaccurate. I refused on public grounds, and very good ones.[1] I deprecate this statement as making it appear that I subordinate the public service to private considerations.

What are you to do with a lying old hand [?] like that? I shall make a statement one of these days which will shake him to his foundations. But what I want to know is how one is to deal with a situation like this. I am not accustomed to have to meet deliberate lies. However, I am keeping calm and no doubt the situation will clear itself . . .

It is an extraordinary lucky thing that we are out here, as Tata[2] in her wrath would surely be indiscreet. She cannot understand that the wisest thing to do is to preserve a dignified silence, which would add immense weight to the blow, should it ever be found desirable to deliver one . . .

[1]See Document 11 above.

[2]Beatty's pet name for his wife, Ethel, only daughter of millionaire Chicago chain-store founder, Marshall Field; it was her wealth which financed their expensive life style and her mental ill-health which caused them both much unhappiness.

21. Memorandum by Local Defence Division of the Naval Staff[1]

[BTY/8/1/9]   10.6.19

SECRET. FORMS OF ATTACK FROM THE SEA AND FORMS OF DEFENCE
[Extracts]

The aim of   2. It is now necessary to determine to what
this   extent, if any, the pre-war standard of defence
Memorandum   requires modification. With this object an endeavour has been made in the following memorandum
to investigate:–

(*a*)   how the above-mentioned Admiralty views
are affected by experience afforded by the
late war;
(*b*)   whether the 'Forms of Attack' contemplated
hitherto are still to be accepted as probable,
and what new 'Forms of Attack' must be
reckoned with;
(*c*)   the new means of defence developed during
the war, and the further developments to be
expected in the future.

Such an investigation at the present time can be
only incomplete and tentative, but it may serve
nevertheless, by collecting material and clearing
the ground, to indicate possible lines for more
conclusive enquiry at a later date. The 'Scale of
Attack' depends on policy; 'Form of Attack' on
materiel. Future policy depends on the Terms of
Peace and the resulting international situation.
Consideration of the 'Scale of Attack' is, therefore, outside the scope of this paper and the
'Scale of Defence' of any particular port is not
touched on.

Developments   3. The course of the recent war has been
in the   marked by many developments in the means
weapons of   available for the conduct of naval warfare; briefly,
naval warfare   these are:–

[1] For the organisation of the Naval Staff see Document 87 below.

(1) The increased range of heavy guns.

(2) Improved methods of precision in the bombardment of enemy coasts.

(3) The rapid development of aircraft, and consequent improvements in aerial observation of fire, reconnaissance, and bombing.

(4) The rapid development of the submarine as a weapon of great endurance and offensive power capable of restricting the movements of capital ships, delivering a series of determined attacks by mine and torpedo on ships entering or leaving harbour, or bombarding the shipping, works, etc, within a harbour.

(5) The great development of mines as a weapon, both of offence and defence, and subsequent progress in minesweeping.

(6) Improvements in the construction of fast motor boats for local patrols, etc.

(7) The elaboration of inventions and devices for the detection or concealment of surface vessels, submarines, mines and aircraft by methods such as hydrophones, wireless directional, listening stations, smoke screens, dazzle-painting, star-shells, paravanes, etc.

An offensive naval policy the main security from attack   4. It is desired to lay special stress on the fact that in the consideration of any scheme for the local defence of our ports and harbours, it has to be realised that an *offensive* and well-directed policy by our mobile forces constitutes the main security from attack from the sea. On the other hand, too great reliance on local defence may tend to a defensive policy at sea, inviting the hostile action it is desired to frustrate.

ATTACKS BY AIRCRAFT

Responsibility of the Air Ministry

1. It is presumed that it lies with the Air Ministry to advise as to the 'forms of attack' to be expected from the air. But as aircraft has been mentioned in connection with many other forms of attack, and constitutes an essential feature of the defences against them, it is necessary to present, with all deference, some indications of the 'forms of attack' that may be expected from the air.

(1) — Attack by aircraft carrying bombs or torpedoes

Bomb-dropping may supersede bombardment by ships

2. This 'form of attack' will require most serious consideration. The development of aircraft may be carried to such an extent that the menace from the air will eventually become greater than that from the sea, and this 'form of attack' in years to come may entirely supersede that of bombardment from the sea. The loss of one or more aeroplanes is insignificant in comparison with the loss of a capital ship or even a monitor, yet an aeroplane is a self-contained weapon of great offensive power, and a well directed bomb from one may effect what hundreds of rounds fired from a ship may fail to achieve. Bombs of 1800 lbs weight have been carried by aeroplanes during the war, and as bomb-dropping sights are improved, considerable accuracy may be looked for.

Foreign Powers will seek advanced bases overseas

3. Attacks must, therefore, be expected from the air either by day or night by squadrons of aircraft carrying heavy bombs or torpedoes. If by night, parachute illuminating bombs would be employed rendering all objects beneath the aeroplane visible. Foreign powers with hostile intentions will endeavour to establish advanced bases from which bombing squadrons could be despatched against our oversea ports and on which aircraft-carrying ships could be based.

Examples of
air
bombardment

4. The results of bombing harbours by aircraft are demonstrated by the attacks on Zeebrugge, Bruges, Ostend and Durazzo, and by the German attacks on Dunkirk. Destroyers, submarines, and other vessels have been bombed and sunk. The bombing of vulnerable points was not so successful. The lock gates were the principal targets at Zeebrugge; but they were most efficiently protected by being run back under concrete shelters during an air raid or bombardment. These gates were damaged on one or two occasions, but no direct hit on them was obtained although several bombs fell very close.

Other uses
for aircraft

5. There are many uses to which aircraft can be put in connection with more extended operations, among which may be mentioned, bombing shore batteries during bombardment, observation of fire, photographic reconnaissance, and illumination of objectives for vessels attacking by night.

*   *   *   *

DEFENCE AGAINST LONG-RANGE BOMBARDMENT BY SURFACE CRAFT

Responsibility
of the
Admiralty

1. It has been shewn that with efficient observation of fire from the air effective bombardment can now be carried out at greatly increased ranges, possibly up to 60,000 yards under suitable conditions. Although it does not lie directly with the Admiralty to decide what is to be the primary means of defence, it is as well to consider whether the experience of the war throws any increased responsibility upon the Navy in repelling this 'form of attack'.

Present
primary
armament
should be
relegated to
position of
secondary
armament

2. Before the war the Admiralty held that where fire can be directed by an observer, so placed as to be able to watch the fall of shot, provision should be made against bombardment up to 18,000 yards. All the arguments in these memoranda assumed the employment of direct observation, the limit of which was taken as 18,000 yards. These arguments may still be

accepted in regard to bombardment by direct observation, Section II (2), page 7. The old primary armament, however, must now be relegated to the position of *secondary* armament, and as such, will still be necessary for defence against other 'forms of attack'. Although with modern mountings and special projectiles the effective range of the secondary armament could possibly be increased to 30,000 yards, the problem of dealing with bombarding ships at ranges of from 30,000 to 40,000 and perhaps 60,000 yards, still has to be solved.

Value of submarines & aircraft

3. In the foregoing pages great stress has been laid on efficient observation from the air as an essential to long-range bombardment, and it has been pointed out that the conditions of accurate firing by ships are such as to invite submarine attack. From this it follows that in favourable conditions a bombarding force can be frustrated, without any help from shore batteries, by the employment of submarines and counter-aircraft.

Submarines as part of the local defences

4. It was considered even in pre-war days that submarines constituted a danger sufficient to deter armoured ships of the line from undertaking bombardments, in view of the subsequent naval action; and the immense development of submarine warfare now gives still greater force to this view. Bombarding forces should now have to reckon with a vigorous attack by submarines forming part of the local defences of the port. In the recent war, Heligoland was not bombarded mainly because of its distance from our bases and the consequent threat of submarine attack on our ships both while on passage to and during their stay on the firing station.

Need of strong air forces

5. Similarly, if the defence holds local supremacy in the air it can render long range bombardment by any ship ineffectual by destroying the hostile aircraft. Long range bombardment is useless without aerial observation of fire. Moreover, it should not be long before aircraft become capable of inflicting considerable damage on

armoured ships and their protecting flotillas by bombing. The use also of torpedoes carried by aircraft will undoubtedly be further developed.

Problem of the heavy gun

6. The problem as to whether it will be necessary to provide a new primary armament of guns of the heaviest type for the defence of our ports against long-range bombardment is not one which the Admiralty will have to solve alone. The great argument in favour of the gun is that it is always there; mines may be swept up, submarines and aircraft may be destroyed or disabled, but it is almost impossible to knock out by long-range bombardment a gun mounted in a modern battery. This was shewn very clearly by the results of the long-range counter-battery work between the German batteries and the British siege guns on the Belgian coast (see Appendix 4). On the other hand, study of the Belgian coast operations shews that not one direct hit was obtained by the German guns on our bombarding ships, in spite of the fact that the coast batteries were brought to the highest state of perfection, on account of the impracticability of employing submarines in those waters.

The submarine our principal weapon against long-range bombardment

7. It may, however, be definitely stated that the submarine is our principal weapon of defence against attack on our defended ports by armoured ships. Any international agreement to prohibit submarine construction would strengthen considerably the case for a new primary coast-defence armament of the heaviest guns available.

*   *   *   *

DEFENCE AGAINST ATTACKS BY AIRCRAFT

Strong local air force the best defence

1. The development of aircraft as an offensive weapon in the last few years has been so rapid that a great increase in size, weight-carrying abilities, and radius of action, may be looked for in the near future. Owing to the limits of their fuel capacity, however, aircraft will be capable of attacks only of the 'raid' type for several years to

come, and against these the best defence is a strong local air force, supported by anti-aircraft batteries, listening and wireless-intercepting stations, etc.

Bomb-proof shelters: isolation of inflammable stores

2. Passive forms of defence would consist of subterranean magazines, work-shops, and stores, and ferro-concrete shelters. Smoke-screens also may be used to protect vulnerable points. Much can be done in peace time by removing inflammable stores, magazines, oil tanks, etc, to positions away from areas of congested traffic or habitation.

Surface vessels controlled by aircraft

3. Against attack by surface vessels controlled by aircraft, the best method of defence is to attack the controlling aircraft with the aircraft of the defences. It may be possible to supplement this by gunfire from patrol vessels and the light guns of the defence.

*　　*　　*　　*

22. *Long to Lord Stamfordham*[1]
[Holograph]
[RA Geo V G.1474/3]　　　　　　　　　14th June 1919

I enclose an account of my recent visit to Ostend and Zeebrugge, which I think may interest His Majesty.

The change in the tone of the Northcliffe Press lately as regards Beatty and Wemyss is very significant. The former has behaved very foolishly and if he does not mend his ways I think he will make it very difficult for him ever to become First Sea Lord. Meanwhile, Wemyss has strengthened his position by the dignified way in which he has borne these undeserved attacks. Whatever justification there may be for dissatisfaction in regard to the Peace terms, the Naval conditions are absolutely satisfactory, and for this we have to thank Wemyss more than anybody else; and, in addition, I should like to say that I find him a most excellent First Sea Lord. I think it will be very difficult to improve upon him, very easy to have a worse one, and I, at all events, am not

[1] A. J. Bigge, 1st Baron Stamfordham (1849–1931): having been private secretary to Queen Victoria he served King George V in the same capacity, before and after his accession; died in office.

prepared to 'put him on the beach' simply because it is thought in some quarters that Beatty ought to come to the Admiralty.

Beatty's statement at the Guildhall that he knew nothing of Admiralty affairs, internal or external, was really a most improper one. He has been regularly and fully consulted as to the post-war Fleet &c and, as you know, I invited him to come to the Admiralty, bringing his whole staff with him, and advise us, after such inquiry as he thought right, as to what ought to be our policy in the future. He declined, and therefore if he does not know what is going on, it is his own fault. The comment of the Press upon his speeches and upon Haig's,[1] are very significant. I heard all the speeches and cordially concur with the verdict of the Press, that the laurels rest with Haig.

23. *Long to Lloyd George*

[Ll.G/F/33/2/54]   15 June 1919

*   *   *   *

Whether it is due to Northcliffe's illness or to some other cause I know not, but he and his myrmidons have certainly been less active of late. There is a very interesting proof of this to be found in the altered situation as regards Beatty. Quite a short time ago there was a very vigorous and determined movement on the part of the Northcliffe Press and in some other quarters to get up a violent agitation condemning the Admiralty and, of course, through them, yourself as Prime Minister, for not terminating Wemyss' appointment and bringing Beatty in as First Sea Lord. I have kept a very close watch on everything that has been going on, and I have been able from time to time to spike the enemy's guns, but this is not sufficient to account for the change, and I cannot help thinking that Northcliffe and his friends and your critics have begun to ask themselves whether the time is ripe for any agitation of this kind.

The reception in the Press of the speeches made by Beatty and Haig at the Guildhall and the Mansion House is very instructive. As I have already told you, in my deliberate judgment, and I think I am quite unbiassed, Haig's speeches were much the best; but, on the other hand, Beatty's were the longest, the most ambitious and, obviously, the most carefully prepared, and it is not too much to say that they have fallen quite flat. Northcliffe

[1]Douglas Haig, Field Marshal and 1st Earl (1868–1928): commanded 1st Army in British Expeditionary Force 1914; succeeded Sir John French as C-in-C 1915.

and Garvin[1] were Beatty's chief supporters. The 'Times' and the Northcliffe papers are more or less silent about Beatty, such references as they make are very cold. Garvin has dropped the subject, while Gerard Fiennes has a most illuminating article in today's 'Observer' in which he takes quite the right line. Beatty has certainly played his cards very badly. I do not suggest for a moment that he has had any share in the Press agitation, but he is of course aware of it and he has not done anything to check it, while there is a very general impression that her Ladyship has been extremely active. But, as I have said, they have played their cards very badly. Beatty was prepared to go to the various functions in plain clothes, on the ground that he is unemployed. It is difficult to imagine that he did not intend by so doing to call attention to his unemployment and give the signal for an attack upon the Government. We forestalled this at the Admiralty by giving him authority to wear uniform on these occasion and reminding him of an old Admiralty Order on the subject; but at St. Paul's Cathedral he objected to the place which had been assigned to him among the other Admirals of the Fleet, and insisted upon having a seat given to him further back, to quote his own words, 'as a private individual'. Of course this kind of conduct injures him with his best friends, the sailors, and his position to-day is certainly nothing like so strong as it was three months ago. Lady Beatty, on the other hand, has on two occasions openly cut me — about as silly a thing as a woman can do. These matters are hardly worth mentioning to you, but they are straws which show which way the wind is blowing, and I think you ought to have this information in your possession.

*   *   *   *

[1] J. L. Garvin, journalist (1868–1947): appointed editor of the *Observer* in 1908 by Northcliffe and continued as such when W. W. Astor became proprietor; supported Lloyd George during war; later, a strong critic of the Peace Treaty and a supporter of Appeasement.

24. *Sir Henry Wilson*[1] *to Lloyd George*

[Holograph]

[Ll.G./F/47/8/27]   36 Eaton Place
                                                                16.7.19

I have just had another talk with Beatty. On reflection, he is more than ever in favour of a proposal for a Minister of Defence, and goes so far as to say that the Admiralty was already lapsing into the pre-war condition and would again become an Office, quite unable to consider war intelligently or conduct it efficiently.

But he made a strong point which I think you should know.

In order to carry the Navy with you he suggests that the Board of Admiralty should first be asked to give their opinion, that is if you decide to go on with the idea, and that you should consider their opinion before taking other advice or action.

This reminded me very much of what you yourself did when you asked Robertson for a paper and then called on Johnnie French and me to write our views.

I promised Beatty I would let you know this.

25. *Long: Memorandum to War Cabinet*

[BTY/13/28/17]   12th August 1919

POST-WAR NAVAL POLICY
[Copy to Beatty]

Before the Board of Admiralty can draw up a definite programme for 1920/1921, there are certain questions which they would desire to have answered by the Government, as these questions involve the consideration of the general policy of the Government, especially in regard to foreign relations.

(1)   What is to be the policy of the government as regards the supremacy of the seas —

(*a*)   over the United States of America?
(*b*)   over any probable combination?

We have held the supremacy of the seas for some 300 years,

---

[1]Field Marshal Sir Henry Wilson (1864–1922): commanded 4th Army Corps 1915; mission to Russia 1916; British representative on Allied Supreme War Council 1917; CIGS 1918–22; assassinated by IRA in London 1922.

and hitherto the dispute has been as to how many and what Powers were to be regarded as our potential enemies, over whom we ought to have supremacy.

There has never been any dispute as to the fact that no one Power could be permitted to surpass us in Naval strength.

As things stand now, the Power which caused us the greatest anxiety — Germany — has, for the time at all events, disappeared. France and Italy are our Allies, and are exhausted by the war. In the opinion of the Board of Admiralty, the only Navy for which we need have regard, and in respect of which we desire a decision of the Government, is the Navy of the United States of America.

The facts in regard to the Naval strength of Japan are given in Appendix II, but it is considered that Japan may be put aside for the present, whether as an individual opponent or as a partner in any probable combination against us.

As regards the United States, the situation is difficult. I give in Appendix I the figures which I have already circulated to the Cabinet with my memorandum on the Estimates, but corrected up to date. It will be seen that if the USA carry out their programme of 1916, abandoning altogether their additional [new] programme, we shall have a very narrow margin in 1923–1924, and some of their ships will outclass ours in fighting power.

It will be seen also that the new USA Fleet Organisation provides for 18 Dreadnought Battleships and 11 pre-Dreadnought Battleships being kept fully manned and in instant readiness, as compared with the Admiralty proposal to keep 21 Dreadnought Battleships and Battle Cruisers fully manned and in instant readiness.

It will also be seen that the U.S.A. Naval personnel for 1920 is to be 171,000 men.

It seems unlikely that the traditional policy of the USA should so alter that they should become an aggressive power, but yet it is obvious that if they continue to maintain a Naval Force of this size, a very moderate reduction in the Admiralty proposals in regard to Capital ships would place this country in a position of manifest inferiority.

It is unnecessary for me to remind the Cabinet of the strength of feeling in this country and throughout the Empire in favour of the maintenance of our sea supremacy.

The facts and figures are of course known to everybody who is interested in naval questions; and I think it must be recognised that the Government must now definitely decide whether they are prepared to maintain the supremacy which we have held for so long.

(2)   The second question (which has a very close relation to the first) is, Are we to deal finally with the question of the strength of our Naval forces independently of the provisions of the Covenant of the League of Nations or not?

It will be recollected that Article 8 of the Covenant states that the Members of the League recognise that the maintenance of peace requires the reduction of national armaments to the lowest point consistent with national safety. It then provides that the Council of the League 'taking account of the geographical situation and circumstances of each State shall formulate plans for such reduction for the consideration and action of the several Governments', and that 'such plans shall be subject to reconsideration and revision at least every 10 years'. It further provides that 'after these plans shall have been adopted by the several Governments, the limits of armaments therein fixed shall not be exceeded without the concurrence of the Council'.

Unless we are to throw away the principle of mutual reduction of armaments, I suggest that we should not take any serious action independently of the procedure under the Covenant, but that whatever decision be arrived at, the procedure should be to propose to all the Allied Powers a reduction under the provisions of Article 8 of the Covenant. It might be advisable to sound the USA beforehand as to whether they will take joint initial action with us in putting forward such proposals through the Council of the League. We shall then know whether the object of the USA in projecting this big Fleet (as some people think) merely to have a powerful weapon with which to obtain a general reduction of armaments, or whether it is really their intention to force us to the alternatives of either competing with or accepting numerical inferiority to them.

(3)   There is a third question upon which we seek information. In pre-war days it was necessary for the naval advisers of the Government to decide what risks ought to be run, if it was not possible to provide against them all. An attack by Germany in the North Sea was, as we now know, rightly regarded as the risk which overshadowed all others; and therefore our Navy was built for this particular work — and we largely abandoned the policy which had previously been pursued of 'showing the flag' in foreign and other waters. The information which reaches the Board of Admiralty from many quarters convinces us that the time has

come when it is necessary that the White Ensign should be seen in all these places. This does not necessarily mean a large number of expensive ships; but it does mean a sufficient number of light cruisers to enable us to show the flag in these waters. Only recently we have had evidence of the effect produced by the appearance of our ships in South American waters; and the Board of Admiralty ask the Cabinet to say definitely whether they are in future to pursue the policy known as 'showing the flag'. This, again, is a subject upon which very strong feeiing exists in this country and in the Empire. There is every indication that the USA and Japan are both well aware of the advantages which flow from the presence of their ships in foreign waters, and that they are doing all that they can to push their trade and their general interests, by sending their ships to stations where prior to 1904 we had the monopoly.

(4)   A further question is: What should be the period of time during which we may reckon on immunity from war with a great Power or combination of small Powers giving an equivalent enemy force, and therefore a reduction in our naval preponderance?

It has been suggested that it should be for a period of either five or ten years. On the one hand, we know accurately what the position of the U.S. Navy and the Japanese Navy will be at the end of five years, whereas, unless the League of Nations operates, it is impossible to say what they will be at the end of ten. On the other hand, if we could fix upon the longer period, it would undoubtedly enable us to make more effective reductions at present. The view of the Admiralty is, however, that as our actual information only covers the shorter period, the question whether the longer period can safely be adopted must depend upon whether the Covenant of the League of Nations, which names 10 years as the extreme period at which revisions of Naval and Military strength shall take place, makes an auspicious beginning.

In conclusion, I desire briefly to call the attention of my colleagues to the fact that, while the demands for reductions and economies are made with growing insistence, the demands upon the Navy show no signs of decrease — quite the contrary. We have been called upon recently to keep a large force in Russian waters; to provide a force for Flensburg in connection with the Schleswig plebiscite; we have had to send men to Yorkshire; to have others in reserve for troubles elsewhere; ships to Liverpool; and we have constant demands for the presence of ships by some of our Crown Colonies. If we have to admit that we cannot meet these and other calls, will not the effect upon the Empire and, indeed, the world, be disastrous?

APPENDIX I
United States Navy

The following statement shows the position of our own and the US Navies now and in 1923/24 (i.e., in 4 years' time) in respect of Capital Ships of *Dreadnought* Type, viz:–

1919	Great Britain	USA
Dreadnought Battleships	33	18
Battle Cruisers	9	nil
1923/1924		
Dreadnought Battleships	33	29
Battle Cruisers	10	6

Numbers of Capital Ships to be maintained in commission with full crews by the two Navies

At the time when the Admiralty Memorandum of 19 June was written, no information was available as to the intentions of the United States in this respect, but the information is now available.

The new USA Fleet Organisation is to consist of two main Fleets of practically equal strength — the Atlantic and the Pacific — with a small Asiatic Fleet and still smaller Auxiliary Squadrons in various localities. The Atlantic and Pacific Fleets are each to consist of 4 divisions of Battleship, 2 divisions of Cruisers, 18 divisions of Destroyers, 3 divisions of Submarines, and 2 divisions of Minelayers, together with repair ships and other Auxiliaries.

The USA, therefore, intend to keep in full commission:–

Battleships	(Dreadnought)	18
-do-	(Pre-Dreadnought)	11

The Admiralty proposed to keep in full commission:–

Battleships and Battle Cruisers (Dreadnoughts)   21*

United States Navy Personnel
(according to last hearing before Congress June 21st)

Total personnel at present	241,000
Total personnel 1920	171,000

(This reduction in personnel is on account of the fact that the US Navy transportation service will have completed the repatriation of American troops in Europe by the end of this year.)

USA Capital Ships under Construction (Dreadnoughts)

	Laid Down	Authorised but not laid down
Battleships	5	6
Battle Cruisers	0	6

Mr. Daniels has recommended to Congress that only the ships of the 1916 programme and before should be proceeded with, and it is more than probable that Congress will accept this recommendation.

Under the terms of reorganisation of the US Navy announced during the last fortnight, it appears that the full number − 29 Battleships (15 in Atlantic, and 14 in Pacific) will when completed be kept in full commission.

*(in addition to the *New Zealand* on Special Service with Lord Jellicoe, and the *Australia* in Australasian Waters).

APPENDIX II
Japanese Navy

(Only ships of the most modern type are included)

Ships in commission

Battleships	4
Battle Cruisers	3
Light Cruisers	3
Destroyers	19
Submarines	3

Ships in reserve which can be put in commission at short notice.

Battleships	1
Battle Cruisers	1
Light Cruisers	−
Destroyers	12
Submarines	−

Ships actually under construction

Battleships	2
Battle Cruisers	–
Light Cruisers	2
Destroyers	12
Submarines	9

Ships of which the construction is definitely approved but which were not actually under construction on May 1st 1919. The present state of Dockyard accommodation admits of the construction of those ships according to programme.

Battleships	2
Battle Cruisers	2
Light Cruisers	5
Destroyers	10
Submarines	25

Ships projected for which approval has been given in principle only. Their actual construction depends upon approval being given definitely to undertake it, and on Dockyard facilities permitting of it.

Battleships	–
Battle Cruisers	2
Light Cruisers ⎫	
Destroyers ⎬	Indefinite
Submarines ⎭	

Future strength

The best Japan is considered able to do is to produce by September 1923 a main Capital Ship strength of 8 Battle Ships and 8 Battle Cruisers, of which the oldest ship will be 9 years old.

In the opinion of the Naval Attache, Tokyo, which is concurred in, Japan will not achieve this best, but will in the Autumn of 1925 have a main strength of 16 Capital Ships all under 12 years old. Japan will continue to build at her full capacity, and money has already been voted to increase this capacity.

26. *Long to Beatty*

[Holograph]

[BTY/13/28/11]

Admiralty
24.ix.19

My dear Admiral of the Fleet,
Admiral Wemyss has resigned the office of First Sea Lord.

I have pleasure, with the Prime Minister's concurrence, in inviting you to succeed him sometime in October.

In order to avoid any misunderstanding hereafter it is necessary that the status of the office of 1st Sea Lord should be clearly defined. When we discussed you coming here earlier in the year you will remember you said you 'would be willing to come on certain terms'. They were:

1st   That you should be appointed C-in-C as well as First Sea Lord with power to issue orders on certain matters under your own signature

2nd   That the appointment of the other Sea Lords should practically rest with you.

I pointed out that both these proposals were wholly incompatible with the constitutional position of the Board of Admiralty and of the First Lord, & that I could not agree with them. I added that I should of course be glad to take counsel with you on these and all other questions concerning the Board of Admiralty & the Navy; this being the invariable custom.

I should therefore be glad to know that you accept my views on the above questions.

I must add, that in consequence of the changed conditions resulting from the defeat of Germany & the heavy financial burden we have to bear, it is necessary to effect great economies in the Estimates. We have been compelled to make considerable progress with our plans, but I should however, explain to you that the strength of the Post-War Fleet has not yet received the formal sanction of the Board & suggest that you should see the draft before the orders are actually issued & make any suggestions which you may think proper.

I shall of course be happy to see you & I hope that you will feel able to help the Admiralty & the Navy at what is a very critical juncture, when reductions have to be made to the utmost limit short of sacrificing the security of the country.

I will also say that although our personal relations have unfortunately not been as cordial as I had always endeavoured to make them, I am fully prepared to welcome a colleague of such distinction, who has already rendered such eminent service, & whose presence at the Admiralty would, I know, be most acceptable to the Navy & the country.

I hope & believe that we shall be able to maintain those close & friendly relations which should always exist between the First Lord & the First Sea Lord.

Sincerely yours
WALTER H. LONG

27. *Beatty to Long*

[Holograph Copy]

[BTY/13/28/12]   Brooksby Hall
                                                      26.9.19.

Your letter dated 24th was only received by me late last night.

I have the honour to accept the invitation which you send me, with the concurrence of the Prime Minister, to succeed Admiral Wemyss in the office of 1st Sea Lord some time in October.

With regard to your views as to the status of the First Sea Lord, I would say that I accepted the office from your predecessor unconditionally. In conversation with you subsequently I expressed the opinion that certain modifications in the functions of the First Sea Lord were desirable in the light of war experience. When I understood you to confirm your predecessor's offer, however, I had no idea or intention of making terms or conditions.

As regards appointments of Sea Lords, Flag Officers and Captains, I am in entire agreement with you that they rest with the 1st Lord, who consults with the 1st Sea Lord in accordance with the invariable custom.

I fully understand the necessity of effecting great economies and that the Naval Estimates have to be considerably reduced to meet the altered circumstances.

I note what you say about the strength of the Post-War Fleet, but I feel that without information on general naval policy, my views would not be of value. I would suggest therefore that the final draft should remain in abeyance for the short period which is to elapse before I take office.

I would only add that my one desire is to serve the State and that you can rely on my co-operation and support.

PS   I am entirely at your service and will come and see you when you wish. My present engagements take me to Manchester tomorrow, Saturday, and to Kirkcaldy on Monday, after which I shall be free, and a telegram to Aberdour will be sufficient.

28.   *Beatty to Long*

[Holograph Copy]

[BTY/13/28/21]   Aberdour House
1.10.19

I have received your letter of Sept 30th with enclosures.

It is very difficult for me with my limited information to offer a definite opinion. I can however express general agreement with your memo of August 12th to the War Cabinet.[1] In this memo you ask 4 very important and pertinent questions, to three of which I can find no reply.

The crux of the situation appears to lie in the answers to the second question. The Post-War Fleet appears to me to be sufficient to meet the present situation, but the immediate future depends upon:–

(*a*)   Whether the USA ratifies the Covenant of the League of Nations

(*b*)   Whether Mr Daniels's[2] recommendation to continue the 1916 programme only is approved by Congress

(*c*)   Upon the naval policy of the Dominions with regard to the War Cabinet Memo 616A. I am not clear as to their decision. I concur with the reference to it in the Draft Memo for consideration by the Board, but an answer to your Question 2 in your Memo of August 12th is necessary before the policy on this point can be defined.

[1]Document 25 above. On 30 September Long had sent a draft of a further similar memorandum to Beatty asking for written comments and discussions in London 'in the hope that you may be able to express your views to date' (BTY/13/28/13).

[2]Josephus Daniels (1862–1948): Secretary of US Navy 1913–21; strong advocate of a US Navy 'second to none'; member of Allied Naval Council from its inception in 1917; opposed demands for creation of a separate air service absorbing US Navy's air arm.

As to the suspension of construction and the limitation of recruiting and training, I cannot believe it is wise to stop progress quite so drastically. It might be possible for the next 12 months without much sacrifice, provided experiments and investigations were being pursued.

The remarks of the DNC on materiel entitled 'Future provision for keeping fully prepared' are very important.

As soon as I can get south I will come and see you, but the outlook does not look very bright at present.

29.   *Admiralty Memorandum for War Cabinet*

[BTY/8/1/5]   24 October 1919

NAVAL POLICY AND EXPENDITURE
[Copy to Beatty]

The Board of Admiralty have given careful reconsideration to naval requirements in the light of the decisions arrived at by the Cabinet on the 15th August, and in doing so they have kept before them the desire of the Cabinet that a figure of £60,000,000 should be aimed at for the Navy Estimates of 1920–1921.

2.   The Admiralty have approached the problem by considering in the first place what is the minimum strength of the Fleet which can be regarded as providing in present circumstances for the security of the Empire, and by next proceeding to ascertain what would be approximately the total of Navy Estimates for 1920–1921 if such a Fleet were maintained next year, provision of course being also included for the portion of dead-weight expenditure arising out of the War which cannot be liquidated during the present year.

3.   The revised Post-War Fleet shown as an Appendix to this Memorandum constitutes in the opinion of the Admiralty the minimum Naval Force upon which it is open to them, subject to the grave considerations stated later, to base their calculations. This Force provides for the number of Capital Ships (*a*) in commission and (*b*) in reserve being:–

(*a*)   In Commission: 16 Battleships   4 Battle Cruisers.
(*b*)   In Reserve: 13 Battleships   3 Battle Cruisers,

as compared with which the other great Navy of the World (the United States) comprises:–

18 Dreadnought Battleships $\Big\}$ in full commission
11 Pre-Dreadnought

4.   The personnel required for this British Force in order to
man the ships in commission and to provide two-fifths crews on
mobilisation for the ships in reserve, with a margin sufficient to
work the Fleet under peace conditions, is approximately 126,000
officers and men. The United States naval personnel voted is
171,000 officers and men for the first 6 months of 1920.

5.   A long-service system has been proved to be essential for
a Service like the Navy, and sudden large decreases or increases
in the number of Permanent Officers and Men cannot be effected
by any ordinary means. Should extraordinary means be resorted
to, it would cause unsettlement and detriment to efficiency in the
Navy to a far greater extent than in a short-service system. It
may, however, be possible between now and the 1st April 1920
to get rid of the men in excess of the number required for this
minimum Naval Force, and if Treasury consent is received for a
Retirement Scheme, of a large proportion of the surplus Officers
as well, but this latter forecast is purely conjectural.

The total Navy Estimates for 1920–21 on the basis of this minimum Force and Personnel, and providing for starting no new
programme of construction, would, at the present enhanced
prices, be between £58,000,000 and £59,000,000 approximately, if
there were no dead-weight of war expenditure to fall upon next
year, and if Separation Allowances could be abolished next
March.

6.   It is estimated, however, that there will be £12,000,000 of
dead-weight expenditure arising out of the war which cannot be
liquidated until 1920–21.

Further, it has been decided and announced that the future of
Separation Allowances will depend upon the cost of living, and
at present it does not seem possible to assume that these Allowances will not be continued for 1920–21. The cost of their continuance for that year is between £4,000,000 and £5,000,000.

Taking those two exceptional commitments into account, it
would be unsafe to forecast the total of Navy Estimates for
1920–21 on the basis of this minimum Fleet at less than
£75,000,000.

7.   As already stated, the above figures do not provide for
starting any new programme of construction, but the Admiralty
consider it essential to include adequate provision for preventing

the entire dispersal of the existing facilities for the rapid construction of warships and their equipment in this country as a consequence of the complete break in our Building Programme, and the best way of effecting this is under consideration.

8.   If the Fleet be reduced to this extent, it must be clearly understood that Great Britain will no longer be supreme upon the sea. We shall be supreme in European Waters, but as regards the seas as a whole the supremacy will be shared with the United States. Our immediate position with the United States will be one approximately of equality, but it will rapidly become one of marked inferiority, if we undertake no new construction and the United States continue their 1916 Programme, which consists of capital ships much more powerful than any British ships with the exception of the *Hood*. By the end of the year 1923 we shall have passed to the position of being the second Naval Power unless

> either (*a*)   the United States can be induced by diplomatic means (whether by use of the machinery provided by Article 8 of the Covenant of the League of Nations or otherwise) to abandon or modify their 1916 Programme:
>
> or (*b*)   the decision to start no programme of new construction is reconsidered, in the light of the United States' action, in 12 months' time from now.

9.   Already the mere rumour of the passing of our sea-supremacy has called forth emphatic protests from other parts of the Empire, and it will undoubtedly have important effects on our prestige and our diplomatic and commercial interests.

10.   It has been suggested that it was well understood before the war that the United States did not enter into our comparisons of naval strength. This is not strictly accurate. All that was ever laid down by any Government was that in applying the 'Two-Power Standard' the United States, owing to their distance from Europe, should not be counted as one of the two principal Powers against whose possible *combination* we were providing. The arguments used had reference to the difficulties of effective co-operation between an American and a European Power, though no doubt the fact that up to that time the United States had faithfully followed the tradition of the Monroe Doctrine in having no European interests, was not without its influence. Even this view, however, was hotly contested and would certainly be contested again.

11.   But now it is not a question of our naval strength *vis-à-*

vis an hypothetical combination of two Powers, but in comparison with the United States Navy alone, at a time when the war has had the result of making the United States for the first time a factor in European politics. From their own pronouncements we know that the United States have grasped the truth that a Navy to be an effective weapon should be at least equal in strength to the possible antagonist, and everything goes to prove that their present intention is to maintain their Navy at a strength at least equal to our own. Such a state of affairs might possibly have been viewed with complacency at the end of the war had the United States been in the same position as it was at the commencement. But this is not so. The United States are building up a Mercantile Marine with the idea of competing with Great Britain in the world-carrying trade. They propose to protect that trade with a strong Navy, and the fact cannot be ignored that conflict of interests may arise with the United States in the same way as with other Powers in our history.

12. It is not suggested that this involves war between the United States and the British Empire. Having acquired by peaceful means the supremacy of the sea, their subsequent victories are probably destined to be commercial and diplomatic; but the effect of these upon our trade and Empire may be no less serious on this account.

13. The Board of Admiralty would be failing in their duty if they did not thus point out clearly what is involved in the decisions which the Cabinet now have to make.

14. The Board believe it to be unquestionable that Great Britain owes her leading position amongst the Nations to her long-maintained pre-eminence upon the sea. They believe that this pre-eminence cannot be relinquished without her ability to hold her position being profoundly affected, with all that that position involves in respect of prestige, authority, and commercial advantage.

15. The particular responsibilities of the Board in regard to the safety and welfare of the Empire, impel them, therefore, to urge that the sea supremacy, which is vital to us, should not be sacrificed, and that if the United States cannot be induced to abandon or modify their 1916 Programme, (as indicated in para: 8, Clause (*a*)) provision should be made to undertake the construction required to counterbalance it, (as indicated in para: 8, Clause (*b*)).

W.H.L.

24.10.1919.

30. *Wemyss to Long*

[Add. 62424]   Admiralty
                                                                  31.x.1919

*   *   *   *

I sometimes review the episodes of the last 10 [?] months and wonder whether any of the troubles which arose between Beatty and myself were owing to faults on my side. Honestly I do not think they were, and I was always in hopes of matters adjusting themselves, until those incidents arose which made it clear that no good could come from my taking any further steps. Well, if I committed any errors they were probably those of being too plastic [?] towards him at a time when I thought him a bit over-wrought, and in a state of mind which made it difficult for him to see matters in their true perspective and to judge them clearly.

It was owing to the fact that you were First Lord which made it possible for me to carry on; and, to carry on just then, was, I believe, the best for the Service.

*   *   *   *

I have taken a great deal of trouble during the last weeks to be 'en rapport' with Brock, so that there should be no gaps, and I feel fairly confident that you will not be bothered by finding any fundamental differences between my ideas and those of my successor. There are only 2 big questions of policy outstanding – the Air personnel of the Navy and Jellicoe's report,[1] which is awful! All other big matters are in such a position that Beatty can take them up and deal with them unhampered by any previous action on my part.

*   *   *   *

---

[1] Jellicoe's reports and other documents on his Empire Mission, 1919–20 are in A. Temple Patterson (ed.) (1969) *The Jellicoe Papers* vol II, part III, Navy Records Society (subsequently cited as *Jellicoe Papers*).

PART II

FIRST SEA LORD: MAJOR PROBLEMS EMERGE
November 1919–August 1922

INTRODUCTION[1]

When Beatty took office on 1 November 1919 he was immediately confronted with short term operational problems arising from the government's policy of supporting anti-Bolshevik forces in the Russian civil war which had followed the October Revolution of 1917. Simultaneously he had to tackle the major long term tasks which were to dominate his service as First Sea Lord. Chief among these was to persuade an economy-preoccupied Cabinet to make a clear commitment to maintain Britain's naval supremacy, by funding the modernisation of the Fleet necessitated by the naval ambitions of the United States and Japan. Closely connected to this was the need to analyse and apply the experience of the war, particularly the efficacy of the mine and torpedo against surface ships, and, infinitely more difficult, to assess the future significance of air power in maritime war. This last was bound to raise institutional conflict in the Navy's relations with the newly created Royal Air Force and in Beatty's own relationship with the first Chief of the Air Staff, Sir Hugh Trenchard.[2]

Crucial to success in all of these would be Beatty's ability to gain the support of his own political chief, the First Lord of the Admiralty, in the hope that he would be able to convince Lloyd George, the Prime Minister, now immersed in the critical negotiations of the peace treaty with Germany, and other Cabinet

[1]For the naval background to this section see Stephen Roskill (1968), *Naval Policy between the Wars, vol I, 1919–29*, London, (subsequently cited as Roskill, *Naval Policy I*). The domestic and economic background can be approached in A. J. P. Taylor (1965), *English History, 1914–45*, Oxford; his listing of Cabinet appointments and changes is particularly relevant.

[2]Sir Hugh Trenchard, later Marshal of the RAF and Viscount (1873–1956): failed Dartmouth entrance examination; commissioned into Royal Scots Fusiliers 1893; served in India, South Africa, Nigeria and Ireland; gained pilot's certificate and seconded to RFC and staff of Central Flying School Upavon 1912; commanded military wing at Farnborough 1914; commanded RFC in France and made brigadier general 1915–17; 1st Chief of Air Staff January 1918; resigned due to incompatibility with his minister, Lord Rothermere, April 1918; commanded independent bomber force in France from May 1918; on Churchill's invitation resumed as CAS February 1919 until 1929; Marshal of the RAF 1927; Commissioner of Metropolitan Police 1931–5.

69

ministers obsessed with the country's economic weakness, of the strength of the Navy's case. Fortunately he was able to establish excellent relations with Walter Long, the current First Lord, and, for the time being, to gain the strong support of Winston Churchill, Secretary for War and Air. Moreover Beatty's wartime popularity and professional reputation in the country were factors which could not be ignored by a Liberal–Conservative Coalition government containing strong navalist sentiment, especially when it was subject to attack by a popular Press if it appeared to be weakening the nation's defence, a Press which incidentally, Beatty was always ready to enlist in support of the Navy [107]. The existence of such backing, added to his own rapidly displayed skill in political negotiation and advocacy, resulted in what he saw as a clear success in overcoming the opposition in principle to a capital ship replacement programme. The fact that it was not implemented was due to the decisions of the Washington Naval Conference of 1921, based on the wider issues of the economy and a realisation of the folly of initiating a naval race with the United States.

From his first days as First Sea Lord, armed with his experience in the Grand Fleet and mindful of his own constant criticisms of the Admiralty, Beatty was determined to work through a well chosen and well organised Naval Staff. On arrival he found that Wemyss had already reorganised the greatly expanded wartime Staff to match its peacetime role and, with the appointment of Brock as DCNS and Chatfield[1] as ACNS, and the continuance of Spickernell as his secretary,[2] he soon had a team he could depend upon to react promptly and authoritatively to the heavy demands he made upon them. Throughout his term of office, crowded as it was with disputes with the Cabinet, the Committee of Imperial Defence and a multitude of *ad hoc* committees and conferences, he could rely on not being immersed in detail as had so many of his predecessors and successors, and being free to concentrate on the major issues of politics and policy. Similarly he made constant use of the specialist divisions of the Staff and related Admiralty

[1]Later Admiral of the Fleet Lord Chatfield (1873–1967): Beatty's Flag Captain during the war; Rear-Admiral 1919, joining Beatty at the Admiralty as 4th Sea Lord; appointed ACNS February 1920; 3rd Sea Lord and Controller 1925; Vice-Admiral 1926; C-in-C Atlantic Fleet 1929; Mediterranean and Admiral 1930; 1st Sea Lord 1933–8; Minister for Co-ordination of Defence 1939–40; author of *The Navy and Defence* (London 1952) and *It Might Happen Again* (London 1957).

[2]Fleet Paymaster, later Captain (S), Sir Frank Spickernell (1885–1956): Beatty's secretary throughout the war and during his term as 1st Sea Lord.

technical branches to supply himself with the precise information needed for the probing questioning and telling interventions which characterised his participation in committee [46–46A].

Despite his frequent complaints about the frustrations of these constant political struggles and the inevitable reduction of Britain's naval strength over which he had to preside, the documents show that Beatty derived considerable satisfaction from the successes he achieved in safeguarding the basic strength and morale of the service in such unfavourable circumstances. That he was able to sustain the pressures and demands for nearly eight years despite the additional burden of his wife's increasingly severe mental illness, compels admiration for his patience and devotion, even if one believes that his sense of responsibility for the Navy and his conviction that only he could safeguard its future, provided a compensation which enabled him to surmount his genuine and painful private grief. The pleasures of the hunt and the grouse moor would hardly have been an adequate substitute [44, 70, 73–4, 78, 83, 101, 107]. He also found consolation in his continuing relationship with Eugénie Godfrey-Faussett, with whom he could still share both his official and domestic cares [32, 73, 88].

In October 1921 Beatty became involved in a dispute in which his family origins must have given him a personal interest. Ireland's successful demands for self-government raised questions about the future of the Navy's bases there, and the record of a conference with Churchill and the Irish leader, Michael Collins,[1] shows him in action at the beginning of a long lasting and bitter dispute [92].

INTERVENTION IN RUSSIA[2]

Britain's intervention in Russia after the 1917 revolution originated in the hope, shared by France and the United States, that by backing anti-Bolshevik leaders they could keep her in the war against Germany and Austria and thus avoid the danger of being faced with a superior concentration of force on the Western front.

[1]Michael Collins (1890–1922): Irish nationalist leader and Chairman of the Provisional Government of the Irish Free State 1922; assassinated in August 1922 by irregular forces hostile to the treaty agreed with Britain bringing the Free State into existence.

[2]Roskill *Naval Policy I*, ch. III, analyses Britain's intervention; R. J. Bullen (1983), *The Royal Navy and the Baltic 1918–20*, unpublished Ph.D. thesis London: London University, assesses the RN contribution.

To this was added a strong ideological opposition to a revolutionary creed which appeared to threaten all established regimes. For Britain in particular there was long term apprehension about the threat to her Empire and her global strategic and economic interests. Intervention took place in the North, centring on Archangel and Murmansk, in the Black Sea, the Caspian and the Pacific. When Beatty took office withdrawal had begun. Archangel and Murmansk had been evacuated, as had Baku in the Caspian, and Vladivostock. But land forces remained at Batum on the Black Sea, and, of greatest concern to him, a naval force under his friend Walter Cowan[1] had been operating in the Baltic since January 1919, in support of the emergent new littoral states against both German and Russian threats to their precarious independence. Beatty's attitude to intervention was ambiguous. He was ideologically strongly anti-Bolshevik and particularly concerned with threats to Britain's interests in the Near and Middle East, but at the same time he was anxious about losses to his ships and even more, about the morale of his sailors, whose demobilisation had been delayed since the end of the German war. Ironically, unrest was most apparent in the Baltic squadron where Cowan's exploits had been politically effective, in contrast to the futility of the other interventions. Within three days of taking office Beatty was recommending complete withdrawal and, although this did not happen until 1921, Cowan himself and a substantial part of his force were ordered home [31]. The withdrawal of German forces from the area and the Bolsheviks' preoccupation with more pressing dangers to their regime, ensured that the Baltic republics could begin their twenty years of independent existence. Beatty's attention then shifted to the Near and Middle East. He opposed the evacuation of Batum and recommended reoccupation of Baku. He became most emphatic on the need for a naval presence in the Caspian and on the extreme importance of guaranteeing British access to the Persian oil fields, now that oil was ousting coal in maritime propulsion [34, 36, 37]. Later, he was even prepared to recommend direct intervention in support of the White Russian general, Wrangel,[2] who appeared

[1]Later Admiral Sir Walter Cowan (1871–1956): entered RN 1884 (with Beatty); Flag Captain to Brock in *Princess Royal*; Commodore 1st Light Cruiser Squadron; Rear-Admiral, 1918; commanded RN force in Baltic 1919; Battle Cruiser Squadron 1921; Vice-Admiral 1923; C-in-C Scotland 1925; C-in-C America and West Indies 1926–8; Admiral 1927; retired 1931.

[2]Baron Peter Wrangel (1878–1928): succeeded General Denikin (1872–1947) as commander of anti-Bolshevik forces in Southern Russia in April 1920.

to be gaining significant success in Southern Russia, but Cabinet policy was now firmly against further intervention and Wrangel was finally defeated by the end of the year [42]. Beatty's growing fear of the impact of Bolshevism even led him to fear its spreading to Britain and the Navy itself [43].

THE FUTURE OF NAVAL AVIATION

That Beatty had welcomed the 1917 Smuts Report[1] recommending the incorporation of the Royal Naval Air Service and the Royal Flying Corps into a new service which was to emerge as the Royal Air Force in 1918 should not be interpreted as a lack of understanding of the future significance of maritime air power. An alternative version is that he thought that if the RAF were to undertake responsibility for the air defence of the United Kingdom and for offensive operations against the enemy, it would be possible to make a strong case for a specialised force for naval operations. This would have been in harmony with his clearly expressed views in the later stages of his command of the Grand Fleet that air power was an integral part of its combat equipment.[2] Certainly when he came to the Admiralty he was made thoroughly aware of the difficulties which had arisen with the existing inter-service arrangements. The Naval Staff had opposed the loss of the Fleet Air Arm from the beginning, and with Chatfield's appointment as ACNS in February 1920, and thus responsible for air matters, their criticisms were accentuated, and reinforced by reports from the Fleet of the practical operational and personnel problems which had arisen. It was inevitable that Beatty would now press for some form of designated naval air power. As the debate continued he reluctantly

---

[1]Jan Christian Smuts (1870–1950): led a commando raid against the British in the Boer War; played a major role in the peace negotiations, and in the creation of the Union of South Africa in 1909; supported participation in the war from 1914 and commanded Imperial forces in successful campaign in German East Africa; in January 1917 came to London as South African representative in the Imperial War Cabinet and then, at Lloyd George's invitation, joined British War Cabinet; after the war, active in support of League of Nations and the concept of a British Commonwealth of Nations; opposed harsh peace terms with Germany; South African Premier 1919–24 when defeated by the Nationalist Party. The work of his committee on the organisation of British air power, including Beatty's views, is covered in S. W. Roskill (ed.), London (1969) *Documents Relating to the Naval Air Service, vol I, 1908–18*, Navy Records Society; a second volume is being prepared by Professor Geoffrey Till.

[2]See *Beatty Papers I*, pp. 481–8, Grand Fleet Fighting Instructions.

had to accept that the Government, and any likely successor, would never retreat from the policy of a unified force under the Air Ministry. He and the Naval Staff then began to search for a compromise and started a struggle which was to continue throughout his term of office. Although he deployed considerable negotiating skill and made some progress, it was not until 1937 that acceptable arrangements for meeting the Navy's specialised needs were made. There is no doubt that when war came, the United States and Japanese navies, which had never lost control of their air power, were able to make more efficient use of what was to emerge as a decisive factor in war at sea, than could the Royal Navy.

The Chief of the Air Staff, Sir Hugh Trenchard, determined to maintain the principle of the unity of air power, was prepared for the opposition he was bound to encounter from the Navy and Army. In November 1919 he took the initiative by proposing a period of grace to enable him to get his fledgling service established before he had to face up to public controversy. A personal letter to Beatty [33] gives a clear presentation of his point of view and of the problems he had to solve. Although it contains no recognition of the particular requirements of maritime air operations, his suggestion that in due time, the other two services should include the provision of air power in their own Estimates, could have been interpreted by Beatty as giving the Navy considerable influence over the meeting of its own needs, and could have been a major factor in his acceptance of the truce. But by 1921 the truce was over, and Beatty, on the grounds of operational necessity and in agreement, he claimed, with the Army, pressed the First Lord to raise in Cabinet the whole concept of the need for a separate air service [89, 91]. In the following year he produced the additional argument that Admiralty control of naval aviation would be more economical and thus assist the government to meet the reductions in expenditure urged by the Geddes Report, and asked for a strong committee to settle the matter [106]. At this stage Churchill, now Colonial Secretary, tried to bring the two sides together by informal meetings, as well as by correspondence. In these Beatty showed some willingness to compromise by claiming that he was not seeking to establish an entirely separate naval air service, but only a comparatively small force under Admiralty control as an integral part of the Fleet. By now

Hankey[1] was convinced that no agreed compromise was possible and that a committee should be established to give a clear political directive with Cabinet authority. The Prime Minister's acceptance of this advice was eventually to lead to the setting up of the Balfour Committee [111–14].

THE BONAR LAW COMMITTEE ON THE FUTURE OF THE CAPITAL SHIP

Although relations with the RAF were to occupy Beatty for much of his term of office, his first two years were dominated by wider questions of the size of the Fleet, the maintenance of the One Power Standard, the role of the battleship, and finally, the Washington Conference: a conference which resolved all these questions for the time being, although in ways which Beatty in his heart of hearts could not welcome, although he had to accept their inevitability.

The Bonar Law Committee, formally a sub-committee of the CID, established in December 1920, 'To take evidence on the question of the Capital Ship in the Royal Navy' was a politically strong body. Bonar Law,[2] the Chairman, was the leading Conservative minister in Lloyd George's coalition, and destined to be Prime Minister when it broke up in 1922. The other members were Churchill (at its inception Secretary for War and Air), Walter Long (First Lord of the Admiralty), Robert Horne[3] (President of the Board of Trade), Eric Geddes (Minister without Portfolio), and Beatty himself, as a member and not just a witness. Although the nature of external events, particularly the Washington Conference, made some of its findings abortive, it marked a very significant stage in Beatty's development as First Sea Lord. For the first time it involved him on equal terms in prolonged negotiations with ministers on matters of primary importance to the Navy, and which also forced him to give considerable thought to the relative

[1]Maurice, later 1st Baron, Hankey (1877–1963); entered Royal Marines 1895; served in NID 1902–7; Assistant Secretary CID 1908; Secretary 1912–38; Secretary War Cabinet 1916–18; Cabinet Secretary 1919–38; member of War Cabinet 1939–40.

[2]Andrew Bonar Law (1858–1923): Leader of Conservative Party 1911; Colonial Secretary 1915–16; Lord Privy Seal 1919–21; Prime Minister 1922–3.

[3]Robert, later 1st Viscount, Horne (1871–1940): Scottish lawyer; associate of Eric Geddes in war transport organisation in France; Director of Labour at the Admiralty 1918; 3rd Civil Lord of Admiralty 1918–19; Unionist MP for Glasgow and Minister of Labour December 1918; President Board of Trade 1920; Chancellor of Exchequer 1921–2; held no further office and had successful business career.

responsibility of the Cabinet and the Admiralty for formulating and executing naval policy. His role was the greater because his political chief, Long, was prevented by illness from attending any of the committee's meetings, although he gave strong support in correspondence with his ministerial colleagues. Beatty's very effective presentation of the Navy's case owed much to his successful use of the Naval Staff to produce a constant flow of factual information and rational argument.

The actual subject of the inquiry had already seriously concerned Beatty and the Staff before he took office, and essentially arose out of the lack of battleship building during the war and the evident intention of the United States and Japan to embark on substantial construction programmes [see documents 5, 14, 25, 29]. For Beatty the issue was clear. The government must formally confirm the policy that the Navy would not be allowed to become inferior to that of any other country, including France and the United States, however unlikely it was to become an enemy, and must provide the resources for an appropriate capital ship replacement programme. For the government the situation was much more complex. Beatty's proposed building programme seemed to threaten their plan for economic stringency. The last thing they wanted was unwinnable naval competition with the United States, and they were aware that among a minority of naval officers the view was growing that the emergence of air power and of effective underwater weapons was casting doubt on the future efficacy of the battleship as the determinant of naval power. It was this doubt in particular that Beatty, in the absence of Long, had to persuade the committee to reject, and he did so with evident enjoyment both in planning the questioning of witnesses and in making substantial oral and written contributions to the proceedings [38, 45, 46, 73]. The final result was inconclusive. There was general acceptance that no case had been made for the obsolescence of the battleship, but Law, Geddes and Horne could not accept Beatty's argument that an immediate building programme should be authorised. Beatty, Churchill and the ailing Long would not sign a report on these lines and issued their own [74–80, 82, 84–6].

THE WASHINGTON CONFERENCE, 1921

As early as May 1919 Churchill had recognised the danger and folly of a Naval race with the United States and urged the necessity of agreement on naval arms limitation between the two countries.[1] By 1921 the British government, led by Lloyd George, was so strongly in favour of this that it was determined that no objections from the Navy would be allowed to stand in its way. The same opinion was held by the United States government and Congress, although they firmly felt that American public opinion would not accept any continuance of British claims to naval superiority, and that equality must be achieved. This approach was demonstrated when the Conference assembled in November. The British main delegation was entirely civilian, led by Arthur Balfour,[2] Lord President of the Council, while Arthur Lee,[3] who had succeeded Long as First Lord of the Admiralty and Auckland Geddes,[4] Ambassador in Washington, made up the membership. Beatty and Chatfield were merely in support, to provide expert advice to the politicians. The same approach was made by the Americans under the leadership of Charles Evans Hughes,[5] Secretary of the Navy, but naval officers figured in Japan's delegation.

Beatty's discomfort at the whole pattern of the Conference was increased by his failure to achieve a good relationship with Lee. A strong mutual antipathy between them developed as the Conference proceeded, which contributed to Beatty's early return to London, although there was much truth in his claim that he would

[1]See pp. 35–6.
[2]Arthur, later 1st Earl, Balfour (1848–1930); Conservative MP from 1874; Chief Secretary for Ireland 1887; 1st Lord of Treasury in his uncle Lord Salisbury's government 1891 and again in 1895; Prime Minister 1902–5; at the beginning of the war, at Asquith's request, active in CID; 1st Lord of Admiralty 1915–16; Foreign Secretary 1916–19; Lord President of Council 1919–22.
[3]Arthur Lee, later Lord Lee of Fareham (1868–1947): military career 1888–1900; Military Attaché in Washington 1899; retired from Army and elected MP (Conservative) for Fareham 1900; Civil Lord of Admiralty 1903; rejoined Army, served on General Staff in France 1914; at Lloyd George's invitation became Parliamentary Secretary, Ministry of Munitions 1915; Military Secretary to Lloyd George as Secretary for War 1916; Director-General of Food Production 1917; peerage 1918; President of Board of Agriculture 1919; 1st Minister of Agriculture 1920; 1st Lord of Admiralty 1921; resigned on break up of the Lloyd George Coalition in 1922 and held no further political office.
[4]Sir Auckland Geddes (1879–1954): brother of Sir Eric Geddes (see p. 4); although a medical man, served in Army as AAG at GHQ in France; Director of Recruiting at War Office 1916; Director of National Service 1917–19; MP for Basingstoke 1917–28; President Board of Trade 1919–20; Ambassador to United States 1920–24.
[5]Charles Evans Hughes (1862–1948): successful commercial lawyer in New York; Governor (Republican) New York State 1906; Supreme Court judge 1910; unsuccessfully contested Presidential election against Woodrow Wilson 1916; Secretary of State 1921–5; his opening speech at the Washington Conference was the high point of his career.

be better employed in saving the Naval Estimates from suffering fatally under the Geddes Axe. He was happy to leave the detailed naval negotiations to Chatfield once he was convinced that the politicians could not be deflected from their overall aims. What he most strongly objected to was the ten year 'holiday' on battleship construction, on the grounds that Britain had already had a five-year 'holiday' and that if it were prolonged the future capability of industry to satisfy the Navy's requirements would be destroyed. He admitted the justification for a reduction in capital ship numbers but proposed a steady gradual replacement programme rather than a complete cessation of building. The Cabinet accepted the logic of his arguments but decided that the overall advantage of accepting the American proposals and thus securing the signing of the treaty should be given priority [90, 93, 100].

THE GEDDES AXE

The Commitee on National Expenditure under Sir Eric Geddes issued its interim report dealing with the armed forces in December 1921. Its basic contention was that economic collapse and high taxation could only be avoided by significant cuts in government expenditure. Its 'axe' was to be swung against all departments. Five were to be abolished, including Transport and Labour, and heavy reductions made in education and public health expenditure. For the Navy, the Admiralty's proposed Estimates for 1922–1923 were to be reduced from £81 to £60 millions. With Lee fully occupied in Washington, Beatty was solely responsible for saving the Navy from what he regarded as unacceptable blows to its personnel and equipment. He handled the task with great skill, particularly by gaining the powerful support not only of Churchill but also of Birkenhead, the Lord Chancellor.[1] In the consequent negotiations Churchill recommended cuts to £62 millions but insisted that the major personnel reductions must be rejected. He accepted the force of Beatty's argument of the necessity to counter the Japanese threat, including the construction of the Singapore base, and also commended the Admiralty for the economies it had already achieved and planned. When the Estimates were finally presented to Parliament in March 1922, to Beatty's satisfaction they totalled just under £65 millions. This

[1] F. E. Smith, later 1st Earl of Birkenhead (1874–1930): eminent lawyer and Conservative politician; Solicitor General 1916–19; Lord Chancellor 1919–22; Secretary for India 1924–8.

achievement, demonstrative of Beatty's now proven political skills, was the more remarkable as it coincided with his wife's suffering a period of intense depression which taxed him sorely – even to the extent of telling her that it was only due to his personal devotion to her that she was saved from having to be admitted to a nursing home [101–5, 107–10].

31. First Sea Lord: Memorandum for Cabinet

[Copy]

PROPOSAL TO MAINTAIN A NAVAL FORCE IN THE
BALTIC DURING WINTER 1919–20[1]

[ADM/116/1774]   4.11.19

It is understood that the main reason advanced in support of this
proposal is to show the flag. The latter proceeding is of undoubted
value in normal times of peace in waters like the Baltic.

Experience has, however, shown that the presence of an odd
light cruiser or destroyer in the various ports has little or no
stabilising effect on local affairs since the German aggression
became pronounced. The inability of HM Ships to do more than
advise and the necessity for removing themselves when matters
become threatening have tended still further to emphasise the fact
that a weak naval force is only effective as long as the other side
chooses to allow it to be so – in short, 'the bluff has been called'.

If a British force, however small, remains in Baltic waters
during the winter months it appears certain that there will be calls
on this force from the various Baltic States for protection and
assistance. Refusal of such requests would inevitably lessen British
prestige in these States; acquiescence would equally inevitably
lead to operations on an ever increasing scale culminating eventually in the presence of a force similar to that now employed.

All light cruisers and destroyers have had a particularly arduous
period of service in the Baltic during the past eight months. The
conditions, which are unavoidable, are described as far worse
than war. Further service there throughout the winter would be
extremely unpopular, and it is distinctly undesirable to expose
men to further contact with the various political elements which
obtain in those ports. As an instance of this danger, Bolshevik
propaganda has already been found in the possession of British
seamen, which would obviously have had its effect on the weaker
elements.

It would be necessary to limit the period of service to one

[1]R. J. Bullen, see p. 71 n. 2, gives a detailed account of the political and
operational problems encountered.

month, bearing in mind the considerations outlined and the unsuitability of light cruisers and destroyers to very cold weather.

It is considered that the minimum force that it would be worth while retaining there would be –

2 light cruisers
5 destroyers   } based at Copenhagen

The destroyers are necessary on account of the danger from mines; it is not fair under peace conditions to ask cruisers to run the risk of being mined without some escorting force in attendance.

It would be necessary for a force equal to the above to proceed to the Baltic and return at frequent intervals for relief purposes, involving great expense. This expense would be added to by the necessary provision of fuel at the base; canteen stores, provisions, etc. would also be required should one of the ships have to proceed to Libau, etc.

It is estimated that the cost for three months would amount approximately to £140,000 for fuel alone. There would undoubtedly be other expenses, but these are so vague that anything nearer than the merest guess is impossible. £50,000 soon slips away in these indefinite expeditions.

In conclusion the Admiralty desire to point out that they are unable to see that the maintenance in these waters of what is really, in view of its size and combination, a non-fighting force, would result in any gain which is not more than counter-balanced by the objections set forth above.

In consideration of the considerable cost involved and the pressing need for economy, the Admiralty recommend that the entire force be withdrawn.

(Intd.) B.

4.11.19

Forwarded.

(Intd.) W. H. L.

32. *Beatty to Eugénie Godfrey-Faussett*

[SLGF 15/2]   Brooksby Hall
                                                    Sunday [9 Nov 1919]

My first week at the sink of iniquity has gone, and left me cold. From 10.30 to 7.30 every day in that spot is not my idea for the future. But it was necessary to become acquainted with the personnel and what they were doing.

I just itch to blast the whole place and begin afresh, but with a great machine which has to function hourly one cannot destroy until one can create immediately the machine to take its place, and therefore I have to move slowly.

This is the first moment I have had time to write anything but the official type of outpourings. However, I am getting hold of things and begin to see daylight, and once when we can start [?] it will be comparatively easy.

*   *   *   *

33. *Sir Hugh Trenchard to Beatty*

[Copy]

                                                         Air Ministry
[AIR 8/17/2A]   Kingsway WC.2
Personal   November 22nd 1919

Dear Admiral,
    The view I have of the future Air Force is as follows:
    There will be three branches of the Air Service:

(*a*) That portion which will be trained for, and work with, the
        Navy, as an arm of that Service.
(*b*) That portion which will be trained for, and work with, the
        Army, as an arm of that Service.
(*c*) The main portion, which will be an Independent Force,
        (that may work independently, or in co-operation with
        either the Navy or the Army), and Research.

The picture would finally therefore be as follows:

	Independent	
Navy	Force and	Army
	Research	

(*a*) and (*b*) would probably have distinctive badges, to show their distinction from each other, and the whole would be trained and supplied by the Air Ministry. The Air Ministry would present the estimates, and justify them.

As time goes on, it may be that the central portion will increase in size until it is as large as, or even larger than, the other two portions.

It may be asked why not bring in this scheme now at once. My answer is that I have already adopted the principle by forming the Coastal Area, and it is only a question of the method and time by which the final organisation should be completed. To form separate branches at once would inevitably result in the absence of any common basis or ideals, and we should return to the old state of affairs with practically separate Services. I am absolutely convinced that in order to form the final conception of the Air Service we must lay the foundation of an Air Force spirit and of a training system common to all in its initial stages at all events. In other words we have to form the centre portion first, with the beginnings of the outside branches, which will grow in size and independence as we develop.

If this scheme were brought in now, there is a danger that, in view of the large number of Naval and Army officers and Members of Parliament who consider that the Air Force should be broken up, endless discussion would ensue with Cabinet, Parliament and Press, and this would result in delay in the formation of the basis of the Air Service which it is so essential to start at once.

It would be impossible now to split up the vote for Air estimates and let the Navy and Army ask for their own, because:

(*a*) Who is to pay for aerodromes and buildings? some of which may be common to all three Services – for example, Malta.

(*b*) How is payment for personnel to be adjusted – say where men are sent to hospital abroad.

(*c*) It is impossible to say what portion of the training would be for the Navy only or what portion would be for the Army only among the officers and mechanics at the various schools. Much of it is common to both, and it would be impossible to make out a fair proportion.

The Air Ministry is now beginning to feel, for the first time in its existence, the novel experience of having permanent people in charge of the various Directorates; political changes do not trouble the departmental work so long as there is no change in policy, but we know full well from experience that these changes usually do mean a change of policy and the inevitable loss of continuity.

No officer, however zealous, can give his whole attention to his work if he feels that his post is not secure owing to continuous changes in method of working. This naturally affects all the subordinates in the department and under these unsettled conditions much valuable time and money is wasted.

I am absolutely convinced that the Air Ministry must exist as a separate department entirely responsible for its own estimates at present, and that any suspicion of a contemplated change in its functions will not only create much unrest in the R.A.F., but will also encourage all the numerous people, such as MPs, many Admirals and Generals, disappointed ex-RAF officers and others who, while professing great interest in the importance of Air matters, are, in reality out to revert to the old order of a divided Service. I think in many cases this is due to ignorance, but whatever the reason may be, I am sure that any alteration whatever at the present time would be fatal.

If there is any change of method the Service would feel, and the old Services too, that you as Frist [sic] Sea Lord had brought about this change, and that you were opposed to the principle of an Air Service – although I know that this is not so – and I am afraid the effect of their feeling that you were against an Air Service, even though it would be untrue, would mean the end of it.

What is wanted in the Air Service is a period of freedom from criticism by Parliament and the public, and this I am sure could be obtained if we continued as we are at present. Everybody would then feel that you were backing us up with all your power, and when the Air Force has been formed, it may be in two or three years' time, then, and not till then, will be the time to consider a modification by which the old Services will pay each for its own portion of the Air Service, without the danger of its breaking up the Air Force.

Another reason for not asking the old Services to pay for their parts of the Air Service now is that if the Admiralty or War Office asked for extra money for the Air Service, the Cabinet would say that this must come out of the total amount already allotted to the Air Force, and this would mean a continued discussion as to how it might be possible to build up an Air Service on a smaller sum, resulting in further delay in forming a basis for building on in the future.

I would therefore most strongly press you to agree to accept this view, if you can see your way to do so. I know the feelings in the Air Service, both in the Naval branch and the Army branch, and there is a feeling of unrest owing to the continued plainly expressed desires of the senior officers of the old services.

I have written this as my personal view and tried to show how the personal element enters largely into my views and how the fact of your being at the Admiralty affects it. So I hope you will not mind the personal aspect of it.

Yours sincerely,

(Signed) H. TRENCHARD

34. *Beatty to Long*

[Memorandum]

[Ll.G/F/34/1/3]   [Forwarded to Lloyd George]   6.1.20

CASPIAN SITUATION

1st Lord

The recent successes of the Bolsheviks in South Russia have profoundly changed the situation since the decision was reached last summer to evacuate the British naval personnel in the Caspian Sea.

2.   Denikin's[1] present situation in the Caspian is serious. He has lost Tsaritsin and Krasnovodsk and the Bolsheviks' fleet in the Volga was reported on December 27th to be only prevented by lack of fuel from coming South. Denikin's fleet, which is at Petrovsk, is reported as unsatisfactory and likely to turn Bolshevik (vide statement by Col. Stokes in Tel. 234 from Mr. Wardrop).

3.   At the same time there are indications, according to Admiralty information, that the Bolsheviks are turning their eyes to the Middle East and particularly to the Mahommedan population there.

We have also assumed responsibility for Persia, whose interest in the Caspian is great.

4.   British control of the Caspian will be an essential condition of any military operations that may become necessary for the

[1]General Anton Denikin (1872–1947): his initial success and subsequent failure are analysed in Roskill, *Naval Policy I*, pp. 155–9, 162–4.

defence of Persia, Mesopotamia or India, or for the protection of the Trans-Caucasian Republics if the Bolsheviks continue their advance southwards.

5. In these circumstances the Admiralty consider that it is of great importance to regain control of the Caspian immediately. In their view the quickest and most effective way to do so is to take over at once as many of Denikin's ships as he will agree to turn over and man them with British crews from the Mediterranean.

6. In view of his critical situation it is anticipated that Denikin may be prepared to accede to this proposal if only to save his ships, but for the same reason the Admiralty consider that the matter will have to be carried through at once, if it is to be done at all. They therefore consider the question as urgent.

7. If General Denikin is either unwilling or unable to hand over his ships, the Admiralty would be prepared to put forward alternative proposals, which would, however, require time to put into effect.

It is to be understood that any proposals for the Naval control of the Caspian are dependent on the use of Baku as a base. No other port has the necessary facilities or communications. This entails military occupation of Baku by British troops.

(Sgd.) BEATTY
6.1.20

Forwarded
(init) W.H.L.

35. Beatty: Minute on Naval Staff Organisation[1]

[Copy]

[ADM.116/1803]   8.1.20

I have had under consideration the necessity of strengthening the organisation of the Naval Staff as regards the Divisions of the Staff charged with the responsibility, under the Chief of the Naval Staff, of formulating the Staff view as to:–

(a) Development of the Air as applied to naval progress.

(b) Types of vessels to meet naval requirements.

(c) Development and use of weapons generally: thus to ensure

[1]See Document 87 below.

correct application of technical experience gained in the
4½ years of war.

(d)   Anti-submarine training and experience.
(e)   Staff questions on Experimental establishments and scien-
      tific research.

2.   For this purpose it is proposed to place under the A.C.N.S.
those Divisions of the Staff dealing with the following:–

(a)   Types of ships, including submarines, as required by
      policy.
(b)   Material generally, so far as its tactical requirements are
      concerned and its quantity and distribution, including:–
      Guns
      Torpedoes
      Mines
      Anti-submarine weapons
      Gas
(c)   Signalling, in connection with tactics
(d)   Development of air material to meet policy requirements
(e)   Regulation of Fleet practices: co-ordination between fleet,
      [sic] and standardisation of method.

*   *   *   *

4.   The ACNS under the new organisation would remain a
member of the Board, in charge of the Divisions of the Staff
referred to above, and responsible to the CNS for the work outlined.

36.   Report of Cabinet Conference on oil supply and control of Caspian

[Copy]

[BTY/8/1/11]   [Extract]   Paris – 18.1.1920

Lord Beatty said that he would like to add an additional danger
to those that had already been mentioned as involved in the loss
of control of the Caspian.[1] This was a Naval strategical question.
During the last five years our command of fuel and particularly
of coal, was one of the factors which had helped us to control the
seas. This power was passing, owing to the fact that oil was rapidly
taking the place of coal. Not only was the mercantile marine using

---

[1]See Document 34 above.

oil as its fuel to an increasing degree, but the Navy was now dependent to the extent of 75 per cent on oil supplies which were not under British control. He believed that at the moment he was correct in stating that only 4 per cent of the oil output of the world was under British control, although if the proposed agreement with the French were signed this percentage would be considerably increased. It was very important to the Navy that this control should not be in foreign hands. Of course the output of the United States of America was entirely in American hands. The Americans could also at any moment control the Mexican Eagle supplies, and owing to its geographical position the same applied to Trinidad. The other sources of supply which we could control were very small. One of the problems of the Naval War Staff had been to ascertain where oil was to be found which could be obtained without control by other Powers. Of these sources it was found that Persian oil was by far the most important. In Persia there were great oilfields not as yet tapped, which experts believed were more extensive than those in existence elsewhere. To hold the Caspian meant that these oilfields would be relatively easily defended. From the commercial point of view it was most important to hold them. If, as the Secretary of State for War had suggested,[1] it might be desired to re-capture the Caspian in the face of opposition, this might prove well-nigh impossible. At the present moment time was a very important factor. If no decision were reached within three days time, he believed it would not be possible to hold the Caspian. A good deal had to be done. Among other things, General Denikin's consent had to be obtained. (Mr Churchill observed that there was no difficulty about this.) The representatives of the Azerbaijan had informed him that they would agree to hand over their ships. We should have to put ourselves in a position to repair them, and they would have to be got into condition for use not later than March 10th, when the ice would melt on the Volga. If no decision were taken within three days he repeated it would be impossible to effect this.

[1]Winston Churchill.

37. *Long's Private Secretary to Lloyd George's Private Secretary*

[Ll.G/F/34/1/8]   February 12th 1920

Mr Long would be glad if the enclosed copy of a Memorandum from the First Sea Lord could be brought to the Prime Minister's notice.

Mr Long strongly recommends that the action suggested by the Commander-in-Chief Mediterranean should be taken. [Marked 'Approved']

Memorandum by Beatty

[Copy]   12.2.20

With reference Memorandum by Secretary of State of Foreign Affairs on evacuation of Batum, in which he quotes the opinions of Admiral de Robeck and Admiral Webb,[1] that the removal of these troops would be a grave mistake at this juncture, a telegram has been received from Admiral de Robeck urging that the First Battle Squadron should proceed to Constantinople. General Milne[2] has telegraphed similarly . . .

The First Battle Squadron is at Malta and is ready to proceed on receipt of orders.

The presence of this Squadron at Constantinople would enable the British garrison to remain in Batum, and the Naval force in the Black Sea would ensure their safe withdrawal in emergency.

If necessary, it would be possible to land upwards of 1500 men from these ships.

---

[1]Later Admiral of the Fleet Sir John de Robeck (1862–1928): entered RN 1875; Rear-Admiral 1911; Admiral of Patrols; commanded 9th Cruiser Squadron 1914; 2nd in command and eventually successor to Vice-Admiral Carden in the Dardanelles and Vice-Admiral 1915; commanded 2nd Battle-Cruiser Squadron Grand Fleet 1916–19; C-in-C Mediterranean 1919–22; Admiral 1920; C-in-C Atlantic 1922–4; Admiral of the Fleet 1925. Rear-Admiral Richard Webb (1870–1950): had acted as Deputy High Commissioner at Constantinople pending de Robeck's arrival; the High Commissioner was responsible to the Foreign Office and not the Admiralty; Webb subsequently was the SNO afloat at Constantinople.

[2]General Sir George Milne (1866–1948): later Field Marshal and 1st baron; at this time commanding British land forces in Near East; CIGS 1926–33.

38. Beatty to First Lord

[Copy of Memorandum]

[ADM 1/8602/54]   8.7.20

Secret. NAVAL POLICY AND CONSTRUCTION

First Lord

In a memorandum to the Cabinet dated October 1919,[1] on Naval Policy and Expenditure, the minimum Naval force necessary in the then existing circumstances for the security of the Empire was given as follows:–

In Commission	16 Battleships	4 Battle Cruisers
In Reserve	13 -do-	3 -do-

With these minimum numbers it was pointed out, however, that Great Britain would no longer be supreme upon the sea. These words were used:–

We shall be supreme in European Waters, but as regards the seas as a whole the supremacy will be shared with the United States. Our immediate position with the United States will be one approximately of equality, but it will rapidly become one of marked inferiority, if we undertake no new construction and the United States continue their 1916 programme, which consists of Capital ships much more powerful than any British ships with the exception of the *Hood*. By the end of the year 1923 we shall have passed to the position of being the second Naval Power, unless –

either (*a*) the United States can be induced by diplomatic means (whether by use of the machinery provided by Article 8 of the Covenant of the League of Nations or otherwise) to abandon or modify their 1916 Programme:

or (*b*) the decision to start no programme of new construction is reconsidered, in the light of the United States' action, in twelve months' time from now.

2. In the further memorandum to the Cabinet on Naval Estimates and Naval Policy dated 13th February, 1920, the foregoing argument was emphasised, and it was again pointed out that if an understanding with the United States was not possible, then it

[1]See Document 29 above.

would be necessary definitely to lay down that a 'One-Power Standard' against the strongest naval power is the minimum standard compatible with our vast sea requirements, and that the British building programme in all types of vessels must be such that this 'One-Power Standard' is fully maintained.

3. This memorandum was considered by the Cabinet, and in his speech on the introduction of the Naval Estimates in the House of Commons on March 17th, 1920, the First Lord[1] used these words as indicating the policy of the Government:–

I believe it is a fact that the naval policies of all past Governments, whichever party they represented, have, at least, included this common principle, that our Navy should not be inferior in strength to the Navy of other powers, and to this principle the present Government firmly adheres . . . That is the foundation of the naval policy of His Majesty's Government. This is not a matter for the Admiralty, this is a matter for the Government, and this is the policywhich we have deliberately adopted, and I, at least, think it is a policy which will commend itself to the House of Commons and the Country.

No modification of the United States 1916 programme has occurred, and to carry out the Government policy and maintain a 'One-Power Naval Standard', the commencement of a building programme in the financial year 1920–1921 will be essential.

4. An examination of the relative strengths shows that if we are to maintain this 'One-Power Standard' the essential factor is that we should commence forthwith to replace our older Capital ships. The reason for this is that war experience resulted in a rapid advance in the design of war vessels introducing improvement not only in gun and torpedo power, but also in protection qualities; so much so that the older classes of British War Vessels are rapidly becoming, and in some cases are already, obsolete, and are not fit to hold their position in the Fleet.

In any comparison, therefore, with the United States, it is not sufficient to consider total numbers. The far more important consideration is the comparison between the respective numbers laid down since 1916 and after the experience gained as a result of the Battle of Jutland. This relative position assuming no British building programme is shown in Appendix I. [not included]

If then it is desirable for political or other reasons in considering

[1] Walter Long.

the question of the strength of the British fleet not to refer to the United States or the 'One-Power Standard', (especially may this be the case at this present period prior to the Presidential Elections), and to avoid it being laid to our charge that we are entering upon a building competition with the United States, it would be equally effective to frame our construction programme on a 'replacement' policy, the necessity for such replacement being based on the war experience referred to above, and also the lessened life of our ships consequent on the enormous strain during the war, caused by continuous steaming and high speeds; sea-keeping under all conditions of weather, and refits of a shortened duration and at longer intervals.

It could further be pointed out that a steady replacement of our older ships is an essential and sound financial policy if we are to avoid far heavier expenditure on construction at a later date.

5. It is this aspect of the question which has been most carefully examined by the Naval Staff, and as a result it can be stated that if we adopt a policy of –

(*a*)   15 years age for replacement of Capital ships now in the fleet and completed prior to the War, of the *Dreadnought, Orion, King George V*, and *Iron Duke* Classes (22 vessels in all);

(*b*)   20 years age for replacement of Capital ships now in the fleet and completed after the commencement of the War (*Queen Elizabeth* and later Classes);

then provided no further construction by the United States is undertaken, a 'One-Power Standard' will be maintained.

6. Accepting the above policy of the gradual replacement of Capital ships now in the fleet, with the ultimate object of maintaining a 'One-Power Standard', it will be necessary to lay down 4 replace Capital ships in 1921 and a further 4 in 1922. The relative position at the end of 1925, assuming this building programme, is shown in Appendix 2. [not included]

This is the minimum for safety, and even with such a programme it must be clearly understood that there will be a period (1923–25) when we shall have actually fallen below the 'One-Power Standard' and be somewhat inferior in fighting strength to the United States.

It is proposed, therefore, in the financial year 1921–22 that Parliament should be requested to authorise the building of 4 Capital ships.

7. In regard to Light Cruisers and Destroyers, our position is such that actual new construction will be unnecessary, and it will be sufficient if in the financial year 1921–22 the Light Cruisers and Destroyers already laid down are completed and replace older classes of similar vessels. This will involve the completion of the *Cape Town*, 2 *Effinghams*, 3 'D' Class and 2 'E' Class, and certain Destroyers, progress on which has been suspended in HM Dockyards whilst vessels hired during the War were being reconditioned prior to return to their owners. This reconditioning is now coming to an end and apart, therefore, from the primary consideration of naval strength, there is the secondary consideration that work on the Light Cruisers and Destroyers will prevent unemployment or dislocation of labour in the Dockyard towns.

8. Construction of Submarines will also not require to be undertaken during 1921–22. Important developments in regard to the internal combustion engine and other factors may be expected during the course of the next year, and prior to full consideration of these developments, it would be unwise to embark on a programme of Submarine replacement and construction. The argument of gradual replacement in the case of Capital ships does not apply to Submarines, which are rapidly and comparatively cheaply built, and it is an advantage, therefore, with Submarines to wait and gain the result of laboratory and sea trials now being carried out.

9. There remains the question of special types of vessels required by the sea-going fleet under modern conditions, and the need for which did not exist in the same measure before the War. These include Aeroplane Carriers and Minelayers.

10. On the vital importance of Air power in all Naval work in the future it is unnecessary to insist in this paper. We are at present urgently in need of further data and experience.

The efficiency of the fleet depends now, and will depend still more in the future, upon its being equipped with a sufficiency of aeroplanes.

As a result of this development aircraft carriers have become a necessary adjunct in the organisation of a fleet.

At present we are confined to the possession of one ship only, the *Argus*, and this ship is totally inadequate for the carrying of the number of reconnaissance, gunnery and torpedo aeroplanes required by the seagoing fleet. We therefore ask for monies to complete the *Eagle* and *Hermes* and to render the *Furious* capable of meeting modern requirements.

11.   Similarly as regards Minelayers, the seagoing fleet is without a modern Minelayer, and we require to gain experience in the type of vessel, and the special fittings necessary to carry out this important operation of modern naval strategy, an operation which, so far as can be foreseen, is likely to increase rather than decrease in importance. The construction of one experimental Minelayer 1921–22 is pressed for.

12.   Cabinet authority is therefore requested to proceed with the preliminary inquiries and work necessary to allow of a building programme 1921–22 of:–

4 Capital ships
Completion of Light Cruisers and Destroyers already laid down
Completion of *Eagle* and *Hermes* and alteration of *Furious* as Aeroplane Carriers
1 Minelayer

work being commenced immediately the approval of Parliament has been obtained.

13.   A large addition to the Naval Estimates will be necessary for this purpose.

In this connection it is noted that in Command paper 779 'Further Memorandum by the Chancellor of the Exchequer on the future Exchequer Balance Sheet' issued Tuesday, 29th June, the sum of £60,000,000 is set aside for the Navy as the estimated expenditure in a Normal Year. In regard to this it must be pointed out that in a Memorandum for the Cabinet on 'Navy Estimates and Naval Policy' dated 13th February 1920, these words were used:–

the amount included for the maintenance of the minimum Naval force – which may be regarded as representing normal naval expenditure, apart from the provision for New Construction, is 62½ millions.

and again:–

62½ millions is required for the maintenance during 1920–21 of a fleet of the minimum strength which can be regarded as providing in present circumstances for the security of the Empire, but without any allowance for starting any new programme of construction.

In our opinion the time for the provision of New Construction has now arrived. An increase in the Estimates must be faced, and the measure outlined in this Memorandum given effect to, in order to maintain our Sea Power and to carry out the policy approved by the Cabinet, and of which Parliament has been informed, namely, the maintenance of a 'One-Power Standard'.

39. *To his wife* [Grantully Castle, Aberfeldy, Perthshire]

[BTY/17/53/27]   Hanover Lodge
                                                                 Regent's Park
                                                                 3 Aug. 1920

Darling Tata

       *   *   *   *

Ireland is as bad as it can be & has swallowed up all the available troops in Great Britain which is a serious matter as we are threatened now with general strikes & unrest among the miners, railway men, engineers and general transport workers. On the top of it all comes this trouble in the Navy, the one force they had relied upon for everything, over this blessed Welfare Committee.[1]

However I have wrestled with that question all day & have come to a definite understanding as to how far we can go & no further. If that is turned down, then we really [come to ?] trouble, and I do not mind if we do. As well to have it now as later when it will be more difficult. – I have gone as far as I can to meet them, and discipline must be maintained . . .

ever your devoted
DAVID

[1] In reaction to apprehension aroused by the Sailors' Councils in the German and Russian Navies the Admiralty had established a Welfare Committee in August 1919, with elected representatives of the lower deck as advisers. So many of their requests were refused that the sailors virtually boycotted the committee and the Admiralty suspended it on 3 August 1920.

40. *To his wife* [Grantully Castle]

[BTY/17/53/30–31]
Hanover Lodge
Wednesday
[4 Aug. 1920]

. . . The situation in Poland[1] is reaching a crisis and as always, whenever there is trouble they turn to the Navy.

Consequently it looks as if we are to embark upon a new war. Curious that it should come on the 4th August.

Now we have to make arrangements to send a large naval force to the Baltic for moral effect – what that means to the Bolshie [sic] nobody can say, but I think with them it will carry but little weight. They understand only the results of heavy blows and as they are far from the sea will not [care or] understand the value of Sea Power!!!

The trouble is, what to do? We have tied ourselves into knots trying to temporise, and now it has failed, we can really do nothing. I cannot but believe that the time for bluff & moral effects has passed and we may [sic] look that fact straight in the face.

Winston is in despair and nearly off his head. The only optimist is the Prime Minister, and he is too much so.

It means incidentally that I shall not get up to you on Saturday night – Monday is fixed as the crucial day and I shall be lucky if I can get away then. I hope for the best and much may happen between this and then [sic]. There are so many elements for disturbance that it is hard to foresee what can or will happen 24 hours ahead. In the meantime the men of the Fleet have gone on leave & I have refused to recall them until I know definitely what is required of the Navy . . .

---

[1]In the summer of 1920 Soviet troops had penetrated deeply into Poland and there were pressures from France as well as internally for British intervention. These were countered by threats of a general strike from trades unions and left wing political movements. The government's dilemma was solved by Polish victories and the routing of the invaders; peace was concluded in March 1921.

41. *To his wife* [Grantully Castle]

[BTY/17/53/33–34] Admiralty
5.8.20

The plot thickens as far as Poland is concerned and there is no doubt that we have got ourselves into an unholy mess in that quarter.

We have now presented Soviet Russia with an ultimatum, as you will have seen in the Press. They have got until Monday to answer it, and if unfavourable it seems that we are committed to another War; ie:– against Russia. We have now no men and no money. We have ships, but what can they do against a Power that is without Sea Forces. Blockade, yes, but that amounts to nothing. We can send ships, big ships, into the Baltic to obtain moral effect – but will that accomplish anything? I do not believe the Bolshy [*sic*] cares a cuss for moral effect.

We can assist Wrangel in the south of Russia, ie: Black Sea, and with our support in money, which we haven't got, arms, munitions and food. He can no doubt prove himself a very serious thorn in the side of the Bolshy. Beyond that, we can do little or nothing. On the other hand, Germany looks like playing into the hands of the Bolshy and will make use of the menace to recoup himself out of Poland for all she has lost on the Western front. Indeed there never was such a mess and it is difficult to see a clear way out.

Why in the world all this could not have happened earlier, or later, not just when one wanted a rest and change. All I can hope for is that the Bolshy will see reason and come to terms [–] I can get away.

* * * *

42. *Naval Staff Memorandum*

[Ll.G/F/34/1/37]   Admiralty
                                                                  5.8.20

My Dear Prime Minister,
   I enclose Staff Memorandum on possible action in the Black
Sea. I can't help thinking that a threat to support Wrangel would
have more effect on Krasin[1] & Co. than anything else,
                              sincerely yours
                              WALTER LONG

BLACK SEA
POSSIBLE NAVAL OPERATIONS AGAINST THE
BOLSHEVIKS

1. To convey Wrangel's forces to any part of the Black Sea or
    the sea of Azof they may desire to reach and cover their
    landing. In order to enter the Sea of Azof it will be necessary
    first to reduce the Bolshevist battery of 2 6" guns and an
    aerodrome in the neighbourhood of Tamanskya [*sic*] which
    protect the Kerch Strait.
2. To support the flanks of Wrangel's army where they rest on
    the sea.
3. To harass the Bolshevist forces on the coast roads wherever
    they are to be found.
4. To blockade the Russian coast in Bolshevist hands.
5. The first thing to do is to re-establish our Naval Mission at
    Wrangel's headquarters.

[Beatty's Holograph Minute]

This covers everything that can be done [–]. Para 2 includes the
destruction of the Bolshevist batteries that protect the mouth of
the Dnieper river & which are vulnerable to attack from the sea.
Para 5 covers the possible wish of Wrangel to recapture Odessa,
which could be assisted by HM Ships.
                              B.
                              5.8.

---

[1]Negotiations on re-opening trade with Russia were the first step towards
Britain's full recognition of the Communist regime. Leonid Krasin, Commissar
for Foreign Trade, headed the delegation which reached London in May 1920. A
trade agreement was signed in March 1921. Diplomatic recognition came in 1924.

43. Beatty to Lloyd-George

[Holograph]

[Ll.G/F/4/4/2]   Grantully Castle
                                             Aberfeldy
                                             Perthshire
                                             29.8.20

My Dear Prime Minister,

I am sorry to disturb your holiday with unpleasant reading, but matters have become so serious recently owing to the activities of the Soviet Delegates, that I feel it is my duty to write and let you know what is going on.

I presume you are aware from the Admiralty Memo, that the two Russian Delegates, Rothstein and Milinskoff [sic], who took passage in our destroyer recently, approached the crew en route to Reval on the subject of Bolshevism.[1]

Our District Intelligence Officers inform us that in every naval port Councils of Action have been formed and that the most strenuous efforts are being made to spread Bolshevism amongst not only the men, but the officers in H.M. Navy. The dockyard men are particularly affected by the movement, and at Portsmouth have already held a public meeting on the subject, whilst at Rosyth they have addressed a memorandum to the Admiral Superintendent pledging themselves to carry out any orders received from the Council of Action in London.

From our information the Soviet Delegates have engaged the services of the local insurance agents to distribute their propaganda.

What we have known from our Secret Intelligence has been confirmed by what has been made public in the Papers, ie; that the Soviet Delegates are actively in close touch with the Council of Action. The formation of the London Council of Action is the direct outcome of the presence of the Soviet Delegates in the country.[2]

[1]En route to London the delegation had preliminary talks with the Allies in Copenhagen; this could account for the passage of some members in a British destroyer. H. Ullman (1972), *Anglo-Soviet Relations 1917–21: The Anglo-Soviet Accord*, Princeton, p. 270 names Rothstein and Milutin as trying to subvert the crew.

[2]Throughout the negotiations the British government frequently complained about communist propaganda by the delegates. This included interventions in the Workers' Councils set up to oppose intervention in Poland. Stephen White (1979), *Britain and the Bolshevik Revolution*, London, analyses the extent of British concern about the threat of communism at the time.

As each one of these delegates signed a written undertaking not to indulge in propaganda, or to interfere with the internal affairs of this country, before they were allowed to come to London, they have flagrantly broken this undertaking and should be expelled from [The MS ends here]

44.   *To his wife*

[Incomplete]

[BTY/17/53/45–47]   Admiralty

Friday, 1st Oct. [1920]

No letter from you this morning, but I got one, a very short one from [–] in which he attributes your indisposition to malnutrition which has affected the nervous system and at the same time your intestines function badly which causes autointoxication. I assume that the latter means a form of self-poisoning. But he says that both troubles can be cured by undergoing the treatment; which is very satisfactory, and the more hopeful because he says that organically, as regards heart, lungs, kidneys & liver etc, you are perfectly healthy and well. This is a great relief to know, and when he has overcome the weak spots there is no reason why you should not be as well as any human can be.

I pray that there will not be a set-back to the cure, and that with it, you will regain your normal equilibrium & recognise that we all, the boys and myself, are looking forward to your returning your own sweet self without being afflicted with strange fancies and imaginings, which please believe me, exist only in your imagination. Then let us make a fresh start and do our united best to live in peace and harmony at home.

I am quite sure that we can make things right and have a happy home together and live in perfect harmony, if we make up our minds to do so. In any case, let us start with that idea and intention before us and sink our differences with that end in view.

*   *   *   *

45. *To Walter Long*

[Holograph]

[Add. 62425] Admiralty
1.12.20

My Dear Long,
I do hope that you are progressing favourably and will soon be fit and well again . . .
We had a meeting, Finance Committee and Sea Lords, yesterday to go through the Sketch Estimates, to have a preliminary talk as to how and where we could make cuts. The Spending Lords and the Staff are now going through them piecemeal and I hope will result [*sic*] in being able to make some really valuable recommendations to the Board as to where we can reduce with the least possible loss of efficiency.
You will have seen the attacks in the Press, which I am glad to say are not one-sided, on Admiralty policy. The more there are the better, and it is better we should be taken to task than to have nothing said at all.
I have not heard what effect the Policy Paper has had on the Cabinet, but no doubt you have. I hear the Japanese Naval Estimates are £75,000,000, a very large sum for that country, while those of the United States are round about £186,000! . . .
You may remember that last May I spoke to you of the services rendered to the Navy during the war by Sir Alfred Fripp,[1] and hope you could see your way to put in a word for him to the Prime Minister for the next Honours List.
Yours sincerely,
BEATTY

[1]Sir Alfred Fripp, an eminent surgeon had helped Lady Beatty to equip and man her yacht *Sheelah* as a hospital ship in 1914 and had been appointed an Honorary Consulting Surgeon by the Admiralty (see *Beatty Papers I*, p. 104).

46. *Eustace Tennyson d'Eyncourt[1] to Beatty*

[BTY/8/2/19] 3.12.20

REMARKS ON THE FUTURE DEVELOPMENT OF SUBMARINES FROM A CONSTRUCTIONAL POINT OF VIEW.

CNS

The advocates of the Submarine argue that she has rendered the surface capital ship obsolete.

Before criticising this contention from a purely constructional standpoint, I wish to emphasize my considered opinion that the mine is such a powerful weapon against submarines or submersibles, that any Power which attempts to rely only on submarines will find all her submarine bases completely blocked by mines, with the result that very soon she will be forced to develop surface craft.

The submarine, at her present state of development, relies on submersion for protection, and, as long as she remains a submarine or submersible vessel, this feature must necessitate the serious limitation of her qualities as a surface craft.

To take a few examples, her speed, manoeuvring power, and accuracy of gunfire must be considerably inferior to any surface craft of similar dimensions. – To improve these, it would be necessary to increase her displacement and horse power very considerably, but, even so, she cannot be given the armour protection of a surface vessel, and comparatively slight damage will either sink her or necessitate remaining on the surface.

Further, as soon as her displacement is increased, she begins to lose her qualities as a submarine by becoming unhandy for manoeuvring or diving, and she requires, not only sea room, but very great depth of water in which to operate.

If her power is increased, steam power will have to be introduced, and great difficulties will arise in regard to funnels, venti-

---

[1]Sir Eustace Tennyson d'Eyncourt (1868–1951): naval architect; after apprenticeship at Armstrong Whitworth's on the Tyne and the 2 year constructor's course at the RN College Greenwich, he worked at Armstrong's until 1898 when he moved to Fairfield Shipbuilding Co on the Clyde, and then, in 1902, back to Armstrong's as Head of the Design Office. As Director of Naval Construction 1912–24 he was responsible for the design of all naval vessels as well as contributing to airship and tank design. His papers are in the National Maritime Museum.

lation, etc., and she will become an easier prey to the moderate sized submarine than any surface vessel.

It is therefore considered that the development of the submarine is strictly limited to the following:–

(1) Moderate increase of displacement compatible with handiness.
(2) Increase of surface speed.
(3) Endurance.
(4) Strength of hull.
(5) Weight and precision of torpedo.

These developments have already been considerably discounted by:–

(1) Improved detection apparatus.
(2) Improved weapons of attack in the nature of depth charges and towed explosive charges.
(3) Increased speed of surface vessel which will always be ahead of the submarine.
(4) Improved underwater construction, which, in future capital ships, will render them proof against several torpedoes.

I am therefore of opinion it is not too much to say that the future capital ship is as safe from underwater attack or from submarines as she will be against attack by guns or from the air.

46a.   *Tennyson d'Eyncourt to Beatty*

[BTY/8/2/27]   3.12.20

REMARKS ON PROPOSALS TO REPLACE OUR
OBSOLETE CAPITAL SHIPS DURING THE NEXT FEW
YEARS

AVAILABLE BERTHS

There are in existence in this country the following berths which could, in emergency, be used for the construction of modern capital ships:

Armstrongs	2	only one can be conveniently used at one time owing to the large amount of labour required.
Browns	1	
Cammell Laird	1	
Vickers	1	
Fairfields	1	Space very restricted and this Firm have specially laid out their plant for merchant ship building.
Total	6	

Of these, therefore, only *4* can be conveniently used.

TIME TO COMPLETE

It is probable that it will take three years to complete a capital ship.

TIME TO COMPLETE TO LAUNCHING STAGE

It is economical to complete as much material, hull, armour and machinery as possible on board before launching the vessel, and, in any event, it is difficult to advance the construction to the launching stage in less than 15 to 18 months.

It is probable, therefore, that the actual laying down of the second four ships may not be possible during 1922/1923, although, by collecting material, their completion will not be necessarily delayed.

IMPORTANCE OF COMMENCING CONSTRUCTION AS SOON AS POSSIBLE

It is of great importance to commence the construction of these vessels as soon as possible for the following reasons:–

(1) Special plant and machinery, different from those used for merchant ships, are required for warship construction and are already being scrapped to enable peace work to be undertaken.

(2) Specially skilled labour, accustomed to special warship work, is being dispersed, and the longer warship construc-

tion is put off the more difficult it will be to find suitable skilled labour.

(3)   The boom in merchant shipbuilding is already on the wane, and unemployment of ordinary shipbuilding trades will be avoided by undertaking warship construction.

3   [This paragraph is deleted in the original]

(4)   The Heavy Gun, Armour and Gun Mounting Firms are already asking for subsidies to keep their Armament plant in existence. ie 500,000 per annum; 6% of its value.

(5)   It is more economical in labour, and better for the country, to spread the construction of eight ships over four or five years, than to endeavour to complete them in from three to four years, as the men that have been working on the ships first laid down can be transferred to later ships, and a steadier demand on labour will result.

[This paragraph is deleted in the original]

(6)   The existing Heavy Gun, Armour, Gun Mounting and Shell plant is only sufficient to complete the ships over the longer period mentioned in (5) above.

[This paragraph is also deleted]

If on the other hand this Plant is scrapped from lack of funds & it is again reqd in 1, 2 or 3 years time it will require an expenditure of ten times its original cost: ie £100,000,000.

TO SUM UP

(1)   Six capital ships are the maximum that can be laid down in one year.

(2)   It is undesirable to lay down more than four in one year for the following reasons:–
       (*a*)   There is only sufficient skilled labour for four.
       (*b*)   There is only sufficient special Armour, Heavy Gun, Gun Mounting and Shell plant to deal with four ships a year.

(3)   It is economical to commence as soon as possible, to avoid the special plant and skilled labour being lost.

(4)   If construction is not commenced next year, Armament Firms will have to be paid subsidies for retaining their plant and skilled labour.

47. Beatty to Walter Long

[Copy]

[BTY/13/25/29]   9.12.20

I am indeed sorry to hear you have again had to go back to bed, but earnestly trust that it will be only for a short duration. I indeed sympathise with you and know how exasperating it is.

I took up the matter of the wording of the Resolution on Naval Expenditure, which I said in my note to you yesterday would make you smile.

It was of no use to do so at the Cabinet Meeting, which was very large, and it would have been difficult to explain correctly our point of view. Moreover, I wished to have time to think it over before suggesting an alternative wording. I attacked them this morning and pointed out that as it stood the Resolution was a grave reflection upon the Admiralty. The words 'The Cabinet are by no means convinced that the lessons of the War have as yet been definitely ascertained' and 'They are not satisfied that our Naval position can best be secured by adopting a programme of Capital Ship construction' meant one of two things: either the Admiralty have failed in their duty, or the Cabinet had no confidence in their Naval Advisers, after some discussion and some heart burning it was altered as in typed copy enclosed, which I think meets our views. I was particular in adding the words 'and the Admiralty welcomes the decision', to indicate that in no way was our hand forced.

I am preparing a digest of the whole question for the CID which will make our views plain and simple and really ought to finish the whole thing. If they appoint a Sub-Committee of the CID to go into the whole matter and take evidence, it is very important as to who the President of the Sub-Cttee would be. I do not think we ought to submit to an outsider being brought in, such as Lord Grey or Mr McKenna,[1] whoever it is should be of the CID. If this move is intended to waste time we must combat it for all we are worth. We have already fallen behind time and we cannot get our ships laid down for 6 months after the Cabinet give their approval. Loss of time means waste of money, because the ships will have to be completed by [the] end of 1925.

---

[1]Edward Grey, 1st Viscount Grey of Falloden (1862–1933): Liberal politician; Foreign Secretary 1905–16. Reginald McKenna (1863–1943): Liberal politician; 1st Lord of Admiralty 1908–11; Chancellor of the Exchequer 1915–16.

I feel that the situation is truly serious and I earnestly hope you will be able to be present. If you cannot, will you write a very strong and urgent letter to the Prime Minister, send me a copy and ask him to see me so that I can lay the situation before him. He said yesterday he wished to see me to talk the matter over, and I have twice sent over to his Secretary to say I am available when he wants me, but nothing is doing.

I am sending a paper representing that the Japanese have already given an order to Vickers for ½ their output in armour for the next year, which will militate very gravely against the rapid construction of our ships. While we are wrangling the Japs are acting.

48. *Long to Beatty*

[BTY/13/28/31]   December 10th 1920.

I am very much obliged to you for your long letter telling me the whole story.

I can only say for myself that if the original wording of the Cabinet Minute had stood I should have resigned within 24 hours and nothing would have induced me to alter my mind; as it is I don't feel by any means too comfortable.

We have given periodically every warning to our colleagues, to Parliament, and to the Country; we have constantly referred to the action of the USA and Japan, we have discussed the question of the 'big ship' repeatedly, I personally have discussed it at length with the distinguished naval representatives of other countries including France, America, Japan, Italy, Chile and it is not our fault if my colleagues in the Cabinet have suddenly awaked to the true position of affairs.

However, there is nothing as you say to which we can legitimately object in the present decision, although I am afraid I detect in it a desire to postpone things. So far as I am concerned I regard a policy of postponement as almost, if not quite equivalent, to turning down our proposals; however I shall now await your digest for the CID and do my best to get to London in time to take part in your discussions. If I am unable you may depend upon it I shall write a very strong letter, but I mean somehow to be there.

I have a consultation to-day and must await their pronouncement, but I somehow think that I shall manage, at all events, to be able to give the best hours of two or three days next week.

* * * *

I resume this letter after my ordeal in the form of a consultation by three doctors from London, Bath and my own.

I would much rather jump the biggest fence in Leicestershire both ways than go through these infernal ordeals. However, they assured me that I had no desperate disease in the shape of cancer, etc., – an assurance I did not require – but they told me emphatically that it would be impossible for me to go to London next week. In these circumstances, I am sending you in the pouch, tomorrow, the letter I am proposing to send to the Prime Minister on Monday. If there is anything in it which you would like altered, please do not hesitate to make your suggestion.

I feel that while, of course, the responsibility must be mine, as the First Lord of the day, the real responsibility of the future will rest with you as the First Sea Lord, and recent victorious Commander-in-Chief, and therefore I am most anxious, so far as I can, to work in absolute agreement with yourself.

I am afraid, as I have said, there is no chance of my getting to London next week, though I really would give my soul to do so, in these circumstances the letter must be the substitute but can you, if necessary by telegram, tell me if you agree in these opinions –

First. We cannot possibly allow anybody to be Chairman of the Sub Committee unless he is really a man of independent views, and where is he to be found? To appoint McKenna is ridiculous, at least I would not stand it. He is a Fisherite and from my point of view, as a politician, a Little Englander, but I believe he is popular with the Navy and therefore I am sure he has good qualities which I do not recognise, therefore it might be possible for you to accept him while impossible for me. What do you say about this from your point of view?

You say in your letter to me 'if they appoint a Sub. Comm: of the CID to go into the whole matter and take evidence it is very important as to whom the President of the Sub Committee would be. I do not think we ought to submit to an outsider being brought in, such as Lord Grey or Mr. McKenna; whoever it is should be of the CID.' I very largely concur in this view but I am not sure whether we can insist upon the Chairman being a Member of the CID as I do not know who there is among them to whose

Chairmanship, and therefore absolute control of the conduct of the Committee's proceedings, I would be prepared to submit.

A possible Chairman to my mind, is Lord Crewe,[1] possibly some other fairminded politician, who does not at the moment occur to me, but of this I am quite clear, so far as I am at present advised, and before getting your final opinion, namely, that we cannot subordinate our responsibility to anybody else except the Prime Minister.

Yours ever
(Signed) WALTER H. LONG

49. *Beatty: Memorandum for Cabinet and CID*

[Copy]

[ADM 116/1176/275]   10 Dec. 1920

SHIPBUILDING POLICY

With reference to Cabinet Conclusion No. 4 of 8th December 1920, the Admiralty desire to bring to the notice of the Cabinet and the Committee of Imperial Defence the extreme importance of coming to a very early decision in regard to the question of Shipbuilding Policy, remitted by the Cabinet. As an illustration of its extreme urgency, attention is drawn to the serious position which has just arisen in regard to a vital factor in ship construction in this country, *viz* armour-plate production.

Ever since 1919 the Admiralty have frequently invited the attention of the Cabinet to the question of Shipbuilding Policy. In August 1920 it was made clear that the great armament firms in this country could no longer afford to maintain their armour-plate plant and hold it at the disposal of this country, unless subsidies were paid to them; and since that date frequent attempts have been made to obtain a decision in regard to this matter.

What was anticipated has now occurred. One of the largest armament firms in the country has closed down its armour-plate works. Another of the great firms has within the last few days, accepted a large order from a foreign government. This has so reduced the effective output of armour-plate in this country, that

[1] Robert Crewe Milnes, Marquess of Crewe (1858–1945): Liberal politician; succeeded his father as Lord Houghton 1885; Lord Lieutenant of Ireland 1892–5; Lord President of the Council 1905; Leader of House of Lords 1908 and Secretary for Colonies 1910–14; Secretary for India 1915–16; Lord President of the Council 1916–22; Ambassador in Paris 1922–8.

unless immediate steps are taken in regard to this matter it will entail serious delay in the completion of the capital ships which the Admiralty have proposed as the minimum necessary to maintain a Navy at a standard of strength which will adequately secure the safety of the Empire and its maritime communications.

BEATTY.

50. Walter Long to David Lloyd George

[Copy]

[BTY/13/28/36]   December 13th 1920

I am profoundly sorry that I cannot attend the meeting of the CID tomorrow, but I am confined to my bed and practically on my back, and it is quite impossible for me to come.

I am not quite sure what is the proposal to be put before the CID tomorrow, for, as you are aware, I have not been consulted since the question was first raised.

It never occurred to me that our scheme of Naval Policy would be dealt with in the Debate on Economy, and, of course, it would never have been mentioned had it not been for the unprincipled action of the 'Times' newspaper; they, at all events, are entitled to claim that they won a victory.

There is, so far as I know, no precedent for the present position, but I have, of necessity, to remember that the CID is of comparatively recent creation and therefore a question of this kind may to-day very properly be submitted to them.

The Committee quoted by the *Times* is no precedent for the step which it is now proposed to take.

I am, of course, away from my Office and my papers, but I have not been able to ascertain that the Committee, set up by Lords Selborne[1] and Fisher, was anything but an ordinary Committee, *set up by the Admiralty themselves* to advise them. However, this is as I understand it, already settled, and the Board of Admiralty, of which I have the privilege to be the representative, are to be put upon their trial. The question therefore arises, by whom are they to be tried?

[1]William Waldegrave, 2nd Earl Selborne (1859–1942): Liberal Unionist politician, succeeded to title 1895; Under Secretary for Colonies under Joseph Chamberlain 1895; 1st Lord of Admiralty 1900–05, where closely associated with Fisher's reforms; High Commissioner in South Africa 1905 and active in facilitating creation of the Union in 1909; President of Board of Agriculture 1915; refused to serve under Lloyd George whom he mistrusted, and resigned office 1916.

I am informed that it is suggested that the enquiry should be conducted by a Sub. Committee of the CID.

It is therefore clear that the question at issue, viz. whether the Board of Admiralty have given full and proper consideration to the question of whether or no the big ship is to be retained in the Navy, is one which must turn upon evidence; but I presume that the Sub. Committee will consider it to be their duty to conduct their own enquiry into the value of the big ship; until this is completed it is impossible for me, or any Member of the Board of Admiralty, to say what course of action they will take if another Body is called upon to perform their duty.

By accepting this form of enquiry I feel that I am entitled to make a very urgent request to you to the following effect:–

That the Sub. Committee shall be small and shall not be composed of Members of the CID who want money for their own branch of Defence; not because I have any want of confidence in their ability or their fairness, quite the contrary, but because I feel that in the present circumstances it is inevitable that the Head of each Department must press for money for himself. It may not be possible to grant this portion of my request and I shall not quarrel with the decision if this be so, but I do press to be allowed to name the Chairman of this enquiry, as it is of vital importance, not only to the credit of my Colleagues and myself, but in some respects even to our good faith.

It is impossible, of course, for you to preside yourself.

The Committee must sit soon and often and I therefore most urgently beg that you persuade the Lord Chancellor[1] to act as Chairman.

51. *Beatty to Long*

[Copy]

[BTY/13/28/35]   Admiralty
                                        13th December, 1920

I am indeed grieved to learn from your letter and also from Craig[2] that it is impossible for you to come up to take part in the discussion which is to take place to-morrow.

I have not received a copy of the letter which you are sending

[1]Lord Birkenhead.
[2]Sir James Craig, Parliamentary and Financial Secretary to the Admiralty: the future Lord Craigavon, prominent Ulster leader.

to the Prime Minister. I am fully alive to the possibility of the endeavour being made to delay coming to a decision, which I agree would be nearly as bad as turning down our proposals altogether.

We simply cannot, if we are to be within measurable distance of the United States in Sea Power, afford to waste another year.

I have sent you two telegrams to-day regarding the Chairman of any Sub-Committee that may be appointed, and I feel that we shall do well if we can secure the Lord Chancellor for that purpose. He is sympathetically inclined, will be quick in coming to a decision and will be logical in his summing up, which is all in our favour.

I do earnestly pray that you will very soon mend but in any case I trust that you will not think it necessary to resign. Such action would I feel sure increase our difficulties enormously. You are always available to guide us in the way we should go, and, if necessary, I can always come down and see you. I personally should far rather continue as at present. And I am sure that the whole of the Board are with me in this view and would look upon it as a disaster if you thought it necessary to withdraw from the Headship of the Admiralty.

I can well understand your mental tribulation at being laid by the heels at this juncture which is of vital importance to the future of the Navy and of the Empire. A mistake now and we shall and can never recover from it.

52. *N. J. S. Barnes[1] to Walter Long*

[Copy]

[BTY/13/28/39]   Admiralty
                                                    13th December 1920

The First Sea Lord is anxious for your views on the composition of the Sub-Committee of Enquiry which will meet at noon to-morrow, Tuesday:

(1) It is agreed that we will not consent to any but a senior Member of the Cabinet in the Chair. We press for the Lord Chancellor;

(2) As to the other members: The First Sea Lord feels that they should be Members of the Cabinet, himself, with CIGS[2] and

[1]N. J. S. Barnes, Private Secretary to the 1st Lord.
[2]CIGS, Sir Henry Wilson.

CAS if desired, and possibly a legal Member or servant of the Government to elucidate evidence. He thinks we should demur to appointment of Naval Officers not Members of the Board, or of representatives of firms, such as Trevor Dawson, or, indeed, to any outsiders; that if any such members of the Committee are proposed, we should record a protest, but otherwise accept the decision.

He asks if you will telegraph or telephone your opinion to-morrow morning.

As you are aware, his general view is that this is an enquiry by the Cabinet into the Admiralty's proposals, and the First Sea Lord thinks it is for the Cabinet themselves to institute that enquiry; and that it would be wrong for the Board of Admiralty to be subjected to a Committee of investigation consisting of outside persons. His own suggested Committee, in fact, would be the Lord Chancellor, two other Members of the Cabinet, himself, with of course no objection to CIGS and CAS if desired.

Of course you would be a member if you were able to be present.

53. *Lloyd George to Long*

[Add.62425]   10 Downing Street
                                              14th December 1920

My Dear First Lord,

. . . As I have had no opportunity for personal consultation I feel I owe it to you to give some explanation as to how this Inquiry was initiated. Last week, in view of the forthcoming Debate on Economy, first the Finance Committee and then the Cabinet had to take stock of the financial situation as a whole. The Cabinet unanimously agreed, that in order to satisfy the very strong feeling in favour of economy, it would be essential for the Chancellor of the Exchequer[1] to be in a position to announce such hopes as we were able to find that every possible economy would be introduced for the Budget for 1921–22, and that the Government were giving the closest consideration to them. It is difficult to exaggerate the strength of opinion, not only in Parliament, but in the country at large, on this question . . .

When we came to review the financial situation for 1921–22

[1]Austen Chamberlain.

we were all very painfully impressed with the magnitude of the prospective Estimates of the Fighting Services, and in this connection we naturally had to give the greatest consideration to the Memorandum by the Admiralty on the subject of ship-building policy.

As a result of prolonged discussion in the Finance Committee and the Cabinet, we all agreed that in the present state of public feeling on the subject of expenditure, we should have to be very sure of our ground before committing ourselves to a large programme of naval construction. On this occasion there is a new element in the discussion, namely that the United States of America have become the second Naval Power. We felt that this in itself introduces considerations that go far beyond the technical questions of the form in which naval superiority is to be ensured. In order to appreciate this it is necessary to recall that, as far back as 1904, when Mr Balfour was Prime Minister, the Committee of Imperial Defence, when considering the defence of the various naval bases in American waters, deliberately decided that 'an attack from the United States need not be taken into consideration', and I myself recall, in 1912, when considering an important naval question, the Committee of Imperial Defence based its inquiry on the assumption that the United States of America should be omitted from the argument, although America was at that time the second strongest power. Apart from this, however, we had to remember the fact that we owe America a thousand millions of money, and if we were to enter into anything in the nature of a competition of armaments with them, they would demand payment and make things very difficult for us. I need not dwell on the immense wealth and resources of America which render a single-handed competition in naval construction with them extremely onerous. In view of these and other similar considerations we felt that the Government were up against a decision of the very first magnitude, involving questions of highest policy going far beyond those which ordinarily arise when considering a question of the naval programme. Consequently, without in any way prejudicing our ultimate decision we thought it best to set on foot this Inquiry.

*   *   *   *

I do hope therefore that you will not allow yourself to think that in this matter the Admiralty is being put upon its trial.

Our idea is solely to conduct the Inquiry in the light of the wider considerations I have touched on above.

I cannot say how much I regret that the Cabinet were obliged to initiate the Inquiry, much less to begin it, without my having an opportunity for consultation with you. Once the Inquiry was decided upon however, Lord Beatty gave pressing reasons as to why it should not be postponed.

*   *   *   *

54. *Beatty: Admiralty Memorandum*

[Copy]

[BTY/8/2/18]   14.12.20

HAVE SUBMARINES, AIRCRAFT AND MINES ARRIVED AT SUCH A STATE OF EFFICIENCY THAT THE CAPITAL SHIP IS AN OBSOLETE TYPE?

1.   The term 'Capital Ship' is applied to the vessel which, for the time being, embodies the maximum concentration of offensive power, defensive capability and mobility which can be contained in any single ship. Its object is to command the surface of the sea as far as its power of mobility and the range of its weapons permit it to do so, and to be proof against attack from the depths of the sea and the air.

2.   The arguments adduced against the retention of the capital ship resolve themselves into statements that she is, or shortly will be, incapable of fulfilling her function through the menace of submarines, aircraft or mines.

THE SUBMARINE

3.   The submarine is at a disadvantage when on the surface as compared with ships and aircraft whose offensive weapons drive her to submerge. When in this condition her mobility relative to surface craft is limited, and her power of observation and offensive capability are restricted. It cannot too clearly be realised that the Germans were forced to undertake the laborious task of attacking our vessels with the submarine on account of their inability to employ surface vessels which would have accomplished the same amount of work in a far shorter time.

4.   It may well be asked how these statements can be reconciled with the fact that during the late war the submarine was able to inflict such heavy damage upon our merchant vessels as

to produce a very serious situation. The main reason was that the anti-submarine work had not kept pace with the development of the submarine, and it was only towards the end of the war that the improvement in weapons and devices, and the adoption of the convoy system for merchant vessels, sensibly eased the submarine menace. In this connection it will be remembered that the American Expeditionary Force was transported to Europe with the loss of only one ship through submarine action.

5. It should be remembered, also, that the enemy's initial success against merchant ships was achieved in much the same way as his initial success with gas on the Western Front, that is by his decision to disregard completely all conventions and international law when it suited him to do so.

6. So far as men-of-war were concerned, the submarine in spite of its many opportunities, did not sink a single capital ship in the main fighting fleet. Moreover, at no time was the Grand Fleet deterred from proceeding to sea by the menace from submarines, notwithstanding there were, on occasions, known to be a concentration of these vessels in the narrow waters of the North Sea for the express purpose of carrying out an attack.

7. Starting with the experience already gained, and the further improvements which have been, and are being, effected by experimental and research work, the submarine menace should be kept within measurable limits in any future war.

8. The policy recommended by the 'Submarine School' is that submarines should be built instead of Capital Ships, the theory being that the latter is an easy prey to the submarine.

9. This policy would give comparative immunity to the enemy's light surface craft whether engaged in destruction of our commerce or hunting our submarines.

10. Our light surface craft would be in constant danger of encountering the heavier surface craft of the enemy, the enemy's light craft would run no such risk.

11. Surface craft, owing to their superior mobility, are much more destructive of commerce than submarines. The greatest protection of heavy surface ships against submarines is their mobility, and in this connection it must be pointed out that one of the fundamental difficulties in the strategical and tactical employment of submarines is that of placing them in the decisive position.

12. That it is impossible to arrest development at, say, the light cruiser, is evident when the conditions are considered in which a fleet of all arms, but without the nucleus of capital ships,

is opposed to a corresponding fleet containing such vessels. In these circumstances, the weaker units must always be driven to seek the protection of stronger units, until we once more arrive at the capital ship, the main bulwark of defence, which is capable of defeating all other types of surface vessels.

13. If the dictum that the capital ship is obsolete be accepted by all maritime nations, then the capital ships of all nations would be scrapped, and the submarine would rule the seas. Imagining this to have been accomplished, how are submarines to give expression to naval power? They would presumably do so by waging war on commerce and preventing any surface ships, either merchant ships, store-ships or transports belonging to the enemy to put to sea.

14. Possessing only submarines, the British Empire would be unable to prevent this, and would, therefore, be obliged to attempt to destroy the opponents' submarines. It is a proved fact from war experience that submarines are not the most effective vessels for attacking other submarines. They can be more effectively and extensively attacked by means of surface vessels of high speed carrying offensive weapons. The country, therefore, which has most to lose by being driven off the surface of the sea, that is, the British Empire, would have to build surface vessels of some type to attack the enemy's submarines. These craft would have to be more powerful than the enemy's submarines on the surface, and would also have to have great mobility, endurance, and sea-keeping qualities. They, therefore, could not be smaller than the torpedo-boat destroyer as used in the late war. (The question of Aircraft v. Submarine is referred to later.)

15. The enemy in retaliation, would have to build other surface craft to destroy the destroyers, leading to the counter reply of even larger ships, and, by proceeding round the inevitable circle, we arrive again at the Capital Ship.

16. To approach the question from another standpoint —

The latest type of Capital Ship is so well protected that she can be hit by a considerable number of the most effective torpedoes now existing without being sunk.

17. To make the submarine more effective against the Capital Ship, therefore, it would be necessary to increase the size of the torpedo which she carries, and we will suppose that it is possible to design one to contain one ton of explosive, that is four times as much as at present.

18. This would necessitate a large increase in the dimensions

of the submarine. In many respects increase in size renders her less effective; it takes her longer to dive, makes her a bigger target for depth charges or gun attack, and her cost becomes excessive if she is to be built in large numbers.

19.   But neglecting all these difficulties and assuming that an efficient submarine is achieved which will carry torpedoes with one ton of explosive, the situation as regards the building of capital ships would in no way be affected.

20.   The protection of the modern capital ship is designed chiefly to withstand the attack of heavy guns, the principal armament of surface vessels, while a smaller proportion of her displacement is devoted to protection against the torpedo.

21.   If the torpedo arrives at the state of efficiency suggested above, it will be necessary to consider a redistribution of protection to meet the new conditions, but the capital ship would remain.

22.   It must be understood that the larger the surface vessel the more efficient she can be made, not only against gunfire, but also against torpedo attack. This fact in itself indicates the probability that those who assert that the torpedo will drive the capital ship from the sea have not sufficiently investigated the question.

23.   The possibility of technical science enabling the submarine to be detected so that she can be destroyed has not been touched upon in detail as it does not affect the principle governing the problem, but it is an aspect of the question to which the Admiralty attach great importance and look forward to important developments. Such developments will, however, increase the value of the surface capital ship, as opposed to the Submarine, for purposes of attacking the latter.

24.   From the foregoing considerations it is the Admiralty view that the surface ship still retains an incomparable advantage over the submarine. If, therefore, the command of the sea which has been the outstanding principle of our Naval Policy for the past 300 years is to be maintained, it will be necessary to continue to rely upon surface vessels. It follows, then, that the Capital Ship, which represents the most powerful expression of tactical effort, is also necessary as the logical outcome of the various types of surface ship.

AIRCRAFT

25.   During the late war the operations of aircraft at sea were circumscribed by their susceptibility to bad weather, their small flying endurance, and their consequent dependence upon shore bases or aircraft carrying vessels.

26.   Great development in the flying endurance of aircraft may be expected, but years will elapse before aircraft working from shore bases are capable of operating far afield in the Pacific, Atlantic, or Indian Oceans. Meanwhile, to enable them to do so, they have to be carried near their objective in surface ships, and then, step by step, we once more arrive at the eventual provision of the capital ship.

27.   As regards their offensive capabilities, future aircraft will carry heavy bombs and large torpedoes. Precision with a bomb dropped from a height can never be compared with that of a projectile propelled from a gun, and with the greatly improved anti-aircraft armament of modern surface vessels, aircraft will be kept at such a height as will render accurate bomb dropping a matter of great uncertainty.

28.   The torpedo carrying aircraft must come close to the surface to discharge its weapon, where again it becomes a target for gunfire. Torpedo attack from aircraft will also be made more difficult by the use of smoke screens and other protective devices. In either case the only effect of developments in bomb dropping and torpedo firing from aircraft will be again to alter the construction of the capital ship to enable her to withstand their attacks.

29.   The Admiralty are of the opinion that there is nothing in the present offensive qualities of aircraft which render them a menace to the existence of the capital ship.

30.   The primary aerial defence of the surface ship is the counter-offensive by air, and the nation which possesses the surface ship will be in a better position to develop this offensive in the open sea.

THE MINE

31.   In regard to the Mine, the shallow water round the United Kingdom and the proximity of the enemy's bases accentuated its potency and utility during the late war. The mine, however, is a passive obstruction as opposed to a mobile danger, and as such its effect cannot be comparable to that of the submarine or aircraft.

Protective devices evolved during the late war, coupled with an efficient minesweeping service, went far to overcome the mine danger, and there is no reason to suppose that this type of weapon will ever be more than an impediment to the free movement of a fleet. The mine cannot be regarded as a threat to the continued existence of the capital ship.

CONCLUSIONS

32.   From the above it will be seen that we are still at a period in the world's history when all defensive, and the majority of offensive, operations at sea can be carried out more efficiently by surface vessels than by the submarine or aircraft. These conditions will certainly remain the same for the normal life of the ships for which the Admiralty are now asking the sanction of the Government, that is, for about the next 20 years.

Whatever the means adopted to the end, the end of naval policy remains the same, namely, the maintenance of our own sea communications and the severance of the enemy's. The strength and the nature of our Fleet is determined by what is necessary to effect this.

Nothing is at present in sight to give reason to think that trade will be carried otherwise than in surface ships during the next 25 years.

Any maritime power which is compelled in war to defend its surface vessels, commercial or transport, is driven to the necessity of having fighting surface vessels for the purpose, and as long as fighting surface vessels are a requirement the construction of the most powerful type must inevitably ensue.

(Sgd) B.

55.   *Admiralty Memorandum for the Cabinet*

[Copy]
[ADM 116/1775]   NAVAL CONSTRUCTION 14–15 Dec 1920
SECRET

It has already been agreed by the Cabinet that the Naval Shipbuilding enquiry entrusted to the Committee of Imperial Defence shall be regarded as a matter of urgency. This phrase, however, is capable of different interpretations, and the Admiralty desire to point out how necessary it is that a decision should be arrived at *in time for effect to be given to it in 1921–22.*

In the first place, the following limiting facts must be stated:–

(*a*)   It takes from 15 to 18 months to advance a Capital ship to the launching stage, and 3 years to complete her.

(*b*)   There are only 6 berths in this country which could be used for the construction of modern capital ships, and of these only 4 can be conveniently used. To adapt other berths than these 6 would involve great expense and delay.

(*c*)   There is only sufficient skilled shipbuilding labour, and only sufficient special armour, heavy gun, gun mounting and shell plant, to deal with 4 such ships a year. To expand these facilities would involve great expense and delay.

At the present moment, therefore, it must be accepted that 6 capital ships represent the maximum that can be laid down in one year, and 4 capital ships represent the maximum that can be laid down *under economical conditions of building.*

It has already been pointed out in the Memorandum to the Cabinet that the position in 1925, assuming that we lay down 4 capital ships both in 1921–22 and in 1922–23, will be as follows:–

	Great Britain	*United States*	*Japan*
Class A	9	12	8*
Class B	13	11	4
Class C	4	4	4
	26	27	16*

*8 others to be completed by 1928

If a decision is so delayed that we are unable to lay down 4 capital ships in 1921–22, it must be accepted that our facilities will not allow us to lay down more than 4 in 1922–23, quite apart from the obvious political objections to a greater programme. The position in 1925 would then be:–

	Great Britain	*United States*	*Japan*
Class A	5	12	8*
Class B	13	11	4
Class C	4	4	4
	22	27	16*

*8 others to be completed by 1928

Several of the new US Ships will be completed in 1923–24, and possibly some of the Japanese, and it would be easy for either or both nations, having established this lead, to match any subsequent shipbuilding by us and thus to relegate Great Britain permanently to Third Naval Power.

Moreover, it cannot even be treated as certain that if the commencement of building is deferred until 1923–24, facilities for laying down 4 capital ships in a year will still remain available in this country, unless exceptional steps are taken to ensure this. The Admiralty entertain on this point grave apprehensions, which are based on the following considerations:–

(1) Special plant and machinery, different from those used for merchant ships, are required for warship construction and are already being scrapped to enable peace work to be undertaken.

(2) Specially skilled labour, accustomed to special warship work, is being dispersed, and the longer warship construction is put off, the more difficult it will be to find suitable skilled labour.

(3) The heavy gun, armour and gun mounting Firms are already asking for subsidies to keep their armament plant in existence, i.e. £500,000 per annum, or 6 per cent of its value. If this plant is scrapped from lack of use and it is again required in 1, 2, or 3 years time, it will require an expenditure of ten times its original cost, i.e. £100,000,000.

In short, in delaying new capital ship construction until 1921–22, we have held our hand up to the last possible moment, and the loss of the year 1921–22 would be nothing less than disastrous to our chance of retaining our naval equality with the Strongest Naval Power.

The suggestion has been made that the result of hesitation on our part might be to encourage the United States to modify their 1916 programme.

It is important, therefore, to point out that of the 12 United States ships classed above as 'A'

5 Battleships are well advanced and due for completion in 1923–24.

1 Battleship and 4 Battle Cruisers are less advanced but due for completion in 1924–25.

2 Battle Cruisers are about to be laid down: material is being collected; and they also are due for completion in 1924–25.

It is inconceivable that the United States would scrap the 5 Battleships which are well on the way to completion, and most improbable that they would take off the slips the sixth Battleship and the 4 Battle Cruisers actually laid down.

Any change of policy on their part would be likely, therefore, only to affect the 2 Battle Cruisers not yet laid down.

But assuming for the sake of argument that it extended to the whole of their Battle Cruisers, and that they not only abandoned the 2 not laid down, but removed the other 4 from the slips, such action on their part would not obviate the necessity for our laying down 4 capital ships this year. By doing so we should barely maintain our supremacy, as is evident from the following figures, which would then represent the position in 1925.

	Great Britain	United States	Japan
Class A	5	6	8
Class B	13	11	4
Class C	4	4	4
	22	21	16

On the other hand, the political objections to our laying down 4 capital ships *after* the United States had abandoned 6 of theirs would be enormous. It might, in fact, *pay* the United States to take this step, relying on the effect being to make it politically impossible for Great Britain to lay down any capital ships at all. The resulting position in 1925 would then be:–

	Great Britain	United States	Japan
Class A	1	6	8
Class B	13	11	4
Class C	4	4	4
	18	21	16

These figures suggest that the only wise course is to announce our policy before the United States discuss any modification of their programme, assuming that any modification is in contemplation, in which case we shall be free subsequently to make whatever reductions are reasonable in view of their action.

(Signed) BEATTY

56. *Admiralty Memorandum for the Committee of Imperial Defence*

[Copy]

[ADM 116/1775]   15 Dec. 1920

NAVAL CONSTRUCTION — ARMOUR PLATE

With reference to the question which was raised as to the authority for the Admiralty statement at the meeting of the Committee of Imperial Defence yesterday in regard to the Armour Plate position of this country, contained in CP 2278 of the 10th December 1920, the actual facts are as follows:–

   1. *'One of the largest Armament Firms in this country has closed down its armour plate works'*

This refers to Messrs Armstrong's works at Openshaw near Manchester. The armour plate plant has been dismantled. The only portion of the plant in use are the rolling mills, which are being used for making railway material. The skilled workmen have been dispersed. The firm has ceased to supply even armour plate for experimental purposes, and at the end of this month the Armour Plate Department will have ceased to exist.

   2. *'Another of the great Firms has within the last few days accepted a large order for armour plate for a Foreign Government'*

This refers to Messrs Vickers' contract for 7,600 tons of armour for the Japanese Government.

The annexed letter from the Admiralty Overseer dated 7th December 1920, explains the position.

B.

15 December 1920.

COPY

Sir,

With reference to my recent correspondence respecting Japanese armour at Messrs Vickers, I can now definitely say that Messrs Vickers have a signed contract with the Japanese Government for 7,600 tons of armour, included in which is some 6″, 8″, 9″ and 11″ thick.

I have not yet seen details in connection with this armour but I understand that the largest dimensioned plates are about 13′6″

× 9′0″ × 11″. I also understand that Messrs Vickers at the present time are tendering to the Spanish Government for armour.

(Sgd) Ed. J. Hill
Overseer.

57. *Beatty to Long*

[Copy]

[BTY/13/28/41]   Admiralty
15th December, 1920.

The following is a brief statement as to what occurred at the meeting of the CID yesterday morning.

The Prime Minister commenced by a long dissertation on the subject of policy, stating that the issue of the decision would be of the greatest magnitude, and that any shipbuilding programme that was introduced would be a direct threat against the United States, who would in retaliation insist upon our paying them over a thousand millions which we are in her debt before commencing any building operations.

He further stated that in the past the United States had never been considered in relation to our naval strength, and he did not see why she should be considered now: that the only reasonable or possible thing to do was to endeavour to come to some arrangements with the new administration of the United States as to naval armaments between the two countries and the control of the seas in which the two countries were particularly interested: that the United States would never tolerate our being superior in naval power in seas in which they had the greater interest. He considered that it was very necessary that we should collect and understand all the lessons of the War.

He was followed by the Secretary of State for War, who stated that it would be nothing less than a calamity to surrender our sea supremacy which we had held for so many centuries to any other Power, and that he could not agree to any such decision: that he was not of the opinion that it was necessary to have a superiority of battleships of the post-Jutland design: that the superiority might be made up of a proper proportion of other units — Cruisers, Destroyers and particularly submarines.

I was then asked to say something. I pointed out that in October

1919 the Admiralty in a Memorandum to the Cabinet[1] stated that one of two things had to happen: either we had to come to some arrangement with the United States as to curtailing shipbuilding, or in the autumn of 1920 we should have to consider what steps were necessary to maintain our position of equality. This was emphasized in February in a further Memorandum, and again in August.

You will observe that the discussion was up till then confined to policy. I stated that in the Admiralty Memorandum were the measures which the Admiralty considered as necessary to give effect to the policy of the Government as we understood it to be: that in arriving at these measures we had taken into consideration all the lessons of the war which had been considered and absorbed by the Admiralty during the past two years. During the past summer we had arrived at definite conclusions which enabled us to formulate the measures we proposed.

I referred to the reasons why the United States had not been included in any consideration of Naval power before the war. I stated that the Admiralty in no way aimed at superiority in all seas, and therefore we are in no way treading upon the toes of the United States or of any other sea power: indeed the Admiralty measures did not aim at a superiority even of the collective naval forces over those of the United States. As regards the Secretary of State for War's plea that superiority in Post-Jutland battleships was not necessary, I pointed out that the Admiralty were not hide-bound in regard to this matter. Our proposal was to have 9 ships, Class (A), as opposed to 12 of the United States, which was indeed a marked inferiority. We could afford to be only inferior by a very small margin, and equality would be made up by superior design, a better proportion of other types, and superior personnel, but this latter was not to be gambled with and was one which we had always kept up our sleeve.

Lord Curzon[2] referred to Japan. This gave me the opportunity of stating that Japan's naval power was almost as great a menace as that of the United States, and possibly might even become greater.

The Prime Minister then spoke about the possibility of the new administration coming to some agreement as to stopping their construction, and instructed Lord Curzon to communicate with our Ambassador at Washington to enter into pourparlers with the

[1]Document 29 above.
[2]Foreign Secretary.

possible members of the new administration. As he was returning
to England in the next fortnight it was very important that he
should arrive at some idea or arrangement with the new administration as to what will be possible in this direction.

I pointed out that whatever the new administration of the
United States would be prepared to do, it would be most unlikely,
almost incredible, that they would stop the building of the ships
which are already laid down and for which they had voted money,
and under these circumstances any agreement would make no
difference to the measures which the Admiralty considered necessary to take in 1921–22.

I pointed out that time was a factor of the utmost importance:
that we had delayed to the last possible moment, and that unless
we were authorised to commence building ships in the summer of
1921, we should drop from the position that we have held for the
past 300 years to that of taking the third place as a sea power in
the world, and that we should never be able to regain our present
position without incurring great cost and causing the very greatest
suspicion amongst the powers of the world. I pressed most earnestly that a definite decision should be come to at the earliest
possible moment.

I informed the meeting that the Admiralty's views as to the
position of the Capital Ship as a basis of sea power was contained
in a paper which I circulated;[1] that as regards this vital question
the Admiralty's mind was made up and that we did not consider
it necessary to make any further investigations into the lessons of
the war than those that we have already made to arrive at this
principle, i.e. that the Capital Ship was or was not the basis of
sea power. Of course our investigations and studies would continue, to enable us to improve matters of detail.

58. *Churchill to Beatty*

[BTY/8/2/2]   17th December 1920

I have been reading this morning your paper on the Capital Ship
and I should be glad if you could procure me, for the information
of my colleagues on the Committee, further information on one
particular point.

It is stated that the size of the explosive charge of the torpedo

[1]Document 55 above.

can conceivably be raised to four times its present size, i.e. to one ton of explosive. What would be the alterations in the dimensions of the submarine required to carry such a torpedo and tube? I should suppose there would be no insuperable difficulty in carrying it as a bow tube, although it would no doubt be very large and heavy on the beam. If a submarine can carry a 12″ gun there ought to be no impossibility in her carrying a torpedo which carries a ton of explosive, so long as she carries it fore and aft. Anyhow, I should like the approximate legend of a submarine that would fire such a torpedo through her bow or stern tube.

Secondly, how does the explosive effect of a ton charge compare with that of the existing torpedo? How does it compare with the charge carried by an ordinary mine? What is the effect anticipated on the structure say of the *Hood*, which I presume has longitudinal bulkheads? Would these longitudinal bulkheads be forced in? How many compartments would one expect to have flooded by a hit with such a weapon amidships?

Thirdly, but on this same point, your memorandum speaks of the need of building a ship if necessary to stand the explosion of one or more of these one ton charge torpedoes. Can you give any idea of the legend of such a ship? It seems to me that it would be incomparably larger than anything previously conceived, and that all our conception of docks would equally have to be enlarged.

My apprehension is that the investigation of these points may show that it is much easier to construct a submarine carrying such a torpedo than it is to construct a ship which could face the explosion of one or more of them.

There is so much in your argument with which I agree that I am very anxious that what seems to me to be its weakest part should be effectively explored.

59. *Chatfield (ACNS) to Beatty*

[Holograph Minute]

[BTY/8/2/2]   20.12.20
IMMEDIATE

ISL

The facts in this matter are herewith. I feel it is not altogether desirable to discuss these matters by letter; firstly because it is a very confidential matter & secondly because the Admiralty are to produce their official views before the CID. We do not want to arm our interrogators with ammunition to fire at us in advance.

×

> It is necessary to explain that the suggestion in the Admiralty Memo as to a torpedo with a 1 ton warhead is purely an imaginary one. Any such weapon is unlikely to be produced for a long time, *if ever*. It would be the counterpart of the 2 18″ guns in *Furious* which to the layman seemed a magnificent idea, but which the so called unintelligent naval officer ridiculed, & they were soon removed.
>
> Everything shows that the S/M will have ever greater and greater difficulty in approaching close enough to her target to make sure of a hit & only the certainty of a hit would make it worth while to build such a vessel. If however a 1 ton torpedo is ever decided on as an *aim* it will have to be achieved by stages & the capital ship can be altered to meet it.

Suggest some reply as at × be sent & it be added that the Admiralty will produce more detailed evidence if asked for by the CID.

60. *Beatty to Churchill*

[Copy]

[BTY/8/2/2]   22nd December 1920

I have been away for a day or two or would have answered your letter before. I will answer your three questions as they come:–

1. To carry one ton of explosive would require a six ton torpedo.
2. To provide the tube for a six ton torpedo would necessitate reconsideration of entire design of submarines, and would affect very considerably their speed, diving power, and the other qualities which the submarine relies upon for efficiency.
3. One ton of explosive would probably cripple the *Hood*. There is no difficulty, however, in designing a ship of the dimensions of the *Hood* to withstand a blow from a one ton torpedo, in fact, from our experiments, it may be said that we are well ahead in point of time as regards protection as against the design of such a large torpedo and its tube, which would require much experiment.

As you are well aware, the torpedo is not, like the gun, a weapon of precision, and this must be borne in mind when thinking of putting one's faith in a vessel with but one shot in her locker, such as the submarine which you foreshadow.

61. Brigadier-General S. H. Wilson[1] to Beatty

[BTY/8/2/4]   1st January 1921

WITNESSES FOR BONAR LAW COMMITTEE

Dear Lord Beatty,

I am sending you herewith for your information a provisional list of the witnesses which it is suggested should be examined by the Sub-Committee of the Committee of Imperial Defence, which is taking evidence on the question of the capital ship in the Royal Navy.

This list has been prepared by Sir Maurice Hankey after a discussion with Mr. Bonar Law, and Mr. Bonar Law has instructed me to tell you that it is purely provisional as he naturally wishes to consult you in the matter.

In accordance with Mr. Bonar Law's instructions I have arranged for Rear-Admiral Hall to give evidence to the Sub-Committee at the meeting which is taking place on Monday next at No. 11, Downing Street, at 3.0.p.m., and I have asked Sir Percy Scott if he could give evidence on Wednesday next the 6th instant.

As regards the witness to be examined on Tuesday I have written to you another letter today asking you whether if you have no objection, you would arrange for Admiral Brock, the DCNS to give the Sub-Committee his views.

LIST OF WITNESSES TO BE EXAMINED BY THE BONAR LAW COMMITTEE

Admiral Sir Frederick C. D. Sturdee, Bart, KCB, KCMG, CVO, LLD, C-in-C, Nore
Admiral Sir Charles E. Madden, Bart, GCB, GCVO, KCMG, LLD, C-in-C, Atlantic Fleet
Admiral Sir Percy M. Scott, Bart, KCB, KCVO, LLD (Retd)

[1] An Assistant-Secretary of the CID.

Vice-Admiral Sir Osmond de B. Brock, KCB, KCMG, KCVO, Deputy Chief of the Naval Staff
Rear Admiral Sir Roger J. B. Keyes, Bart, KCB, KCVO, CMG, DSO, HMS *Hood*
Rear Admiral F. L. Field, CB, CMG, Controller of the Navy
Rear Admiral H. W. Richmond, CB, President, RN War College
Rear Admiral Wilmot S. Nicholson, CB
Rear Admiral H. F. P. Sinclair, CB, ADC, Director of Naval Intelligence
Rear Admiral Sir W. Reginald Hall, KCMG, CB, DCL (Oxon), MP (Retd)
Rear Admiral Sir Charles M. de Bartolomé, KCMG, CB (Retd)
Rear Admiral S. S. Hall, CB (Retd)
Commodore W. W. Fisher, CB, MVO, HMS *Iron Duke*
Captain A. D. P. R. Pound, CB, HMS *Repulse*
Captain Barry E. Domville, CMG, Director of Plans, Naval Staff
Captain M. E. Nasmith, VC, CB
Captain G. C. Stevenson, CMG, Deputy Director of Torpedo Division, Naval Staff
Commander J. G. Bower, DSO, Plans Division, Naval Staff
Commander J. C. Tovey, DSO, Operations Division, Naval Staff
Air Marshal Sir H. M. Trenchard, Bart, KCB, DSO, Chief of the Air Staff, or a nominee
Sir Eustace H. Tennyson d'Eyncourt, KCB, Director of Naval Construction

and/or

A. W. Johns, Esq, CBE, Assistant Director of Naval Construction
Sir Philip Watts, KCB

62. *Questions for DCNS*[1] *at Bonar Law Committee*

[BTY/8/2/9]   [January 1921]

1. Is it not a fact that both Canada and Australia are very sensitive to the possibility of aggression by Japan?
2. Therefore if the USA becomes the predominant Naval power both Australia and Canada may be expected to seek a close understanding with that Power with a view to gaining its protection?

[1]Osmond de Brock.

3. This means nothing more or less than the dismemberment of the Empire.
4. The Empire therefore depends on the maintenance of an efficient and sufficient Navy.
5. Are the steps necessary to achieve this contained in the paper on Naval policy and Construction dated 22nd November, and the other papers sent to the Cabinet during the last 17 months?
6. Are not these the considered opinions of the Board of Admiralty, based on the lessons of the War?

63. *Beatty: Notes for Bonar Law Committee*

[Holograph]

[BTY/8/2/10]   [January 1921]

Questions that will be asked:
 With the US Fleet completed as intended in 1925, and if we build no capital ships at all, would you fear for the safety of the Empire?
This presupposes we increase very considerably our submarine and air forces.
 What can the US Fleet of superior battleships do to inflict a severe blow to the British Empire?
 Can the British Navy do nothing to oppose them and defeat their objective?

II

Admiral Madden's paper deals with the comparative cost of building and maintaining a fleet of capital ships & other vessels as we conceive it, and that of a fleet of submarines and aircraft capable of doing the same work, *ie*; producing the same military effect, assuming it were possible.
I assume it wd. be possible to prepare an estimate such as he suggests on Page 6 & if it were within reasonable limits [?] of that reqd. for the capital ship programme, the idea wd. be killed instanter.

III

Naval reasons for not including US in calculations for naval expansion: smallness of her navy; geographical position made a combination with another power impossible.

We make no arrangements for producing superiority in all seas. We are in fact not proposing measures to be superior anywhere even the collective massing of our fleets. Equality is what is aimed at.

IV

The Admlty are not hide-bound on the question of whether superiority or equality is absolutely necessary in post-Jutland battleships. The inferiority must & cannot be great, and we accept numerical inferiority of 3 ships, but no more. Superiority in other units and other qualities make up the equality.

V

There is no reason why bomb-dropping should not be as accurate as shooting with a gun. (This may be correct, but every ship carries 800 projectiles and an aeroplane only 1 bomb. To get the same result you must have 800 aeroplanes.)
There is nothing to prevent aircraft from firing a torpedo greater in size than can be fired from a surface vessel. Radius of action is not 500 miles [?] now; there is great difficulty in increasing distance; unlikely to exceed 500 in next 10 years.
Gun attack against aircraft not likely to be effective defence, either when Fleet engaged in battle or at anchor.
Fleet wd. be unsafe at Bermuda without a very large air establishment. 6 small machines equal to ½ the price of a big machine cd. defend Bermuda against attack of 12 big machines.
Aeroplanes could be used in the convoy to assist protection, armed with a bomb or torpedo, or to protect convoy against attack from aircraft. It may be that any fleet, unprotected by aircraft, approaching within the radius of the aircraft shore base wd. be destroyed by aircraft.
Sir H. T.[1] stated that no improvement of gunnery wd. prevent aircraft from firing his torpedo: supported by Sykes.

VI

Are you prepared to advise that the time has arrived for us to build up our Air Power at the expense of the Navy?
Are you prepared to undertake with Air Forces the responsibilities which have hitherto been borne by the Navy of guarding all parts of the Empire and protecting our sea communications?

[1]Trenchard.

VII

If a torpedo directed by W/T from an aeroplane is fully developed it must inevitably hit the ship and, if sufficient numbers are employed, they must destroy the ship.

There must be an answer to this by [— —] of the W/T as well as aircraft defences.

64. Bonar Law Committee

[BTY/8/3/19]   [January 1921]
SECRET

Questionnaire prepared in the Admiralty
for Rear-Admiral S. S. Hall, C.B.[1] whom it is proposed
to examine on Monday, 3rd January 1921

1. Do you consider that the Capital Ship is no longer the dominating factor in Naval warfare?
2. What do you consider has taken its place?
3. Supposing we had fought the late war with no Capital Ships, but with only light surface craft, Submarines and Aircraft, what effect do you think it would have had on the result of the war?
4. Would the country have then been exposed to the danger of invasion?
5. Would the Germans have been in a position to attack our trade all over the world with surface vessels?
6. Can you give any idea of the number of submarines that would have been required to bring the *Emden* to account?
7. If we had only been in a position to send Submarines against Von Spee's Squadron, would there have been the same certainty about the result of the Falkland Island Battle?
8. Had there been no Allied forces in the Mediterranean other than Submarines, would the *Goeben* and *Breslau* have stayed behind the Dardanelles defences or would they have come out and attacked our convoys?
9. Supposing in the late war that Germany had had no Capital

---

[1] Hall had been Commodore of the Submarine Service 1915–18; along with Rear-Admirals C. de Bartolomé, a former 3rd Sea Lord and Controller, and Herbert Richmond, President of RN College Greenwich, he expressed doubts on the continuing dominance of the capital ship.

Ships to put against our Battle Fleet, what effect would that have had on the course of the war?

10. Would not the effect have been to release a large amount of personnel, a quantity of surface vessels for the anti-submarine campaign?

11. Would it not have been possible to more closely invest the German sea-board?

12. Do you consider that Submarines and Aircraft in themselves constitute an efficient protection for merchant convoys under all weather conditions both by day and night?

13. In the event of an enemy fast cruiser meeting a convoy, by day or night, could Submarines with certainty afford protection to the convoy? Answer is NO.

14. If very large Submarines are employed can they be sufficiently protected against gunfire to be able to fight out a surface action with a surface ship similarly armed?

15. Did our Submarines have to face an intensive anti-submarine campaign?

16. What prevented the enemy from carrying out an intensive anti-submarine campaign against our Submarines?

17. Is it not a fact that the German surface craft were only at liberty to carry out an intensive anti-submarine campaign in the vicinity of their own bases?

18. You do not consider that the existence of the Grand Fleet Capital Ships had anything to do with this limited action of the German surface vessels?

19. Do you consider that surface war vessels of any type are necessary?

20. If so, what?

21. Why do you draw the line at such types? Does not the existence of any surface ship lead logically to the maximum expression of power — the Capital Ship?

22. Do you consider that the free action of a battle fleet by day or night is definitely prevented by the presence of Submarines, either outside the base or in the open sea?

23. Assuming, for the sake of argument, that the Submarine will eventually replace the Capital Ship, do you consider that this time has actually arrived; if not, is it within sight?

24. Do you advocate the Capital Ship being abandoned today?

25. In regard to Aircraft, do you consider that they have, or are likely to reach such a stage of development in the next few

years, as to be a serious menace to the continued existence
of the Capital Ship?

26. Do you consider that Aircraft are a greater menace to the
     efficient employment of Submarines than they are to the
     Capital Ship?

27. If the war is overseas, presumably Aircraft must work from
     surface aircraft carriers?

28. What will afford protection to these carriers from the attacks
     of enemy vessels?

65.   *To his wife* [Brooksby]

[BTY/17/54/2]   Admiralty
                                              Monday [3 Jan 1921]

. . . We sat for 3½ hours and had a very hostile witness to the
Admiralty but I think we dished him in the end.[1]

The Prime Minister saw me after & have just come from him.
Walter Long is very seedy but he, the PM, does not want to lose
him yet, and this suits me very well. He was very complimentary
& said he had the fullest confidence in me and was quite prepared
to go on giving me the full powers. This is surely much better
than having another man hoisted in at this juncture who knows
nothing of the business and wd. have to be educated and be an
awful hindrance to me. . . .

66.   *Beatty to Long*
[Copy]

[BTY/13/28/49]   Admiralty
                                                       3 Jan. 1921

Have just got back from a long Sub. Ctee. Meeting examining
Hall S.S. (Rear Admiral). He was not convincing and made no
great claims for the submarine but pinned his faith to the air, of
which he admitted he knew but little. I think on the whole as he
is one of our most antagonistic critics he did us little harm.

I really do not think that we have very much to be afraid of if
they are all like him.

Mr. Bonar Law was anxious I should give evidence at once so

---

[1] Presumably Hall.

as to indicate the lines on which they should proceed to ask witnesses questions. I demurred and said that as the Admiralty were on the defence we had the right to reserve our defence until all the hostile witnesses had been examined. They particularly want some guidance though as to the Admiralty policy of what the Battle Fleet is for in a war with USA and Japan. They have our papers on Imperial Naval Defence in fact they have had it for a year but dont [sic] read it. I'll give them copies on Empire Naval Policy and Co-operation which was prepared for the Colonial consumption and is just ready. I will also have a simple form of war plan produced to set forth simply our policy in the event of a war with USA or Japan and the DCNS can give evidence which will help them. I see their point of view and understand their difficulty which seeing that they have read nothing we have provided them with and have never thought of the subject before is bound to be great.

Generally speaking they all seemed inclined to support Admiralty point of view and I think it will come alright. Adml. P. Scott[1] has caused them much indignation. His letter in *Times* was monstrous and I am not sure does not call for disciplinary measures from the Admiralty; I am enquiring into the matter and finding out if there is any precedent for removing him from the Retired List with the loss of his Pension. That I think would have to be a Cabinet decision as it is the Cabinet he has flouted and insulted but will keep you fully informed.

I do hope you are better and will soon be well again. The DCNS has had a bad chill and is laid up.

Time is not being wasted as we sit every day and I hope will get through two witnesses each day after this.

---

[1]Admiral Sir Percy Scott (1853–1924): entered RN 1866; a great instigator of gunnery improvements; Captain of *Excellent*, the gunnery school 1903–4; Rear-Admiral and Inspector of Target Practice 1905; commanded 2nd Cruiser Squadron, began bitter dispute with Lord Charles Beresford, C-in-C Channel Fleet 1907; Vice-Admiral 1908; hauled down flag 1909 and continued campaign for adoption of director gun control system which he had developed; Admiral 1913; recalled to Admiralty for special service 1914–18; from 1915 organised AA defence of London; after war publicly advocated abandonment of battleship in view of submarine and aircraft improvements. From December 1920 he wrote frequently to *The Times* including contemptuous references to Bonar Law Committee on 3 January 1921.

67. Plans Division Naval Staff

[BTY/8/1/7–8]   4.1.21
SECRET

HEADINGS: WAR WITH USA AND JAPAN

War with USA

Political Situation
War probably largely unpopular — We should desire to terminate
it as soon as we had shown Empire was able to contend against
USA — Time all on side of USA.

Naval Situation
Early successes important. Fleet must seek out enemy Fleet.
Very possibly US Fleet will be in two squadrons, one in Atlantic,
one in Pacific. US Fleet will probably remain divided so long as
Japan's attitude is unsatisfactory.

British Fleet
Composition and strength — Mobility — large endurance —
ability to take on US Battle Fleet and also attack US trade.

Main Fleet Base
for offensive operations.
Bermuda.
Halifax should be also available. Jamaica unlikely to be used by
main fleet — too close to US territory — but useful for submarines
and aircraft.

British Main Fleet — Operations
Prevent junction of US Pacific and Atlantic Squadrons and fight
them in detail if possible. British Fleet must be capable of taking
on whole US Fleet.

Consequences of defeat of US Fleet
No invasion of Ireland or other portions of Empire across sea
possible — Makes it safe for us to transport Empire armies to
Canada, Phillipines or elsewhere — put all our energies into anti-
submarine operations and cutting off U.S. sea communications —
Trade between Canada and UK made possible, also between S.
America and UK and other parts of Empire.

Other operations
Attack Panama Canal and attempt to stop through communication — this might be possible. Rapid blows at enemy trade — Intensive submarine campaign in Gulf of Mexico from Jamaica especially against Tankers — (importance of oil imports to USA especially in future) — such campaign, if successful, might hit her hard.
Submarines in Carribean [*sic*] and Straits of Florida.
Attack on US trade by cruisers all over the world — Empire much better placed for attack on US trade on account of numerous and scattered bases than vice versa.

Naval Situation in Pacific
Either US Pacific Squadron would be watching Japan, or it would proceed into Atlantic.
We should have little to fear.
Both sides would raid with cruisers and submarines.

Defence of Trade
USA not well placed for intensive anti-British trade war. Very few bases near trade routes. Germany with North Sea and Adriatic ports much more dangerous. Anti-submarine war should prove less difficult than in late war.
Convoy system and Empire co-operation as regards defended ports and control of local waters should keep casualties moderate.

War with Japan

General Situation
US, if not actually with us is likely to be benevolently neutral to us — Japan would be handicapped and would be most unlikely to undertake large distant operations — such as attack on Australia — her eye would be on US Pacific Fleet — Chinese and Dutch neutrality would probably favour us — We can assume Japan would wish to take Hong Kong, either to keep or to bargain with — She might seize Singapore by coup de main, but this is unlikely.

Naval Situation
A Fleet larger than Japanese Main Fleet ready to move to Singapore — all arrangements for fuelling on passage prepared in peace time — Ships need great endurance — mobility of fleet of utmost

importance — on mobility depends retention of Singapore. Even Hong Kong could be saved if mobility great.

Main Fleet operations after arrival at Singapore

If Hong Kong still holding out, fleet proceeds there — A Base further north — such as Samsah will be necessary — Japanese Battle Fleet must be sought out and defeated at first opportunity — that done, other operations, especially such as seizure of bases near Japan, from whence blockade and anti-submarine become simplified.

Other Operations

Japanese trade will soon be stopped in all seas except Pacific — Vice versa in our case — Japan being an Island Power, our object to stop all her communications. If we defeat her main fleet it should not take long to stop her Pacific trade also. Co-operation of Dominions of great use in this war — Australian and Canadian ocean-going submarines could harrass Japanese Pacific trade — Fuel reserves in all Dominions would ensure supply of convoys and warships acting on trade routes — Australia and India could largely assist in maintenance of main fleet in East.

Maintenance of Fleet in Far East

Difficult but not impossible — Singapore must be permanently well equipped — India could co-operate by keeping Bombay up-to-date — Australia should be able to send floating docks and dockyard machinery, mechanics etc. to Singapore.

Japanese submarine war on our trade

Unless she had vast numbers, harm done outside Pacific would be very limited. No Foreign bases — Convoy system and co-operation of all Dominions and Colonies as regards defended ports and control of focal points in their Waters would keep danger down — anti-submarine operations near Japanese Coast desirable as soon as possible — much simplified if Japanese main fleet destroyed.

68. *Captain Roger Bellairs to Beatty*[1]

[BTY/8/3/16]   8th January 1921

During the first part of your conversation this morning the telephone was very faint, but later the Exchange Operators evidently improved the line and it became most clear. I received fully your instructions.

Enclosed with the papers yesterday I wrote you a short letter which I hope you received. In it I informed you that Mr. Bonar Law had decided to take the evidence of Admiral Madden on Thursday next, the 13th, and Admiral Brock's on Tuesday next. It was considered by the Committee that at least a whole morning would be taken in hearing the evidence of each of these important witnesses.

I enclose herewith a copy of a paper which Admiral Madden wrote some days ago at the request of the 1st Lord. This is not the paper which he is putting before the Sub-Committee, and which he is now preparing. The DCNS tells me that this latter paper will not now reach the Admiralty until Monday, so I will retain it here for you; as Admiral Madden's evidence is delayed until Thursday, there is not any immediate hurry in your receiving it.

I enclose also the following papers: —

(*a*) Minutes of evidence of Sir Roger Keyes.
(*b*) Memorandum by DCNS to Departments concerned to prepare an estimate of expense involved in preparation for war overseas.
(*c*) Memorandum from the Secretary of CID stating officially that the next meeting will be at 11 am on Tuesday.

As regards (*a*), you will be able to judge for yourself by reading the evidence. DCNS is exceedingly pleased from the Naval Staff's point of view with Sir Roger Keyes's statements.

As regards (*b*), the DCNS informed me that the Sub-Committee are particularly anxious to have some sort of idea of the expenditure involved in docking accommodation, fuel and other matters referred to in his memorandum in preparing for a war overseas. He has seen the 4th Sea Lord, Director of Naval Construction,

---

[1]Roger Bellairs had been Beatty's War Staff Officer in the Grand Fleet and was now his Naval Assistant.

and the AG this morning, and an estimate is being prepared at once and will be ready for the Sub-Committee by Monday.[1]

The DCNS is not himself writing a paper for the Sub-Committee, but he has informed Mr. Bonar Law that he proposes to make a general statement regarding the Naval Staff's appreciation of the strategic aspect of a war against either the United States or Japan. He then proposes to answer with the aid of a chart any questions on the strategy involved which the Committee may care to put. He does not feel it necessary himself to add a written statement to those which you, as Chief of the Naval Staff, have already sent to the Cabinet, and which of course embody his considered opinions.

As regards the preparation of a questionnaire for you to have when taking the evidence of Admiral Madden, I saw the Director of Plans[2] and enclose his remarks. The point is that it will be desirable for the same procedure, if possible, to be followed with Admiral Madden as with the DCNS, that is, to hear the C-in-C's general views regarding the strategic aspect of a war against either the United States or Japan, and then to ask him such questions as may arise. It will be found that the C-in-C is in the most complete agreement with the Naval Staff, and will pour scorn on those who would risk our sea supremacy at this present period by staking their faith on submarines and aircraft alone.

There is one other point which DCNS has been asked about by the Sub-Committee, and that is the possibilities of the internal combustion engine and electric drive. He has seen the Engineer-in-Chief, who is preparing a memorandum.[3] I fancy that the line taken by the E-in-C will be that the internal combustion engine is not sufficiently far developed, and that the electric drive is greatly inferior to the present steam turbine.

If I may say so, I think it will be necessary to go very carefully into this, before committing the Admiralty to the opinions of the E-in-C, and it would seem a subject on which the Admiralty might well form an outside committee of the very best technical engineering brains of the country. In other words, in this respect

---

[1] 4th Sea Lord and Chief of Supplies and Transport was Rear-Admiral Algernon Boyle; DNC was d'Eyncourt and the Accountant General was Sir Charles Walker, a civilian official.
[2] Director of Plans was Captain Barry E. Domville.
[3] Engineer-in-Chief was Engineer Vice-Admiral Sir George Goodwin.

to follow the precedent of the Dreadnought Committee.[1] In regard to the Internal Combustion Engine, I am by no means satisfied that if it is put to the Engineering world that we must have some more economical system than the present which will permit of our Capital Ships vastly extending their radius of action, and also of economising fuel by being able to immediately work up a full speed without the necessity for continuously keeping all boilers alight, that a design in the next 2 or 3 years will not be forthcoming.

I believe it may be found that this is the history of the opposition to the introduction of water tube boilers and turbine machinery repeating itself.

As regards the electrical drive, I know that some of the existing engineers brought up in a particular school are against it, but I also know in confidence that the present Director of Electrical Engineering, who in a sense is under the Engineer-in-Chief, and who, therefore, possibly finds it difficult fully to express his opinions, is not in agreement, and in fact firmly believes in this form of motor power.[2]

At all events we have the object lesson of the United States fitting it and continuing to fit it to their latest vessels, and we have a report of the late Vice Admiral Napier pointing out what advantages accrue from such a system of propulsion. In any case it appears that both these questions are ones which should not be settled off-hand, and in which the Admiralty are capable of receiving great assistance by means of an outside committee on which, of course, Admiralty representatives would sit.

I also enclose a letter just received from Admiral Richmond,[3] and in addition a letter received from the Foreign Office relative to services rendered by the British Navy in the Baltic. You will see the DCNS's remarks on this, and if you concur the summary can at once be prepared.

I have just phoned up the Cabinet with regard to Admiral Bartolomé's evidence, and I am informed that the taking of this is postponed indefinitely. Mr. Bonar Law wishes in any case to hear Admiral Brock and Admiral Madden first of all.

---

[1] The organisation of consultations involved in the design of the *Dreadnought* is described in Ruddock M. Mackay (1973), *Fisher of Kilverstone* Oxford, Chapter 7.

[2] The Director of Electrical Engineering was W. McClelland, a civilian official.

[3] The future Admiral Sir Herbert Richmond (1871–1946), President of the Naval War College. See *Beatty Papers I* p. 521 n. 1 for his full career.

69. *Draft Naval Staff Memorandum*

[Copy]

[BTY/8/3/22]. 13.1.21

NAVAL STRENGTH

*Consideration of the Evidence given before the Sub-Committee
appointed to enquire into the Capital Ship*

In placing the views of the Naval Staff before the Committee
of Imperial Defence on the evidence which has been given before
the Sub-Committee, it is necessary to make the two main issues
clear.

The first and primary issue is — DOES OUR EMPIRE REQUIRE, for
the exercise of naval power, CAPITAL SURFACE SHIPS? or have such
ships been rendered obsolete by the advance in Submarines and
Aircraft?

The opinion of the Naval Staff on this matter was expressed in
Command Paper 619, 1920, page 4, Section C, and was summed
up in the statement that THE CAPITAL SHIP REMAINS THE UNIT UPON
WHICH SEA POWER IS BUILT UP.[1]

The principal exponent of the opposing school whose evidence
has been taken is Admiral Hall. Sir Percy Scott's evidence has
not been available and his opinion can only be gauged by vague
assertions in the Press.

As regards this latter school, the Committee is referred to
Admiral H. W. Richmond's (President of the Naval War College)
paper in answer to the question by the Chief of the Naval Staff —
'Was he or was he not in agreement with the views expressed by
Sir Percy Scott, and if not, why not?' This paper embodies the
doctrine of the Naval Staff as expounded to the sub-committee
by the Deputy Chief of the Naval Staff: the doctrine endorsed
not only by the President of the War College but by the Commander-in-Chief of the principal fleet, vide: Sir Charles Madden's
evidence in the paper before the Committee.

It is for the Committee to determine on this evidence whether
the opinion of the Naval Staff as to the value of the Capital Ship
is justified.

A second issue which has arisen during the course of enquiry,
assuming the Committee endorse the Naval Staff view as to the

---

[1]First Lord's Statement on the Naval Estimates 1920/21.

necessity for the Capital Ship, is — 'Does the present type of battleship meet our prospective requirements?'

Admiral Richmond, in the course of his evidence, viewed the strategic and financial sides of this question. He pointed out that: —

(a) Our strategy must include an active offensive with light craft and submarines on American forces.

With this the Naval Staff fully agree.

(b) Since it will not be possible to blockade America, we must concentrate on defending the focal points at which trade approaches these islands.

America, to keep up constant pressure against this trade, could not maintain more than two or three heavy ships in position, and despite superior material efficiency of such ships, they could not hope to stand up to our present fleet with attendant craft working from a West Coast base.

(c) The whole position will be modified if we can construct a Capital Ship which has considerably greater sea-keeping capacity and carries its own offensive against submarines, and that our energies, with such financial resources as we have, should be devoted to developing a new type rather than to building the present type.

(d) Our geographical position enables us to contemplate a possible inferiority in numbers of the Post-Jutland type of Capital Ship, provided we maintain a superiority of Cruisers and light craft.

The Naval Staff fully appreciates these arguments, but it is necessary to remind the Committee that in a position of grave responsibility as the adviser of the Government on the maintenance of Sea Power it is necessary for the Staff to deal with the facts of the situation as they are and so far as they can be foreseen without too great a stretch on the imagination, and with these facts in view to inform the Government of the Naval necessities to carry out the Government policy. The Naval Staff are not in a position to gamble.

What are the facts of the situation?

Firstly, the Government policy is that 'our Navy should not be inferior in strength to the Navy of other powers', in other words, we have adopted as the foundation of our Naval Policy the maintenance of a One-Power Standard as against the next strongest Power.

Secondly, the Naval Staff is confronted with an American Shipbuilding programme which will mean that in the year 1925 America will have 12 Post-Jutland Capital Ships against this Country's 1, and in their whole strength of Capital Ships will, viewing the question solely for the moment from the material point of view as opposed to the strategic, be greatly superior.

Thirdly, the Navy Staff have always held that the Capital Ship is the unit on which sea power is built up. They cannot view, therefore, with equanimity, if the Government policy is to be carried out, the American shipbuilding programme, without considering a reply.

Fourthly, continuous investigation has been carried out in the various scientific fields which hold out hope of improving the strategic qualities of the Capital Ship. Electric drive, internal combustion power and other sources of energy are under consideration, but the Naval Staff are advised that despite great future possibilities the time is not yet for the practical application of these developments, and that the type of Capital Ship in the course of the next few years can undergo no profound modification other than those it is proposed should be adopted in the direction of increased offensive and defensive qualities.

Fifthly, the strategic aspect of the question referred to in Admiral Richmond's evidence has had always the most serious attention of the Naval Staff, as being the primary consideration in the preparation of plans. Our geographical position does permit of accepting a slight inferiority in types of Capital Ships, and the proposals placed before the Cabinet for the maintenance of our Naval Strength actually contemplated an inferiority in numbers of such ships, and falls considerably short of equality during the building period 1923–25.

If, however, as has been suggested, no building programme is carried out during the next financial year, the inferiority in Capital Ships would then be too great for the Naval Staff to be in a position to inform the Cabinet that the One-Power standard was being maintained.

Further, if, as has been suggested, the building programme should be postponed one year so as to concentrate in research and experiment with a view to evolving a new type, the position would be, according to the information at the disposal of the Naval Staff, that the shipbuilding and armour plate firms on whom the Admiralty rely would be obliged to close down for lack of work, and considerable expenditure and delay would be incurred in commencing building. Also, one year's delay will not evolve the new type, the requirements of which are clearly in the minds of the Naval Staff, but which cannot be embodied in the present state of technical science. Three to five years' delay rather than one year's delay would be required. If the Government policy of a One-Power standard is to be maintained, delay for the sake of research is impossible. WE MUST COMMENCE BUILDING NOW.

Sixthly, the financial side of the question has not been lost sight of. The proposals of the Naval Staff have been framed to carry out the Government Policy with the minimum expenditure. If the Government considers this expenditure cannot be faced, then the only alternative to reduce the money required is to alter the policy to one-below a One-Power standard.

This is outside the responsibility of the Naval Staff, which can only state to the Government, what the Government must be fully aware of, that this Empire depends for its existence on the sea, that under such circumstances less than a One-Power Naval standard can hardly be contemplated, and that if economy on the nation's budget is to be effected, it should be looked for in other directions than in curtailment of the Naval shipbuilding programme designed to maintain our sea power, on which our whole prosperity is built.

This then is the situation in the Staff opinion as the result of the Enquiry: —

1.   The Capital Ship is, and remains, the unit on which Sea Power is built up.

2.   We require to evolve a type of Capital Ship of large radius of action, economical in fuel, and carrying its own anti-submarine offensive. Research and experiment must be, and is being, pursued to this end.

3.   Whilst keeping the ultimate requirements in view, the Naval Staff have to keep before them the practical fact of the situation that the entirely new type is a vision of the future, and that in the meantime the American shipbuilding programme is proceeding.

4.   The Government have laid down a One-Power Standard for this Country, and, after examining the strategic and tactical aspects of the problem, the Naval Staff consider the shipbuilding programme already forwarded to the Cabinet is necessary to meet this policy. A year or more of delay and our position would be jeopardised. In that time the armament and building firms would

have closed down and could only be restarted with difficulty and expense.

Nor, in the present state of technical science, would the evolution of a new type, such as has been visualised by writers in the press, be a practicable possibility.

5.   If finance does not permit of the building programme, then the Naval Policy of the Government must be altered and the position of a second or third Naval Power accepted. This is a matter for Government decision, and for approval by the House of Commons. The Naval Staff are not in a position to accept responsibility for advising such a decision. This, however, is not their function. It is entirely a Government responsibility.

70.   *To his wife* [Hotel de France, Pau]

[BTY/17/54/27–30]   Brooksby Hall
Leicester
Sunday [23 Jan 1921]

*   *   *   *

The Secretary is a great help and I am able to do some work with him, and he is nice and plays with the boys and they love having him.

Lloyd George is going over today for the Conference and it is while he is away that I hope we shall get on with finishing the work of the sub-committee. If I was to go with him we sh. never get the really important questions finished and should have to come back to do it instead of coming over to Paris.

As far as I can see events now, I ought to be able to leave London the night of Tuesday the 1st March, but my dear, you know my difficulties, and the importance of getting this question settled satisfactorily. The whole of the future of the Empire depends upon it, and incidentally our future also, because if it goes against the Admiralty I do not remain as 1st Sea Lord. You may today think that would be a very good thing, but you would not think so in six months time, and you would also not wish me to be false to the trust that is imposed upon me all for the sake of 48 hours. I shall then come away with a clear conscience and leave the matter in the laps of the Gods — *ie:* the politicians — to take upon themselves the responsibility of seeing the Empire become dismembered. In any case I know in your heart of hearts you would not have me go down to history as the 1st Sea Lord of the day who made so bad a struggle that our rulers gave up the heritage of Command of the Sea which we have held for over 300 years.

You won't say you are always putting your wife 2nd and that I ought not to bother about it, or, if you did, you might do so today, but in a few months time you would think differently, and you would condemn me for not having played the game. So, Sweetheart mine, do not make my task harder than it is and trust me a little more to come to you as soon as I possibly can.

We have had a terrible disaster in the loss of a big 'K' submarine which was lost with all hands for no known reason. It shows quite clearly the unreliability of these much talked of craft.[1]

*   *   *   *

71. Beatty: Notes on Technical Evidence given to Capital Ship Committee

[Extracts]

[BTY/8/3/1]   [January 1921]

[Admiral C. de Bartolomé]

Admiral Bartolomé's statement that Capital ships require protection by an ever increasing number of small craft was based upon past experience in the War.

The Admiralty contention is that with the aid of scientific methods we reduce the number of small craft required for screening Battleships (vide evidence of Captain Waistell) and, by improvement of design, provide protection to the ships themselves to resist attack by submarines and aircraft.

Admiral Bartolomé's evidence as to the value of the bulge shewed that he was one of the principal advocates of this form of defence, thus modifying the impression conveyed by his written Memorandum.

He laid stress on the dangers of the magnetic torpedo. It must be borne in mind that a torpedo which explodes without being in direct contact with its objective loses much of its destructive force. When in contact, the water provides the necessary tamping effect, but when not in contact the explosion is dissipated. Experiments have been carried out, and it is the considered opinion of the Director of Naval Construction that the damage caused by a

---

[1] Submarine *K5* sank in the Bay of Biscay on 20 January 1921.

magnetic torpedo exploded only 10 feet from a ship would not seriously endanger her.

The case of the magnetic mine is similar.

The witness enlarged on his proposals for keeping open our trade communications in the event of war with the USA. His only hope of achieving this, which he admitted was a very slender one, was to place a torpedo-carrying aeroplane in every Merchant Ship, so that it could look after itself. He suggested that submarines and small armed craft should cruise in the vicinity of convoys as an additional protection.

Air Marshal Trenchard pointed out the impossibility of the Torpedo Aeroplane being carried on the Merchant Ships.

Such strategy hardly requires comment. It should be remembered that even Admiral S. S. Hall admitted that the submarine was a poor protection for a convoy.

History shews that the most effective method of protecting trade is to defeat the enemy's Fleet or contain it by a superior force so that forays can only be carried out at great risk.

Admiral Bartolomé expressed many opinions on technical subjects which have been dealt with by the ACNS. He admits that his whole argument is based upon what he considers to be the prospects of successful development of aircraft and submarines. If these craft do not come up to his expectations during the next few years, he agrees that his argument falls to the ground.

Captain A. K. Waistell, CB[1]

Captain Waistell commanded our most important submarine Flotillas during the first half of the period of the war. Of the successes achieved by our submarines against enemy ships in Home waters the great majority were scored by units under his command. He therefore had every opportunity for realising the utility of these vessels. In his present appointment he has had full knowledge of the development of anti-submarine warfare, and is in consequence an important witness.

His statement that the newest anti-submarine devices show promise and that they will be of more use to hunting or other surface vessels than to the submarines themselves is concurred in. One point in his evidence was important and desirable to remind

[1]The future Admiral Sir Arthur Waistell (1873–1953) was at this time Director of the Torpedo Division, Naval Staff.

the Sub-Committee, that the use of asdics by Destroyers would lessen the number required to screen Capital Ships.

Like Captain Horton[1] (the submarine technical expert) he saw no development in sight which would enable the Supersonic Ray to assist torpedo firing from a submarine submerged.

The connection between his evidence and that of Captain Horton should be noted. Captain Waistell's examination showed that whether from fixed or mobile antidotes the greatest danger to submarines is found near land or in shoal waters. Captain Horton spoke of submarines operating in focal areas, adding that their opportunities in the open sea would be few.

In short, the greatest opportunity for the submarine is coincident with the greatest opportunity for defeating its activities.

72. Beatty: Concluding Remarks to Capital Ship Committee with Comments by Bonar Law and Churchill

[Extract]

[Cab. 16/37/555–9]   27 January 1921

With regard to Air Marshal Trenchard's evidence it appeared to me that this was purely of the 'may be' type and that given a certain set of circumstances and a large expenditure of money, he claimed that the Air Service *might* be able to perform *some* of the functions which are now carried out by the Navy. Even the Air Marshal, enthusiast that he is, was very definite in his opinion that the Air Service of the future could not possibly be made a substitute for the Navy in providing complete protection to the British Empire and its sea communications. On the contrary, the Air Service would be an additional form of defence, and this view, I understand, was shared by Sir Frederick Sykes.

On the technical points raised and the claims made by the Air Marshal, perusal of the questions asked and the answers given, supplemented by the evidence of Admiral Chatfield, provide sufficient material upon which to form an opinion. His view that a fleet coming within the radius of action of an air base, equipped

---

[1]Later Admiral Sir Max Horton (1883–1957): entered RN 1898; submarine specialist; commanded submarines throughout the war, particularly distinguishing himself in the Baltic. At this time he was Assistant to the Rear-Admiral, Submarines. He commanded the *K* class flotilla in 1922; Rear-Admiral 1932; Vice-Admiral 1936; commanded reserve Fleet 1937; Flag Officer Submarines 1940; C-in-C Western Approaches 1942, responsible for defeat of U-boats in the Atlantic; retired at end of war.

as he visualised it, would be destroyed, cannot be accepted so far as it is possible to foresee developments at the present time. Such a form of attack will naturally be met by the development of methods of defence. The Air Service is obviously very susceptible to weather conditions. Even the Air Marshal qualifies his suggestions for the employment of flying boats by postulating favourable weather and this must apply equally to the use of airships. He apparently had not contemplated the need for operating with his craft in the vast expanses of the oceans, where continued favourable weather cannot be expected. The Admiralty entirely concur with the Air Marshal that aircraft will become an increasingly important auxiliary to the Fleet, and as pointed out by Admiral Chatfield, aircraft will surely be regarded as the capital ship's best friend and not its worst enemy.

In view of the widely differing estimates of the future of submarines and aircraft and the nebulous data upon which hopes are based, I ask the Sub-Committee if it is possible for those who bear the responsibility for the defence of the Empire to acquiesce in a policy which would substitute such shadows for the substance of the Navy as constituted today which is the result of the experience of hundreds of years, and of which the capital ship is and has been the basis of its power. The Committee have heard many witnesses and much evidence of a diversified type, and in no case has any witness definitely stated that he considered the capital ship to be dead. In one case the witness deprecated spending sums of money until our designs embodied the necessary improvements to enable it to meet new weapons. I state that the Admiralty designs embody these requirements and are keeping up with the methods of attack. Other witnesses have dwelt on the desirability of delay in building capital ships until research and experiment have developed new weapons. This is not the Admiralty view, which is that research in the matter of new weapons must progress side by side with development of old weapons. Even Admiral Hall, a greater enthusiast than submarine officers themselves, admitted that the battle cruiser type of capital ship must remain a factor in naval warfare.

I would submit to this Committee that no case has been made out to displace the capital ship as the basis of sea power but rather that the evidence has gone to emphasise that the capital ship must remain pre-eminently the foundation of sea power. I understand that the Committee is not called on to give an opinion on this question. This, I think, is most unfortunate because they have had the great advantage of hearing the evidence and putting their own questions to the various witnesses. They must therefore be in an infinitely better position to form an opinion than those Members of the Cabinet or CID who will have to wade through the voluminous mass of evidence without having time to study it and follow the arguments with the care that the matter demands.

I have one word to say on the subject of delaying the carrying out of the Admiralty policy. As the result of this enquiry the Government may decide that the capital ship remains the basis of sea power, but that to put into execution now the programme submitted by the Admiralty would, for various reasons, be untimely and unnecessary.

The Admiralty have given a great deal of thought and consideration to this question of how long action could be delayed, firstly in announcing a policy, and secondly, in carrying it out. As regards the announcement of policy, the Admiralty have already placed their reasons before the Cabinet in a memorandum of the 14th November to which they attach the utmost importance. As regards carrying out the policy, the Admiralty are of opinion that further delay cannot possibly be accepted. Apart from the desirability of maintaining our battleship building capabilities, unless we do commence the programme as outlined in the present year we shall fall so far behind that we shall be unable even with the best will in the world to re-establish our position and carry out the policy of the Government to maintain a One Power Standard.

I would remind the Sub-Committee that the Admiralty policy is not one of adding to the strength of the Navy but of maintaining the necessary strength to carry out the Government policy by replacing vessels which are old, worn out and obsolescent, due to the effects of the war and the advance of the science of ship construction.

I would like to add that the Admiralty as a whole have considered the matter from its economical point of view; that the Department is entirely an economical one. Every question that is put before the Board of Admiralty is looked at from an economical point of view and that in no sense or shape or form can the Board of Admiralty as constituted today be considered 'squandermaniacs'.

MR BONAR LAW: We shall treat this as your summing up of the evidence and I do not propose to add to it.

MR CHURCHILL: I was going to ask whether it is not a matter for us to consider whether it would not be desirable for us to express an opinion. I think there is great force in what the First Sea Lord said. We have seen the witnesses and heard their evidence. None of our colleagues will be able to give anything like the time we have to this question, and to studying it, and I think that without coming to any decision today, we might consider whether . . .

MR BONAR LAW: Whether we might ask the CID to enlarge our terms of reference?

MR CHURCHILL: Yes.

MR BONAR LAW: I think that is worth considering, but I think what the First Sea Lord said is met to a large extent by the fact that the CID is a comparatively small body and we shall constitute a large part of it. We are not to make a report but we shall give our opinion on the subject derived from our information obtained from the evidence and it is worth while considering whether we shall enlarge our terms of reference.

LORD BEATTY: It would seem to be the logical outcome.

MR BONAR LAW: The real evil is not great because our opinion would be given to the Committee, the numbers of which are comparatively small and if we agree here I think they would take our opinion.

There is only one thing I thought I would like to know – what is the personnel now of the American fleet as compared with ours.

LORD BEATTY: 171,000 as compared with 127,000. I am not certain but I think at the present time it is 125,000; I can obtain that information, but what they eventually aim at is 171,000.

(The meeting then terminated).

73. *To Eugénie Godfrey-Faussett*

[SLGF 15/4/3]   Hotel Ritz
Paris
Wednesday [2 Feb 1921]

Eugénie Darling,
    Here I am en route to Biarritz to join Tata for ten days or so. I am greatly afraid that I shall not be able to squeeze more as there are more troubles at home which I must be there to tackle.

Nobody else can do it. Walter Long is down and out and we shall be having a new First Lord. I do not suppose I shall be consulted as to who it is to be, they come [*sic*] to the Navy for advice unless they get in a hole. However we defeated the attack on the capital ship with great slaughter, and, although I say it myself, I think we handled the situation with considerable tact and skill and have not rubbed anybody up the wrong way. Having got an advantage over them I do not want to lose it by not being there at a critical time.

It has been a tough job though and Tata's condition and the worry connected with it did not make it any easier.

*   *   *   *

[Signed] Ever your David.

74. *Long to Beatty*

[BTY/13/28/52]   February 12th 1921

You must forgive me for sending you a dictated letter, for at present I am quite unable to write more than a line or two, and that very illegibly, in pencil.

First let me say how rejoiced I am that Lady Beatty is showing signs of real improvement. I know what this means to yourself, what a weight of anxiety it will take off your mind, and I can only hope that it may be very rapid and very real in its continuance.

I shall certainly give myself the pleasure of writing, and you the boredom of reading, my letter on the topic of the termination of our colleague-ship. I am more thankful than I can say now to know that I have filled, what I have always conceived to be the right part for the First Lord of the Admiralty, i.e. by giving the First Sea Lord all your support and assistance in carrying out his Naval policy so far as it is clearly consistent with the general policy of the Government of the day.

I think it is much better that I should send my statement to my successor. There is no necessity to send it to B.L.;[1] I can do just what I like, and the moment it is announced — I think there is no doubt it will be Lee — I will write the letter.

I agree as to the circumstances attendant upon Admiral Brock's position and will certainly include this in my letter to my successor.

I cannot tell you how grateful I am to you for the attitude which

[1]Bonar Law.

you have invariably adopted towards me, it might easily have been loyal, correct and everything else that it ought to have been without being what it was.

If ever I can be of service in the House or out — and I am not sure that I cannot do more as a private Member than I can as a Front Bencher — let me know and I will be at your service.

75. *Note by Churchill to Members of the Sub-Committee on the Capital Ship on his rejection of the Draft Report*

[Beatty's Copy]

[BTY/8/4/14]   War Office
[Beatty's Copy]   13 Feb 1921

I do not wish to associate myself with this report which does not to my mind represent the general character of the evidence. I was not at all impressed with Admiral Richmond's evidence, the value of which was greatly reduced by the fact that he was mixing up financial and political considerations, of which he was no particular judge, with the matters upon which he has professional credentials. I observe that Admiral Richmond has since circulated a paper which is practically a reasoned retraction of his previous arguments. This important fact is not even referred to in the draft report.

Generally I think the draft report lays an undue emphasis on any evidence which may have been obtained against the capital ship, and in consequence gives the impression that the question was more or less evenly balanced, that there were high authorities on both sides and as much argument one way as the other, that possibly there was a slight preponderance in favour of the capital ship.

I hold, on the contrary, that the Admiralty have made out an overwhelming case for the retention of the capital ship as the foundation of sea power in the period with which we have now to deal. They have been supported by the evidence of almost every naval officer in the Service, even those representing submarines. I feel that this volume of responsible professional opinion, expressed as it is on the morrow of a great war by the men who actually handled the weapons of which they are speaking and faced the real conditions, constitutes the only basis on which the Government can respond. Against this opinion has been marshalled the views of officers who have left the service without attaining high command, who are to a large extent not informed on the most recent developments of naval science, and who in some cases are embittered and in all cases without responsibility. I cannot feel that there is any parity or appearance of parity either in the arguments or in the authorities as they have been brought before us.

On the whole I have been greatly reassured by the increasing power of the means to deal with submarines and by the evidence of the limits of the power of these weapons and of the torpedoes they carry. My feeling is that it is more probable that the submarine era will pass rather than that the battleship will pass. I base this opinion not only on the evidence which I have heard at this Committee but on the study and thought of the last ten years. I think the picture of the improved capital ship able to locate by asdics any under-water craft within two or three thousand yards and to hurl an enormous depth charge with great accuracy to the point located is at least as probable as any other forecast which has been made.

A more formidable attack upon the battleship has been made by the air, and in this case responsible officers like Sir Hugh Trenchard and Sir Percy [sic] Sykes have given evidence. Obviously there is a more hopeful future before an arm which is all-seeing than before an arm which is all-blind. This development must of course be watched with great care. But I do not feel that within the period with which we are concerned anyone could confidently rely upon the Air Service to take the place of the British line of battle as the foundation of our safety and authority throughout the world. I expect that a system of general air defence, the great bulk of which would inevitably be localised and consequently multiplicated, would cost enormous sums in stations, in material and in skilled mechanics of all kinds. The wrong principle is to try to be prepared to defend yourself at an indefinite number of points. The right principle is to have some particular weapon which will proceed to attack the enemy's strongest force wherever it presents itself.

Of course it is quite true that once you abandon the idea of being the strongest power at sea and definitely accept a minor role, a lot can be done to annoy the stronger enemy by subsidiary weapons like the submarine. If we found ourselves unable to maintain a fleet which could fight a supreme naval battle with reasonable prospects of success, it would of course be better to give up the competition and fall back upon the weapons of the weaker. I do not, however, see how recourse to these weapons could be more than a deterrent upon the stronger naval power in going to war nor how if war broke out it could do more than somewhat delay our defeat. I do not at all admit that we are at all unable to maintain British sea power. On the contrary, I am confident that the nation has both the means and the will to do so and that it is our duty to make every sacrifice for that purpose.

76. *Notes by Beatty's Secretary on Draft Report of the Capital Ship Sub-Committee*[1]

[BTY/8/4/17]   14.2.[21]

This is sent as a draft for consideration by Members of the Sub-Committee.

It has, however, been 'finally' approved by Mr. Bonar Law, which may mean that he wishes it to go forward as it stands, accompanied by such comments as other Members may wish to make.

Paragraph 22 of the Report is the most important, as it professes to set forth the general impression made on the minds of the Committee. It is no doubt the impression which the Government would like the Committee to have gained, but is quite at variance with the facts represented by the Admiralty.

It is difficult to see how such an impression could have been conveyed by the evidence as recorded.

It is presumed that the Admiralty comments required by the Terms of Reference will be prepared on the *final Report* as agreed to by *all* the Members of the Sub-Committee, if an effort is to be made to produce a unanimous Report. Assuming that such comments are required, it would be unsatisfactory to base them on this particular draft.

OTHER NOTES ON DRAFT REPORT

Para.
6. This paragraph admits that all Naval Officers on the *Active List*, except Admiral Richmond, consider that the Construction of Capital Ships must proceed without delay.
9. Says how much Admiral Richmond's evidence impressed the

[1]See Document 84 below.

Committee. It was exactly the type of evidence the Political element hoped for!

10. Would it not be more accurate to say that the development of certain new methods of attack etc. is in its infancy? Some of them are well developed already.

13. Contains a frank admission that if no new Capital Ships are laid down, the British Navy will be inferior to that of the US in 1924.

It is difficult to reconcile this admission with the statement in para. 22.

14. Seems to indicate a misunderstanding of the evidence, which was to the effect that a knock-out blow against the United States Fleet would not be equivalent to a knock-out blow against the US as a nation. I do not remember evidence to the effect that a knock-out blow against the US *Fleet* was impossible.

As regards destruction of our trade by the US, it is not correct to say that if international law were respected supplies could be brought to the United Kingdom in Neutral Ships. In wars between nations the distinction between contraband and conditional contraband has necessarily disappeared. Neutral ships would be as liable to stoppage as our own.

16. The wording of the latter part of this paragraph gives the impression that the Committee bowled out a lack of co-operation between the Admiralty and Air Ministry.

It was not a case of being 'apparent from the evidence'; it was stated quite definitely that the matter had not yet been considered jointly, and a reason was given.

19. It is fair to record a divergence of opinion among witnesses when Admiral Richmond was the only one who held that a superior US Fleet could not play ducks and drakes with our South American Trade? So far as I understand, the other anti-capital-ship witnesses merely thought that nothing could be done to stop their doing so.

21. This merely shows the avidity with which the politician absorbs the view which suits his political convenience.

[Initialled] F. S.

77. *To his wife* [Biarritz]

[BTY/17/55/9–10]   Hanover Lodge
                                                  Tuesday Midnight
                                                    [15 Feb. 1921]

The Secretary has just gone and we have waded through a lot of stuff and I am more or less 'au fait' with what has been going on.

Bonar Law has cooked the report of the sub-committee to meet with political requirements. This of course I cannot agree to and consequently will have to write another one. It really is monstrous the dishonesty of these political rascals. They simply cloud the issue, draw a red herring [—] the trail and sit tight.

I am afraid that we have not an easy time in front of us.

*   *   *   *

Lee is the 1st Lord. I saw him this afternoon, very pleasant and easy. If he is an honest man he has a tough time in front of him, if he is not — his bed will not be one of roses.

*   *   *   *

78. *To his wife* [Biarritz]

[BTY/17/55/13–14]   Hanover Lodge
                                          Wednesday 16th [Feb 1921]

I was glad to get your letter of Monday this morning . . .

I am disturbed however to realise by the substance of your letter that you were still cross with me. I am not going to lecture you as you suggest I might, but I *am* going to say that you are unjust. Dear Old Girl, do look at things from a broader aspect. It is not really in you to be narrow and carping. You complain of my being hard and indifferent; you little know the strain going on inside and the restraint I have to put on myself to prevent me from bursting out against the injustice of all your remarks. I keep on saying to myself, she doesn't really mean what she says. Now, dear heart you know in your heart of hearts that I never think of anybody except you and the boys, and honestly you cannot be jealous of my love of them or would have it otherwise. Equally I am sure you would never wish me to be an idle man, or if you did and I were, you would regret it the very next day.

*   *   *   *

You dear Old Silly Billy, you say you will never get any happi-

ness, what nonsense that is when you have everything that makes
for happiness to look forward to. We are not old and we have
many years before us in which we can enjoy things together if you
will only let us and look at things from a generous broad minded
point of view.

I have been very busy all day. We certainly have a tough job
in front of us and it is going to take some pushing to get our views
accepted, but I am not letting the grass grow under my feet. If it
goes against us, then you will have your wish and I shall join the
unemployed, but I am not going down without a big fight for it,
and I still have some people who believe in me. I had a long talk
with Winston who will support me, but he thinks it is going to be
a hard fight and we can give nothing away.

Now, cheer up sweetheart mine and look at the bright side
of things & the dark clouds will soon roll away.

Bless you darling mine and don't always think crossly of,

Your devoted
DAVID

79. *To his wife* [Biarritz]

[BTY/17/55/20–22]   Hanover Lodge
Friday, 18th [Feb. 1921]

*   *   *   *

We are getting ready for the Joint Allied Conference on Tuesday and we are [–] about the result of the Sub-Committee
Report. We have had some acrimonious arguments on the subject
and I have disagreed with Mr Bonar Law & his [–]. Luckily, as
I said before, I have Winston on my side, so it may become
necessary, if we cannot come to agreement, to have a minority
Report, which I am preparing. On the whole things are not looking too rosy and I am afraid next week will be a very hectic one,
and we shall have many sharp engagements. If it comes to the
worst they can kick me out, and you will have your wish, but it
will not be a pleasant way to end my period of office and I should
feel that I had been a failure. But I do not think honestly they
will go to that length. I don't care if they do as I shall feel that I
have done my duty and am consoled by the thought that in any
case you will be pleased . . .

80. *To his wife* [Paris]

[BTY/17/55/37–38]   Hanover Lodge
                                                  Wednesday [23 Feb. 1921]

*   *   *   *

I had a long talk with the King this morning, who asked after you, was very nice and sympathetic, and was really pleased to hear you were better, and said you must be very careful not to do too much when you come back to England. He was very strong in his support of the Admiralty policy and said he had tackled the PM – not that that is worth very much but it is better to have him for, rather than against us. Lee I cannot yet make out and do not altogether trust. I think he imagines he sees a way to get credit with the PM by cutting down, and is out to do so. Well, we are ready to meet him in so far as it is possible, but not beyond a certain point. At present he is suffering from Laryngitis. It seems that all that come to the Admiralty have a microbe put into them of some sort . . .

81. *Admiralty Memorandum for CID*

[Copy]

[BTY/8/2/13]   23.2.21

ANCILLARY SERVICES OF THE FLEET
(135th Meeting of CID)

Papers in connection with the Naval Policy of the Empire have been prepared at the Admiralty for the Imperial Conference next June.

A preliminary paper on the general policy entitled 'Imperial Naval Defence' was sent to the Committee of Imperial Defence over twelve months ago, and the Admiralty has been awaiting a decision on this important question before presenting a more detailed policy.

In brief the recommendations are that, for the present, the Dominions and Colonies should limit their shipbuilding programmes to the provision of light cruisers and submarines, expending the remainder of their available funds on the development and protection of their naval bases, and the building up of reserves of fuel and stores.

The United Kingdom would remain responsible for the provision of the main battle force consisting of battleships, battle-cruisers and their attendant vessels, the whole force being sufficiently mobile to move to any threatened portion of the Empire.

The two principal foreign Naval Powers – the USA and Japan – are rapidly increasing their naval strength. The Admiralty shipbuilding programme now before the Cabinet aims at maintaining the One-power standard laid down by the Government and since a division of our main fleet into two portions inferior to the fleets of either USA or Japan is opposed to sound strategy, the mobility of the main body is a most important factor in Admiralty policy. The fleet will be based in a central position in home waters and the Mediterranean, ready to move to the east or west as required.

In addition to the provision of the main fleet, the United Kingdom will have to maintain certain other light forces, consisting of cruisers, submarines and other small craft to guard the sea lines of communication for our own purposes, to attack the military and commercial sea routes of the enemy, and to provide for the local defence of ports and other auxiliary services.

The existing number of light cruisers, destroyers and submarines would not be sufficient to meet the requirements of another big naval war, at the commencement of which the Admiralty would have to ask the Government's sanction for the construction of large numbers of light vessels.

The numbers now available are however sufficient to deal with peace requirements all round the world and to ensure adequate training and progress in the seagoing fleets. They would also be sufficient to deal with the corresponding forces in hostile fleets at the commencement of war. The Admiralty will be in a better position to advise as to the total requirements in light forces when it is known to what extent the Dominions and Colonies will contribute.

These smaller vessels are on a different footing to the capital ship of to-day, which takes a long period to construct and which must therefore be kept on a war footing in time of peace, as it is the main bulwark of our naval strength, and therefore of the safety of the Empire.

In the uncompleted war programme there are the following vessels under construction:–

> 8 Light Cruisers
> 8 TBDs
> 6 Submarines
> 2 Aircraft Carriers

It is not considered that replacements need commence for some time. At a future date it will be necessary to begin a regular policy of replacement.

This policy must, however, depend, as above stated, to some extent on amount of co-operation by the Dominions.

As regards Docks, there are four German floating docks, all of which can be adapted to take our largest ships.

The places to which they should be sent depend on the answer given by the Government to the proposals put forward by Admiralty to establish a base at Singapore and possibly also at Bermuda.

Reserves of ordinary 'H' Mines are sufficient, and it is not proposed to add to them, but a Reserve of 'L' Mines, i.e. those used for Harbour defence, is in processs of formation; the cost (which is not very large) is being spread over several years.

[Initialled] B.

82. *Beatty to Long*

[Typed and Holograph]
[Copy]

[BTY/8/4/10]   1 March 1921

We had a stormy meeting of the Sub-Committee of CID yesterday afternoon.

I definitely stated I could not agree to Mr Bonar Law's Report. Mr Bonar Law said he could not amend it. The result is an impasse.

Horne, who has I believe, given very little attention to the whole thing, seems merely to follow Bonar Law.

Geddes, I fear, will do the same.

Churchill associates himself with my report, and it is proposed that Mr Bonar Law's Report shall go in signed by –

Bonar Law
Horne
Geddes (if he will do so, he was not at the meeting, but I expect
   he will sign it)

I send you my version, and if you agree with it I suggest you say so. They may not agree to your eligibility to sign it, but as you were appointed by name and not as 1st Lord of the Admiralty, and have studied all the evidence, and had all the experience acquired by continuous study of this very question, I cannot feel that they could rightly ignore your interpretation of the evidence.

[1]It would be of the greatest help if you signed my Report. In any case the British public would not split hairs on this point, though Bonar Law and others in the Cabinet may do so.

I do earnestly hope that you are progressing and will soon be able to actively take part in the struggle which is bound to ensue in the House in the near future.

PS Churchill has just sent me the enclosed draft with slight amendments, which are acceptable. Will you, if you think fit, sign it and return it by the Messenger who brings it. [not included]

83. *Lady Lee of Fareham's Diary*

[Extracts]

[Lee]   March–April 1921

March 2 1921

A. tells me that the civilian people at the Admiralty and certain of the Sea Lords are very pleased at the settlement which A. has effected, but others of the Sea Lords, including Beatty and Brock are inclined to be chilly and ungracious. He thinks B. is suffering from swollen head, that he is of the dashing 'cavalry leader' type, without deep or great intelligence, and that Brock is really the *brain*.

April 2 1921

During the next few weeks A's troubles at the Admiralty centred mainly on his difficulties with Beatty, who has apparently been talking a great deal to the Press about his desire to bring in a large Naval building programme. Admiral Bentinck (A's Naval Secretary), who is very cautious, admits that Beatty has never been loyal to anybody. To A. his manner is nearly always bad, sulky and almost insubordinate, but A. is being superhumanly patient with him and refuses to give him any opening for a resignation.

[1]Holograph for rest of letter.

April 24 1921

A. and I 'pro bono publico' went down to luncheon with the Beattys at Esher Place, which they have taken for the season. A. had Lady Beatty on one side of him and Lady Edward Lascelles (Lord Balfour's niece) on the other. Lady B. as usual complained to A. with much violence about the shocking way 'David's war services had been unrecognised by the country'. This seems strange seeing that amongst other things he has been made an Earl, an Admiral of the Fleet, a GCB, an OM and has been given a grant of £100,000 by Parliament. What he now wanted, it appeared, was a KG, and this, the King quite rightly, refused to consider . . .

84. *Admiralty Remarks on Draft Report of Capital Ship Sub-Committee*[1]

[BTY/8/4/3] [March 1921]

Para. 2

The evidence called by the Admiralty was confined to the subject of the enquiry as set forth in the Terms of Reference to the Sub-Committee.

The Terms of Reference contain no instructions to call into question the advice of the Board of Admiralty as to the measures necessary to preserve the One Power Standard adopted by the Government.

Such instructions would have indicated that the Board did not possess the confidence of the Government and would have created a different situation.

The Admiralty, therefore, had no reason to feel called upon to produce evidence in support of the advice which it had tendered in Memoranda to the Cabinet to the effect that it is necessary to lay down Capital Ships without delay.

It cannot be admitted that investigation was held into this question, or that views expressed by irresponsible individuals can be weighed against those put forward by the responsible Department.

[1]On 9 March 1921 General Wilson sent Beatty an advance copy of Bonar Law's Report and wrote 'before circulating it to the Committee of Imperial Defence I should be very much obliged if you would let me know if you approve of it in its final form'. This covering letter and the Report itself are in BTY38/4/2 of 9 March 1921.

Para. 8

Rear-Admiral Bartolomé is not in touch with recent developments in weapons or in warship construction. In considering his evidence it is necessary to bear in mind that of Rear-Admiral Chatfield, who is the officer particularly responsible for the study of developments of this nature. The comparative value of the evidence of these two Officers can best be gauged by consideration of the extent to which it was based upon fact, experiment, investigation and research.

Para. 9

Rear-Admiral Richmond in his evidence admitted that if the design of future ships could embody increased radius of action and protection to make Capital Ships fairly safe against Submarine attack, it would be desirable not to delay their construction.

The reasons which he gave for not proceeding with construction immediately are not concurred in by the Board of Admiralty which is responsible for advising the Government on this vital question.

Para. 10

The wording implies that methods of attack and defence by Submarines, aircraft and mines, as a whole, are in their infancy. This is not correct. Some are already well developed, and there was no evidence to indicate the probability of epoch-making development in the near future.

Para. 11

It should be noted that another expert witness was emphatic in his opinion that development of Asdics would assist defence against Submarines rather than increase the latter's offensive capabilities against Surface Ships.

Para. 12

It is important to bear in mind that the statements of Rear-Admiral Chatfield upon this subject were based upon the results of investigation and experiment, while the views put forward by Air Marshal Trenchard and Major Sykes were not so substantially supported.

Para. 13

Admits that if no Capital Ships are laid down now, the British Navy will be definitely inferior to that of the United States in 1924.

This means that the Government policy of maintaining a One-Power Standard will not be fulfilled.

Para. 14

There was no evidence to indicate that under the circumstances referred to a knock-out blow against the US Fleet was impossible. This must depend upon the strategical and tactical handling of both fleets and their efficiency.

The wording of the paragraph as it stands indicates a misunderstanding of the evidence, which was to the effect that a knock-out blow against the US Fleet would not necessarily constitute a knock-out blow against the United States as a nation. On the other hand a knock-out blow against the British Fleet would mean the inevitable defeat of the British Empire.

With the disappearance of the protection of the British Fleet our vital supplies would be cut off and the British Islands would be starved into submission in a very short time.

The latter part of this paragraph indicates a misconception. Without transgression of international law, neutral ships carrying contraband to this Country would be as liable to stoppage by a superior Surface Fleet as ships flying the British flag. Neutral ships were constantly intercepted by the British Navy during the late war and condemned in the Prize Courts. In wars between nations the distinction between conditional and absolute contraband necessarily disappears.

Para. 16

Exception is taken to the wording of the latter part of this paragraph, which implies failure on the part of two Departments to co-operate satisfactorily.

It was not a case of being 'apparent from the evidence', it was stated quite definitely that the matter had not yet been considered jointly, and a reason was given.

Para. 18

Postulates indecisive encounters which cannot be contemplated.

Para. 19

It appears hardly fair to state that there was divergence of opinion as regards the interruption of the South American Trade. Admiral Richmond was the only witness who held that a superior US Fleet would be unable to interrupt this trade. The other anti-Capital-Ship witnesses merely held that nothing could be done to prevent it.

Para. 20

Would be better worded – 'The Committee, having heard the evidence, is convinced that the Capital Ship remains the basis of Sea Power.'

Para. 21

Neither Admiral Richmond nor Admiral Bartolomé are fully

acquainted with the factors which govern the situation, and are not, therefore, in a position to advise as to the possibility of adopting a policy of delay. The Admiralty has pointed out in Memoranda to the Cabinet that unless a start is made at once it will be impossible, without recourse to war measures, to give effect to the Government's policy of maintaining a One-Power Standard.

As stated above, it is a primary function of the Admiralty to advise as to the measures necessary to give effect to the Government's Naval policy, and rejection of their advice can only mean withdrawal of confidence in the Board.

While assured that it is not the intention of the Sub-Committee to suggest that confidence should be withdrawn from the Board, or to abrogate the Board's responsibility in the matter, it is not understood why such undue stress should be laid upon the evidence of comparatively irresponsible Officers.

Para. 22

Is not concurred in. It is not considered that the evidence in any way led to this conclusion.

The Government has affirmed its intention of maintaining a One-Power Standard, and the Admiralty has stated the programme necessary to maintain this standard.

85. *Beatty: Memorandum to the Sub-Committee on the Capital Ship*

[Copy]

[BTY/8/4/16]   10.3.21

I have no observations to make with regard to the advance copy of the report signed by Mr. Long, Mr. Churchill and myself.

As regards the report signed by Mr. Bonar Law, Sir Robert Horne and Sir Eric Geddes, I desire to point out what appears to be a mistake in a matter of fact in the latter part of paragraph 14.[1]

Neutral Ships carrying absolute contraband or conditional contraband to this Country in time of war would, without transgression of international law, be as liable to stoppage by the enemy as ships flying the British flag.

They would not, of course, be liable to be sunk indiscriminately

---

[1]Para 14 of the Report had not mentioned the legality of the seizure, but not the sinking, of neutral ships carrying goods defined as contraband, absolute or conditional.

at sight by an enemy who respected international law, but it is obvious that capture of neutral ships carrying contraband by a belligerent is much more advantageous than sinking them. It was only because the German Submarines were largely unfitted to effect captures on any scale that they resorted to the policy of indiscriminate sinking.

A belligerent with a superior surface fleet would, therefore, suffer no temptation to emulate German methods, as it would benefit him materially as well as 'morally' to conform to international law in this respect.

It seems possible that this misconception as regards the immunity of neutrals carrying contraband may have weighed considerably in the minds of the signatories of the report in gaining the impression that it is possible to postpone construction of the most powerful type of surface vessel, and I therefore feel it my duty to draw attention to the point.

It must be remembered that the belligerents decide what is contraband and what is not, that during the last war all articles of trade were forbidden entrance by sea into Germany, and that a precedent has thus been created; also that in a war in which all the nationals are organised there is prima facie reason to presume that every article is destined for the use of the armed forces or by a Department of the State, i.e. as intended for the purposes of the war and therefore liable to capture.

86. *To Long*

[Holograph]

[Add. 62426]   Admiralty
                                                          16.3.21

Thank you for your letter and for your very kind and welcome congratulations. But without your invaluable support and the assistance I received from everybody at the Admiralty, it might well have gone against us. However, for the moment, everything has come right, although we have suffered from delay and shall not be able to live up to the dates precasted [?] in our policy paper. There will be no postponement in laying down the ships as soon as we can get the contracts signed, which we are setting about at once, and therefore I do not think it will be necessary to circulate your memo. I will keep it up my sleeve though & if there is any baulking at the last moment, will send it in.

The two Reports on the results of the labours of the sub-committee are to be printed and issued simultaneously.

The Cabinet having accepted the Estimates however have made the labours of that sub-committee somewhat abortive and it was, as I originally pointed out, just a waste of time, and the only effect it has had is to delay the commencement of construction from 1st July to 1st October, in itself a very serious handicap . . .

87. *Organisation of Naval Staff*[1]

[Extracts]

[Parliamentary Papers 1921   [May] 1921
Cmd.1343 XXI(797)]

Distribution of the Duties of the Naval Staff

[Note by Lord Lee of Fareham]: The detailed information in this paper is furnished in fulfilment of an undertaking given by me in the House of Lords on 4 May 1921.

L of F

General Distribution of Staff Duties

FIRST SEA LORD AND CHIEF OF NAVAL STAFF
All large questions of naval policy and maritime warfare. Organis-ation, distribution, and fighting and sea going efficiency of the Fleet.
Advice as to, and general direction of, operations of war.
Internal organisation and general direction of the work of the Naval Staff and the co-operation of the Naval Staff with the Material side of the Admiralty.
(To be kept informed of all important matters by the DCNS and ACNS.)

DEPUTY CHIEF OF NAVAL STAFF (DCNS)
Naval Intelligence; its collection, utilisation for naval operations; and superintendence of Naval Intelligence Division.
Principles of training of the Navy in combatant and staff duties and superintendence of Training and Staff Duties Division.
All operations and movements of HM Ships and co-operating Aircraft, including auxiliary craft.

[1]See Document 35 above. Marder, *From the Dreadnought I* pp. 218–19 has diagrams of the development of the Naval Staff, 1887–1919.

Consideration of strategic policy and plans relating to such operations.

Distribution of the Fleet as affecting operations and movements.

Dates of refits and repairs (in conjunction with Controller).

Strategic aspects of Land and W/T telegraphy.

Policy in relation to Sea-borne Trade and Maritime Transport.

Maritime International Law.

ASSISTANT CHIEF OF NAVAL STAFF (ACNS)

Methods of fighting at sea generally. Tactical investigations.

Requirements of design of vessels and material in relation to policy and tactics.

Signalling, in connection with tactics and weapons.

Fleet practices, co-ordination and standardisation of methods.

Staff questions dealing with research and experiment.

Air development in relation to Naval warfare.

DIVISIONS WORKING UNDER THE DCNS

Naval Intelligence Division, Training and Staff Duties Division, Plans Division, Operations Division, Local Defence Division, Trade Division.

*   *   *   *

[Detailed functions of each Division omitted here]

The three Duty Captains work under the orders of the DCNS and one of them is to be continually on duty, day and night. During the silent hours, or in the absence of the CNS, DCNS, and ACNS, the Duty Captain is their representative, and he will exercise his discretion as to whether he deal himself with any immediate matter or inform them by telephone or messenger.

DIVISIONS WORKING UNDER THE ACNS

Gunnery Division, Torpedo Division, Tactical Section, Air Section.

*   *   *   *

[Detailed functions of each Division and Section of which only those of Air Section included here]

NAVAL AIR SECTION

1. The Naval Air Section assists the ACNS in the consideration of all Air questions relating to Naval warfare. Its functions are:–

    (*a*) to deal in the first instance with all Air information and reports and co-ordinate all Air matters dealt with by the Naval Staff.

(*b*) to advise generally on the Naval side of questions of Fleet Air Warfare.

Note Advice on the Air side is the province of the Air Ministry.

(*c*) to keep in touch with Air progress.

(*d*) to assist by information, or in any other way required, any branch of the Naval Staff that is concerned with the Air weapon.

2. The Naval Air Section will maintain touch, through the liaison officer especially attached for the purpose to the Air Officer Commanding Coastal Area, with the various branches of the Air Staff which deal with the Air side of Fleet Air Warfare, and, as necessary, with the technical branches of the Air Ministry which deal with material.

Appendix
Detailed Instructions for Naval Staff Divisions

1. The Operations Committee consists of the following members of the Board

The First Lord (*ex officio*, Chairman)
The First Sea Lord and Chief of Naval Staff
The Deputy Chief of Naval Staff
The Assistant Chief of Naval Staff

It deals with questions of Naval Strategy and subjects connected with the provision, training, equipment, efficiency, organisation and utilisation of the Navy as a fighting force, and meets periodically as necessary.

* * * *

2. The Superintending Lords (DCNS and ACNS) to whom the superintendence of the several Divisions of the Staff is assigned, are primarily responsible for the workings of these Divisions. This does not however preclude the CNS from dealing direct with a Division if necessary, nor the DCNS and ACNS from dealing direct with Divisions not under their immediate superintendence. Divisions are enjoined to refer freely to other Divisions when the matter in hand requires such consultation. Under the CNS, the DCNS is particularly

concerned with strategy, policy, general principles of training and the conduct of operations.

The ACNS is particularly concerned with questions of tactics and fighting efficiency, the development of weapons and training in the use thereof, and of all questions of Naval co-operation with Air Forces; he superintends the Gunnery and Torpedo Divisions and is assisted by the Tactical and Air Sections.

3. Staff meetings attended by Directors under the presidency of one of the Superintending Lords are held periodically. Directors of Divisions may be accompanied by Heads of Sections of that Division when necessary.

4. In order to avoid overlapping and duplication of work, each Director must at all times communicate freely with other Divisions concerned with the matter in hand, care being taken that none interested is omitted. Close touch with Plans Division must be maintained by all other Divisions, so that action taken by them may be consonant with approved plans for possible hostilities and for future types of ships and material, and with Naval Intelligence Division, to ensure that they are in possession of the latest intelligence bearing on the matter in hand.

Inter-divisional minuting should always be avoided when verbal communication can replace it, joint minutes being prepared when matters concern more than one Division. Separate minutes should be limited, as far as possible, to cases in which agreement cannot be reached, and it is then the duty of the Division last dealing with a question to submit it for decision before it leaves the Naval Staff.

5. In the same way close touch must be maintained by all Divisions of the Staff with the Supply and Technical Departments that translate the principles approved into action, in order that the policy recommended may be compatible with material development and that the direction of development may be guided by the requirements of policy.

* * * *

[Concludes with details of office practice and further details of Divisional tasks]

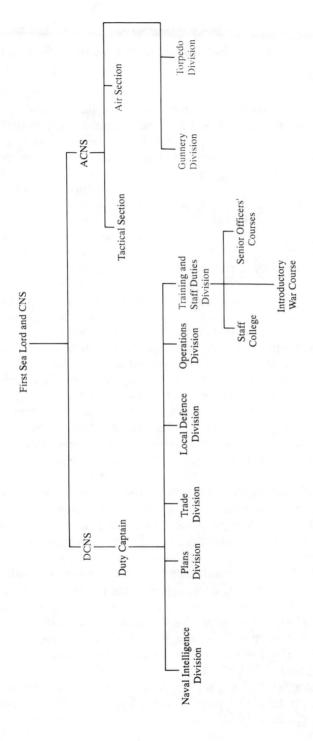

Distribution of the duties of the Naval Staff, 1921

87a.   *Beatty's Address to the Imperial Conference*

[Cab. 32/2]   July 4th 1921

LORD BEATTY: Mr Prime Minister, I should like to make a few remarks on the subject of Sea Power before dealing with this specific question on Strategy in the Pacific, because there is one point which requires to be cleared up. It has been said too often that command of the sea means control of communications. This in itself is correct, but control of communications can only be effected by the destruction of the enemy force. Therefore, the real object of the British Navy is the destruction of the enemy force, as a result of which, it will control communications. Unless this destruction can be achieved, the enemy force must be neutralised as completely as possible. There is in some quarters a general idea that until the enemy be properly contained, his destruction is a kind of luxury which may be indulged in only on the condition that the containing force is not unduly risked. This is a fallacy which it is most desirable should be dissipated, because whilst the enemy has a force in being it can never be completely contained and the attempt to do so is fraught with the greatest difficulty, which involves great efforts and great expenditure. The command of the sea is determined by the result of great battles at sea. To any naval power, the destruction of the Fleet of the enemy must always be the great object aimed at. Stress is laid on the importance of the great battle for supremacy. The development of the navies of the United States and Japan indicates the possibility that such battles may have to be fought in the future. Battles are fought by battle-ships and it is the battle-ships which will have to be concentrated before a decisive battle, and arrangements which have this object must be made during the peace. Geographical conditions and the varied interests of the maritime powers prevent such complete concentration today as has been practical in the past. The United States divides her force between the Atlantic and the Pacific, but the construction of the Panama Canal makes it possible for her to concentrate in one or other at the shortest possible time. On the other hand, Japan is concentrating in the Eastern waters, that is, in the Western Pacific. Therefore, the British Fighting Fleet consisting of the battle-ships is concentrated in Home and the Mediterranean waters ready to move either to the East or West. Fleets are essentially mobile and can be moved with facility from one point of the world to another, providing fuelling arrangements and facilities are made beforehand. The first requirement with such a mobile force is, however, to ensure concentration and complete unity of effort. It is, therefore, necessary to ensure that the various navies of this Empire be similarly trained and that they adhere to a common doctrine and a common system of command and staff. Only by so doing can co-operation after concentration be efficient, and allow of the unity of command and strategic direction when undertaking together naval operations, but the adhering to similar principles in this respect should not in any way interfere with the control of Dominion governments over their own navies, or the internal administration of Dominion navies by their own officers. Dealing with the outline of the main consideration governing naval strategy in a war with Japan, I would like to say beforehand this, that in considering what dispositions are necessary, the Admiralty view the British Navy as an Imperial weapon to defend the British Empire. We do not dispose of our forces to protect the British Isles. We look upon the British Navy just as much for the defence of any other portion of the Empire as of the defence of the British Isles, and, therefore, it is just as much the Navy of Australia, of Canada, of South Africa and of India as it is of the British Isles, and in all dispositions that we make for the purpose of carrying out a war with any power, we are governed by the factor that where the enemy is, there the British Navy shall be also. Owing to the financial stringency which has been explained by the First Lord, we are unable at the present time to maintain our naval forces at a strength sufficient to enable us to station strong fleets within striking distance of the fleets of potential enemies. As I stated before, our main Fleet therefore is kept in a central position where adequate bases for fuel and repair facilities exist today. One of the essential qualities of the Fleet must therefore be, again I repeat, its mobility or its power of rapid transfer to any threatened portion of the Empire. In the event of a war with Japan, it is all-important that the Fleet should be able to reach the Far East in the shortest possible time, and provisions to enable them to do so must be made today. Also provision must be made to maintain them in bases fully equipped with fuel and repair facilities when they get there. Japan may be expected to strike quickly directly hostilities commence. Hongkong [sic], our furthest position primarily, and Borneo and Singapore to a lesser degree, are exposed to attack, and their safety will depend upon the rapidity with which the Fleet can reach the Far East. On its

arrival there the main object of our Fleet is the destruction of the
Japanese Fleet, with a view to holding the sea communications.
Japan depends on other countries for many essential commodities,
and being an Island Power, these commodities have to arrive by
the sea. Hongkong is essential to the conduct of offensive operations against Japan, and every endeavour must be made to put
it in such a state of defence as to make it reasonably probable
that it will be able to hold out until relieved by the Fleet. An
element of doubt, however, with regard to the security of Hongkong on account of its proximity to Japanese territory precludes
its development as our main naval base, and it is essential that
the Fleet should be provided with a secure base further to the
southward, and for this purpose Singapore possesses far greater
facilities than any other possessions in the Islands[1] (position
explained on the map) [not reproduced]. Singapore stands at the
western gateway of the Pacific. It flanks the route from Eastern
Asia to Australasia and covers the main entrance to the Indian
Ocean from the eastward. In many respects it occupies the same
position as Gibraltar does in the west. Of the other conceivable
sites for our main naval base in the East, one in Australia would
be too remote, and to station our Naval Forces in those waters
would be tantamount to the adoption of a purely defensive naval
strategy by which our vital interests to the north and west would
be left uncovered, and therefore Hongkong would fall an easy
prey to leisurely attack, which would be certainly followed by
other attacks on Borneo and Singapore. A base in any of the
islands to the northward of Australia would be open to similar
objections, and a base in Borneo would be too exposed and too
difficult to defend. With Singapore firmly held there is no danger
of a Japanese attack in force upon Australia or New Zealand.
Even with a Fleet in home waters at the outbreak of hostilities,
the limited time available to the enemy during which his sea
communications would be safe would render it folly for him to
attempt a sea attack, conveying military forces across a distance
of 4000 and more miles of water; and the Japanese, being what
they are, would not attempt to snatch an initial advantage at such
a great distance from their main base. Hongkong is obviously
indicated as the most probable object of attack. Considerations
of time and distance render an attack upon Singapore a difficult
undertaking in the interval available before the Fleet arrives on

[1]Documents on the development of the Singapore base are in Part IV below.

the scene, and automatically affords immunity. This is on the assumption that its defences are made sufficiently formidable as advocated by both the Admiralty and the War Office. It cannot be too strongly emphasised that without Hongkong we are not in a position to bring reasonably effective economic pressure to bear upon Japan, and its safety is imperative to the conduct of offensive naval operations. With the Fleet once at Hongkong, it remains to be seen what we can do to distress Japan to the uttermost. Invasion is out of the question, and the proximity of the mainland, and the protection afforded by the Korean Straits to the Sea of Japan renders it impracticable to cut off Japan from intercourse with the outer world. We can hope, however, to sever her sea communications across the Pacific, and to render them hazardous in the Yellow Sea and Sea of Japan.

If you look at the map on which are marked the imports and exports of Japan, you will see that the imports are marked in blue and the exports in red. The only supplies which we could not prevent getting into Japan would be those through the north of Japan, through Pusan and right along to Vladivostock. By doing that we bring very great pressure to bear on Japan. In the Pescadores, which is in the mouth of the Straits of Formosa, Japan possesses a naval base of great potentiality, and it is in close proximity to Hongkong. The distance is about 300 miles. It is capable of basing light forces there, and the harbour can accommodate a certain number of Capital Ships. It is not anticipated, however, that Japan would commit the folly of dividing her fleets, and as it is not capable of taking the entire Capital Ship Fleet, they would probably only use it for the purpose of basing light craft and submarines. However, that force alone would be a very serious menace to the British Fleet. It is a threat to our own communications, and its destruction would probably be the best operation open to combined naval and military effort, and might have the effect of bringing on the desired Fleet action; that is to say if Japan was not prepared to lose without a struggle. In any case, it would probably not be feasible to move our own Fleet north of Hongkong at any rate until a Fleet action had taken place.

A base in the vicinity of Japan could only be found by seizing a harbour in China, or in one of the off-lying islands. The Fleet could not do much more harm here than it could from Hong Kong, and the advantages to be gained would not counterbalance a long and vulnerable line of communications. From HongKong the Fleet can protect all our own sea communications, whilst attacking those of the enemy with light craft and submarines, and bringing economic pressure to bear, as I suggested, by pointing to this diagram of the imports and exports of Japan.

On the west coast of America the outlying squadrons working from the Canadian Pacific ports and in the neighbourhood of the Panama Canal and the Sandwich Islands would endeavour to stop all the trans-Pacific trade at its source, and a fair measure of success, we calculate, could be counted upon in doing this. By these means considerable economic pressure could be brought to bear upon Japan, but it must not be imagined that this will be sufficient to force a conclusion. One fact emerges clearly from a consideration of the naval strategy in a naval war against Japan, and that is that it should be a cardinal factor of our policy to prevent the expansion of Japan to the southward, which would increase the threat to our interests and involve a greater risk to the security of our other possessions. That is to say, that in the event of a war between the United States and Japan, if Japan were to seize the Philippines, from a British naval point of view it would be a menace to our possessions in that part of the world to have a Power in command of the Philippines which would be capable of menacing those possessions.

To summarise the important points in our naval strategy, I would label them as follows:–

(A)   We must have the Fleet in a central position in peace time –

(B)   We must have all oil fuel arrangements in and on the route to the East such that the Fleet's mobility is assured –

88.   To Eugénie Godfrey-Faussett

[SLGF 15/4/8]   Friday [July 1921][1]

*   *   *   *

Also I am overwhelmed with Conferences with the Dominion Prime Ministers, which keeps me very busy, and they are of the greatest importance, & I hope to gain much from the Naval point of view by their presence at our deliberations. They have already had the effect of producing a Jingo spirit in the Prime Minister,

[1]Roskill, *Admiral of the Fleet*, p. 402, n 1, dates this letter March 1921. The reference to the Imperial Conference points to this later date.

which astonishes everybody, and might be of the greatest value, as he will surely give himself away, and if it were not for the tragic side, would be almost humorous. I am sure he pronounces these violent opinions with his tongue in his cheek, & will be ready to repudiate them as soon as they have gone.

*   *   *   *

War is a wonderful thing, far more so than is ever credited to so sombre and baneful a set of circumstances.

It is responsible for crediting many among us with qualities of which we have no real claim [*sic*] and stirs the emotions to such an extent that it creates an atmosphere among human beings, which in the cold and calculating periods of peace are so often shown to be false, or at least are over-estimated. I feel that I am one of those that have reached a pinnacle in the minds of some to which I have no real claim. For instance it was responsible for your placing me on a pedestal which is slowly and surely crumbling away from under me and I am gradually falling to the level of the common herd to which I probably really belong.

From all that has passed between us of late, I am shattering that pedestal and it wd. appear that my own acts are responsible for the destructive force. You are so generous & sincere that you transpose the effects and read it the reverse way. I pray that you are right but am beginning now to have doubts as to myself and my capabilities to make good. Life under prosaic peace conditions is much harder, the issues are not so clear cut and there is time for doubts to creep in, and the vast number of small voices which are only heard in peace, undermine the firm convictions which one possesses in time of war.

It is the same with the human feelings. There is so much more time to think, there are so many more voices to hear that they tend to kill faith, inspiration and everything worth trusting. However your dear letter reinspires & shows you can see clearly, notwithstanding the many handicaps which surround our lives in these more prosaic times. I am encouraged and I thank you for your letter and all that it means.

89. *Beatty to First Lord*

[ADM 1/8611/155]   21.9.21

Necessity for Naval control of maritime aircraft

1st Lord

The remarks of the ACNS demonstrate clearly the degree to
which naval gunnery is dependent on the use of aircraft. He points
out that aircraft are as much an integral part of gunnery material
as range-finders and other essential instruments, whilst from the
tactical point of view their functions are as purely naval as those
of light cruisers and other Fleet units. They are an indispensable
arm of the Fleet, and, if their efficiency is to be equal to that of
the other arms, their training must be equally continuous and as
much a part of the general Fleet training. Failure of any one unit
of a fleet in action would spell disaster, and yet, under present
circumstances, the officer in command of the Fleet cannot be
considered responsible for the efficiency of the Air Unit.

The 2nd Sea Lord deals with the question from the point of
view of the personnel and shows the practical difficulties which
confront us in endeavouring to work the present unworkable
system.

The report of the C-in-C Mediterranean exposes the impracticability of the present order of things in the light of actual experience. He emphasises the fact that failure to achieve success is not
due to any lack of cordial relationship between the personnel of
the Navy and Air Service, but to the inherent impossibility of
forming a homogeneous force from two completely separate
Services.

I am aware that the Government has frequently reaffirmed its
determination to perpetuate the existence of the RAF as a separate Service, but the practical objections to this policy are so
obvious that it would be a dereliction of duty on the part of those
responsible for advising the Government in matters of Imperial
Defence were we to cease to press for its reversal.

The efficacy of the Fleet is being jeopardised, and I understand
that the highest Military opinion holds that the efficacy of the
Army suffers in like degree.

I cannot believe that the Government will attribute the earnest
and reasoned representations of the Naval and Military authorities
to mere prejudice or conservatism; if indeed this is the belief, it

is clear that they no longer possess the confidence of the Government.

I am alive to the embarrassment which the Government would suffer in reversing a decision which it has affirmed and reaffirmed so frequently, but it would suffer no real discredit by boldly facing the facts and acting in the light of experience which was not available when the original step was taken.

It is possible that the examination of the situation by the Committee on National Expenditure might result in recommendations which would smooth the path to the change we advocate.

As to the desirability of continuing the Air Ministry as a Supply Department, I am not at present prepared to comment.

During the war I expressed the opinion that it would be advantageous to centralise the services of supply in this manner, but it is a question which would have to be examined anew.

Minute by 1st Lord's Private Office [Holograph]

First Sea Lord has since prepared a memorandum embodying his views which First Lord has sent to the CID for circulation. Copy enclosed.

A. W. Street
10.10.21

90. *To his wife* [Ritz Hotel, Paris]

[BTY/17/57/13–14]   Tuesday–Wednesday [27–28
Sept. 1921]

*   *   *   *

Wednesday
We are having words about the constitution of the delegation to visit the USA, which is not too nice, and I am not going to play 2nd fiddle in this matter to Arthur Lee, or anyone else, except the Prime Minister or his representative. The whole question has been [burked up to now?] and nobody apparently has taken the Conference seriously in this country.

They are making the greatest mistake of their lives if our political leaders allow the idea to get into the heads of the American public that we are not serious about it and are not going to be all out to make it a success. This idea is creeping in due to the fact that the Prime Minister and Curzon have both refused to go, whereas Briand and Berthelot[1] are going for France and Japs and Italians are treating it with greatest respect. At present the Irish Question has shut down and everything is devoted to Trade and Economical situation . . .

91. *Beatty to CID on Inter-service Relations*

[ADM 1/8511]   7.10.21

(*This Document is the Property of His Britannic Majesty's Government*)

SECRET

COMMITTEE OF IMPERIAL DEFENCE
The Air Force in relation to the Navy and Army

I forward, for the consideration of the Committee of Imperial Defence, the following note by the Chief of the Naval Staff.

L of F

October 10th 1921.

Note by the CNS on Mr Balfour's Memorandum (CID 149C) of 26th July, and on the Note thereon by the CIGS, dated 16th September 1921

I am in complete agreement with the remarks of the CIGS.[2] Most of the arguments are applicable to the Naval point of view.

There are some points, however, of which the Naval aspect requires amplification.

1. Quoting from Mr Balfour, paragraph 3, 'Supposing the main operations are carried out by the Air Force, while the Navy and Army play a relatively unimportant part in the operations – what then?'

It is *not possible* to visualise a combined Air and Naval Operation in which the Navy play a relatively unimportant part.

2. Paragraph 4 of Mr Balfour:–

Parenthetically I may observe that the permanent tendencies have not always been towards unification. Up to the 17th century, for example, Fleets were navigated by Sailors, while Naval Strategy and Naval Tactics were determined by Soldiers.

I am not in agreement with this statement. Since Queen Eliza-

---

[1] Aristide Briand (1862–1932): French Prime Minister 1921–2. Philippe Berthelot (1866–1934): diplomat; Director General of the Ministry of Foreign Affairs.
[2] CIGS, Sir Henry Wilson.

beth's time it has been a fundamental principle that the personnel on board ship must be under the complete control of the Captain, must be trained to take a full part in the general work of the ship, and must be habituated to a sea-faring life. Drake and his contemporaries owed much of their success to making the Soldiers and Military Officers take their part in working the ships; in fact they turned them into sea-faring men. The Spaniards did the opposite because their Navy was run by Authorities who did not understand sea-faring people. The Soldiers took no part in working the ships, and the Seamen hated them. The same relations obtained between the Officers; contentment and cohesion were absent, and in the time of trial they were defeated.

As regards Strategy and Tactics at the time to which Mr Balfour refers, these were, in our Navy, determined by Military gentlemen, who were as much Sailors as Soldiers. It cannot be gainsaid that Admiral Blake was much more a distinguished Sailor than a distinguished Soldier.

The same can be said of General Monk, who became a sea-faring Commander and achieved greater fame as an Admiral than he ever did as a General.

3. In paragraph 5, Mr Balfour asks a question. The CIGS answers this in some detail from the Military point of view.

From the Naval point of view, I know of no operation in which the Navy and Air have to co-operate in which the Navy would not play a more important part than the Air Service.

Take the case of the bombing of an Enemy Naval Base. If the Air Forces can start from their own Bases without assistance, then it is a purely Air operation. But if they require the assistance of the Navy to convey them to a point from which to commence the attack, or to pick them up on completion of their attack, then the co-operation of the Navy is required to command the Seas. This may mean the employment of a Force up to the full strength of the Navy in those waters.

Mr Balfour gives the example of a Convoy proceeding up Channel to show that the Air Force may sometimes assume the major role in Sea Operations. The protection of a Convoy must be primarily in the hands of the Navy. Air attack on the Convoy is incidental, there are other forms of attack to be guarded against both by day and *night*, such as from surface vessels of various types and of submarines, adequate protection against which can only be rendered by Naval Forces both by day and night.

I would add that to-day Aircraft are as much an integral part of the Naval Gunnery material as range-finders and other essential instruments, whilst from the tactical point of view their functions are as purely naval as those of Light Cruisers and other Fleet Units. They are an indispensable arm of the Fleet and, if their efficiency is to be equal to that of the other arms, their training must be equally continuous, and as much a part of the General Fleet Training. Failure of any one unit of a Fleet in action would spell disaster, and yet under present circumstances the Officer in Command of the Fleet cannot be considered responsible for the efficiency of the Air Unit of his Fleet.

(Int) B

92. *Conference on Naval Defence of Ireland*

[Ll.G./F/25/2/32]   October 13th 1921
SECRET

CONFERENCE ON IRELAND.
NAVAL DEFENCE

CONVERSATIONS held in the Secretary of State's
Room at the Colonial Office, on Thursday,
October 13th, 1921, at 3.15 pm.

The Meeting was held at the Colonial Office in the Room of the Secretary of State on October 13th at 3.15 p.m. for the purpose of informal conversations on Naval questions.
There were present:–

   Mr. Churchill
   Lord Beatty
   Mr. Michael Collins
   Mr. Childers[1]

---

[1]Churchill had become Colonial Secretary in February 1921. For Collins, see note 1 on page 71 above. Robert Erskine Childers (1870–1922): served in RNVR during war but became a militant Irish nationalist over Britain's failure to grant Home Rule at the end of hostilities; elected to Dail Eireann and made Minister of Propaganda in 1921; acted as Secretary to the Committee negotiating treaty with Britain 1921–2; later joined those who rejected the Treaty and after capture by Free State troops was court-martialled and shot in November 1922. His novel, *The Riddle of the Sands* (1903 and reissued 1914) prophesying a surprise German raid on the English coast attracted wide attention.

Lord Beatty was accompanied by a Naval Officer, Mr Collins by a Secretary who took brief notes.

Mr Churchill opened the discussion and explained that as Lord Beatty was about to leave the country the conversation had been arranged for that day. He asked Lord Beatty to explain what the British Government wanted in respect of naval requirements and why.

Lord Beatty said that the naval requirements were demonstrated by the late war. We could not fight a naval war unless we controlled the Irish coast. Numerous vessels could recoup in its numerous inlets. He then produced the German chart of the British Isles, showing where each vessel had been sunk by submarines.

Mr Childers, looking at the chart, observed that Irish sinkings were a small element in the problem.

Lord Beatty remarked that the enemy could use the inlets unless we could go in and hunt them out.

Mr Childers rejoined that the same applied to neutral ports.

Mr Churchill pointed out that neutrals were supposed to prevent this sort of thing.

Mr Childers observed that Ireland could be dealt with as a belligerent if it failed to do so.

Lord Beatty held that Ireland would neither have the power nor the capability to deal with submarines. They could come in to refit and replenish, to meet supplies brought either by their own ships or in a neutral. One small ship could carry enough to replenish submarines for a considerable time. Ireland could not prevent the use of these inlets, so we must. They could begin their operations in one inlet and finish in another.

Mr Childers maintained that they could not be supplied without the people knowing it.

Mr Churchill remarked that our ships must have bases on the Irish coast.

Mr Collins asked in what way would a neutral Ireland be a menace to British security.

Lord Beatty replied that we should have to lose too many ships before a neutral Ireland came into the war. The loss of a few more ships would have turned the scale against us in the late war.

Mr Collins: 'When the British Navy is beaten, the neutrality of Ireland does not matter a damn.'

Lord Beatty repeated his point and Mr Childers again rejoined that the people may not prevent the supplies being sent for submarines.

Lord Beatty said there were no people on many parts of the Irish coast. The same thing had happened in Norway.

Mr Collins: 'Norway is not so dangerous.'

Lord Beatty: 'No.'

Mr Churchill said that we wanted bases on the coast more especially on the south-west extremity of Ireland.

Lord Beatty named Berehaven, Lough Swilly and Queenstown.

Mr Childers asked whether it was necessary to occupy the coast of Ireland.

Mr Churchill replied that it was no use talking on the basis of neutrality. England would not accept it. Ireland could not be neutral. She may be inactive, but England must have the right to defend Ireland as well as herself.

Lord Beatty: 'From the naval point of view it is a strategic necessity that we should have stations in Ireland for offensive and defensive purposes. Berehaven and the South-west of Ireland are absolutely essential to us. To sacrifice it we should have to sacrifice something of infinite value which might be vital and would have been vital in the late war.'

Mr Collins: 'If England had not had these ports would the sinkings have been greater?'

Lord Beatty: 'Infinitely greater.'

Mr Churchill: 'That is our case.'

Mr Collins: 'Why do you never make a real naval base?'

Mr Churchill: 'Queenstown is a real naval station and an important one. In peace it is not wanted very much.'

Lord Beatty: 'For peace purposes we should dispose of all property except at Berehaven. Generally, in peace, everything would be in the hands of caretakers.' At Queenstown we should maintain fortifications and certain mooring-buoys. The establishments at Lough Swilly would be the same as at Berehaven. There were oil fuel stores at Haulbowline and at Rathmullen. These might be sold to private persons, subject to a contract to keep a minimum supply of oil fuel. The wireless might be run by the Irish Government subject to Admiralty inspection.

Mr Churchill then sketched the history of these things in the Dominions illustrating by reference to Simons Town in the hope that this would happen in the case of Ireland. We should want signal stations.

Mr Collins: 'The Irish want to avoid any lowering of Irish political status.'

Mr Churchill and Lord Beatty together: 'That is a basis.'

Mr Churchill expressed the hope that Ireland would not want Queenstown to go to rack and ruin. In his day as First Lord of the Admiralty, Cork had been most anxious that the establishments should be maintained and he had seen to their maintenance. 'What,' he asked, 'about an Irish Navy?'

Mr Collins: 'What did Norway use to deal with submarines?'

Lord Beatty. 'Some light cruisers and destroyers. They did not add to their naval expenses for the purpose.'

Mr Collins: 'People in Ireland have no desire to build submarines, it would be a madcap thing.'

Mr Churchill observed that the right to do it would be regarded as a menace in England.

Mr Collins had not much fear about that. He summed up Lord Beatty's statement of requirements with the words: 'Anything less than that you consider would be a definite menace to English safety?' He then asked about air stations.

Lord Beatty replied that power must be reserved to control air stations which were inseparable from submarine war.

Mr Childers asked about coast stations.

Mr Churchill replied we should end coast stations. The Curragh and military cantonments would go. Nothing was wanted for coercion of Ireland, he referred again to the Simons Town basis. When the King declared war, everyone in the Dominions was at war.

Mr Childers rejoined that Laurier[1] had denied this.

Mr Collins asked whether the stations handed over to South Africa would be subject to inspection.

Mr Churchill and Lord Beatty replied 'Yes.'

'That,' said Mr Childers, 'is a free agreement.'

The question of lights was mentioned.

Mr Collins observed that it might be taken for granted that these must be looked after.

---

[1]Sir Wilfred Laurier (1841–1914): Canadian Prime Minister 1896–1911; had advocated creation of a Canadian Navy and supported immediate entry into war in 1914.

93. *Beatty to King George V*

[Holograph]

[RA Geo V O.1735/74]

British Delegation
Franklin Square Hotel
Washington
Saturday 12 November [1921]

Sir,

I present my humble duty and inform your Majesty that in accordance with instructions, I yesterday decorated the coffin of the Unknown Soldier with the Victoria Cross.

Since my arrival in the United States I have indeed had a very busy time, mostly taken up with travelling, eating dinners and making speeches. The welcome accorded to me as the representative of Your Majesty's Navy has indeed been very warm and sincere, and the further West we went the more they appeared to appreciate the work of the Navy during the war, and the fact that not only the British Empire but the world in general was greatly indebted to it for the work it did. This was particularly so at Kansas City where I went to attend the Convention of the American Legion, and also among the great business men in Chicago whom I met at a banquet of considerable importance.

Since my trip to the Middle West I have been in Washington preparatory to the commencement of the Conference. This morning it opened with the address of the President and speech of Mr Hughes.[1]

The latter, by its extensive proposals certainly caused considerable surprise in many quarters, not excluding the American naval clique. It has of course caused much satisfaction in the minds of many. The principle can be accepted, but the difficulty will be in carrying out the proposed 10 years Naval Holiday. We have already, as Your Majesty is aware, had a holiday of 5 years, the result of which has almost broke the armament firms of the country. Another 10 years would require a large subsidy from the Government, which would defeat the economical object. The years of no construction would be followed by a hectic period of feverish [?] building of the navies of the world which would be very heavy in its demands on the public purse, and on the whole,

[1]Harold E. and Margaret T. Sprout, (1940 and later editions) *Towards a New Order of Sea Power; American Naval Power and the World Scene*, New York, is a good introduction to the significance of the Washington Conference. For Hughes, see note 4 on page 77 below.

be greatly more expensive than a steady but small building programme.

The whole question is fraught with snags and will require very careful watching.

Your Majesty will be kept informed as to how we progress.
                    With my humble duty I am Sir,
                              Your obedient & devoted servant.

94. *Balfour to Lloyd George*

[Telegram Copy]

[ADM 1/8630]   Washington
                                          13 November 1921

Report of 1st Conference of British Empire
Delegation to Washington Naval Conference

First Lord and First Sea Lord met British Empire Delegation in the afternoon, when Lord Beatty gave views of Naval Staff on American proposals for limitation of armaments. He is satisfied as regards number of capital ships to be retained, arrested in construction or scrapped, as summarised in paragraph 10 of American plan, but when scheme is discussed in detail in committee, he proposes to urge additional condition that only 2/3 of capital ships be left in commission and 1/3 in reserve.

He accepts proportion of five, five, three for replacement of capital ships (para 12(a)), but prefers to apply these proportions to numbers rather than tonnage. His principal criticism relates to proposed naval holiday of ten years (para 12(b)) which would result in decay of naval ship-construction and armament industries, unless firms were heavily subsidised. Towards end of ten year period these industries would have to be reconstructed at great expense in order to build ships required for replacement. For Great Britain, 12 capital ships would have to be under simultaneous construction in order to complete replacement at the end of ten years. This burst of feverish shipbuilding would set in at end of each period of ten years, followed by relapse and comparative somnolence. Lord Beatty suggests alternative scheme, substituting slow and steady replacement for spasmodic building. His plan would permanently reduce shipbuilding capacity of nations and would be more economical, and better calculated to lead to settled and peaceful atmosphere among naval nations.

Lord Beatty insists that strength of European navies must be taken into account from first in any scheme of value.

As regards cruisers and other auxiliary vessels, Lord Beatty accepts proportions in para. 14, so far as concerns those classes of auxiliary vessels which are complementary to the battle fleet, but he insists, that over and above these, British Empire requires other cruisers for protection of communications.

Lord Beatty is prepared to urge far greater reductions of submarines than proposed in American plan, in fact he would welcome total abolition of submarines, provided all nations agreed. As many maritime nations are not represented at Washington Conference, this proposal is not susceptible of immediate application, even if accepted.

Views expressed by Lord Beatty were generally accepted by British Empire Delegation. With their concurrence, I propose to give warm welcome on principle to American proposals, and definitely accept their plan as regards numbers of capital ships. At the same time I shall emphasise widespread and special responsibilities of British Navy, and, without dwelling on points of detail, I shall indicate that certain aspects of the scheme require fuller examination, and that the scheme should be referred to a commission.

BALFOUR

Report of 3rd Conference of British Empire Delegation

[Extract]   16 Nov 1921

*   *   *   *

Lord Beatty thought that if a ten year holiday was agreed to, Britain should insist on the abolition of submarines.

*   *   *   *

Report of 4th Conference

[Extract]   17 Nov 1921

*   *   *   *

Lord Beatty referring to the last paragraph of the telegram from the Cabinet referring to aeroplanes, said that the only way to deal with the aeroplane menace was by and through the development of the capital ship. There was a risk that if the capital ship did not go on developing, it would become useless to compete (as it alone could) with the menace. He said that in the opinion of his

Naval Staff a ten years' holiday would as a consequence affect the personnel of the Navy. [*sic*]

In consideration of the fact that the US proposal would in effect be that both the US and Japan could continue to build improved combatant craft, whereas we, having our full ration already, would have to continue as we were. Lord Beatty strongly advised that if the ten year holiday were to be accepted at all, it should be accepted only if applicable to all vessels of every class, including submarines.

*   *   *   *

95.   *Beatty to Admiralty*

[Copy Secret Cypher Telegram]

[ADM. 116/3445/93]   Washington
                                                                                15.11.21

We are faced with the following alternatives for replacing capital ships.

Firstly: to accept the US proposals for a 10 year holiday, with all its obvious impracticability.

Secondly: to accept a policy of steady continuous replacement of laying down two ships every three years commencing immediately.

Thirdly: to agree to a holiday of, say, three years, and then to proceed to lay down 2 ships every three years.

Request you will consider these three alternatives and advise us with all dispatch, from the point of view of the effect on specialised warship construction.

Third alternative is preferred if subsidy questions could be satisfactorily settled . . .

96.   *Balfour to Cabinet and CID*

[Copy Cypher Telegram]

[ADM. 116/3445]   Washington
                                                              November 17th 1921

Your telegram No. 7.

British Delegation have carefully considered the views of Cabinet Committee and Committee of Imperial Defence, and desire to make the following observations thereupon:

We fully appreciate the moral appeal of ten years holiday proposal and volume of support which it is likely to evoke throughout the civilized world. Before accepting it, however, it is essential to examine (? danger)s involved in it and not to imperil future security of the British Empire. Further, we have positive information that American Naval Department had not realized the serious defects of its own proposal and may itself propose a more practical and less dangerous alternative. It is also probable that Japan, France, and Italy will independently raise objections. Meanwhile, our experts have been instructed to avoid premature discussion of this particular subject pending our further deliberation and consultation with Cabinet and present position is that they are awaiting promised elucidation by American experts of their own proposals which may be spontaneously modified.

We note that Cabinet is prepared to contemplate keeping British plants necessary for replacement purposes in existence by subsidies and that Admiralty is preparing estimates of cost. Latter, if maintenance is to be effective, must be very heavy and we cannot ignore obvious risk that a subsequent Government might be unwilling or unable to get parliamentary approval for necessary annual subsidies. On the other hand, richer countries like America or some other Power under militaristic control, might keep in existence building facilities which would enable them to proceed after long intervals and at short notice with construction of new fleets which could (? dominate the) seas. In any event, as pointed out in my telegram, I would (? group omitted) present ten years proposal would involve periodical and violent spells of armament activity at immense cost and recurring disturbances to peace of the world. This could only be avoided, if American plan is to stand, by complementary and equally drastic proposal, that all heavy armament and armour plants should also be restricted and that none other than Government-owned facilities, sufficient for replacing one or two ships at a time, should be maintained. Further, we strongly urge that in the event of America standing for ten years naval holiday, as at present, we should demand it should be applied to other combatant craft as well as to capital ships. In this connection we would observe that United States and Japan, under American scheme, would be at liberty to continue construction of light cruisers and aeroplane carriers, whereas Great Britain would not be permitted to build any. We think that naval holiday should be complete. With reference to your remarks, to the effect that character of fleet would not be improved appreciably if Lord Beatty's proposals were carried into effect, Lord Beatty observes that under his scheme, six capital ships would be built in ten years, each one of which would be constructed to meet the dangers you contemplate, from development of submarine and attack from the air. We shall, however, make proposal in a more explicit form, although opposition is certain from lesser naval Powers, and United States Government would probably wish not to go further than a reduction of tonnage originally proposed. Public opinion in all countries, however, seems likely strongly to endorse abolition.

97.   *Beatty to DCNS*

[Copy Secret Cypher Telegram]
[ADM 116/3445/104]   Washington
                                                      18.11.21

No Naval Staff views are to be placed before Committee of Imperial Defence without previous communication to the Naval Staff at Washington. Otherwise there is a danger of staff advice at home, which is not in a position to be so well informed as Staff advice tendered on the spot, being at variance, thus opening a vista of cross purposes which it is desired to avoid. Naval Staff views should continue to be forwarded to Washington, and are expected.

You will be kept informed as closely as possible by the Naval Staff at Washington.

98.   *Beatty to Controller*[1]

[Copy Cypher Telegram]
[ADM 116/3445/105]   Washington
                                                      19.11.21

12. Following for Controller from First Sea Lord.
Adoption of numbers basis for relative strength will probably necessitate adoption of a maximum limit of size for each type of vessel. American proposal for capital ship ?(limit) is 35,000 tons.

---

[1]Rear-Admiral Sir Frederic Field (1871–1945): 3rd Sea Lord and Controller April 1920–May 1923; commanded Special Service Squadron on world cruise and Vice-Admiral 1923–4; DCNS 1925–8; C-in-C Mediterranean and Admiral 1928–30; 1st Sea Lord 1930–33.

Consider it will be necessary ?(repeat) ?(necessary) to accept this for any replacement of ships which may be built in the next three years, the limit being revised from time to time should capital ship be endangered by progress in other types of vessels and weapons ?(used) generally. As regards cruisers consider 10,000 repeat 10,000 tons limit would be suited to our interest, as regards flotilla leaders propose about 2,000 repeat 2,000 ton limit and destroyers ?(about) 1500 repeat ?(1500) tons. Desire your opinion and that of ?(Director of Naval Construction) as to the suitability of these limits from a design point of view with especial consideration to increased endurance future designs. It is not repeat not proposed to accept any of the United States proposals limiting size weapons in ships or their speed etcetera. Constructors must have a free hand to utilise the tonnage limit to the best advantage. As regards airplane carriers, American proposal of 80,000 tons is based on two carriers of 40,000 tons each. I consider a limit of 25,000 repeat 25,000 tons per ship would be more satisfactory as we require not less than five repeat five carriers since our fleets might have to be divided between Eastern and Home waters. In consultation with Staff and Director of Naval Construction desire view on this question. Also with regard to maximum repeat maximum limit of displacement, repeat displacement, for various types; what do you consider the best rule for calculation of displacement from an international point of view, that is, the relative simplicity ?deep load displacement, or any other variations should be considered.
Message ends.

99. *Prime Minister to Balfour*

[Copy Cypher Telegram]
[ADM 116/3445/73–4]   1 Dec. 1921

CID further considered subject of your telegram No 73 (CID Paper No 29–B) this morning. First, we have signified our agreement to the original American proposal of relative battleship strength, and that is still our definite policy.

*   *   *   *

Secondly: Admiralty representatives are all naturally strong partisans of the intermediate and gradual replacement policy in accordance with views expressed by the First Sea Lord. They have adduced many powerful arguments showing advantages of this course. Nevertheless, we feel that the advantages of a ten year absolute naval holiday in capital ships are so great for the cause of peace and disarmament throughout the world, that we are prepared to face the technical objections and inconveniences inseparable from it. We feel strongly that Great Britain should stand firmly on this ground and not mar in any respect her moral position, and that if this grand project should break down it should be on account of American or Japanese afterthoughts, and that we should to the end of the discussion adhere to our full and unqualified acceptance, offering no support to these technical objections.

*   *   *   *

100. *Beatty: Memorandum to Cabinet*

[ADM 116/1776]   10th December 1921
SECRET
C.P.No.3542

I have read Telegram No. 101 to Mr. Balfour with the utmost amazement, and I desire to place on record that there is no foundation in fact for the statements therein made, that the British Naval experts are working in collusion with the United States Naval experts to frustrate the views of the Governments of both countries.

The further statement that they have indulged in professional undertakings and confidences which are 'admittedly' to the detriment of the interests of this country is a grave reflection on the intelligence and the patriotism of the British Naval Officers concerned.

I cannot but regret that I was not given an opportunity of clearing away the misconceptions which appear to exist as to the conduct of affairs in Washington.

I was available from noon onwards on the day on which the telegram was sent.

101. *To his wife* [Biarritz]

[BTY/17/58/19–21]   Brooksby
                                                          Friday [20 Jan. 1922]

                         *   *   *   *

Now my dear heart you must not be so despondent. You are in
a far better place as far as the weather is concerned than this and
you really must make up your mind that, come what may, you
are going to help yourself, nobody else can, and unless you make
a real struggle for it I do not know what is going to happen. You
have got a great deal to live for. I am a public man, and I have
a right to ask you to do all you can to make yourself well so that
you can be of assistance to me in my life. I know you are suffering
from a complaint which precludes you from helping me today,
but instead of aggravating that complaint by sitting down wringing
your hands and declaring that you are the most miserable of
women, make up your mind you are going to win through.
Nobody can help you but yourself. If I were to sling in my appointment now, I would not help you. You would only have me to
abuse and revile at and pour out your woes to. And, if I slip out
of the picture now, I go for ever. Today I am fighting a terrible
battle to preserve what can be saved of the Navy for the Empire.
It is the most difficult task I have ever had to do & more depends
upon the results than anything we can imagine. I can throw up
the sponge and retire from the contest – resign my appointment.
I have no doubt somebody will be found who could do it equally
well, but what sort of figure should I cut in the eyes of the Service,
the country, the world and in history if I were to do? What little
reputation I have would be blasted for ever. What use should I
be to you in the future, a discredited, disgruntled human being
without occupation & with no future.

   If you were your old self, you could help me much & if you
could see your way to take a grip of yourself _now_ and make up
your mind to throw off all the imaginary bogies which upset you,
and which are like [*sic*] to ruin our lives & destroy the work of
my life, you could still help, first, by taking a great weight off my
mind, and secondly, by recovering your equilibrium render me
that assistance and support which you alone could if you were to
set your mind to it.

   I have made a name and a reputation that might well lead to
bigger things. If I sling up everything now, what would be the

result? I should not help you, nobody can do that but yourself, and for the rest of our lives we should be a disappointed and discredited couple. I, because in the hour of need I slung up my office and you, because you made me do it.

My dearest heart, you, with all your understanding, will readily recognise this. I pray you not to let your personal feelings overcome every other thought but that or your trouble. If I was a physician or had any power of bringing relief or assisting you in any way, then there would be something for it. But we know from bitter experience that I am no use to you. In this instance I aggravate the trouble and nothing is gained. You must look facts fair & square in the face and make a supreme effort for all our sakes and not spend your thoughts on evolving new grievances & means of giving effect to them. If you were an American, living in America, you would have been put in a nursing home, shut off from this world and all you love for six months or more. We can't do that, & don't want to do that, here, but we do ask you, David, Peter & I, to make an effort yourself to try, for a short period of say six months, to cut yourself off and try and re-establish yourself in mind & body to take your place in this world and by [–] be of some use to us all in our struggle in life. You can if you make your mind up to it. Ask Rosamund, she is wise and sensible and will agree with everything I have said, I am sure.

The future is in your hands, nobody else's, and on what steps you take depends the whole of our lives, your sons & husband.

Bless you dear heart, take courage, use determination & the great gifts God has given you of great common sense & you will win through.

102.   *To his wife* [Biarritz]

[BTY/17/58/40–41]   Hanover Lodge
                                                    27.1.22

*   *   *   *

I intended going down to Brooksby tonight to have a hunt, get some fresh air and exercise, and was going to take Roger Keyes with me.[1] But at the last moment press of work prevented us from going, which was a great disappointment. However, if we can get

---

[1]Keyes was DCNS November 1921–5.

on with our replies to the Geddes Committee we are moving in the right direction.

Churchill's Committee which is enquiring into it is treating us sympathetically and I hope we shall be able to convince them that we are doing our best – but we have to safeguard the Empire, a fact which the politician is apt to lose sight of.

*   *   *   *

103. Beatty and Keyes: Memoranda on Reductions in Naval Staff[1]

[ADM 116/2105]   28.1.22.
                                                              7.2.22.

I realise the low cost to the Country of the Naval Staff. It is, however, imperative that the numbers should be reduced to the lowest limit possible with efficiency, taking into consideration the instructions of the Government that no great war is anticipated in the next 10 years, although provision should be made for possible expansion of trained units in case of an emergency arising.

Any reduction made in the personnel of the Staff creates an increased reduction both in the Naval and Civilian personnel in administrative departments at the Admiralty, and the financial effect is therefore accumulative.

Intelligence Division I consider yet further reduction should be made in this Division. If necessary the intelligence activities must be limited and the greatest care taken that this Division does not overlap and carry out duties pertaining to the Plans, Trade, or Operations Division. DTSD should look into this with DNI and report through DCNS to me.

Plans Division
Training and Staff I concur that no further reductions can be
Duties Division made.
Trade Division
Operations Division I understand that the reason given for the numbers in this Division is that the Division must be able to cope with the extra pressure

[1]See Documents 35 and 87 above.

of work which arises suddenly in any emergency.

In a peace organization I cannot concur that numbers in this particular Division should be governed by this consideration.

The Naval Staff must be considered as a whole and if industrial trouble or emergency of such a nature should suddenly arise, work must cease in other Divisions of the Naval Staff and these must lend personnel to the Operations Division.

I wish the possibility of a reduction of 1 Deputy Director and 3 Commanders to be reported on to me by the DTSD after conferring with the Director of Operations.

Local Defence *Division*   A reduction of personnel should be possible here, accepting perhaps a slowing up of work carried out.

DTSD to consider the reduction of 1 Deputy Director and 1 Commander.

Gunnery Division *Torpedo Division*   Here again if some slowing up of the work involved is necessary I consider a further reduction of 1 Commander from each Division should be made.

I concur in the numbers in *Tactical and Air Section* and also reduction in the Duty Captains.

PS [Holograph] If the reduction in Operations makes it difficult for that Divn to carry out duties of Duty Capt, officers from other Divisions should be required to assist.

B
28.1.22

The First Sea Lord has approved of the following reductions in the complement of the Naval Staff:–

Intelligence Division
  1 Captain (Assistant Director).
  2 Commanders.
  2 Captains RM
  1 Paymr. Lieutenant
  1 Instructor Commander

Plans Division
  1 Commander
Training and Staff Duties Division
  1 Lieutenant Commander
Trade Division
  1 Paymr. Lieut-Commander
Operations Division
  3 Captains (Duty Captains)
  1 Commander
  1 Lieutenant
Local Defence Division
  1 Commander
  1 Lieut-Commander
  1 Lieut-Colonel RM
Gunnery Division
  1 Captain
  1 Commander
Torpedo Division
  1 Captain
  2 Commanders
Tactical and Air Sections
  Nil

In signifying his approval, he added the following minute:- 'The Directors of Divisions are to be congratulated on the loyal and whole-hearted manner in which they have met the demands caused by the exigencies of the moment.'

These reductions are to take effect on 31st March 1922. It is desired that the names of the officers who will be reduced shall be communicated to DTSD as soon as convenient.

R.K.
7.2.22.

To Directors of Divisions
and Heads of Sections
of the Naval Staff.
(Copy to each).

104.   *To his wife* [Biarritz]

[BTY/17/58/55–56]   Hanover Lodge
                                    Tuesday 31st [Jan. 1922]

*   *   *   *

Here we are engrossed still with defeating the misstatements of the Geddes Committee[1] and, I think, we are winning a very considerable victory and proving our points up to the hilt.

The Cabinet Committee composed of Winston, Birkenhead, Montagu & Baldwin have been very complimentary and I think we have made a case before them, but it is a little early to state definitely the result.[2] It has been a matter of immense labour and if they (the Cabinet) would only trust those that are running the Show have saved us all the work which it has entailed. However, I think we have knocked the bottom out of the Geddes Report and exposed the fallacies under which they worked which had no relation to the facts.

*   *   *   *

105.   *To his wife* [Biarritz]

[BTY/17/59/1–3]   Hanover Lodge
                                                1.2.22

*   *   *   *

I think we have succeeded in impressing the Winston committee with the strength of our case and of our earnest desire to meet the demands for economy. But we must be allowed to apply them in our own way and not be dictated to by Geddes or any other amateur economist. We have made our last cut and cut [?] back and are now against the wall and can do no more. So they must take it or lose us, just as they see fit.

I really am so tired of the interminable struggle that I am quite ready to leave it altogether and let them find somebody else to try and do what they want. But, whoever it is, they won't succeed

[1] The Reports of the Geddes Committee on National Expenditure are in Parliamentary Papers, Cmd 1581, 1582, 1589 of 1922; Admiralty Remarks on the Interim Report in Cmd 1587 of 1922.
[2] Churchill's Committee set up January 1922 to consider the Services' objections to Geddes's recommendations; Edwin Montagu (1879–1924): Secretary of State for India.

and at the same time have a Navy left with which to safeguard the Empire.

I believe that there will be a General Election this summer, everything points in that direction and that L.G. wants to consolidate his position and secure a new lease of life as the Prime Minister.

However, on the whole they are pleased with the Admiralty.

. . . Winston tells me that Mrs Winston has been suffering badly from nerves and has had a bad breakdown. It is extraordinary what a universal complaint it is and what a lot of people are suffering from it . . . I suppose it is one of the aftermaths [?] of the war which makes it so common. Of course Mrs Churchill has been suffering from it off and on for a very long time, as I remember she had one very bad go when I was Naval Secretary to Winston. So you are not the only sufferer from this damnable complaint.

I have just finished dinner and I quite enjoy spending my evenings at home by my own fire side and not having to make conversation, just reading and writing to you. You would call it dull and lonely, but I am never lonely and am at peace for a bit when by myself.

106.   *Admiralty Memorandum to CID*

[Copy]

[Cab. 21/225]   February 6 1922
SECRET.   RELATIONS BETWEEN THE NAVY
AND THE AIR FORCE

The Committee on National Expenditure, in their Interim Report (pp. 6 and 7), have made some remarks in regard to the future relations of the Army and Navy to the Air.

2.   In accordance with their Terms of Reference, the Committee have restricted themselves to the financial aspect of the question, and find their remedy for existing defects in the creation of a Ministry of Defence.

3.   Apart from this highly controversial remedy, the Admiralty feel that the time has come for bringing to the notice of the Government, with a view to the institution of a thorough enquiry, the defects of the present scheme on the important grounds of efficiency.

A detailed examination shows that considerable economies will result if the views of the Admiralty in conjunction with those that the War Office are putting forward are accepted. In the following remarks only the main principle is dealt with, but concrete proposals in support of this principle are available.

4. The Admiralty is the sole authority responsible for the defence of our sea communications.

5. With this object in view, the Board of Admiralty has, in the past, been responsible not only for advising as to the whole of the requirements necessary for carrying out the Naval Policy of the Government, but also for seeing that the expenditure approved for this purpose is allocated to the best possible advantage.

6. The advent of the air weapon, which has become an integral part of our Fleets, has provided the sole exception to this wise rule. The strength and composition of our Naval Air Units depend on Air Ministry finance and organisation, although the efficiency of the Fleet and its tactical and strategical employment in time of war are largely dependent upon the efficiency of its aerial equipment.

7. The ships used for carrying aircraft are, it is true, provided by the Admiralty, but vessels and aircraft are interdependent, and neither can be used without the other; yet they are provided for by two different Departments of State.

8. In regard to personnel, the Navy needs an air personnel totally different from that which the Air Force requires. It needs a comparatively small body of men, highly specialised in their particular work. Elasticity is of much less importance than specialisation; above all, the senior Air Officers of the Fleet should be men who have years of experience of *naval* air work behind them, and the Royal Air Force is unable to produce these without detriment to the air requirements in other directions.

9. It will be seen from the foregoing remarks that although responsibility for the efficiency of the Fleet rests on the Admiralty, they are partly dependent for attaining efficiency in a highly important direction on another Ministry — a situation which is fundamentally unsound.

10. The Admiralty consider that the air weapon will never be developed satisfactorily for naval purposes until they are in a position to supply and administer their own Air Service, employing a suitable co-ordinating medium in those respects in which requirements are common to both the Army and the Navy.

11. In the opinion of the Admiralty this unsatisfactory state of affairs, both in regard to personnel and material, should not be allowed to continue. Experience since the war has all contributed to show the fundamental mistake of the existing organisation.

In Appendix I will be found the views of various authorities well qualified to give them, and naval opinion is unanimous in expressing its dissatisfaction with the present scheme and its grave anxiety should no alteration be effected.

In Appendices II and III are two Admiralty Memoranda in connection with this subject prepared respectively for the Committee on National Expenditure and Mr. Churchill's Committee.

12. It is hoped that the Government will recognise that the Admiralty have done their best to effect the economies necessary to our straightened national circumstances — economies which in many cases have been agreed to with profound regret on account of their adverse effect on the ability of the Admiralty to provide in an adequate manner for carrying out the naval policy of the Government.

13. In the present Memorandum the Admiralty recommend a policy which they are confident will lead to still further economies, whilst at the same time removing a situation which, if allowed to continue, will paralyse the work of our sea forces.

The foregoing considerations encourage the Admiralty to hope that their earnest request for a strong and impartial Committee to enquire into the existing defects in the system of naval air co-operation will not pass unheeded by the Government.

(Initialled) B.

107. *To his wife* [Biarritz]

[BTY/17/59/15–16]   Hanover Lodge
                                                     Monday [6 Feb. 1922]

                    *   *   *   *

In the meantime the situation here is developing in an unpleasant way so far as we are concerned. They are going to publish Geddes's report, but are not going to publish any reply. Anyway, that's what they say. Of course that means we, the so-called spending departments, will come in for a great deal of abuse, and I am afraid that my leaving England at this juncture will look like running away. It is most unfortunate that it should have been brought to a head just now, but it cannot be helped. And whatever the abuse is I suppose I must suffer [*sic*] unless I stop and defend myself and the Admiralty.

If you could hold on for another few days without me, I think I could weather the storm which the publication is sure to produce. But I am quite prepared to leave for Biarritz at a moment's notice and leave the yapping dogs to abuse to their hearts' content.

I have a good case and am prepared to stand by it, but am not so prepared to leave it to others. Intrigue is rife and the only way to defeat it is to meet it with counter-blasts in the press, which I have to engineer myself.

*   *   *   *

107a.   *To his wife* [Biarritz]

[BTY/17/59/23–24]   Hotel Ritz
Paris
Sunday [19 Feb. 1922]

My Darling Tata,

I hope you got over your terrible storm. You certainly sent me off in a hurricane frame of mind. I can perfectly see your point of view, as I have told you, but you never can see mine. As long as I have got a job to do, I have to do it, and in a case like this it did not serve any good purpose your banging away as you did. If I chuck my appointment tomorrow, it would not have changed the fact that I had to go back and stand by comrades & support Admiralty policy when they telegraph for me as they did. All it did was to spoil the last few hours of a perfect holiday.

If your storming could have altered anything, then storm away, but as it could do nothing but make us both perfectly miserable what is the use of it?

All my heart to you
your devoted
David

108. *To his wife* [Biarritz]

[BTY/17/59/29–32]   Hanover Lodge
                                                        Monday [20 Feb. 1922]

I have had a very strenuous day, two meetings, both of which were fairly satisfactory but not final or sufficiently definitive. The Prime Minister is very anxious and overburdened with the economical situation and does not [*sic*] which way to turn.

The Navy of course is a source from which he apparently thinks he will find untold means of acquiring economies, but he won't unless he is prepared to alter the policy of the Empire, which he cannot and dare not do. And, without a change of policy, I can do no more. I think without doubt the majority of the Cabinet are with me, certainly the ones that count, and I do not think I can be forced into a false position. They are sympathetic and appreciative of all that we have done and I think realise that we have gone to the bottom of the well.

Lee is overwhelmed by the attack on him by the *Times*. He can think of nothing else, which is a mercy, as he leaves the things that matter to me and is happy apparently in doing so.

*   *   *   *

109. *To his wife* [Biarritz]

[BTY/17/59/36–37]   Admiralty
                                                                    22.2.22

Just a spare moment to scribble you a line. I think that all is going well, though it is very difficult to say for certain. But our position is strong and I think on the whole has been strengthened by the conversations we have held in the past two days. If the Government go to the extreme of altering their naval policy, as we have said they must do if they expect us to make any further cuts in the Naval Estimates, then I think there will be a split in the Cabinet and certainly a row in the Houses of Parliament. And I do not think that the Government would face that with a General Election looming up in the near future.

But there is no doubt that the financial situation is bad, very bad, and unless a reduction can be made in the Income Tax a good many companies, as well as private individuals, will be broke. The trouble is that they will not tackle a great many departments where great cuts can be made and where they have been overspending the public money with lavish hand for the last 3 years.

I suppose vested interests are too strong and have strong influence to bring to bear on the Powers that Be. It seems very hard that departments like Transport, Education, Housing, Labour, should not be attacked as vigorously as the Services. But it was always the same. In time of peace we have no friends and have no influential Party supporters.

*   *   *   *

110.   *To his wife* [Hotel Plaza Athénée, Paris]

[BTY/17/60/1–3]   Admiralty
                                                                1.3.22

*   *   *   *

The political world is very upset by an internal crisis in the parties, and the Prime Minister is talking of resigning, but of course he won't. They never do when they talk about it.[1]

The Chancellor of the Exchequer[2] is explaining the Geddes Committee Report and I hope is going to support the Admiralty view. He stated that the Geddes figures were quite correct — which we contend is not so, and he spent most of his time eulogising the wonderful work that they performed and then proceeded to hint that they made many mistakes. I could not wait any longer in the House as I had to come back to finish off some work here. But I had Winston promised to get up and defend the Admiralty if it became necessary, and he is quite prepared to do so, and in fact would like to do so. So I hope it does become necessary.

Of course the papers are full of nothing but the Wedding.[3] Thank the Lord it is over and there will be a little more attention paid to the things that really matter. However, I must not grumble as we really have done very well, and on the whole thing I think the Government are very pleased with it. They haven't said so collectively but several members have individually, which is something.

[1]Lloyd George's Coalition was to break up in October 1922 and was replaced by Bonar Law's Conservative government.
[2]Sir Robert Horne had become Chancellor in April 1921 (see note 3 on page 75 above).
[3]Princess Mary, only daughter of King George V had married Henry, 6th Earl Harewood (1882–1947) in February 1922.

110a.   *To his wife* [Hotel Plaza Athénée, Paris]

[BTY/17/60/21–24]   Hanover Lodge
                                              Saturday [11 Mar. 1922]

My Darling Tata,

Your telegrams and letters fill me with joy. I can't tell you or ever explain what a great weight has lifted from my mind and how different everything seems in consequence. I first cried, then laughed, and sent for Mam[1] to tell the great good news and [—] beamed all over and danced round the room and said I must write at once to David. It all seems so very wonderful and yet when you read the little book which I have just done again, so simple and straightforward . . . I think of it all day and say to myself 'She is better. She is better.'

What a wonderman little Coué[2] is. One must never go back on it and one must go through the little ritual every day, morning and evening . . .

Indeed the world seems a different place and I did my work today with a light heart and everything seemed to come easy to me.

*   *   *   *

Bless you dear heart. I am happier than I have been for years.
All my love,
ever your devoted
DAVID

---

[1]Lady Beatty's secretary, Mlle Kambly.
[2]Emile Coué, French psychotherapist (1857–1926): emphasised auto-suggestion as a cure for nervous ailments; his reputation spread widely, especially in the USA. His method was synthesised into patients' constant repetition of the formula 'tous les jours, à tous les points de vue, je vais de mieux en mieux'; Lady Beatty had consulted him at Nancy; his books explaining his technique were translated into many languages.

111. *Churchill–Beatty Correspondence on RN–RAF Relations*

[Extract]

[Cab. 16/48]   March 17th 1922

Annexure No 1.

NOTE BY MR. CHURCHILL

Notes on Admiralty–Air Ministry Relations

1.   The culmination of all naval operations is the supreme sea battle. The study and direction of this battle belongs in its integrity to the Admiralty.

2.   It follows that the rôle of aircraft in the sea battle must be prescribed by the Admiralty, who, for this purpose, should avail themselves of the highest developments of the science of aviation.

3.   It follows, also, that the Admiralty should define the rôle and prescribe the quantity of aircraft employed and also the proportion naval expenditure on aircraft for battle purposes should bear to other elements in the naval battle.

4.   It follows, further, that the Admiralty should ask Parliament for the money to pay for the aircraft they require, and should also have full and unfettered control over the said aircraft while employed for naval purposes.

5.   The Air Ministry, on the other hand, is the repository of the science of aviation in all its branches and aspects and the supreme professional authority on aerial war as a whole.

6.   The relations of the Air Ministry to the Admiralty in respect of purely naval services should partake largely of the nature of a laboratory and a shop for matériel, and a school and Staff College for personnel.

7.   It is important that the general unity of the Air Service should be preserved, even in regard to airmen of naval origin serving under the Admiralty for naval air purposes. For this purpose there should be a certain interchange of personnel between the Royal Navy and the Royal Air Force, and every effort should be made in the system affecting the personnel to prevent crystallization into opposite and rival schools.

8.   In the event of a war against a Power which had no navy, but a very large Air Force, the air squadrons attached to the Navy should be capable of rapidly rejoining the main Air Force. Similarly, in the event of a war against a Power which had no Air Force, but a powerful Fleet equipped with aircraft, it should be

possible for the Naval Air squadrons to be reinforced to the fullest extent, either by additions to the existing seaplane and aeroplane carriers, or by air squadrons operating in conjunction with the Fleets from land.

9. The Royal Air Force should be regarded as the parent service for all airmen in their capacity as airmen.

It is suggested that if agreement could be reached on the above general principles between the high personnel of the Admiralty and the Air Ministry, there should be no insuperable difficulty in working out details. This task could be remitted to small technical committees of subordinates, referring points of difference as they arose to their superiors.

(Initialled) W.S.C.

112. *Beatty to Churchill*

[Copy]

[AIR 8/7/10]   Hanover Lodge
Regent's Park
N.W.
Sunday, 19th [March 1922]

My dear Churchill,

I have received your memo *re* Notes on Admiralty–Air Ministry relations. They are sufficient to indicate that our views are not too divergent. First, I wish to reiterate that there is no desire on our part i.e. the Admiralty to abolish the Air Ministry or break up the Air Service.

The one is a Statutory body created by the Government and it is no business of ours whether the Government consider it desirable to maintain it or not. To break up the Air Service would be a retrograde step from which we should be a considerable sufferer if it came to pass.

What we do desire is to remedy the present state of affairs by which the Personnel and Materiel employed [on] work which is an integral part of naval responsibility, [are] supplied by another service over which we have no control.

To achieve this the Admiralty view is exactly as enunciated by you during our conversation on Friday. That is:–

The Admiralty must be in a position to say what they want, order it and pay for it. In arriving at a decision as to what they want they would be guided by the advice and experience of the

Air Ministry, who will be the responsible authority for Air Science and Research.

The Air Ministry will be the authority responsible for the actual supply of aircraft to the Navy, as to all other Services requiring such supply, thereby avoiding danger of competition in the markets and constituting a means of co-ordinating air thought in one channel.

The Admiralty should provide their own personnel sending those selected to a Central Training Establishment under the Air Ministry for the initial training in the art of flying, and for the technical instruction, subsequently returning to a Naval Training School for instruction in purely Naval requirements.

If these two fundamental principles are accepted there should be no insuperable difficulty in working out details.

113. *Beatty to Churchill*

[Copy]

[AIR 8/7/14]
Admiralty
17th July, 1922.

Thank you for your letter of the 14th enclosing Trenchard's proposals for the Air Staff of a Carrier such as the *Furious*[1] in 1929.

As you wish, I am having prepared a paper showing the organisation which we consider necessary to ensure naval fighting efficiency.

Meanwhile let me say that it appears to me that the attitude taken up by the Air Staff on this matter is based on a misconception of Admiralty requirements and the principle which the Naval Staff considers must be accepted before it is possible to arrive at mutual agreement in regard to common training, administration and co-operation.

Briefly that principle is that the air unit of the fighting fleet is a naval unit similar to the capital ship unit, the light cruiser unit or the destroyer unit, with a definite function, in combination with other naval arms, to achieve victory in the naval battle; and as a naval unit it must be manned trained and controlled by the Navy for the Navy.

And here let me say that the creation of this new naval air unit is not the setting up of a separate naval air service, and in no way

---

[1] *Furious*, originally a battle-cruiser was converted to an aircraft carrier by 1925.

conflicts, so far as I can see, with your expressed views or the decisions of the Government.

Over the vast field of naval operations, including the protection of commerce in narrow waters such as the English Channel and the defence of bases both at home and abroad, co-operation of air forces with the Navy will be essential in any future war.

The Government have decided that for this purpose there shall not be a separate naval air service as at the commencement of the last war, but that such air co-operation shall be provided by the independent air force administered and controlled by the Air Ministry.

For co-operation of this nature it is possible a naval wing of the Air Ministry under Air Ministry control and working on the lines of the present organisation will meet requirements and allow of the necessary expansion in time of war and the avoidance of overlapping and competition and the disadvantages you refer to arising from a separate naval air service.

But this sphere of co-operation with the Navy involving as it does the reinforcement or withdrawal of air forces in accordance with the direction of the supreme executive command, is an entirely different question from the building up of a definite naval unit, an arm of the fighting fleet, a unit which if withdrawn from that fleet destroys its composition and effectiveness.

Expansion of this unit in time of war will be met by the ordinary means adopted for the expansion of the other units; the difficulties you refer to in this respect will not arise in the case of this comparatively small unit: those difficulties arose, as you point out, owing to a separate naval air service, whose major duties were not with the fleet, but in co-operation with subsidiary forces ashore and afloat. Nor for this fleet unit should we experience difficulty in regard to the provision of officers or the flow of promotion.

I have written this with a view to removing any misconception or confusion which may exist in regard to the idea that I contemplated a setting up of a separate naval air service. The decision of the Government in this respect stands, but I do feel that the Government in arriving at this decision never questioned the principle that a naval unit of the fighting fleet must be manned, administered and controlled by the Admiralty.

Accepting this principle, we can go ahead with arrangements for preliminary common air training, co-ordination of design and supply, and the steps necessary to ensure maximum co-operation of air forces with the Navy in the defence of the Empire, such Air Forces belonging to the Independent Air Force and forming no separate air service.

I should like to add the following brief remarks in regard to the particular points you ask me to consider.

(*a*) The waste involved in using only Dartmouth Cadets to form a Naval Air Service.

No naval air service is contemplated; only a naval unit of the fighting fleet, comparatively small in size and definitely limited by Carrier capacity and the Washington Treaty.

No waste will be involved. On the contrary, since all personnel in the Carriers will be naval capable of carrying out naval duties, a considerable saving on total personnel will be effected.

(*b*) The consequent inevitable recourse as before the war, to special entry and short service officer personnel.

This does not arise. Before the war the separate naval air service embraced manifold duties, and the arm of the fighting fleet was only a small part of the whole.

(*c*) The complex position produced by all these different classes of airmen, viz. Dartmouth Cadet airmen, Naval Special Entry airmen, permanent Air Force airmen, short service commission Air Force airmen.

This does not arise. The position of naval personnel manning the naval unit will be considerably less complex than that of air force personnel and naval personnel as at present.

(*d*) The disadvantage of the Navy cutting its personnel off from all interchange with the main Air Force and consequent cliquey jealousies and rivalries.

It will be the duty of the Air and of Naval Staffs to prevent this, and incidentally, I may add, matters are not particularly satisfactory under the present system.

(*e*) The absolute need of providing effective expansive power for naval aviation.

The expansion of the Naval air arm of the fighting fleet will depend on the carrier capacity, and will be comparatively small. It will be met by the ordinary steps taken for expansion on mobilisation.

(f)   The unfairness of the Admiralty picking the brains and using the schools of the RAF while declining to make any use of the RAF personnel or conversely to contribute a certain proportion of officers to the general well being of the RAF, and the ill-will resulting.

This, frankly, I do not understand. For the efficiency of the Service the Admiralty certainly would gladly make the utmost use of the brains and schools of the RAF in developing the Naval Air Unit. It is hoped that the Air Ministry will similarly make use of the brains and schools of the Navy for developing its efficiency in co-operation with Naval Forces. The Admiralty would gladly come to arrangements for assisting the RAF to the utmost.

(g)   The expense and inconvenience of the duplication of establishments and the inevitable divergency between the two forces.

The duplication now exists; with the development of co-ordination of Staff and administrative work of the three Services, Navy, Army and Air Force, as frequently outlined by you in your speeches and letters, I believe the divergency contemplated will never arise.

114. *Hankey to Lloyd George*

[Memorandum]

[Ll.G/F/26/2/10]   Offices of the Cabinet
1st Aug 1922

Prime Minister

   I had a long talk this morning with Ld Beatty. He is very much concerned at the delay in settling the question of the Navy and the Air Force. He says that there is not the smallest chance of Mr Churchill being able to bring about an arrangement between the two Services, who are hopelessly divided on what he regards as a vital question of principle. In fact, Mr Churchill admitted to me yesterday that he hardly expected to reach an agreement and that ultimately a decision would have to be imposed.

   Lord Beatty and Admiral Keyes, whom I saw together, were both very strong that the present system has completely broken down. They say that they have tried their utmost to work it, but they find it impossible to work a system for what is now an essential auxiliary service. They tell me that they have had bitter complaints from every Commander-in-Chief, including Admiral Madden and Admiral de Robeck. In order to give the Air Ministry a chance the Admiralty has up to now always refused to listen to these. The present situation, however, is absolutely intolerable and is making the proper development of aircraft working with the Fleet impossible. Friction is continuous.

Lord Beatty says that settlement of a great number of important questions affecting the Admiralty Estimates depends on a settlement of this question, and he begs that you will do everything possible to get a decision before the holiday, and not postpone it.

Curiously enough, after I had had an hour with Lord Beatty on the subject, Lord Lee rang me up independently to make the same request, that I would do all I could to induce you to settle the question before the holiday.

My own view has for some time been that the decision could only be arrived at by some impartial body such as:–

> The Prime Minister
> Mr Chamberlain
> Lord Balfour,

who could read the papers, hear Mr Churchill, and if necessary, the two participants.

One difficulty is that Lord Balfour is leaving for Switzerland on Friday, and Lord Lee is leaving to visit the Mediterranean Fleet either Thursday afternoon or Friday.

I think it will meet them if you give Lee and Beatty a chance of stating the urgency, and if you follow by stating the greater urgency of other questions.

PART III

POLITICS AND NAVAL POLICY
November 1922–August 1927

INTRODUCTION[1]

Although Beatty was inevitably concerned about the political instability in the Eastern Mediterranean at the beginning of the period
and became increasingly aware of threats to Britain's interests in
the Far East from chronic disorder in China and the growing signs
of expansionism in Japan, it was not these which made the greatest
demands on his time and energy. His major preoccupation was with
matters at home. Chief of these was a continuous struggle to maintain the Navy at a strength adequate to fulfil what he saw as its
global tasks. In essence this was a struggle with successive governments dominated by the determination to reduce national expenditure and difficult to convince of the necessity for modernising the
Navy in a world in which they could see no clear maritime threat to
Britain's interests. This general attitude made the Admiralty's
policy of planning a long term construction programme hard to
implement throughout Beatty's time in office, and his performance
must be judged by his degree of success in achieving it. The task
became particularly difficult with the advent in January 1924 of a
minority Labour government, dependent on Liberal support. The
Prime Minister, Ramsay MacDonald,[2] and many of his supporters
were pacifists at heart, and the Chancellor of the Exchequer, Philip
Snowden,[3] was grimly determined to reduce expenditure on armaments. This first Labour administration remained in office only until
November 1924 and was replaced by Baldwin's[4] Conservative
government which lasted until June 1929. This did give some con-

[1]For the background to this section see Roskill, *Naval Policy I*, Chapters I–XVI.
[2]James Ramsay MacDonald (1866–1937): Leader of Labour Party from 1911;
Prime Minister and Foreign Secretary 1924; Prime Minister of 2nd Labour Government 1929–31; of National Government 1931–5; Lord President of the Council
1935–7.
[3]Philip Snowden, later Viscount (1864–1937): in Labour politics from 1894;
MP 1906–18; opposed war and lost seat 1918; re-elected 1922–31; Chancellor of
Exchequer 1924, 1929–31; followed MacDonald into National Government, Lord
Privy Seal 1931–2; Viscount 1932.
[4]Stanley Baldwin, later Earl (1867–1947); Conservative MP 1908–37; prominent
in break-up of Lloyd George coalition 1922; Financial Secretary to Treasury 1917;
President of Board of Trade 1921–2; Chancellor of Exchequer 1922–3; Prime
Minister 1923, 1924–29; Lord President of the Council 1931–5; Prime Minister
1935–37; Earl 1937.

tinuity of policy and personnel and removed the ideological pressure for disarmament, but it did not automatically open the purse of the Treasury. The new Chancellor was Winston Churchill, now returned to the Conservative Party from the Liberals, and determined to excel as the guardian of the nation's wealth and well qualified by his experience at the Admiralty to fight its demands for funds in detail.

The Washington treaty limited Britain to building only two new battleships, but placed no limit on cruiser construction, and it was over this that Beatty and Churchill had their hardest fight. Of less strategic significance, but fought no less fiercely, was the Admiralty's attempt to bring naval officers' pay into line with the Army and Air Force by paying them a marriage allowance. Beatty failed to win on this issue. He was aware of the fact that his own comparative wealth might lead his fellow officers to doubt his commitment to their cause and this may well explain the angry tone of his correspondence with Churchill [152, 169–70]. It was not until 1938 that the Treasury gave way.

The second great issue involving heavy expenditure which preoccupied Beatty was the construction of a fortified base at Singapore, without which the British fleet could not operate in the Far East. This is treated in Part IV (see pp. 357–413) and it is sufficient here to say that the Labour government cancelled its predecessor's decision to build the base, on ideological as well as economic grounds. Baldwin's administration reversed this but progress was slow. A further burden on Beatty's mind was the mounting intensity of the dispute over the historical treatment of the battle of Jutland [119]. This in turn is treated in Part V (see pp. 415–479). It is noteworthy that in all the financial and policy struggles with governments, Beatty succeeded in gaining positive political support from successive First Lords: the Conservatives Amery[1] and Bridgeman[2] and the politically neutral Viscount Chelmsford,[3] who

[1]Leopold Amery (1873–1955): Conservative politician, supporter of Joseph Chamberlain; MP 1911–45; Parliamentary Under Secretary for Colonies under Lord Milner 1919; for Admiralty 1921; 1st Lord of Admiralty 1922–3; Dominions Secretary 1925–9; Secretary for India 1940–5.

[2]William Bridgeman, later Viscount (1864–1935): Unionist MP 1906–29; Parliamentary Secretary Ministry of Labour 1916; Board of Trade 1919–20; Secretary for Mines 1920–22; Home Secretary 1922–4; 1st Lord of Admiralty 1924–9; Viscount 1929.

[3]Frederick John Thesiger, 2nd Baron and 1st Viscount Chelmsford (1868–1933): Governor of Queensland 1905–9, of New South Wales 1909–13, where supported first Labour Government; 1910 Viceroy of India 1916–21 where furthered moves to self-government; 1st Lord of Admiralty 1924.

accepted office under the Labour government on conditions which included his support of Admiralty policy on Singapore and the cruiser programme [135]. In most important matters they were all content to let Beatty make the running in committee and negotiations, although Amery, a much more powerful political figure than the other two, did not hesitate to bring him to heel on at least one occasion [127, 129].

The third of Beatty's major concerns were the continuing disputes with the RAF on the provision of an effective air component for the fleet, and on the role of air power in the defence of Singapore. His main contention on the former issue was that air power was an integral part of the fleet's fighting capabilities, and therefore demanded naval personnel, command and control. The RAF's case, put forward by Trenchard, was based on his unshifting opposition to any derogation from the unity of air power and on his conviction that in the future at least some of the tasks of the other two services could be more effectively and economically performed by the RAF. The institution of the Chiefs of Staff Committee in 1923 gave Beatty a new forum in which to advance the Navy's claims, and where he usually found himself in alliance with the CIGS against Trenchard [125]. In addition he took the opportunities offered by the Imperial Conferences of 1923 and 1926 and the publicity given to speeches at the Lord Mayor of London's annual banquets to ensure that the Navy's case did not go by default. In accordance with convention he did not speak on naval affairs in the House of Lords until after his retirement, but he was always conscious of the strong back bench support for the Navy in both Houses of Parliament which needed the information and inspiration which he could provide [131, 172, 192].

Besides all this activity at the highest national and imperial level was a troubled conscience at having to preside over the radical reduction in the Navy which cut short the career prospects for many of his fellow officers. Perhaps it was this, despite his inherently authoritarian attitude, which led him to lift the wartime censorship of the *Naval Review*[1] to give them an opportunity to vent their views [174, 176]. And, as always, in addition to all these professional concerns, his correspondence and his daily life

[1] *The Naval Review* founded in 1912 by a group of officers, headed by the then Captain Herbert Richmond, with the object of stimulating free discussion of the general principles of their profession in contrast to the *matériel* matters which had hitherto dominated their training and experience. It continues to thrive as a private quarterly periodical. In addition to naval officers and civilian officials, the Editor can admit 'other persons in touch with and interested in the Royal Navy'.

were increasingly burdened by what he now termed his wife's neurasthenia [164], which he thought at times threatened his own mental stability and reserves of moral strength [119, 139–42, 150–51, 153, 155, 177, 187–9].

STRUGGLES OVER THE ESTIMATES

The Naval Estimates had to be presented to the House of Commons in the Spring of each year and were the fruit of months of detailed calculation and planning followed by hard negotiations with the Treasury, and, if agreement were not reached there, with the Cabinet. In these political negotiations success largely depended upon the joint efforts of Beatty and his First Lord. In the earlier preparations and the provision of papers and oral evidence for related committees and high level enquiries, the quality and organisation of the Naval Staff were of supreme importance and Beatty took particular care over this, as he did over the senior appointments going to men he trusted. In particular he saw the necessity for delegation so as to leave himself free for negotiations with the politicians and his fellow chiefs of staff [115–16, 148, 154, 173].

The 1923/4 Estimates were drawn up and approved with comparatively little opposition.[1] At £58 million they showed significant reductions and Beatty was pleased that the Board's efforts at economy had been appreciated outside the Admiralty [120–21]. Those for the following year[2] were to have a much stormier passage. They were based on the Admiralty's determination to begin a long term building programme for cruisers, destroyers, aircraft carriers and submarines, initially involving expenditure of some £32.5 million over five years. This was not well received by the Chancellor, Neville Chamberlain, who, after pressure by Amery, was apparently willing to accept increased total estimates of over £62 million. This preliminary arrangement was overturned by the advent of the minority Labour government on 23 January 1924; a government ideologically as well as financially opposed to rearmament.

Beatty immediately set about building good relations with his new political masters. He soon revised his initially poor opinion of the First Lord, Chelmsford, and recorded, somewhat patronisingly, how well he got on with the Labour junior Admiralty minis-

[1] *1st Lord's Statement on the Estimates*, Cmd. 1818, 1923.
[2] *1st Lord's Statement on the Estimates*, Cmd. 2071, 1924.

ters. But in the Chancellor, Philip Snowden, he found an un-charmable opponent [133–45]. The Admiralty began by presenting a large building programme costing over £260 million over the next ten years. Their aim was to attain a 25 per cent superiority in cruisers and destroyers over Japan, as well as building 80 sub-marines and 4 aircraft carriers. The government were inevitably hostile and replied by establishing a Cabinet Committee, under J. R. Clynes,[1] the Lord Privy Seal, to consider not only this programme but also the desirability of the Singapore base. Although the Government finally decided against the establish-ment of the base as being contrary to their general policy of seeking international co-operation through the League of Nations and working for a continuing limitation of armaments, the Admir-alty had more success with its cruiser programme. The relevant Estimate went through the House in a vote in which the Govern-ment's decision was supported by the Conservatives against some of its own backbenchers and Liberals. Beatty regarded this as a significant victory. A great deal of the credit must go to Chelms-ford for his success in persuading his colleagues on the Clynes Committee and in Cabinet.

Beatty had congratulated Churchill on his appointment as Chan-cellor in November 1924 but had no illusions that this meant the end of his struggle for naval construction. However, the spirit in which they argued was very different from the cold relationship with Snowden. This is well illustrated in a note from Churchill (unfortunately undated) apparently passed over the table at 10 Downing Street during negotiations, probably early in 1925. 'I thought you were masterly. I have never heard such powerful statements by the 1st Sea Lord.'[2] Of course Churchill was not motivated by the ideological concepts of the Labour government. More telling in negotiation was his long acquaintance with naval matters and his strong suspicions of the Admiralty practice of exaggeration in its claims and calculations, and his determination to maintain the Treasury's drive for economy. Beatty and the new First Lord, Bridgeman, thus found themselves involved in prolonged arguments with Churchill in Committee and Cabinet over the proposed 1925/6 Estimates of some £65 million.[3] This

---

[1] J. R. Clynes (1869–1940): Trade Union and Labour leader; union organiser from 1891, noted for his moderation in negotiation; in 1899 member of Labour Representation Committee which became Labour Party in 1900; MP from 1906; Lord Privy Seal 1924; Home Secretary 1929–31.

[2] This holograph note, on 10 Downing Street writing paper, is in BTY/14/4/6.

[3] *1st Lord's Statement on the Estimates*, Cmd. 2366, 1925.

was an increase of about £9 million over the previous year, but included, for the first time, an item of £1.75 million for the Fleet Air Arm under the Trenchard–Keyes agreement of 1924.[1] Churchill added to his previous arguments that the international situation made it reasonable to project indefinitely into the future, the Ten Year Rule, first adopted in 1919.[2] He offered a sum of £60 million which the Admiralty rejected, countering with a bid of £60.5 million which included nothing for new construction, which would be covered in a forthcoming Supplementary Estimate. To end the deadlock the government appointed a Cabinet Committee, under Lord Birkenhead, Secretary of State for India. Churchill and Bridgeman were members, but it was Beatty, as a witness before the Committee and in related correspondence, who bore the brunt of the arguments with the Chancellor. It must be remembered that concurrently the two protagonists were differing fiercely over naval officers' marriage allowances [152, 169–70]. When the Committee failed to agree, the Prime Minister was persuaded to impose a decision which gave approval for the first five years of the Admiralty's programme at a cost of £58 million, but extended it to seven years. The documents show Beatty at his most effective in political persuasion [149–51, 153–66, 168, 172–3].

There was far less controversy over the 1926/7 Estimates,[3] which showed a reduction, and again Beatty stressed the advantages the Admiralty gained from demonstrating its readiness to economise. So strongly did he feel this that he used it in his arguments with Baldwin about increasing the Navy's control of its air power [177, 179, 181].

RENEWED CONFLICT OVER NAVAL AIRPOWER, 1923–27

In March 1923 the government, aware of growing tension between the Navy and the Air Force, set up a Sub-Committee of the CID under Lord Salisbury,[4] Lord President of the Council, with a wide

[1]See Paul G. Halpern (ed.) (1979), *The Keyes Papers, Vol II, 1919–38*, NRS, pp. 10, 118, 256, 283, 412.
[2]See Stephen Roskill (1972), 'The Ten Year Rule: The Historical Facts', *Journal of Royal United Services Institution*, March.
[3]*1st Lord's Statement on the Estimates*, Cmd. 2595, 1926.
[4]James Gascoyne-Cecil, 4th Marquess of Salisbury (1866–1947): Unionist MP 1885–1903 when succeeded to title; Lord President of Council 1922–4; Chairman of CID Committee on National and Imperial Defence which recommended formation of Chiefs of Staff Committee 1923; Lord Privy Seal 1924–9.

remit on means of securing better co-ordination of defence by closer inter-service relationships and the possible establishment of a Ministry of Defence. At its first meeting this body delegated the specific question of air support for the fleet to a sub-committee chaired by Lord Balfour and with Lords Peel[1] and Weir[2] as members. It was in this body that Beatty was to make his main effort. It reported on 21 July and, although it went some way towards meeting the Admiralty complaints on the faults of the existing system, it rejected their demand for a separate Air Service entirely under Admiralty control. Despite Amery's strong objections, Salisbury's main committee recommended the report to the Cabinet for adoption. This aroused great resentment among the Sea Lords but, under Amery's firm guidance, they accepted that they could not join in a mass resignation against a clear government decision, and reluctantly assured Baldwin that they would make a real effort to make the new compromise work.

Beatty had urged the Prime Minister to resolve the matter before the committee was instituted and was at first confident of a favourable result for what he saw as a modest demand in terms of personnel and resources [118, 121]. This constituted the main thrust of his evidence to the Balfour Committee, supported by a strong demand for a policy decision on personnel to be taken as soon as the plans for carrier construction were well advanced.[3] Also, at the first meeting of the Chiefs of Staff Committee with Salisbury in the chair on 17 July, he made a more oblique move in support of his aim [122–6]. His personal disappointment at the Balfour Committee's report was intense, hence the strong line taken by Amery to prevent a constitutional clash between the Admiralty and the government [127–32].

The advent of the Labour government in January 1924 had brought a lull, as the Board decided to concentrate on the larger immediate problems of the building programme and Singapore, although they did not omit any opportunity to convince the new

[1]William Robert, 2nd Viscount and 1st Earl Peel (1867–1937): Unionist MP 1901–5, 1909–12, when succeeded to title; Parliamentary Under Secretary War Office under Churchill 1919; Minister of Transport 1921–2; Secretary of State, India 1922–4, 1928–9; Earl 1929; high reputation as a Committee man.

[2]William Douglas, 1st Viscount Weir (1877–1959): engineer and industrialist; Director of Munitions for Scotland; Controller of Aeronautical Supplies Ministry of Munitions, and Member of the Air Board 1917; Air Minister 1918; a strong backer of Trenchard; after war returned to industry; remained influential on RAF development, especially on strategic bombing role; Baron 1918; Viscount 1938.

[3]Geoffrey Till (1979), *Air Power and the Royal Navy, 1914–1945*, London, gives a succinct account of British carrier development.

administration of their dissatisfaction on the Air question [138]. Spurred on by Chelmsford, the Cabinet set up a further enquiry under Lord Haldane,[1] the Lord Chancellor and Deputy Chairman of the CID. In Beatty's absence abroad Keyes, the DCNS and Trenchard negotiated under Haldane's guidance a compromise over the differences which had arisen in the interpretation of the Balfour report by July 1924. Although the Fleet Air Arm was to remain part of the RAF, the Navy gained many of their main demands on personnel, especially that all Observers should be naval, as should all the ratings on the new carriers as they came into service. Beatty was not directly involved in the negotiation but there is no reason to believe that he was critical of Keyes's achievement.[2]

LAST YEARS IN OFFICE, 1925–27

These were significant for the additional influence and prestige gained by Beatty from his position on the Chiefs of Staff Committee where he acted as Chairman, except for the rare occasions on which a minister presided. This obviously gave him opportunities to steer the discussions on Singapore in the direction he wanted (Part IV, pp. 357–413) and also on several other major inter-service matters. In 1925 he initiated the discussion which led to the Chiefs producing an 'Annual Review of Defence Policy', and also took the lead in improving inter-service staff planning. In private he was even ready to accept the institution of a Ministry of Defence, but only on the condition that the single service ministers should disappear and leave each Chief of Staff without a political superior in his own department. He also strongly supported the foundation of what was to be the Imperial Defence College, formally created in 1926 under the presidency of Admiral Sir Herbert Richmond. In all these inter-service developments, with the important exception of the defence of Singapore, Beatty seems to have carried Milne[3] and Trenchard with him, and to have worked in close co-operation with Hankey who, as Secretary

[1]Richard, later 1st Viscount, Haldane (1856–1928): statesman, lawyer and philosopher, partly educated in Germany; Liberal MP 1885–1911, when created Viscount; 1905–11 Secretary for War responsible for important army reforms; Lord Chancellor 1912–15 when dropped for alleged German sympathies; Lord Chancellor 1924 in first Labour government.
[2]See note 1 on page 226.
[3]Sir George Milne, CIGS 1926–33.

of the CID, normally attended COS meetings, supported by one of his Assistant Secretaries [171, 180–85].

Beatty's statement on defence as Chairman of the Chiefs of Staff to the Imperial Conference of October 1926, was his swan song on the larger stage. Already in August he had indicated that he would be ready to retire after that Conference [186–7] and by April 1927 Hankey was taking his retirement as an accepted fact [194]. He went on 29 July amid an effusive leave taking with Bridgeman, with whom he seems to have established the warmest personal relations of all his First Lords [197–201].

115. *Beatty: Memorandum on Staff Organisation*[1]

[Copy]

[ADM 116/2683]   17.11.22

With a view to investigating any possible field for affecting further economy in the personnel of the Naval Staff at the Admiralty, it is requested that the following will form a Committee:

> Vice Admiral Sir Roger Keyes, KCB
> Rear Admiral The Hon. A. Boyle, CB[2]
> Sir Charles Walker, KCB[3]

and after taking the evidence of the Directors of Staff Divisions, the Directors of Administrative Divisions and others concerned, will report as to the conclusions they reach.

2.   For the guidance of the Committee it should be pointed out that no departure can be contemplated from the fundamental principle on which the work at the Admiralty is at present organised; namely, the separation of the Staff work of Operations, including strategy, tactics, training and intelligence, from the work of administration and supply.

Nor should any modification be made in the system whereby current and future work are separated within the Staff itself by having separate Operation and Planning Divisions.

3.   Within these limits, however, it may be that there is still room for improving the present organisation both in efficiency and with economy.

In this connection it has been suggested that the number of separate Divisions is too great and that advantage would be obtained if certain Divisions were abolished, the work being performed by Sections of Divisions remaining.

4.   Again it has been contended that under the present organisation, and with the present number of personnel in the Staff Divisions, there is a tendency for the Staff to overlap with Divisions on the technical and administrative side, this applying with

---

[1]See Document 103 above.
[2]Boyle was 4th Sea Lord and Chief of Supplies and Transport.
[3]Sir Charles Walker was Accountant-General of the Navy and later Deputy Secretary of the Admiralty.

particular emphasis to the Gunnery, Torpedo and Local Defence Divisions.

In regard to this, it is to be observed that the duty of the Staff is to deal with the tactical employment of weapons and to lay down the requirements of strategic and tactical policy.

The technical Divisions under the 3rd Sea Lord and Controller are available to give the highest expert advice as to how requirements can best be met.

If Staff Divisions in addition to advising as to requirements are also advising as to how they propose those requirements should be met, then they are exceeding their functions and performing work which does not belong to them.

5.   It is in these directions which the Committee is particularly requested to obtain all the evidence available and to report as to their conclusions as rapidly as possible.

116.   *Admiralty Committee's General Remarks on Report of Lord Weir's Committee*

[Extracts]

[ADM 116/2683]   17.2.23

Whilst the Report of Lord Weir's Committee may prove of value to the Board of Admiralty in their efforts to effect further economy in the administration of H.M. Navy, it is necessary to point out that the composition of the Committee is not such as to lend great weight to any recommendation it may make in regard to that side of the Admiralty Office dealing with the naval policy, strategy and tactics, the work of the Naval Staff under the First Sea Lord.

2.   Lord Weir, the Chairman of great technical and administrative ability, Lieutenant General Sir Herbert Miles, with his knowledge of War Office administration from the point of view of the Adjutant General's Department, Sir R. R. Scott, a highly placed Civil Servant in the Treasury, Lieutenant Colonel Sir J. R. Chancellor, former West Indian Governor and with a knowledge of the Secretarial side of the Committee of Imperial Defence; these personal characteristics may enable the Committee to make useful recommendations in regard to economy and efficiency in matters relating to technique and administration, but they alone are insufficient to make them authorities competent to advise on the economic and efficient organisation of the Naval Staff.

3. It is to be noted that none of the members are conversant with naval strategy and tactics; none of them have a knowledge of the sea or of the requirements of the sea; no evidence was taken by them from the Chief of the Naval Staff, the Deputy Chief of the Naval Staff, the Assistant Chief of the Naval Staff, nor any other Naval Officer who has held high command or Staff position at the Admiralty. The recommendations therefore of that portion of the report dealing with the organisation of the Staff should be received with caution and critically examined before adoption, in order to make certain that fighting efficiency will not be sacrificed for a trifling economy.

4. In approaching this question it is to be remembered that after the Napoleonic Wars questions of economy and administration were allowed to efface considerations of fighting efficiency, with the result that certain so called reforms of the Admiralty Office were undertaken by Sir James Greene.[1]

These reforms were based on administrative convenience. They paid little attention to the lessons of war. Inefficiency resulted. The state of the Navy sank to a low point, and the efforts continued despite the efforts of the reformers, down to the late war, on which we entered with a Naval Staff untrained, and inadequate for requirements.

5. The same tendency is apparent today. We have had the Geddes Committee, and now the Weir Committee; both Committees making recommendations based chiefly on economic and administrative convenience with fighting efficiency relegated to the background.

6. That economy is essential at this present period is perfectly understood, but what is equally essential is a high state of efficiency of the reduced fleet with which the Admiralty is now required to carry out the Naval Policy of H.M. Government. The delicate organism of the Naval Staff hardly lends itself to economic treatment other than at the hands of those who understand its technical organisation and its activities in relation to the sea going fleet and shore training establishments.

Expert investigation with a view to reduction has in fact been

[1]There is a slip-up here. The reference must be to Sir James Graham who as 1st Lord radically reformed Admiralty organisation in 1832. Herbert Richmond (1928), *National Policy and Naval Strength* pp. 231–54, in an article published first in 1925 criticises Graham's policy in terms remarkably similar to those of these 1923 minutes. The slip might have originated in the similar name of a former Permanent Secretary to the Admiralty, Sir W. Graham Greene (1911–17). See Marder, *From the Dreadnought* vol. 4, pp. 215–16.

applied continuously. Prior to each financial year it is the policy of the Chief of the Naval Staff exhaustively to review the organisation and composition of the Naval Staff with a view to effecting the utmost economy consistent with the requirements of Naval policy, and the general political outlook. As a result, the numbers of the Naval Staff, which in November 1918 stood at a figure of 336, was reduced in 1919 to 160 and in 1920 to 118, in 1921 to 87 and in 1922 to 64.

7. In accordance with this policy a committee consisting of the Deputy Chief of the Naval Staff, the Fourth Sea Lord and the Deputy Secretary, were appointed by the Board in November last to enquire into the organisation and personnel of the Naval Staff, with a view to effecting further economy. That Committee, after fully investigating all the recommendations on the subject, have been able to suggest further small savings and certain changes in organisation, which, it is believed, will result in economy and efficiency.

Their reports on the Naval Staff should be closely compared with that of the Weir Committee. It will be found in the Board Committee's report the reasons for and against certain lines of action are fully discussed, certainly more fully than that of the Weir Committee.

8. It would almost appear from the Report of the Weir Committee that a misconception prevails in the minds of the members as to the purpose for which the Naval Staff exists. Thus we find in paragraph 44 the Committee refer to the Naval Staff being the channel through which the imagination of the thinking naval officer is expressed. They go on to say, 'the plea for increased thinking Departments causes us to review the origins of the really big advances or steps in modern naval materiel. The *Dreadnought* was not the product of a Naval Staff. The turbine, the watertube boiler and fire control were the work of those outside the Staff Department . . .'

We are asked here to contemplate the great changes in naval material prior to the war, and our attention is invited to the fact that these changes were made without the assistance of a Naval Staff.

9. This may be admitted, but the functions of the Naval Staff are not only concerned with material. The work of the Naval Staff is directed to ensure that material considerations shall not dominate strategic and tactical considerations, that the weapon does not become the master of the tactician. The three spheres

of Operations, Intelligence and Training, the Naval Staff endeavour to ensure that the requirements of Strategy and Tactics are met, that sufficient types of all units are available to meet the Naval situation and that the training of the personnel conforms to strategic and tactical thought.

Whatever material advances may have been made prior to the war, it is notorious that naval war plans were lacking, that no bases were available for our ships, that there were an insufficient number of destroyers, that the tactical doctrine in regard to the use of destroyers was of a defensive not an offensive nature, that there was a lack of vision in regard to the offensive powers of the submarine, and that our means of attack on submarines were of a primitive nature.

In these and many other directions the fighting efficiency of the fleet was impaired, chiefly due to the lack of a naval staff charged with responsibility in these directions.

Organisation of Naval Staff

10. The organisation of the Naval Staff is the result of war experience, and has been framed by those who have had intimate knowledge of war requirements and the sea-going fleet under war conditions. The organisation was modified in 1920 to embrace more fully the war lessons, and a further slight modification is being proposed in the present year, a modification which it was deemed inexpedient for personal reasons, and until further experience had been gained, to make in 1920.

11. Broadly speaking the basis of the organisation is that the work of the Staff naturally divides itself into two main channels:–

(a) Strategic, including Operations, Plans, Intelligence.

(b) Tactical and Training, including fleet exercises, tactical use of weapons, staff requirements of material.

At the head of the strategic side is placed the Deputy Chief of the Naval Staff; at the head of the Tactical and Training side is placed the Assistant Chief of the Naval Staff, each members of the Board of Admiralty, thus ensuring that the Directors of Divisions on the Strategic and Tactical side have direct responsibility through their Superintending Lord to the Board of Admiralty.

Position of the ACNS

12.   Lord Weir's Committee makes the recommendation that the Division referred to above should no longer obtain and that the work of the Naval Staff, strategic and tactical, should be dealt with by one Member of the Board of Admiralty — the DCNS — the ACNS ceasing to be a Member of the Board, but instead being given the status under the DCNS of a Director in charge of the Training and Staff Duties Division, which Division would include in its functions the work now carried out by the Gunnery and Torpedo Divisions.

13.   Under the Board system, whereby responsibility finally rests with the Superintending Lord, this proposal would result in too much being thrown on the DCNS in that Officer becoming immersed in paper considerations on all aspects of staff work, and unable to devote his energies to the important strategic considerations which now form his responsibility. In this centralisation there would be a loss of efficiency.

Position of the First Sea Lord

14.   It may be argued that under peace conditions the Chief of Naval Staff can personally superintend the Staff work in connection with Strategy, leaving the DCNS to deal with the Tactical side.

But this is to defeat the trend of recent endeavour which is to free the CNS entirely so far as is practicable from departmental work, to ensure that he shall be removed from all detail in connection with Staff work, Strategic or Tactical and that he shall consider only the main and big questions connected with Policy.

It was in this direction that the Hartington Commission of 1896 urged reform,[1] it being apparent to that Committee that the 1st Sea Lord's attention was principally concerned with the small, to the exclusion of the big. Little was accomplished, however, and it was not until the late war and the pressure of events forced a

[1] Spencer Compton Cavendish, Marquis of Hartington, later 8th Duke of Devonshire (1853–1908): Liberal politician, but opposed to Irish Home Rule and joined Liberal Unionists; Hartington's Royal Commission was established in 1888, not 1896, and issued Reports in 1889 and 1890; after rejecting proposals to join the two Services under a Ministry of Defence it recommended the formation of an inter-Service Council under the Prime Minister, not to be realised until creation of CID in 1904; it found little wrong with Admiralty administration but strongly recommended the creation of an Army General Staff; this not established until Haldane's Army Reforms after the Boer War; see note 1 on page 228.

change, that in 1918 the 1st Sea Lord was at length granted that freedom from petty interference essential for the efficient prosecution of war or for efficient preparation in peace.

15. That this Departmental freedom of the 1st Sea Lord is even more important today than formerly can scarcely be doubted. It is now recognised that the 1st Sea Lord as Chief of the Naval Staff is the principal adviser of HM Government as to the naval requirements to meet policy. With the Chief of the General Staff and the Chief of the Air Staff. He is the head of the Combined Staff which advises the Government on the requirements of strategy viewed on [sic] its widest aspects with the political heads of the War Office and Air Ministry and the Chiefs of the Army and Air Staffs, under the Lord President of the Council, and the Sub-Committee of the Committee of Imperial Defence, dealing with all major questions connected with military policy and the co-ordination of military requirements. Responsibility for this work makes it undesirable that the Chief of the Naval Staff should become a departmental head of a side of the Naval Staff. His position must be quite outside the departmental organisation. He must be concerned only with the large questions of naval policy, being advised on these by the DCNS, on the strategic side, the ACNS on the tactical side, who, under the Board system of responsibility, should each be members of the Board.

* * * *

Trade Division

22. In regard to the Trade Division Lord Weir's Committee state that, similarly to the Local Defence Division it is part of the War organisation concerned with plans for the control and protection of merchant shipping and with economic questions connected with naval operations. They consider a separate Division is undesirable and that one Officer on the Staff of the Plans Division should be able to maintain a skeleton scheme as a foundation on which the organisation that would be required in a great war could be built up.

23. The Trade Division do not, as suggested by the Weir Committee, collect commercial and economic statistics, but leave this work to the Overseas Trade Department, Board of Trade and various other Government Departments, making use of the statistics so supplied for general naval purposes in connection with

plans for the stopping of enemy trade and the protection of British Trade.

24.   The Admiralty Committee reported that they were unable to recommend the amalgamation of the Trade Division with the Plans Division, considering that in view of the supreme naval importance of the attack and defence of commerce the inter-dependence of naval operations and mercantile movements, and the specialised nature of the work involved, it was desirable to retain the present arrangement of a separate Division.

Concluding remarks

25.   The main recommendation of the Weir Committee dealing with the Department of the 1st Sea Lord (paragraphs 44 to 49 of the report) have been referred to in the foregoing and compared with the Admiralty Committee recommendations.

Briefly Lord Weir proposes that:

(*a*)   The ACNS should cease to be a Member of the Board.

(*b*)   The Training and Staff Duties Division should include sections dealing with Gunnery and Torpedo staff questions, the ACNS being the Director of the Division.

(*c*)   The work of Local Defence Division should be merged in that of Plans and Operations Division.

(*d*)   The work of Trade Division should be undertaken by one Officer of the Plans Division.

It is considered that (*a*) would react on efficiency, would over-burden the DCNS and would tend to throw departmental work on to the CNS.

(*b*) would prevent direct responsibility to the Board of the Heads of Sections dealing with Gunnery and Torpedo efficiency two principal staff subjects concerned with fleet tactical and fight-ing efficiency. The Head of the Division would have more to deal with than a single individual is capable of with maximum efficiency. No economy would result from the proposal.

(*c*) should be adopted.

(*d*) would prevent that full attention being given to plans for the attack and defence of commerce which its naval importance requires.

26.   The difference in the effect of the recommendations of

the Admiralty and Weir Committees on Vote 12 is shown in the table.

	Saving effected by Weir Committee per annum on Vote 12	Saving effected by Admiralty Committee per annum on Vote 12
ACNS to cease to be a member of the Board	£720	
Local Defence Division to be merged in Plans and Operations Division	Proposed by both Committees.	
Training and Staff Duties Division to be reduced		£4500
Trade Division to be merged in Plans Division	£5800	———
	£6520	£4500

That is, assuming that the fullest effect can be given to the Weir recommendations, there would be a saving of £2000 a year over the Admiralty proposal.

It should be observed, however, that the Weir proposals give no actual figures. It is almost certain under their recommendations that the staff of the Training Division would have to be increased, and even if the Trade Division was amalgamated with the Plans Division one additional officer as suggested in the Plans Division could not cope with the work involved.

Practically to carry out the Weir proposals would require at least two officers additional to the Staff of Plans Division and one officer additional to Training Division, and no saving would result.

117. Admiralty Minutes on Lord Weir's Report

[Copy]

[ADM 116/2683]   19.2.23–24.3.23

Staff Organisation

I have fully considered Lord Weir's proposals and disagree with the suggestion that ACNS should go off the Board.

I agree with our own Committee's recommendations as to the organisation of DCNS's and ACNS's branches. But I should like you to go more closely into the question of possible further reductions in the actual personnel. Accepting the view that Trade Division should remain as a division, it should be reduced as far as possible, to a skeleton organisation and be worked by junior officers. Again admitting the strength of the proposed new Local Defence section under Plans, I should like you to consider how far the section could be made up (or compensated for) by reductions in the rest of the staff of Plans. I only give those as instances — what I want is to be in a position when justifying my rejection of Lord Weir's proposals to be able to say that our scheme is not only more efficient but as economical as it is possible to be consistently with the efficiency of this most vital element of the Service.

Intd. L.S.A.
19.2.23

CNS

The Admiralty Committee met again to consider the points raised in the First Lord's minute and as to whether further economies in the Naval Staff as suggested therein could be carried out without undue loss of efficiency.

After again closely considering the organisation and reviewing the work carried out, the Committee decided it was impossible for them to suggest further reduction.

With regard to the Trade Division, it is to be observed that this Division is in fact now a skeleton organisation barely able to meet the requirements of peace; very great expansion will be necessitated in war; comparison of the numbers in this Division during the late war and now is instructive in this respect.

Again as regards the Section of Plans to deal with Local Defence; the Committee only recommended this organisation to meet the imperative needs of economy, and the numbers which they put forward are, in their opinion, the minimum which can be accepted if the requisite efficiency is to be maintained.

Nor are the Committee able to recommend that Junior Officers should be employed on the Admiralty Staff. They consider that it is greatly to the advantage of the Service the present rule which ensures that only Naval Officers of experience are appointed to the important Admiralty positions, Officers with ample sea experience and in a position to speak with knowledge and authority on sea requirements.

The only direction in which the Admiralty Committee saw the means of making a possible economy was the substitution of a Civilian for the 2nd Paymaster now employed in the Trade Division. The duties here are mostly of a clerical nature, involving being able to obtain quickly statistical information and records required by the Senior Officer of the Section or by the Director of the Division. Such a change, however, would give no reduction in numbers of the Naval Staff, and only result in a very small economy.

In regard to the last sentence of the First Lord's Minute, the Committee are fully of the opinion that the 1st Lord can certainly say to-day when justifying his rejection of Lord Weir's proposals, that the Admiralty scheme 'is not only more efficient, but as economical as it is possible to be consistently with the efficiency of this most vital element of the Service.'

C.W.	A.V.B.	R.K.
8.3.23	8.3.23	8.3.23

1st Lord

Herewith the Committee's remarks on the points raised by you. They have gone very carefully and fully again into the question and their decisions are as indicated with which I fully concur.

(Intld) B
8.3.23.

As proposed.

(Intld) L.S.A.
23.3.23.

[*Secretary's Minute*]

Immediate action should be taken to carry out the changes approved by the First Lord on these papers; and an advance acquaint should be sent to 1st SL, 2nd SL, 4th SL, DCNS and ACNS and Naval Secretary informing them that these changes have been approved and that steps are being taken to give effect to them, so that there may be no possibility of appointments of officers being made in the meanwhile which are not in accord with the changes.

There is no need to wait for Treasury concurrence before putting the transfers and reductions into effect.

(Intld) O.M.
24.3.23

118. *Beatty to Bonar Law: Minutes*

[Holograph]

[BL/111/5/24]   Admiralty
Wednesday [21 Feb 1923]

In thinking of our conversation yesterday it occurred to me that you were under some misapprehension as to what the withdrawal of machines and personnel meant to the Air Service, and that if we took from them what is required for the Naval Air requirements they would be left with nothing.

Actually, as regards machines, we should take from them 4½ Squadrons, leaving them with 32½ Service Squadrons, not including Reserve Squadrons or Establishments.

As regards personnel we should take over under 5%. This can hardly be considered as wrecking the Air Service.

Bonar Law to Beatty

[Holograph Draft]

House of Commons
21.2.23

I thank you for the letter & although the numbers are smaller than I imagined, the differences are still there & I sincerely [?] trust it may be possible for a compromise to be arranged.

119. *To his wife* [Golf Hotel, Hyères, France]

[BTY/17/63/13–15]   Admiralty
                                                                         6.3.23

I am very distressed at your last letters which indicate that you are still obsessed with all manner of fears which have no substance in fact, although no doubt very real to you. I do not know how to combat them beyond stating that they are purely of an imaginary character upon which you build to such an extent as to cause you real suffering.

. . . When you worry about such trifling subjects it naturally has a very depressing effect upon your whole outlook of life. It is too silly and childish, & you are always looking for a grievance where no grievance exists. All this has a very depressing effect upon me and causes me much more worry than you can ever possibly think of.

$$* \qquad * \qquad * \qquad *$$

I get so weary in thinking of it all, and the utter foolishness of it all, that at times I feel quite sick and am incapable of doing my work properly, and I have a good deal on my hands just now. We are preparing for another great battle in Cabinet Committee on the Air Question. It is a momentous question and we cannot afford to be beaten over it. It takes a vast amount of preparation, and that alone occupies most of my time, and we stand or fall by the result.

There is another question which also is a source of annoyance and anxiety and that is the Jutland question which is ever present & must be brought to a head.[1] The solution is not easy, there are so many interests involved. The outstanding one & only one which should be considered is what is best for the Navy. That is my guiding consideration.

Now cheer up for heaven's sake & help me by being more reasonable and taking a more reasonable view of life . . .

---

[1] In February 1923 circulation of drafts of Corbett's account of Jutland and the Dewar brothers' *Staff Appreciation* fanned the flames of the controversy; see *Jellicoe Papers*, vol. II, Part IV; and also Part V of this volume.

120.   *To his wife* [Hyères]

[BTY/17/63/26–27]   Hanover Lodge
                                                                    9.3.23

. . . The Naval Estimates were completed and laid on the table
of the House of Commons yesterday afternoon, and of course
appeared in the Press this morning. They were well received and
at last our efforts in the direction of economy are being really
appreciated. It's as well because we had reached rock bottom and
can go no lower, & in fact they must increase from now on. It
has always been represented to us by a succession of Chancellors
of the Exchequer that the financial year 1923–24 was the critical
one, that is the one in which we shall have greater difficulty than
in any other to make the Budget meet. So it is to be hoped that
in the coming years we shall have more scope and be able to
begin building up. We have the principles accepted which is the
great thing, and 2 battleships laid down & commenced,[1] and next
year we must begin a light cruiser programme. But our action up
to now has carried the people with us & we shall more likely to
be justified for an increase of expenditure [*sic*] next year than if
we had failed to find some relief in naval expenditure this year.
The next thing I hope we shall see which is more than likely, is
an attack upon us for not doing more. The great thing is for the
public to think that they are guiding our policies & either checking
our extravagance or urging us to greater endeavours, & then they
are quite happy.

*   *   *   *

[1] *Nelson* and *Rodney*.

121. *Beatty to Osmond de Brock*[1]

[Copy]

[BTY/13/4/3]   Admiralty
                                                  13th March 1923

I must apologise for the length of time taken to answer your letter, but I had hoped by the delay to be able to give you more definite information than I am capable of at the moment.

First, let me congratulate you on the result of the Smyrna incident. The firmness there displayed and the quick strengthening of the Smyrna Force enabled the situation to be cleared with considerable credit to us generally and the Navy in particular.

Second, as regards the future of Constantinople and Chanak, the situation remains much as it was, with the addition that I think it is beyond doubt that there is no strong likelihood of events reaching a point in which force will be exerted, that is, a condition of war, and it is believed here that the more moderate counsels of Mustapha Kemal and Ismet Pasha will prevail and that there is little chance of our drifting into war.

I entirely concur in all that you say as regards the policy of bluff having been carried to its limit, and we can do no more. If perchance the worst was to happen, we can but revert to the policy, with which you agree, to withdraw from Constantinople and concentrate at Gallipoli and Chanak.

I fully realise the monotony and that pressing condition of life it is for all concerned, but I hope the time is not far distant when we can withdraw and you can continue the ordinary work of the Fleet on the Station. I am afraid it will be necessary for you to remain a little longer, but I hope not for long.

We have just completed our Naval Estimates and laid them on the table. We have as usual, as you will see, made great sacrifices to meet the economic conditions, and in doing so we have reached rock bottom. In succeeding years the estimates must increase to make up the leeway lost in the last three years.

The First Lord made a very clear and lucid statement which

---

[1] The Near Eastern crisis of 1919–23 originated in Turkey's resentment of the peace terms imposed by the Treaty of Sèvres in 1920, particularly the territorial concessions to Greece, and in the military action taken by Mustafa Kemal to reverse them. Lloyd George's extreme pro-Greek attitude took Britain to the brink of war at Chanak in September 1922. See A. J. P. Taylor (1965), *English History 1914–1945*, Oxford, pp. 190–91; Roskill, *Naval Policy I* pp. 181–203, describes the British Army and Naval involvement.

has placed our position clearly before the world. On the whole it has been well received, and I think that the public at large now realise that as far as economies are concerned we have done all that is humanly possible.

We have at last succeeded in getting a Committee to be appointed to enquire into our demand that we should have our own Naval Air Arm without interference from or by the Air Ministry. I think the Prime Minister realises that the feeling in the Navy is very strong on this point, and admitted to me personally that our case was a very strong one.

I have no fears as to the result, but I am apprehensive of waste of time, and on every occasion where it is possible I impress, as do all of us, the necessity of coming to a decision as early as possible. I hope, therefore, in the next two months to have the matter finally decided.

Our small point of insisting upon our Naval Air Arm, they try to swallow up in the big question of the general consideration for the defence of the Empire and the part that should be played by the Air therein. On this large question we have strong views which have a naval aspect, but we hope to keep them clear of the smaller question which has raised the whole issue.

I have in mind, and indeed in hand, a scheme for the re-distribution of the fleets, with the view of reducing the forces in the Atlantic Fleet and consequently increasing the strength of the Mediterranean Fleet, using Gibraltar and Malta for their repairing bases.

However, I will write to you about this more fully later, and certainly shall not do anything until I have talked things over with de Robeck, who naturally will be interested and may not wish to continue the command, conditions of which would be altered so much from that which they were when he accepted his present appointment.

Many thanks. I have quite recovered from the motor accident, but it took a long time.

The work here never seems to lessen, and we no sooner find a solution to one problem than we are faced with many others. However, I feel that if I can get the Air question satisfactorily settled and a reasonable programme made out for increasing our Light Cruiser strength, I can remove myself without leaving any outstanding problems of magnitude to be tackled in the future.

I am afraid you have had a poisonous winter, and your first year of command has been anything but an enjoyable one.

I hope, however, the next two years will make up for it, and during them you will be able to re-constitute the training of your fleet under the most favourable conditions.

122. Committee of Imperial Defence National and Imperial Defence Committee

Sub-Committee on Relations between the Navy and the Air Force
[Cab. 16/48]   [Extract]   March 22 1923
SECRET
N.D.(R)/2nd Mtg.

Shorthand notes of evidence given by the First Sea Lord and Chief of Naval Staff before the Sub-committee at their **second** meeting held at 2, Whitehall Gardens, SW1, on Thursday, March 22, 1923 at 11.30 a.m.

Present:
The Right Hon. The Earl of Balfour, KG, OM
(in the Chair)
The Right Hon. Lord Weir

The following were also present:

The Right Hon. L. S. Amery, MP, First Lord of the Admiralty
The Right Hon. Sir Samuel Hoare, Bart, CMG, MP, Secretary
of State for Air
Admiral of the Fleet, Earl Beatty, OM, GCB, GCVO, DSO,
First Sea Lord and Chief of the Naval Staff
Rear-Admiral C. T. M. Fuller, CB, CMG, DSO, Assistant Chief
of the Naval Staff
Lieutenant-Colonel Sir M. P. A. Hankey, GCB, (Secretary)
Major L. A. Clemens, OBE, MC (Assistant Secretary)

1. **Lord Balfour** explained that, although at an appropriate stage of the enquiry the two Departments would be given an opportunity of stating their views on the general question before the Committee, at the moment, however, the members of the Sub-Committee wished to acquaint themselves with a number of details. In this connection the Secretary had prepared a questionnaire (Appendix),[1] which he suggested might be taken as a basis for discussion.

[1]Not included here.

2. **Lord Beatty:** As you have already said, the views of the Admiralty have been put forward in many papers on many occasions extending over a period of years, but perhaps it is as well to restate the Naval point of view, which is – shall the air unit of the fighting Fleet be manned by Naval personnel under the Admiralty, specialised in their particular branch, similar to the submarines and such units, or shall it be manned principally by personnel of the Independent Air Force under the Air Ministry?

3. **Lord Balfour:** That is the broad outline?

4. **Lord Beatty:** That is the broad outline. The reason why we have now got to this state of affairs is that last year we fired off Memoranda at the devoted heads of the late Government, and stated we could not go on as we were, and asking definitely for an enquiry. That enquiry was promised, but, as you know, owing to certain circumstances, it never developed. The reason was that the late Secretary of State for the Colonies[1] thought that he had powers of persuasion greater than those of any other man, that he was going to be the angel of peace, was going to rule out all the difficulties without any trouble, and that it would not be necessary to go through this procedure of having a Committee. Of course, we did get a little further in the matter. It was conceded by the Air representative – on that occasion the Air Marshal, the Chief of the Staff – that on the question of material they would give way, that we should have all we asked for in the way of material and that sort of thing, provided that we paid for it. The stumbling block, of course, was the question of personnel. We never got over that. Then, when we were going to set about actually constituting the Committee – I think Sir Maurice Hankey will say it was actually constituted – it was about to begin its deliberations when the political crisis occurred and the Government disappeared, and so left the burden to the next Government. So here we are again in precisely the same position as we were twelve months ago, twenty-four months ago, and thirty-six months ago. During the period of the last two years there has not been quite the same urgency in the matter as obtains at the present moment. I may say that at the very commencement of 1919 the Chief of the Air Staff came to see me on this particular point and requested me to hold my hand in this matter, and said, 'We will endeavour to meet you in every sort of way; here we are, a new Service, we are starting on our legs now, and if you set about

[1]Winston Churchill.

trying to take away everything we have got, for the Naval purposes under your own control, it will break up what appears to be a promising young Service; therefore I ask you not to do this now, but in a year's time it will be different, and no doubt we shall be able to come to terms and meet you in that direction.'[1] He practically embodied that in a White Paper, which was issued to the Cabinet, in which he outlined the probability of the Naval Service having its own Air arm. Therefore, with that before us, I, perhaps unwisely, counselled the Admiralty to take a generous view of the situation and not to harass the unfortunate Air Ministry, struggling to gain their feet, and that sort of thing. Unfortunately, in the years that have passed, nothing was done and the opposition only stiffened as I have already outlined. Months have slipped by, and it is now a period of two years since we took up the cudgels vigorously on behalf of achieving what we want. To-day the situation has been made acute by the fact that, owing to the very large number of reductions in the personnel of the Fleet, we have a great many valuable officers, who otherwise will have to go ashore, who could be retained in the Naval Service if we achieve what we hope to achieve – that is, our own Naval air arm. Moreover, our programme of construction includes producing a number of aircraft carriers, which will come into being at the end of this year and the beginning of next, which makes it imperative that any change shall take place before these aircraft carriers are fully equipped and manned, and so forth. We should begin now. The psychological moment has arrived, and if a change is to take place, it should take place now. So that is why we have pressed – the First Lord will agree with me, for I addressed a letter to him on the subject, which he considered and talked to the Prime Minister about. The outcome, of course, is the present big Committee of the Committee of Imperial Defence, which is sitting, and the Sub-Committee over which you are presiding on that particular point. It is no use my going over and elaborating all the papers; you have them before you, and it is much easier for you to read them than to listen to me on the points as to the principles which are involved and the Admiralty point of view. It would only waste time and you could do it much quicker by reading them.

5.   **Lord Balfour:** I do not think you need be at all afraid that Lord Weir or I think we have got an easy job before us, which is apparently the view you took of the late Colonial Secretary. We

[1]See Document 33 above, a letter from Trenchard largely confirming Beatty's version of their conversation.

do not think we have, and I am sure I speak for Lord Weir when I say that we recognise that this question is not only excessively difficult, but excessively urgent. I presume it is because it is excessively urgent that this Sub-Committee has been appointed to try and deal with it. What I want, as you truly say, is the broad outline of the Admiralty case to be quite easily and rapidly collected from the excellent papers which they have circulated. The same is true of the Air Service, but as regards the details of these questions, I do not think any information can easily be extracted from the papers to which you refer. I do not say it could not be extracted, but it would take a long time, obviously, and Lord Weir, who has looked through the large papers, will admit that these questions are not answered in the large papers, which deal with broad questions of policy.

6. **Lord Beatty:** Exactly. I say we have never in the past attempted to deal with these questions in detail.

7. **Lord Balfour:** And most rightly.

123. *Beatty: Statement to Balfour Committee 9th Meeting*

[Cab. 16/48]   June 18 1923

314 **Lord Beatty:** I should like to say one thing more before we finish. I have spoken of the question of principle; I have talked about the importance of the Navy being responsible for the efficiency of its own personnel. I should like to call to the mind of the Committee the very distinct position in which a Naval Commander-in-Chief lives. It is quite apart, quite different from that of a Commander-in-Chief in any other Service. For instance, in an Army the Commander-in-Chief is in the rear, sometimes in one position, sometimes in another. He has no tactical control. A land battle is spread over many miles – 100 miles. It may last for weeks. The Commander-in-Chief has no forces under his personal observation. Now, in the Navy a Commander-in-Chief commands a Fleet and has that Fleet more or less entirely under his own observation. I speak from experience. I have commanded a Fleet in action. I know what is happening. I know that I have to make up my mind as to the disposition of my forces. I have to make up my mind as to how those forces are to be used. I have to make up my mind as to whether I can rely upon this or upon that. I have to make up my mind as to whether *that* Destroyer Flotilla is a better one than *that*, that I can tell this fellow to go

all out and that fellow not. I have complete control, and I can trust implicitly every unit because I have trained it myself and can therefore rely upon them. I have not got to rely upon the co-operation of a unit which belongs to another arm. Therefore, I point out that the case of a Naval Commander-in-Chief is a very important one in the fact that he can rely upon units which he himself has trained; he himself knows all that goes to make the efficiency of that unit, and in the present circumstances, under the existing scheme and under the existing conditions, no Naval Commander-in-Chief can rely on his own personal touch being conveyed to a unit, and a very important unit, of the Fleet, so long as it remains under another Department. I have to say this, that the Admiralty are responsible for Naval strategy in its broadest sense; that is, that in time of peace we are responsible for the composition and the disposition of the Fleet that we control. To-day part of the Fleet, an integral part of the Fleet, is an Air Arm, which is just as much a part of the Fleet as the guns that are in the ships, or the Submarines, or the Destroyers, or any part of it. If the Admiralty are permitted to develop their own Air Arm in the same way that they develop every other component part of the Fleet, they would know how much they could depend upon the Air Arm to do the work of, and possibly replace other units of the Fleet. In doing so it is conceivable that great economies might arise which to-day are impossible under the existing régime. We are fully alive to the present possibilities that are claimed in the future for the air, and we realise the important part that the Air Arm must play in any future Naval operations.

But unless and until the Admiralty themselves can develop as rapidly as possible our Air Arm, keeping step with advancement with other branches of the Service and utilising the whole to meet the strategic requirements, the full power of the air will fail to be effective in the Navy. In time of war Naval strategy will depend very considerably on the Admiralty having control of its own Air Arm, complete control as we asked for it, and if the Air Arm is in the hands of another Department the Admiralty can have no assurance in regard to the success of their strategy. It means that, if the efficiency of the Air Arm is in the hands of another Department, the Admiralty cannot lean to any extent on that Air Arm in framing its strategic policy. Developed for the use of the Navy to meet strategical and tactical requirements, it would be the aim and the object of the Admiralty to ensure that a complete understanding of the possibilities of the air and the air sense itself should permeate the Naval Service, and for this reason the Admiralty should endeavour to create a Naval Service a proportion of the officers of which who should attain high rank and command, should have a complete understanding and knowledge of the requirements of the Navy and its equipment of the Air arm. We feel that can only be obtained by the Admiralty controlling and providing its own air work, and by no stretch of the imagination do we conceive that a similar condition can be arrived at under the system which prevails at the present time.

124.   *Beatty: Memorandum to Balfour Committee*

[Copy]

[Cab. 21/266]   July 10 1923
SECRET
ND(R)19

I assume that the summary of the Air Ministry case as set out in ND(R)18 brings to a conclusion the evidence and data required by the Sub-Committee enquiry into the relations of the Navy and the Air Force.

The Naval Staff are in complete readiness to controvert in detail the loose arguments and misstatements of facts to be found on almost every page of ND(R)18. There must be some finality to this enquiry and, unless therefore specially requested to do so by the Committee, I do not propose to forward a further Naval Staff paper.

I desire however to take this opportunity of stating once more, and with greater emphasis after reading ND(R)18, and the evidence of the Chief of Air Staff at the ND(R) 10th meeting, my conviction that the present system cannot continue without the gravest consequences ensuing to the Navy and the Empire.

Throughout, I find the argument for a central Air Ministry controlling a vital arm of the Fleet is evolved solely to fit in with the Air Ministry's conception of what is required to provide for the local defence of these islands *vis à vis* a near Continental Power – France.

During the course of the enquiry the Admiralty has concerned itself not with the question of a separate Air Force for such defence purposes, but with the wider defence issue which arises

consequent on our Empire responsibility [*sic*] and the vital necessity of keeping open the lines of communication between component parts of that Empire.

This wider issue is primarily an Admiralty responsibility, a
responsibility which carries with it full and absolute control of
every arm of the Fleet, operational and administrative.

It is well to point out that it is a divergence of principles alone
which underlies the divergence of views between the Admiralty
and the Air Staff.

(Initialled) B.

125. *Chiefs of Staff Committee*
Minutes of 1st Meeting[1]

[Lord Salisbury, Lord President of the Council, in the Chair]
[Cab. 53/1]   [Extract]   July 17 1923
SECRET

[*Air Requirements of the Army*]

*   *   *   *

Lord Beatty doubted if the problem was being attacked in the
right way. He considered that the best plan would be to ask
the Foreign Office to specify the wars against which provision
should be made. This having been done, the Navy, the Army and
the Air Force should work out their plans. During the working
out of these plans the War Office would obviously say they wanted
a certain force consisting of so many divisions with certain artillery, tanks and Air Forces attached to them, but whereas the Chief
of the Imperial General Staff would obviously be responsible for
the artillery and tanks for the expeditionary force, he did not
understand who would be responsible for the air allotment. It was
necessary to consider the question . . . to have a definite problem
to work on so that the Staffs might evolve concrete plans.

*   *   *   *

Conclusion
That the responsibility for fixing the total air requirements of the
Army and the total air requirements of the Navy have to meet
any particular eventuality rested with the Chief of the Imperial
General Staff and the Chief of Naval Staff respectively, but that

[1]The COS Committee emerged from the recommendations of the Salisbury
Committee of 1923; see note 4 on page 226.

in the working out of these requirements the Air Staff should be consulted.

*   *   *   *

126.   Beatty: Additional Statement to Balfour Committee

[Cab. 32/48]   July 21st 1923

Lord Beatty: Because the principle was one which is the most important one – the principle that the Admiralty should be solely responsible for the efficiency of the Fleet – the principle that we have advocated from start to finish. May I say, as regards the question of urgency, there is the point that I did not mention at the time, which is a matter of the gravest consideration – the development of the Naval air units in the United States and Japan, which are advancing very rapidly. They are giving a great deal of serious thought and consideration to the whole problem of Naval air expansion and advancement, both from the research and technical point of view and from the personnel point of view.

*   *   *   *

127.   Amery: Diary Extracts

[Typescript]

[Amery Papers]   July–November 1923

23 July 1923
Had a good talk with Beatty who is naturally very upset and talked very freely about a general resignation of Sea Lords . . .

25 July 1923
Very anxious special Board meeting to consider the Report of the Sub-Committee. Fuller,[1] Keyes and some of them were all for claiming our maximum and nothing else. Beatty I think would be willing to find a compromise. Stayed on at the Admiralty afterwards starting my Memorandum for the morning, while Beatty prepared another which he and I agreed upon just before 8.

---

[1] Admiral Sir Cyril Fuller (1874–1942): entered RN 1887; gunnery specialist; Rear-Admiral 1921; ACNS 1922; 3rd Sea Lord and Controller 1923–5; Battle Cruiser Squadron 1925; Vice-Admiral 1926; C-in-C North American Station 1928; Admiral 1930; 2nd Sea Lord 1930–32.

27 July 1923

Had a long palaver with Beatty and Oliver,[1] impressing on them the disastrous results of using the threat of resignation, equally disastrous if we failed or succeeded. I made it clear throughout of course that there could be no question of their resigning without my doing the same. And, I think, made them understand something of the attitude of mind of the Cabinet and the Public towards an attempt to force their hand.

28 July 1923

Worked in the morning at a memorandum to the Cabinet summing up the situation. Board at 12 where I put the general situation before them pointing out what I would still try and get through the Cabinet but deprecated all talk about anything in the nature of resignation. The Sea Lords had trooped straight into the Board from a prolonged conference in Beatty's room and I gather that that particular danger was ruled out. Unfortunately an awful lot of nonsense got to the papers, some of it through young Curzon who runs in and out of the office far too much. About one o'clock I got an urgent message from Chequers with regard to things in the 'Daily Express' and other papers which amounted to practically a verbatim transcript of 20 lines or more of the latest Admiralty memorandum to the Committee. This sort of thing is an infernal nuisance and seriously weakens our case with the Cabinet. I sent for Beatty at once and he made inquiries but could find out nothing and this morning (30th) reports that he is quite sure that no unauthorised copy got out or was shown to anybody. I have also asked young Curzon who swears he has not seen it. Beatty in fact suggests that the leakage was deliberately done by the Air Ministry. Meanwhile my anxiety over this tiresome business has been greatly lightened by the fact that someone in the PM's own office seems to have given away that I asked in the morning whether he could see me and Beatty at Chequers over the week-end and this has got into the Central News as an attempt to way lay the PM and courteously refused by him . . .

[1]Admiral Sir Henry Francis Oliver (1865–1965): entered RN 1878; navigation specialist; Naval Assistant to Fisher and Wilson as 1st Sea Lords; Rear-Admiral and DNI 1913; Chief of Admiralty War Staff and Acting Vice-Admiral 1914; DCNS 1917; 1st Battle Cruiser Squadron 1918; C-in-C Home Fleet 1919; 2nd Sea Lord 1920; Admiral 1923; C-in-C Atlantic Fleet 1924–7; Admiral of the Fleet 1928.

1 Aug. 1923

The Sea Lords came to me in a deputation, very distressed and restive and, through Beatty, laid a special stress on the necessity of its being made clear in the Prime Minister's statement, that the settlement was only provisional.

*   *   *   *

And then, back to the Admiralty where I saw Beatty, who gave me a couple of sheets with certain points, which, he insisted, ought to come into the Prime Minister's statement, failing which the Sea Lords would resign. I went down to the House to see Baldwin about these points, but hearing that I could not get at him and that Salisbury was drafting the statement, went to see him at the Cabinet offices. Meanwhile, I got a letter from Beatty definitely asking me to tell the Prime Minister unless these points were met, the Sea Lords would consider they had lost the confidence of HM Government and would have to make room for others. I pressed Salisbury very strongly on the main point, which was to make clear that the settlement was not final.

Salisbury did not like the tone of Beatty's letter at all, which was not surprising, and when I saw the PM later in the evening, I did not actually show it to him, though I read him out the sentence about their feeling that they had lost the confidence of HMG. Baldwin refused to be seriously perturbed and I did not press matters, rather agreeing with him, and also unwilling to make him angry with the Sea Lords. I had by now clearly come to the conclusion myself that, unsatisfactory as the compromise was, there was no justification in it for anyone resigning.

2 August 1923

Saw Beatty and had a pretty stiff altercation with him as to the right of the Sea Lords to resign if they did not think that the statement was sufficiently satisfying in its tone. Down to the House by 11.30 for the statement, which I think sufficiently met the point as regards non-finality. It was received without enthusiasm by the House, which, I think, shared the Naval view.

*   *   *   *

Saw Beatty at the Admiralty and found him more amenable, but still complained very much of the ungraciousness of the statement, and of the absence of any assurance that the Board still had the

Government's confidence. I subsequently rang up Davidson[1] and got him to draft a suitable letter from the Prime Minister, and also tried to get him put in something to meet the point that the view of responsibility had not been accepted and that there was now an element of dual responsibility, which I read out at the Board next morning.

3 August 1923
Board at 11.30; made a brief statement on the Air question before reading out PM's letter, and there was no dissent from my view, that we try and work as well as we can, and the better we work, the more likely it is to break down in our direction before long.

1 November 1923
We had a Board this afternoon at which Beatty reopened the whole air question, on general principles. We argued the matter at great length, my main point being that we cannot go back directly on a Cabinet decision without giving it a reasonable trial, and that after all, either way, a period of transition was inevitable. I was clearly not disposed to even consider the memorandum; Beatty suggested the Sea Lords should think over the matter further, and we left it at that.

128. Beatty: First Sea Lord's Proposed Memorandum for the Cabinet

(Item 4 for Board Agenda)
[ADM 167/68]   5.11.23

The Admiralty has given long and earnest consideration to the recommendations set forth in Command Paper 1938 for determining the relations between the Navy and the Air Force, and, in compliance with the decision of the Cabinet, to adopt these recommendations for the time being, is formulating proposals for putting them into effect. This is being done on the understanding that their adoption is regarded as an experiment.

2.   The Board is however bound to represent that this decision will prolong still further the period during which there will exist

---

[1]J. C. C. Davidson, later Viscount (1889–1970): Conservative politician; MP 1920; Parliamentary Private Secretary to Bonar Law and then Baldwin 1921–2; Parliamentary Secretary to Admiralty 1924–6 and a strong supporter of Beatty against Churchill on the cruiser programme; relinquished office to become Chairman of Conservative Party 1926; Viscount 1937.

a division of responsibility, which is definitely and inevitably prejudicial to the efficiency of the Fleet in time of peace, and would
invite disaster in time of war.

The Lords Commissioners of the Admiralty have the honour
to request that this serious representation may be placed on
record.

129. *Admiralty Board Minute 1747*

[ADM 167/67]   8 Nov. 1923

The First Lord stated that he did not think that the case of the
Admiralty would be any further advanced by repeating to the
Cabinet in a Memorandum views which he had already personally
expressed to the Cabinet. He agreed however, that notwithstanding this point, it was open to the Sea Lords, should they deem it
their duty to do so, to put on record the views expressed in the
draft Memorandum, in the form of a Memorandum addressed to
himself, with the request that he would forward it to the Prime
Minister. He was prepared to forward such a Memorandum by
the Sea Lords to the Prime Minister and call the latter's attention
to the serious nature of the representation.

The First Sea Lord stated that the Sea Lords would prepare a
Memorandum accordingly.

130. *Memorandum by the Sea Lords on the Balfour Committee's Report*

[Copy]

[Cab. 21/267B]   9.11.23
[(CP 464(23)]

The Sea Lords have given long and earnest consideration to the
recommendations set forth in Command Paper 1938 for determining the relations between the Navy and the Air Force, and, in
compliance with the decision of the Cabinet to give these recommendations a trial, are in communication with the Air Ministry
with a view to putting them into effect.

2.   The Sea Lords are however bound to represent that the
decision will prolong still further the period during which there
will exist a division of responsibility which is definitely and inevi-

tably prejudicial to the efficiency of the Fleet in time of peace and will invite disaster in time of war.

(Signed)   A. K. WAISTELL
ROGER KEYES
ALGERNON D. BOYLE
CYRIL FULLER
H. F. OLIVER
BEATTY

131. Beatty: Speech at Lord Mayor's Banquet 1923

[Draft Text]

[BTY/11/8/23]   [9] November 1923

It is my proud privelege [*sic*] to reply to the toast of the Royal Navy, and in occupying your time to listen to me, which I will endeavour to make as short as possible, I assume that the interest of the peoples of this Empire is as great to-day in the well-being and efficiency of the British Navy as it ever has been in the past; and therefore if you will permit me, I will touch on some of the questions which have struck me will be of interest.

After the war quite rightly and properly we commenced on the Navy, as did other Departments, with the reduction of ships, personnel and material.

This policy, fateful as it was, has been carried out thoroughly and effectively, having due regard to the commitments of the Empire which it is the duty of the Navy to safeguard.

In 1921 at the Imperial Conference which was then held, the naval policy of the Empire was laid down that the needs of the Empire require the maintenance of a Navy at least as strong as that of the greatest Naval Power.

This was followed by the Washington Conference, where, as is well known, the strength of the Navies of the Great Powers was definitely laid down and accepted in so far as capital ships and aircraft carriers were concerned, in the ratio of 5 Great Britain, 5 United States, 3 Japan, 1.7 France and Italy. To all other vessels such as Light Cruisers, Destroyers, Submarines, etc., there is no limit beyond that of limiting the size of the Light Cruiser to 10,000 tons.

It was recognised that our peculiar situation as an Empire called for very different treatment in the matter of Light Cruisers to other nations. This can easily be recognised as essential when it is understood and realised that this Empire of ours is a Commonwealth of Nations spread all over the world whose lines of communication are the sea; and it is for the protection of those lines of communications that Light Cruisers are all important.

Owing to the need for economy, our Light Cruiser building programme has not kept pace with the needs of the Empire. The Light Cruisers are wearing out; their lives are short and the time has arrived when it is necessary to replace these worn out vessels by new and up-to-date ships. The Prime Minister has already announced the forthcoming replacement of the old County Class which were specially laid down in 1901 for trade protection.

As I have said, the situation as regards Capital Ships was agreed to and decided for us at the Washington Conference, and the necessary steps have already been taken to provide the British Empire with her allowance of this type of vessel.

I think it would be as well to say something on this type of vessel. It is a type which has caused considerable controversy and comment, and therefore it would seem desirable that something should be said.

The question arises – what is a Capital Ship? – and it seems to me that it can be no better expressed than by defining it as an inexpugnable ship combining the greatest offensive powers with the greatest powers of defence, with the addition of speed and good sea keeping qualities.

The Capital Ship of to-day has to meet very different forms of attack than 10 years ago. Not only have guns and torpedoes developed immensely, but submarines and aircraft are additional weapons with which to threaten the life of the Capital Ship.

The gun of to-day has greater velocity and bursting charge. The protecting armour has had to be increased accordingly; this armour helps to deal incidentally with other forms of attack.

The increase in the efficiency of the torpedo has led to the adoption of new methods of protection. The submarine, which has increased the attack from that particular weapon, has necessitated the development of these new methods of protection. Anti-submarine methods have had to be devised to minimise this form of attack. These methods have made great progress, and the race between the submarine and the anti-submarine devices is somewhat the same as that between the gun and the armour. To-day the development of the anti-submarine is more than keeping pace with the submarine, and to the Power in command of the surface of the sea the submarine is not a great menace. To a

Power weak on the surface of the sea it must remain a serious menace.

Then we come to the Air.

In a certain limited radius of action aircraft are a menace to ships, but are not a menace sufficiently great that means cannot be devised whereby the Capital Ship cannot counter and defeat this form of attack.

In any case, the great oceans upon which our trade and communications are maintained are as free from air influence as ever.

In arriving at the decision that a Capital Ship can be produced which can withstand all the attacks to which it may be subjected, the opinions of Naval Officers who have had the greatest experience and are best qualified to judge both at the Admiralty and in the Fleets, have been taken into account. These opinions have been confirmed by the decisions of the United States of America and Japan.

Turning again to the question of the Air as a new weapon of the fleet, I would like to say that nowhere is the importance of this arm more fully recognised than in HM Navy, the development of which must be all-important to naval forces. It is not too much to say that in the future no ship and no fleet will be fully equipped for war without aircraft. Aircraft have become an additional naval weapon required by ships working on the surface of the water. A unit of the Fleet, such as a Light Cruiser Squadron, would not be complete without these aircraft any more than it would be without guns or torpedoes, and the fleets of the future will be commanded by officers with as intimate knowledge of the Air as of the gun and the submarine. The intelligent use of the Air for reconnaissance purposes will improve the quality of the information which the Admiral now possesses derived from Light Cruisers; and it may well be that in the future the Commander-in-Chief of a fleet with his staff may be quartered on board an aircraft carrier; during operations his Staff Officers being in the Air, far in advance of the fleet, giving information which will enable him to so dispose his forces to obtain strategic and tactical advantages which would culminate in great victory. But let me add this – as in the case of the submarine the full use, the freedom of action, and the value of aircraft working with the Navy, can only be secured by the Power which commands the surface of the sea; without command of the surface the Aircraft could not function. For these reasons it is of paramount importance that the Air Arm of the Navy shall be developed and improved side by side with the Gunnery Arm, the Torpedo Arm, the Submarine Arm, and all the other arms which go to make up the efficiency of the fleet.

We will now pass to another naval question which is exciting considerable interest and comment – Singapore – This project of developing Singapore, or I might say of putting Singapore in order so that it shall be of use to the Navy, has been attacked by many as if it was something new. This is far from the case; for many years it was a naval base, a base which was recognised by many of the most astute as being the best strategical position in the Far East; indeed the gate of the East – (quote Sir Stamford Raffles).[1]

The Western Pacific has always been a Station for strong British Forces. The needs for this strength are surely as strong to-day as they were in the past. Our possessions are no less, and have become more valuable.

The Empire was founded on commercial enterprise. It was considered in the past necessary and desirable to protect that enterprise. The Flag followed the Trade and not the Trade the Flag, and our commitments in the Pacific are now greater than they were before.

Australia and New Zealand have increased in population and prosperity. They are portions of the Empire which require as much protection or more protection to-day than ever they did in the past. The wealth of the Crown Colonies has increased and our trade in the Indian Ocean is more important.

If protection was required 20 years ago, how much more so is it required to-day. If those who are responsible for our destinies say that protection is not required, that we can afford to live on the good-will of others, then Singapore is not necessary; but if on the other hand we think it is desirable to safeguard our interests in that part of the world, then Singapore is necessary, for without it they cannot be secured.

132. *Admiralty to Air Ministry*

[Copy]

[ADM. 116/2236]   13 Nov 1923

In reply to Air Ministry letter 447/85/23/56 of 12th October 1923, I am commanded by My Lords Commissioners of the Admiralty

[1]Sir Stamford Raffles (1781–1826): clerk in East India Company aged 14; recommended purchase of Singapore from Sultan of Johore, 1819, recognising its strategic and commercial importance, which he developed 1822–3.

to state that they have given most careful consideration to the Air Council's proposals for implementing the recommendations of Cmd. 1938.[1] In Enclosure I, herewith, will be found the Admiralty's views on the Air Council's proposals, together with Admiralty proposals for giving effect to the recommendations.

2.   My Lords desire to point out that the Report contained in Cmd. 1938 does not dispute the principle that the Admiralty ought to be solely responsible for the fighting efficiency of the Fleet, and, consequently the Admiralty proposals have been drawn up with a view to ensuring this, as far as the provisions of Cmd. 1938 allow.

3.   Further, although every effort will be made by the Admiralty to make the scheme work on the basis herein proposed, it is recognised by Their Lordships that such a trial must be regarded as an experiment.

4.   When the Air Council have expressed their agreement with the proposals herein, a Joint Committee can then be formed to discuss the details arising therefrom.

[O. M.]
[Secretary]

133.   *To his wife* [Paris]

[BTY/17/64/4–7]   Hanover Lodge
23.1.24

Such a day, the old 1st Lord out and the new 1st Lord in. Two Board meetings, and taken old Peter[2] off to Eton and planted him securely there.

*   *   *   *

Today, as I have already said, Amery has departed and one called Lord Chelmsford,[3] who distinguished himself as a complete failure as the Viceroy of India, and has now thought fit to be a renegade from the ranks of Conservatism and join Labour and the Socialists. I should have preferred to have had a real Labour man to a hybrid of this nature. The Parliamentary Secretary is a gentle-

---

[1] The Report of the Balfour Committee, 1923.
[2] Beatty's younger son, born 2 April 1910: suffered poor health; became a racehorse trainer and in 1938 produced the Derby winner.
[3] See note 3 on page 222.

man!! called Mr Ammon[1] who was in the Post Office as a clerk some years ago and was kicked out for trying to raise a mutiny among the employees there. The Civil Lord is one Mr Frank Hodges,[2] an out and out Labour man who organised the big strike the summer before last. So, we have a really bright lot to deal with, and the Lord only knows what the outcome will be.

However, we must wait and see and not be too precipitate in our view or in our actions.

134. *To his wife* [Hyères]

[BTY/17/64/9–10]   Admiralty
                                                                  25.1.24

. . . I have made the acquaintance of Mr Hodges, the new Civil Lord, a regular Labour man with an intelligent face and good head on him. We made friends and he seemed grateful that I didn't bite him or was disagreeable. He evidently has brains and a will of his own. Also I received the new Financial and Parliamentary secretary, Mr Ammon, who I told you of. He also is a typical Labour MP, and I think we shall get on alright when we once get to work.

I had a long conversation with Chelmsford and I like him. He seems reasonable and open-minded, but is in a very difficult position. I think he will see things from our point of view and it remains to be seen what strength he has in the new Cabinet and if he carries enough guns.

*   *   *   *

Generally speaking there is no news of interest. Everybody seems to be waiting for the Government to move now they have filled up all the appointments. We shall have a [–] further struggle over the Naval Estimates, which were already cut to the bone, and I suppose we will have another struggle . . .

---

[1]Charles Ammon, later Lord Camberwell, had to defend Beatty's cruiser programme in the House of Commons. He was again Parliamentary Secretary 1929–31.
[2]Frank Hodges, then secretary of the miners' union had in fact been a moderate in the lead-up to the coal strike of 1921.

135. *Sir Alan Lascelles*[1] *to Sir Owen Morshead*[2]

[Memorandum]

[RA Geo V K.1918/184A]

Buckingham Palace
3rd June 1952

* * * *

As regards Lord Chelmsford's acceptance of office under Ramsay Macdonald, Lord Stamfordham only tells half the story. Chelmsford's main reason was that, as Ramsay and Haldane had already told him, the first Labour Government could not be formed unless some other peer would agree to accept office and so provide the necessary quota of Secretaries of State in the House of Lords. Chelmsford, (who had never mixed in party politics) thought it would be very dangerous if a Labour Government were to be shipwrecked on this particular rock, and so agreed to fill the gap as First Lord of the Admiralty. He stipulated that (*1*) the cruiser programme should be carried out; (*2*) the fortification of Singapore should continue; (*3*) he should never be asked in Cabinet to give an opinion on any party question.

Chelmsford told me all this at my son's birthday party on January 11th, 1924; all his conditions were loyally observed by Ramsay.

136. *To his wife* [Hyères]

[BTY/17/64/11–14]

Admiralty
Saturday [26 Jan. 1924]

* * * *

I have had some trouble with the new Chancellor of the Exchequer who says he cannot accept the Naval Estimates, but I don't think his opposition will come to anything very serious, and I am sure the Cabinet will not wish to face the new Parliament with an immediate break with the Admiralty. But still, it all makes work, for they have to be convinced, and this continual arguing & wrangling with successive governments is very wearing and trying.

[1]Sir Alan Frederick Lascelles (1887–1981): Private Secretary to King George VI 1943–52. In 1924 he had been Assistant Private Secretary to the Prince of Wales, the future Edward VIII.
[2]Royal Librarian and Archivist at Windsor Castle.

I am afraid Chelmsford is not a strong man but we shall see, and very soon find out if he is worth anything at all.

*   *   *   *

137. *To his wife* [Hyères]

[BTY/17/64/35–42]
Mentmore
Leighton Buzzard
Saturday night
[undated]

Here I am after a very bad day's hunting. Harry Dalmeny[1] very kindly asked me to come here after hunting & stay the night . . .

I have to go to London tomorrow because I have to prepare for the first assaults on the Navy by the new Cabinet and we cannot afford to be defeated in the 1st round. There is a decided Press campaign, one half of which (the stable half) represented by *Times* [*sic*], the *Daily Telegraph, Morning Post*, and some of the picture papers are on the side of the Admiralty, and the other half against us. They try to represent that I am a dictator and have bullied two Cabinets into swallowing schemes for the aggrandisement of the British Navy, but now I am up against the Labour Cabinet I am to face defeat. It is unfortunate because it prejudges the situation and puts the Labour Cabinet on the defensive and makes them think they have to withstand the wicked machinations of an unscrupulous Board of Admiralty. However I dare say they will listen to reason especially as I have a good deal of support in the House of Commons.

*   *   *   *

---

[1]Harry Primrose, Lord Dalmeny (1882–1974): son of 5th Earl of Rosebery, Liberal Prime Minister 1894–5; succeeded as 6th Earl 1929.

138. *Notes of Sea Lords' Meeting*[1]

[Extract]

[BTY/8/5/21]   28 January 1924

CRUISER BUILDING PROGRAMME

The question of the new construction programme was considered by the Sea Lords in view of the new situation consequent on the change of Government.

This situation was a changed one, as it was not now the intention to consider the question of relieving unemployment. The sole consideration was the minimum requirements of the Admiralty to meet the naval situation.

After discussion the 1st Sea Lord requested the 3rd Sea Lord to confer with the ACNS and the Naval Staff and put forward for the consideration of the Sea Lords a proposed programme based on the construction in 1924–25 of five light cruisers, 1 submarine depot ship, 1 destroyer depot ship, 2 destroyers, and such other additional units as might be considered necessary.

It was suggested that the aim should be to foreshadow a total construction programme for ensuing years up to 1926–27 of approximately £10,000,000 annually, and after that year, £7,000,000 annually.

Fleet Air Arm

The Sea Lords had under consideration the situation as it now existed between the Admiralty and the Air Ministry as regards the Fleet Air Arm. It was decided that this question must be put aside for the moment whilst Singapore and the construction programme required priority. It was agreed however, that the time had arrived for the Cabinet to be informed that the Admiralty found it impossible to carry out the recommendations of the Sub-Committee. That a complete deadlock had been reached, and that they were unable, owing to the attitude of the Air Ministry in regard to the question of allowing Naval Officers to fill the higher appointments in the Fleet Air Arm, to call for volunteers.

Further, on the vital principle of finance, the Air Ministry refused to consider the essential principle that the responsibility

---

[1]A further extract from this document, dealing with Singapore, is Document 204 below.

should be invested in the authority on whose estimates the money was taken.

The deplorable state of the situation, its reaction on naval efficiency, the dissatisfaction of the Admiralty in regard to the position, the failure to take advantage of the Imperial Cruise to gain naval air experience, all these factors should be developed in a letter to the Cabinet, and the attention of the Cabinet should be drawn to the Sea Lords' former memorandum stating their grave anxiety at the departure from single control, which they look upon as vital.

The 1st Sea Lord undertook himself to write a memorandum to the 1st Lord as a preliminary measure, inviting the attention of the 1st Lord to the Sea Lords' memorandum, and asking that the attention of the present Cabinet should be called to this, which was circulated to the late Prime Minister and his colleagues only a few days before the dissolution of the last Parliament.[1]

139.   *To his wife* [Hyères]

[BTY/17/64/29–34]   Hanover Lodge
                                    Thursday [31 Jan. 1924]

*   *   *   *

Surely it would be the height of unreasonableness to go all that way to find the sun and then to turn round & come back again in a fortnight. The very fact that such an idea should obtain in your mind indicates quite clearly that you are not fit to do such a thing. What does the Doctor say?? You are an ill woman and yet you will not be treated as an ill woman. If you could only bring yourself to live the life, unexciting as it is, of an invalid for a short time, you would store up enough good health and reserve of nerve strength that would help you to get well in no time . . .

I am having a pretty bad time just now and the Press are attacking the Admiralty in general and me in particular because of the Naval Estimates of which they know nothing. And they say I am trying to browbeat a well-meaning, long-suffering Labour government. I can stand a lot of that kind of abuse. But we are having an anxious time just now, and shall have, until Parliament meets on the 12th, when I hope for some relief.

---

[1]The General Election of December 1923 had resulted in a Conservative defeat in the Commons on 21 January 1924 by a combined Labour/Liberal vote and Ramsay MacDonald's 1st Labour Government's taking office.

I am not pessimistic though and think we shall win through in the end.

I like the 1st Lord, he is reasonable and a help, but it remains to be seen as to what firmness he possesses and whether he can stand against the whirlwind of assaults that are sure to be hurled at us in the next fortnight.

. I keep receiving letters from Admirals and others who are interested in the Navy, urging me to stick to the ships and saying that they trust me to save the naval situation. Very flattering, no doubt, but they do not contain much helpful suggestion. However it is something to know that one's efforts are appreciated by somebody. And it cheers one up and gives one heart to continue the struggle.

I think I have succeeded in making Mr Ammon and Mr Hodges our staunch supporters, and they carry some weight in the Labour councils [sic].

*   *   *   *

In these days we want all the courage we possess, they are difficult indeed & you would help me so much, far more than you can ever think, if you could write me a cheerful, reasonable letter. The accumulated weight of all my troubles are [sic] heavy and you could lighten them if you would.

140.   *To his wife* [Hyères]

[BTY/17/65/2–3]   Admiralty
Friday [1 Feb. 1924]

*   *   *   *

The struggle between the Admiralty and the Government grows acute and the more we examine it the more we see that we must stick our toes in, stick to our guns, and if necessary they can kick us out. I won't mind if they do, personally, and would immediately come to join you, so don't come rattling home in a hurry as I might be coming out to join you. Of course it would be a lamentable thing from the Service point of view, but I cannot do more than I have done and intend to stick to.

The Press are getting very busy and the large majority uphold the Admiralty, but a violent and unpleasant section of course put the worst construction on our motives and our actions but that really doesn't matter either one way or the other. The 1st Lord is upholding us in so far as he can, but I don't think he is strong enough, and before the whole thing is decided against us I shall demand to see the Prime Minister, so that he at least shall be under no misunderstanding as to what it all means.

So, there it is and the next week will I trust see us either out of the picture or in a stronger position . . .

141. *To his wife* [Hyères]

[BTY/17/65/4–11]   Hanover Lodge
Saturday night
[2 Feb. 1924]

I got your two letters of Wednesday and Thursday today and am greatly distressed at all you say. It seems so hopeless to make you understand my position and the very real difficulties that are in front of me.

I have tried to explain to you that things being as they are, it is quite impossible for me to get away at this juncture, *but* that if the Government persist in the attitude they are adopting at present I shall be a free man in a very short time . . .

It seems to me I have been trying to get you well for the last four months, but you give me no credit for my endeavours. My dear sweetheart be reasonable. I offered to take you out at the only time I could get away, but you would not get away. Then you said you must go just when the time came that I could not go. We got Eugénie to go with you, and now you say she hates you. All I can say is that in the two letters I have had from her, nothing could be nicer than the way she writes of you, and how well you have struggled to get well and how hard it is for you. Now you say she knows very much more about me than you do, because she told you I was an ill man. Well I suppose Godfrey[1] told her that, — *I did not.* When I was thanking Godfrey for letting her go, I did tell him that the Doctor told me that if the strain of looking after you of the last 4 months went on, I should break down; there was nothing so catching and that I simply could not go on doing it and doing my work with insufficient sleep, and the strain on the mind was terrific & nobody could foresee what the result would be . . .

You say, I can hunt, yes, the very little I have had has helped

[1]Captain Bryan Godfrey-Faussett, whose wife, Beatty's mistress, Eugénie, had been persuaded to accompany the mentally ailing Lady Beatty to France. See *Beatty Papers I*, pp. 375, 426–7, 551–4, 572–4.

me to stand the strain and I can work well. My dear heart that has had the effect of taking me out of myself and making me forget temporarily the troubles at home, & kept me from brooding over them. I did not tell you all these things. I did not want to add to your unhappiness.

*   *   *   *

I went to see the King this morning, and he is very troubled with the situation and what may come out of it. He begged me for the good of the Service and the State to remain at the Admiralty. The Navy was the only stable thing left and it would soon crumple up if I left. He was very nice & complimentary and very much moved and asked me to treat our conversation as private, so please remember not to mention it to *anybody*.

I have had a combined letter from some Admirals, the most prominent on the list, begging me to remain firm; 'that the Service is fortunate in my being its head and however disinclined I may be to continue the wearisome work, it would be a material disaster if I left; the Service trusts me and knows that I will never permit its discipline to be undermined or its strength reduced to dangerous limits' — That is a quotation paraphrased. So you see, dear heart, somebody trusts me and I should be unworthy of my trust if I left them in the lurch now. And I cannot do my work properly when my mind is unsettled and harassed by private affairs. If you will hold on for another week or ten days things may be entirely different.

I want to go to Malta to see about changing the distribution of the Fleet and O. de B. has written to say that he would send the *Bryony*, the C-in-C of the Mediterranean's yacht, to anywhere I liked for me. And you could come too, and we could sail from Cannes or anywhere along the coast. But I could not fix anything up for certain until the present situation is cleared, but another week or ten days should do that.

*   *   *   *

Bless you dear heart, it won't take you as long to read as it took me to write this long epistle, but I earnestly pray that you will understand not only what is written but the spirit and the motives which lie behind the words. And the only one that moves me or can count, is that we shall dig ourselves out of this slough of despond into which we are sinking, face the facts with courage & determination, and remember that our lives are intended to be useful, not only to ourselves in providing enjoyment, but to the world at large & our own portion of it in particular, and we have many happy years before us to live with the Boys and see them grow up into useful men, happy and contented, and this all depends upon us doing the right thing _now_, and making no mistakes.

142.   *To his wife* [Hyères]

[BTY/17/65/18–21]   Admiralty
                                                                          [4].2.24

Just returned from hours of unpleasant and very controversial arguments with the new Chancellor of the Exchequer in particular and the whole Cabinet in general. Nothing was decided and we have to go back again later on a day to be fixed. It was most unsatisfactory but there were gleams of hope of being able to arrive at a compromise, but it was not encouraging. You will see how perfectly impossible it is for me to come rattling out to join you at Hyères and I am between the devil and the deep sea. The First Lord supported me nobly, but he is very pessimistic and has just informed me that he did not see how he could possibly stop on in a Cabinet with the views expressed by Mr Snowden, the Chancellor of the Exchequer. Of course, if that is the case there will be a débacle, and I do not see how anybody can continue to attempt to administer the Navy under such conditions. In that case you may very well see me coming out to you, having wiped the dust of the Admiralty off my feet. So, for heaven's sake do not be in a hurry to post home. The next week should decide things one way or another.

*   *   *   *

If you could see the letters I get and the appeals I receive from many quarters to stick it out & try and save the situation, you would realise the magnitude of my task and the heavy responsibility that lies on my shoulders just now. And I think you would be pleased that so many people have faith in me & would be proud of the part I am able to play in the affairs of our distraught & wretched country, instead of trying to goad me into being a traitor to the Service and the Country. For heaven's sake be reasonable sweetheart mine and be a help instead of a hindrance to me just now.

*   *   *   *

143. *To his wife* [Hyères]

[BTY/17/65/23–24]   [Hanover Lodge]
                                                                   Tuesday night
                                                                   [6 Feb. 1924]

I have had a very strenuous day and am now writing to you after
dinner before going to bed. There is no doubt that the advent of
the Labour Government has added to our troubles and very much
to our work. But that was only to be expected at first. It is to be
hoped that as time goes on and they have to act on the defensive
in the House that our situation will be relieved and their time
more fully occupied in defending themselves in the House, that
we shall be relieved to a great extent. Our trouble lies in the fact
that we have got to educate them and in doing so we have to
disabuse their minds of a great many fallacies that exist, and
substitute the questions which are of real importance to the
Empire. In fact, we have to teach them Imperialism. With some
it is easy, but with others it is difficult. For instance, Mr J. H.
Thomas,[1] Stephen Walsh[2] and Clynes are already very sound on
these questions, and Lords Haldane and Chelmsford ought not to
require any teaching, merely being brought up to date. With these
five thinking together we shall start with a fairly good nucleus to
deal with the remainder. It is quite extraordinary the amount of
real ignorance that exists in their minds on questions of the greatest importance.

We had another long sitting today of an educational character,
and although it seemed a waste of time, I hope most sincerely it
will bear fruit. I already see signs that they as a whole are beginning to grasp some of the essentials. But it is wearing [*sic*] kind
of work and leaves me rather like a piece of chewed string at the
end of it.

---

[1]J. H. Thomas (1874–1949): Railway trade unionist and Labour Leader; MP
from 1910; led railway strike of 1919; Colonial Secretary 1924; Lord Privy Seal
1929; Dominions Secretary 1930; followed MacDonald into National Government
as Dominions Secretary 1931–5; Colonial Secretary 1935–6; resigned after Budget
leak.
[2]Stephen Walsh (1859–1929): Trade Union and Labour leader; MP 1906–29;
Parliamentary Secretary Ministry of National Service 1917; an advocate of compul-
sory military service; Secretary for War 1924.

144. *To his wife* [Hyères]

[BTY/17/65/35–38]   Turf Club
                                                                Piccadilly W1
                                                                  Friday night
                                                                [8 Feb. 1924]

I have had a wearisome and tiring day of endless discussions and
did not get away until 8.30, and as I have to go back to see the
Sea Lords I came here to get some dinner. We shall have to come
to some understanding as to whether we can go on or not. The
new Chancellor of the Exchequer, Mr Snowden, is a bitter pacifist
and would do away with the Navy altogether if he had half a
chance. I told them that if they wanted to be defeated in the
House they were going the right way about it. That is the last
thing they want. They are just beginning to realise the sweets of
office and the advantages of possessing £500 a year, and most of
them have no desire to relinquish that.

   If they give in, well and good, if not we can but go, and they
will find some difficulty in finding others to take our place.

*   *   *   *

145. *To his wife* [Hyères]

[BTY/17/65/58–59]   Admiralty
                                                                       15.2.24

. . . I do like our new First Lord, he is a gentleman & is as straight
as a line. He might not be of a very strong character but we can
help him in that direction and we can believe what he says. He
is also a hard worker and gets through a lot and grasps the salient
points of the various questions which come up. The thorn in our
side is Mr Philip Snowden, the Chancellor of the Exchequer who
is an out and out pacifist. Some of the others like Thomas, &
Walsh are quite reasonable & sound men, and old Haldane has
been a great help to us and supports us on every occasion. But I
am afraid they are going to be difficult as there are many pacifists
among the junior officials. However my two, Mr Ammon and Mr
Hodges, both men that count in councils [*sic*] of the party are
seeing reason and are a help. I like Mr Frank Hodges especially.
He was the leader of the miners and led the big strike two sum-
mers ago, a fine fellow with a good head on him, and I think he
is a friend of mine now, you would like him.

*   *   *   *

I asked old Asquith how long he gave the Government to remain in office, but he wd. not commit himself, Lloyd George has prophesied 6 months, as I think I said before, this is either too much or too little. They will either go in the next month or hang on for 12 months.

*   *   *   *

146. *To his wife* [Hyères]

[BTY/17/65/79–79]					Admiralty
						21.2.24

*   *   *   *

We have won our first victory over the Government, but they have had some trouble over it in the House this afternoon and I had to go down to bolster them up and give them material. They are beginning to lean on us now, so that is to the good. The Liberal party tried to play a dirty trick on them and thought they would bring about their defeat, but we have had to whip up the Conservative party to come to their rescue; the irony of fate, their friends have attacked them & their hated enemies have to rescue them. It was on the building of the Lt. Cruisers, 5 in number. The Government gave in to Admiralty demands and are being attacked by the Liberals for doing so.

*   *   *   *

147. *To his wife* [Hyères]

[BTY/17/65/88–91]					Hanover Lodge
					Saturday [23 Feb. 1924]

. . . I am moving [?] for all I am worth to get the Committee which has been appointed to enquire into Singapore to begin at once, and two or three days at the outside will be sufficient to deal with that question. It is extraordinary to note the result of the Division in the House of Commons on the question of cruisers. Only 73 Liberal members supported the motion, that is voted against the Admiralty. Over 20 Liberal members and the whole of the Labour party & the whole of the Conservative party supported the Admiralty, including extremists of every description, pacifist, communist, socialist, etc. It really is a very remarkable result and one which gives ample food for thought. That they should have done so is registered against them, and they can't go back on it, and it can always be held up against them should occasion require. The Prime Minister should see, & I think does, what an immensely strong position it puts him in. Who would have thought a few years, or even months ago that we should see an overwhelming majority of the House support the proposition of a strong Navy. They have no doubt been manoeuvred into this & probably is against the grain, but there it is. To save themselves, they are committed to the maintenance of Naval strength. It is a great triumph and one that we must not lose sight of. We couldn't have done so well with a Conservative party in power.

On the whole the Prime Minister has strengthened his position, both personal and political, in the country as a conscientious practical ruler, but I don't believe he sees that. Still, we can point that out and it will help with the big problems that lie before us. I have had an exhausting day of getting ready for the next round and we shall be ready for them as soon as I can get them ready to start. The Admiralty are working like one man and no stone is being left unturned. Our Labour confrères are as enthusiastic as anybody else and are wholeheartedly in the job. So we ought to win through, but of course one can never be quite certain what wind will deflect the political mind.

Lloyd George neglected to vote, but his son[1] & his secretary & henchmen all voted for the Admiralty & he abstained himself, but went away. I suppose he did not wish to show himself as being in entire opposition to his own Party . . .

148. *Beatty: Minute on Naval Armaments Limitation*

[ADM 1/8683/131]   23.4.24

Controller

ACNS

The Cabinet has directed the Admiralty to prepare a Memorandum on the question of the limitation of armaments, which, so far as can be seen at present, will resolve itself into proposals for the extension of the Washington agreements.

All means by which the financial burdens of naval armaments can be reduced without endangering the safety of the Empire, must be explored.

In the case of capital ships there appear two possible methods:—

---

[1]Gwilym Lloyd George, later Viscount Tenby (1894–1967): second son of David Lloyd George; Liberal MP 1922–4, 1929–50.

(a) By reducing the present tonnage limits of 35,000 tons to something in the nature of, say, 25,000 tons.

(b) By extending the age of replacement from 20 years to 25 years.

The interests of the Empire require that the limit of tonnage should not be reduced to such an extent as to:–

(a) Decrease the power of capital ships to withstand air or under-water attack.

(b) Put the limit at such a low figure that 3rd rate Naval Powers can afford to construct such ships.

The endurance and speed of capital ships should closely approximate to that of *Nelson*.

In the case of cruisers the limits of tonnage and armament might be reduced from 10,000 tons and 8″ guns to, say, 7,000 tons and 6″ guns, if good endurance and sea-keeping qualities can be maintained.

What should the tonnage be under these circumstances?

On the supposition that cruisers would be limited to 6″ guns, what limits should be placed on flotilla leaders and destroyers, as regards tonnage and armaments, and on submarines as regards armament?

Please report on the above as soon as possible as the preparation of the Memorandum is a matter of urgency.

B. 23.4

149. *To his wife* [Cap Ferrat]

[BTY/17/69/18–21]   Hanover Lodge
                                                     Friday [9 Jan. 1925]

. . . You will have observed in the papers the wrangle that has been going on in the USA over the American Navy & now they are voting enormous sums of money to build a lot of cruisers and are to lay down 8 at once. This makes it very awkward for us both in the political world and the naval world, and I am hoping it will assist us in the demand for 6 cruisers to be built this coming year. I do not think we shall have difficulty in making a really strong and sound case, but the economists have got their mind on a reduction of the Income Tax for which they anticipate receiving much applause and a great deal of credit and simply cannot

& will not look at any other point of view. If they persist it will show once again how penny and pound foolish our legislators are, and in the end they will incur a considerable amount of odium, but there are none so blind as those who won't see, and that I fear is the case just now.

Winston is spreading himself in Paris just at present, and being very much in the limelight is very pleased with himself in particular and the world in general.

* * * *

150. *To his wife* [Cap Ferrat]

[BTY/17/69/76–79]   Hanover Lodge
Thursday Morning
[22 Jan. 1925]

. . . I've had a very strenuous day battling as usual over the problems of the Estimates. They called a meeting to deal with them this afternoon, that is Wednesday afternoon, and for 4 hours we argued with Winston and the Treasury Myrmidons & I think on the whole were successful. But it was a hard struggle, and takes a lot out of me, to concentrate on gigantic figures for a prolonged period, and have to battle with those whose life is spent in a maze of figures. There is no doubt that we have all got our crosses to bear, but mine seem so varied and different that it is bewildering at times. The problems are so different and each one so difficult. If they were all of the same kind it would be comparatively easy, but what with my public difficulties and private problems, they seem incapable of solution.

* * * *

151. *To his wife* [Cap Ferrat]

[BTY/17/69/98–99]   Admiralty
Monday 26th [Jan. 1925]

* * * *

That extraordinary fellow Winston has gone mad, economically mad, and no sacrifice is too great to achieve what in his short-sightedness is the panacea for all evils, to take 1/- off the Income Tax. Nobody outside a lunatic asylum expects a shilling off the Income Tax this Budget. But he has made up his mind that it is the only thing he can do to justify his appointment as Chancellor of the Exchequer, and is prepared to throw everything, all his ideas of Imperialism etc, to the winds to achieve this one thing. The result will be a split in the Conservative party and nothing else.

As we at the Admiralty are the principal spending department he attacks us with virulence, and now proclaims that a Navy is a quite unnecessary luxury. This as you may imagine does not go down very well with the die-hards which are a very considerable portion of the Conservative party, who already hate Winston like poison, & consequently the silly fellow is providing them with fresh ammunition with which to destroy him. Of course we are after him & do not give way, and there is likely to be a deadlock of a sensational kind before long.

Poor old Bridgeman our 1st Lord takes a very gloomy view and sees his job fading away from him. But I have heartened him up a lot, and I think he will stand firm. It's then a case of Winston coming off his perch or a split in the Government followed by the resignation of the Board of Admiralty.

Every year it is the same struggle, we have won through up to now, but we are up against tougher stuff just now, and it requires very careful watching, and a false move will court disaster – it's a very interesting situation, but fraught with difficulties. However I am full of hope. We stick together . . .

152. *Beatty to Bridgeman*
[Copy]
[BTY/8/7/2]   27th January 1925

In order that you may be under no misapprehension as to the strength of my views on the question of marriage allowance for Naval Officers, which we were discussing this afternoon. I am writing this note to say that it is a matter which affects vitally the wellbeing of the whole Service.

The Officers have been very patient and have behaved exceedingly well. They have made no efforts by sub rosa methods or otherwise to air their troubles in public, in the press, or in any other way, but the fact that they have refrained from giving publicity to their grievance does not mean that their feelings are less strong.

They have very properly relied on the Admiralty to fight their battle, and they know that the Admiralty has had the question in hand. They know that a Committee has sat under the Presidency of Admiral Goodenough, and they know that that Committee could have come to only one possible conclusion.

They are therefore relying quite definitely on things being put right. The whole Board, after exhaustive enquiry is completely satisfied as to the facts of the situation, and I should regard it as a betrayal of the Officers to acquiesce in any proposal to drop it out of the estimates.

The loyalty, which has been strained unduly by delay in doing justice, cannot be taxed much more, and I feel I cannot remain responsible for the discipline of the Navy if the question is ruled out in face of the overwhelming evidence which has been produced.

153.   *To his wife* [Cap Ferrat]

[BTY/17/69/102–104]   Admiralty
Wednesday [28 Jan. 1925]

Two very sweet and dear letters from you yesterday, which have cheered me up and made me feel a lot better, and of course we are going to live happily together . . . The only thing after all in life to achieve perfect happiness is to have occupation of a kind that one feels that one is really doing something for the good of something or somebody as well as for oneself, coupled with perfect happiness in one's [—] inner life. We are far more fortunate than most in that we can have these conditions at their best. I do try never to cause you anxiety about my personal actions, and you must realise that I have nothing else to live for but to make you and the Boys happy, and do the work for which I am best fitted which will be of benefit to the country in general and to the Service in particular.

In the course of this work I have many ups and downs and many disappointments, and some successes, and I am always battling with entirely changed conditions and points of view. Of course being a public man I am prepared to meet or ignore a great deal of criticism, some fair and honest, but a great deal of which is neither. I try not to take notice of the latter, and have succeeded to a certain extent, but little drops of water wear away a stone and when one is unhappy in one's family life & have private worries, one becomes less capable of throwing off or ignoring the beastliness of personal attacks. At the present time when I am having some bitter struggles over the many questions which go to make up the Naval Estimates, one feels that these personal attacks are inclined to influence & reduce the authority with which one speaks and defends the policy adopted.

* * * *

154. *To his wife* [Cap Ferrat]

[BTY/17/69/107–112]

Marlborough Club
Pall Mall
Thursday [29 Jan. 1925]

* * * *

We are having a rotten time here because all the government workmen have gone on strike and refuse to stoke the fires for the central heating and hot water for the government buildings, so everybody goes cold. I got up some stokers from Portsmouth and was told that I was using Imperial Forces for strike-breaking purposes which was illegal. I have now got volunteers, so can release them . . .

I've had a rest from Winston the last two days, but it is the calm before the storm which will burst out next week. I think I have collected much evidence which will defeat him & gradually am overcoming the views of the waverers who are undecided. By putting the whole thing on a higher plane and appealing to their patriotism I find a successful method, provided one is emphatic enough.

I shall lose Roger Keyes shortly as he is going to relieve O. de Brock. I have got Field,[1] who was the 3rd Sea Lord two years ago and who commanded the Special Service Squadron which went round the world, coming to replace Roger, but I shall be sorry to lose him.

Then my Controller, or 3rd Sea Lord, Fuller,[2] is going, which is an awful bore as he deals with the material side, a most important side which takes a lot of head work & brains to run properly. But my consolation is that I have Chatfield coming to take his place, and you know I am very fond of him and think a great deal of his capacity, both in brains and in the amount of work he can

---

[1]Later Admiral of the Fleet Sir Frederick Field (1871–1945): entered RN 1884; torpedo specialist; commanded *King George V* at Jutland; Rear-Admiral 1919; 3rd Sea Lord and Controller 1920–23; Vice-Admiral 1923 commanding Special Service Squadron's world voyage 1923–4; DCNS 1925–8; C-in-C Mediterranean Fleet 1928–30; Admiral 1930; 1st Sea Lord 1930–33; Admiral of the Fleet 1933.

[2]See note 1 on page 253.

get through. Then I have little Brand[1] coming as Naval Secretary to the First Lord, so shall have a lot of good fellows to help who are all willing and will soon learn their jobs. But changes are a nuisance when one is struggling all the time and have to have all the details of many questions at one's finger tips.

We shall battle through somehow. Old Mike Seymour is doing very well [?] as 2nd Sea Lord, although he suffers much in this weather and goes sick every now and then . . .

155. *To his wife* [Cap Ferrat]

[BTY/17/69/115–120]   Hanover Lodge
Friday [30 Jan. 1925]

. . . I of course darling heart understand your full desire to do all in your power to help me in every way. As you must realise, my life is not a bed of roses or my path easy just now. And we have suffered a severe disappointment, indeed a blow from the Government when they have evinced a complete indifference to our naval commitments and necessities and are actually behaving far worse to us at the Admiralty than the Labour party. Of course it is all Winston as Chancellor of the Exchequer, he has just gone economy mad, and the result is that the Government as a whole cannot see any use in a Navy at all and are not proposing to build any cruisers at all. Well, this obviously has got to be fought and if I have never done anything else of any value for my country, I *must* withstand this at all costs and simply cannot let it go. I must stand and fight or get out. In any case it means that I cannot possibly leave the scene of action until a conclusion has been arrived at, some way or the other. If I stand, I do not admit defeat, it is not to be thought of, and that means I cannot get away the beginning of February as I anticipated. But I shall remain and win through at all costs. I can do no less.

*   *   *   *

---

[1]Hubert G. Brand, as Commodore 1st Class had been Beatty's Captain of the Fleet when war ended. Rear-Admiral and 1st Cruiser Squadron 1919; Vice-Admiral 1924 but no appointment until 16 April 1925 when became Naval Secretary, but only six days later, consequent on the death of Vice-Admiral Sir Michael Culme-Seymour, became 2nd Sea Lord, until August 1927.

156.   *To his wife* [Cap Ferrat]

[BTY/17/69/123–126]   Saturday
[31 Jan. 1925]

*   *   *   *

I am very busy tackling the Chancellor of the Exchequer who has burst a bomb on us which he thinks will pulverise us, in the [—] of a memorandum setting forth the extravagance of our claims. I am answering that tomorrow, in the meantime I've persuaded the First Lord to go and spend the weekend with the Prime Minister at Chequers, and take him for a long walk and talk sense to him. I hope by these means to arrive at creating a better atmosphere in the Prime Minister's mind. We have had some bitter struggles in the past but never so bitter a one as this, although there is no bad feeling about it. Winston and I are very good friends and there is no malice or bad feeling attached to it, and we meet on the very best of terms. I am afraid he is in for a great disappointment as he [— —] that he would take a 1/- off the Income Tax, and he can't do it or go anywhere near it.

*   *   *   *

157.   *To his wife* [Cap Ferrat]

[BTY/17/70/3–5]   Hanover Lodge
Monday [2 Feb 1925]

I had a bad day yesterday and it continued until the small hours of this morning, that is until 2 am.

Bridgeman the First Lord went down to Chequers to see the Prime Minister, to spend the weekend and table our [?] Naval Estimates. In the meantime Winston had launched a Memorandum to the Cabinet against naval expenditure which brought Bridgeman galloping back & of course, being a Sunday, it was difficult to put hands on anybody and to prepare our case which they want for the Cabinet tomorrow. However I got hold of some assistance and we sweated at it until the small hours of this [?] morning; Bridgeman in despair at finding a *modus vivendi*. The poor Sea Lords very nervous at losing their jobs, which means bread & butter to them.

Today I had a long & wearisome day going over all the old ground, finishing up with 2½ hours with Winston, very amicable

& friendly. But, as he says, he is in a very difficult position, and it is not easy to bring our difficulties into line. But we were friends, and I think I can see my way, but there has [?] to be a lot of understanding [?] to get over the many obstacles in the way.

In the middle arrived your telegram [*sic*] and I wired back an answer at once. I will look into the matter as to dates for the *Bryony* and wire you Wednesday, if I can get her then [?]. The object was to visit the Fleets and witness the exercises, when we could see David . . .

158. *To his wife* [Cap Ferrat]

[BTY/17/70/12–13]   Admiralty and Hanover Lodge
                                      Thursday [5 Feb 1925]

I am having the devil's own time over Singapore.[1] For 2½ hours we argued and talked at the Committee of Imperial Defence today on a question which was settled, and has been again raised, principally with the object of gaining time. It simply is monstrous and means a mass of work to prove what has been proved over and over again. It has a depressing effect, which, added to the depressing weather, is hard to bear.

I had to stop writing to you and go and see the Prime Minister about the Estimates and so brought this home with me and am writing after dinner . . .

Little Bridgeman is leaving all the conversations about the Estimates with me, and so I have to keep my wits about me. But I think we are getting on. I do not think that Winston will go into the last ditch, and, although we are a long way apart just at present, we shall come together and find agreement somehow. But we have said our last say and if he won't come to terms, it will have to go to the Cabinet and they must decide, unless I can persuade the Prime Minister to use his good offices with Winston to settle it outside the Cabinet.

. . . He [Lord Curzon] has been very useful to me and supported me nobly on more than one occasion, principally because he dislikes Winston, so that he finds pleasure in our continued opposition. But as a matter of fact we, Winston and I, are very good friends through it all.

*   *   *   *

[1] Lord Curzon's sub-committee established in January 1925 to reassess the siting and defences of Singapore base.

159. *Beatty to Bridgeman*

[Holograph Photocopy]

[BGMN/3]   [Mediterranean]
Sunday 8th [Feb 1925]

. . . My interpretation of the sense of the meeting of Thursday is as contained in my telegram sent by the *Bryony* via Malta which you should have tonight.

Namely, that Churchill's proposals cut at the root of the Naval Policy of the Empire. If the Cabinet decide to alter the Policy of Naval Defence (and only the Cabinet can make this decision, not the CID) then the Admiralty will make new proposals to give effect to the policy. This, I think, your letter to Birkenhead makes clear. If this is the case, then it seems useless to waste time considering Admiralty proposals to give effect to the existing policy, which is not going to be carried out.

The Admiralty have alone [*sic*] the responsibility of giving effect to the Government's policy, not the Chancellor, supported by Sir George Barstow.[1] There is nothing more we can do until the Government make up their mind on the policy to be pursued, and it is a waste of time to continue investigation of proposals which are based upon a policy which apparently is not recognised or accepted by the Government. And it should be definitely stated that we are unable to discuss any programme which is not based upon the present accepted policy.

As I have said, this is a Cabinet question, and until it is decided, we can and must mark time, and I see no object in talking about destroyers, submarines etc.

You can reach me by wireless to the *Bryony* direct, and consequently I can get home in 48 hours from the receipt of any message from you. Is Winston only trying to kill time and cause delays? It looks like it, because I cannot believe that he believes all the rubbish he has talked.

My little lady is not very well and I am very anxious about her, but hope for a change for the better in the course of the next few days. Do not however hesitate to recall me if you should think it necessary.

I am very distrustful of CID meetings and hope that the Cabinet

---

[1]Sir George Barstow (1874–1966): Treasury official since 1898; during war involved in Service supply matters; in charge of Service supplies 1919–27; on retirement appointed to Board of Anglo-Iranian Oil Company.

will not try to foist what is their responsibility alone on what is after all only an Advisory Committee.

160. *Beatty to Bridgeman*

[Holograph Photocopy]

[BGMN/3]   [Mediterranean]
Sunday 8th [Feb 1925]

As I said in my letter to you by Fletcher,[1] he was here such a short time that I had no time in which to read and comment on Churchill's statement. However, I have now done so, and the first thing that strikes me is that his [?] statement is going to be very helpful.

It is a clear lucid statement for the layman [?], but more than that, it indicates the many [?] points on which the Treasury needs education and enlightenment. There should be no difficulty in the Naval Staff providing answers, with arguments, to the contentions which he raises. It has in fact brought the whole question to the point at which we have been endeavouring to bring it for a long time, and it is to be hoped that the Government will recognise the importance of the issue raised. Indeed it can no longer be shelved.

The Chancellor has recognised the importance of the question and all it involves, so much so that he has gone so far as to propose a change of policy. With this, the Admiralty are on a different [?] ground, but when it comes to a question of the abandonment of any provision for the defence of our Eastern interests, it is apparent that the Admiralty must have the clearest instructions on these vital questions. At present the Admiralty's responsibilities are very different to those that the Chancellor envisages. This is the main question & no other.

On questions of detail in which the statement abounds, and in which the Chancellor exercises his humour at the expense of the Admiralty, very complete answers can be provided in which I have no doubt we can indulge in a little humour, if so disposed.

I am writing to DCNS to get his Naval Staff busy as to this, and to provide answers, complete and effective to the various points which the Chancellor thinks he might have made.

But these are really beside the point &, while providing plenty

---

[1]E. Fletcher, Paymaster Lieutenant, serving in 1st Sea Lord's office.

of padding which might impress Wood, Peel etc, it must be remembered by the Committee that the only responsible authority are the Admiralty, & not Chancellor of Exchequer [sic] with his naval adviser, Sir George Barstow.

Generally speaking, I feel happier that Winston should have burst his bomb at this stage in the proceedings, it should help us considerably. We know the worst, and if it had come later it would have been greatly more embarrassing.

It seems to me that the Admiralty line should be that the whole question of Government policy is under review, and that until we are given a decision on the points of policy that Winston has raised, we hold our hand, as it is futile to waste our time in considering our responsibilities when we do not know what they are going to be.

It is true that we have the responsibility in guiding the Government in cardinal facts in Naval Defence, and this I consider we have done & can do no more. We have endeavoured to show that there is no fallacy in the fact that Japan is a potential danger and that we cannot produce the necessary protection to the Empire at short notice & must therefore take a long view and endeavour to meet the danger by precautionary measures in advance.

As I have already said, I am happier after reading Winston's effort than I was before . . .

161. *To his wife* [Cap Ferrat]

[BTY/17/70/40–43] Brooksby
Saturday [14 Feb 1925]

I heard from Molly who tells me that you are thinking that I am playing with you & tell you things to keep you over there, and mean something different. Dear heart, this is not fair and is so far from the truth that I feel it is an injustice and not worth replying to. Actually however I feel that it is better to swallow one's pride and meet any charge of that kind by a plain statement of the facts.

You must have realised from my letters that I have been passing through a pretty hard time & from day to day have not known what the outcome would be. I have a great responsibility on my shoulders, not only affecting the Service, but the future of the Empire, and moreover affecting the lives and careers of many distinguished officers serving under me at the Admiralty, to whom it means a great deal more than you can understand. They are all poor men with wives and families and their bread and butter is dependent upon the success of what I have set out to do, consequently decisions are not taken lightly. And it was not humanly possible to definitely state that by a certain date, or at all, that I should be free from the struggle to get away.

It was only recently that I was able to definitely fix a date which I communicated to you at once, *ie:*– the 1st or 3rd March, and to that date I am prepared to stick. My task this year has been infinitely more difficult and I think I have now overcome them [*sic*] all and saved the situation. My meeting yesterday with the Prime Minister and the Chancellor of the Exchequer was very fruitful and the way is clear to an understanding which will preserve the issues for which I have been struggling. The struggle has been long and difficult, but I think all is well and I shall certainly come to you in a fortnight's time for three weeks of peace, and visit the Fleet.

            *   *   *   *

It will be fun seeing David[1] and all the sailors again & that is good for them and good for me too — the Admiralty and Sea Service get into close touch by such meetings and confabulations. . .

162. *To his wife* [Cap Ferrat]

[BTY/17/70/65–66]   Admiralty
                                               Friday 20th [Feb 1925]

The poor old King is very sorry for himself and is an awful patient. He immediately thinks when anything goes wrong with him that he is going to die and I hear they have had an awful time with him. He has been [—] tiresome [?] over the Naval Estimates, putting his finger into the pie and can only think of the economical side of the picture and not of the Imperial side, because principally the economic side is the popular side and to advocate money to come off the Income Tax seems to him to

---

[1]Commander David Field Beatty (1905–72): Beatty's elder son; 2nd Earl 1936; entered RN 1918; retired 1930; Conservative MP for Camberwell 1931–6; Parliamentary Private Secretary to Financial Secretary to Admiralty 1931–6; recalled to RN, served at sea 1940–43; Deputy Director Combined Operations 1944–5; retired after war and became Joint Parliamentary Secretary Air Ministry 1945.

be the popular move. He is also moved by the possibilities of another Washington Conference, and because the United States achieved a certain amount of credit by a 'beau geste' in the last one he wants to go one better and advocate no battle-ships at all. He has of course no Naval advisers of any quality and they all have hurried schemes without knowing or even understanding the principles at stake. *But* he is alright when I get at him and put him wise on the situation, which I will do as soon as he is again fit to see anybody.

This Washington Conference which is on the tapis is going to be a nuisance. First of all it is doubtful whether they will be successful in getting all the Powers to attend, and it would be out of the question to have one unless all the Powers that were at the last one turned up for this one. The conference it is anticipated would take place in June, which is unfortunate in many ways. I have no desire to go there in June and will send my assistant, who will then be Admiral Field, a first class fellow who I am sure will do it very well. He commanded the Special Service Squadron that went round the world and has had plenty of opportunity of widening his outlook and gaining knowledge from the Imperial point of view, and moreover, is a good speaker and able to keep his end up. Of course all this is in the very initial stages and it is doubtful what will come of it.

Keyes goes out to the Mediterranean in May when Field comes to the Admiralty to take his place. Chatfield comes to the Admiralty in April, and Tommy Brand as Naval Secretary in April also, so I shall have men I can trust round me, which is something. In the coming struggle with the Committee Cabinet [*sic*] on new construction and on the manning of the Fleet I shall want all the help I can get . . .

163. *To his wife* [Cap Ferrat]

[BTY/17/70/94–95]   Admiralty
                                                                 27.2.25

. . . We had a final meeting this morning on the Singapore question and at long last they have definitely & irreversibly given in and agreed to our demands. So that is that, I am glad I've got that settled & off my mind.[1]

[1]The background to these discussions on Singapore is given in Roskill, *Naval Policy I*, pp. 445–66, 536–9, 556, 562–4; and in Part IV below.

As I told you, on Monday they open the ball on the Admiralty Construction Plans, and that will be the commencement of another campaign which I am afraid will be long & bitter, and even if the committee will not accept the Admiralty views, we are still free to say that we cannot abide by their decisions — that is to say give up our prerogative of being the deciding authority on questions of naval defence, although, no doubt, it will make our position more difficult and incense the members of the Little Navy Brigade. The only thing that seems to obsess the minds of everybody at present, even the most [—] is to take something off the Income Tax and Super Tax. I am all for the latter which would affect only a small proportion, but the latter [sic] is not really much help, and yet they could not do the Super Tax without [—] so much more off the Income Tax.

On the whole, the situation bristles with difficulties and it is very difficult to see daylight, or a way out. But my job is to fight to the last gasp for the Navy, the only stable thing left in the country & consequently the only Service left to attack. The Press are too ridiculous and unfair and are of no use as leads to the country. They only [—] & publish what they think will please the Public instead of leading thought & trying to educate the Public . . .

164.   To Eugénie Godfrey-Faussett

[Holograph]

[SLGF 15/6/2]   [No address]
                                                    Saturday [April 1925]

*   *   *   *

I have really been very busy and worried to death, first of all by Ethel and her continued attacks of neurasthenia which has at last been getting a hold of me. I never thought it would, but it has, and there is no blinking the fact. I have never admitted it before to a human soul, either verbally or in writing, and I get frightful waves of depression.

My work, which has saved me from it for so long, is not doing the same now, and that in itself has become much more difficult & I find things which were easy to combat before are not nearly so easy now. I am more sensitive to attacks and [—] push them on one side as I used to do. This bl—dy Bacon book[1] annoys me and has added to my despondency, and the difficulties I am having with the government are not so easily overcome, & I think they don't pay so much attention to my advice as in the past. Very silly no doubt & I am quite sure it is silly, but it has the effect of driving me into a hole and not seeing anybody . . .

165. *Birkenhead Committee – 8th Meeting Record of Proceedings*

[Extracts]

[Cab 27/273]   30 June 1925

The Chairman: I understand what the Chancellor of the Exchequer wants is to know primarily what construction is looked forward to in the next three or four or five years.

Mr. Churchill: And the resulting cost.

The Chairman: And the resulting cost. But there are also these other questions which do not entirely depend on construction, namely, manning and oil reserves.

Mr. Bridgeman: And the Fleet Air Arm.

The Chairman: We shall have to take those in time, but you will probably agree that the best thing is to begin on the four or five years' programme of construction first.

Mr. Churchill: I would like Lord Beatty's general statement.

Lord Beatty: As I understand the situation, I had a short conversation with the Secretary of State for India, and what he said was required from me, more or less to open the proceedings, was to state to the Committee the factors which governed the Admiralty in formulating the requirements of the Navy to carry out the policy of the Government in the matter of Naval Defence. That is what he said he would like me to do.

The Chairman: Over a period of years?

[1]Admiral Sir Reginald Bacon (1863–1947): entered RN 1877; Naval Assistant to Fisher as 1st Sea Lord 1904 and member of Committee on Designs; Rear-Admiral and retired, to become managing director of gun manufacture at Coventry Ordnance Works, 1909; recalled by Churchill to command Dover Patrol, and Vice-Admiral 1915; dismissed by Geddes 1917; made Controller of Inventions by Churchill as Minister of Munitions; retired 1919; author of biographies of Fisher (1929) and Jellicoe (1936). The second edition of his strongly pro-Jellicoe book, *The Jutland Scandal* (1924), was published in 1925.

Lord Beatty: Over a period of years. To do this shortly and briefly is not easy. First of all, what is the policy of the Government in the matter? It is not necessary for me to enlarge upon it beyond saying that the Admiralty interpretation of the one power standard as regards the United States of America, and the 5 to 3 ratio as regards Japan, which are the two strongest Naval Powers, is confined to capital ships and aircraft carriers.

The Chairman: When you say that is the Admiralty interpretation, I understand there is no dispute?

Lord Beatty: There is no dispute about that.

Mr. Churchill: That is the law.

Lord Beatty: That is the law.

The Chairman: It is accepted by everybody.

Lord Beatty: And as regards that type of vessel, equality in the one case, and the ratio of 5 to 3 in the other, shall be interpreted in the most literal sense, and that we should not be allowed to fall below these standards in any sense of the word; I mean to say by that, not only in numbers but in efficiency and equipment, in training and all that goes to make up the efficiency of the Fleet. I touch upon this at the outset because although it is not necessary to open the question of the numbers which is, as you say, the law laid down at the Washington Conference, it has a very important bearing on the number of men that will be required for the manning of the Fleet which, as you have said, is one of the questions which is to come before this Committee subsequently. Now the strength of the Navy in every other class of vessel, that is cruisers, submarines, destroyers, mine layers, mine sweepers and all the mass of auxiliary craft which go to make up the Fleet, such as depot ships, repair ships, victualling ships, &c., is not laid down or restricted by any international agreement. The Admiralty are therefore governed in assessing our requirements in this respect by the knowledge attained through a great number of years, years of experience such as no other Power possesses, supported and sustained by the experiences of the late war. In talking with the Secretary of State for India he thought that it would be sufficient for me to outline the case of the cruisers as an example of what was in the mind of the Admiralty, and so I propose to take the question of the cruisers which, I understand, is causing the Government the greatest concern because of the cost and the numbers that we at the Admiralty consider are necessary. It has been accepted that the numbers of this class of vessel which are required are not to be measured by the numbers possessed by other Powers entirely, but also by the length of our lines of communication, which it is an Admiralty responsibility to protect. To fix this number correctly and adequately we are dependent upon the sum of our knowledge and our experience in the past, and more especially upon experience we acquired during the late war. The number of cruisers which are required to give reasonable protection to our lines of communication, as well as those required to work with the Fleet on the basis of the one power standard with the United States and the 5 to 3 ratio with Japan, is a matter and a question which can be decided only by the Admiralty. The situation as regards cruiser construction has been growing steadily more acute every since the termination of the war. We are faced to-day with a rapidly declining cruiser strength. A steady policy of replacement pursued from the end of the war would have been the most economical way of meeting the situation, and, as is well known to many members of this Government, this course has been continually advocated by the Admiralty during the past five years. We now find ourselves faced with the alternative of leaving our lines of communication at the mercy of an enemy or of applying ourselves resolutely to remedy the situation. As I have said, this will surely be recognised by members of the Government because it has been represented by the Admiralty again and again, so much so that the actual situation was recognised by the late Conservative Government, and it will be within the recollection of those who were members of it that they decided to take strong measures and lay down eight cruisers in the autumn of 1923. But one of the disadvantages that the Admiralty is continually suffering from is change of Government, and again the Government changed and that policy fell to the ground. The succeeding Government, after again further exhaustive enquiries — we are always having enquiries on these questions and we are always having to point out the situation as it is — they were sufficiently impressed by the urgency of the situation to authorise the laying down of five cruisers, and it is to continue this rectifying of the situation that we have put forward the proposals we have. It might be said, 'Well, we have accepted the situation for so long, why not continue to accept it for another year?' and the answer to that is that the time is too short. Vessels which are now on the effective list are in nearly all cases part of the late war programme, that is to say, they were built simultaneously and therefore will wear out simultaneously, and in a period that falls within the period which the Admiralty have under review, that is, a ten years' period. The Chancellor of the Exchequer has asked for a period of three or four years. The Admiralty have to take an even longer period than that, and our view is a ten years' view. Of course, it is true that no Admiralty, no Government, can be committed to a policy over a certain length of time, but in dealing with great questions of administration and supply of vessels involving such cost and such vast expenditure of money, it is true to say that the Admiralty have always taken the longest view that is possible in this matter.

I have just spoken about the fact that the cruisers — not only cruisers but other vessels — were a part of the late war programme, and I might call attention to the fact — a very important fact — that cruisers and destroyers and submarines which were included in the war programme were built for North Sea conditions, whereas in the future all these vessels must be able to work on oceanic conditions, for which a greater mobility and endurance are essential. The ten years' replacement programme which I have referred to has been drawn up to carry out the Government policy, and in doing so two most important principles have been observed, first, that it is adequate — and it is no more than adequate — to meet the minimum requirements for the Naval Defence of the Empire, taking into account the known building programme of other Powers; and no allowance is made for any continuance of building by other Powers.

The Chairman: What do you mean by that phrase, that no allowance has been made for any continuance of building by other Powers?

Mr Churchill: There may be a larger increase.

Lord Beatty: Even greater demands may be made upon this country to build more ships.

Mr Bridgeman: You are only counting those either built or under construction by a foreign country?

Lord Beatty: Exactly. No allowance is made for any continuance of building, and if Japan or other countries go on building cruisers — take Japan, for instance. We are safe in taking Japan within these four walls. If she continues building cruisers at the rate at which she is building them now, the Admiralty, in duty bound, will have to come to the Government of the country and say, 'We shall require more than what is included in the ten years' programme that we put forward.' The second factor is that construction should be spread, so far as possible, equally over the period under review, whilst remembering that a heavy replacement programme for capital ships commences in 1931, which will be a still further charge. I have referred to the fact that cruisers, &c., would have to work in the future under oceanic as opposed to North Sea conditions. This is a very important fact, and perhaps it requires some explanation, as it has an important bearing upon the value of the cruiser in any war that can be contemplated in the future. In the late war, owing to our geographical position, we were able, after the first few months, to confine the enemy's naval operations to the North Sea, with the exception of an odd raider, which was a disguised merchant ship of slow speed. The depredations on our trade committed by this disguised merchant ship of slow speed should be a continual reminder of what we might expect should it have been possible for them to have despatched modern powerful fast cruisers for the purpose of attacking our trade. In any war that we can contemplate in the future our geographical position does not place us in such favourable circumstances, and an enemy will be free to launch —

Mr Churchill: You are speaking of Japan, practically?

Lord Beatty: I am talking about Japan or the United States, which are the only other two naval Powers that exist. If France had a big naval force I would refer to her too, because it would be the same thing. If Spain or Italy had great naval power, as Spain had in the middle centuries, the situation would be just as difficult as it is with Japan, except that she would be nearer. But in any war that we can contemplate our geographical position does not permit of such a favourable view, and any Power that possesses naval strength can launch powerful cruisers on our ocean trade routes, and therefore the demands for our cruisers for oceanic trade protection would be far greater in any future war than it was in the last war. The majority of our present war built cruisers have insufficient sea-keeping qualities for this work, and that is a very important factor. In deciding the number of cruisers — which we have to come to in the end — we are, as I have already said, guided by the experience of the past. For the ten years prior to the German menace we possessed over 100 cruisers, whereas today we have 48 completed —

*   *   *   *

Lord Beatty: As I said, the position now is that we have 48 which, with the completion of the 3, *Effingham, Emerald* and *Enterprise*, will grow into 51, the lowest number we have possessed, the lowest number of cruisers that we have possessed since 1889, and this is at a time when we are more dependent than ever on the importation of our foodstuffs and the other essentials which are necessary to these islands, and at a time when the merchant tonnage of the British Empire has increased from approximately 10 million tons in 1887 to 21½ million tons in 1924. I think it would be right for me to say something which will be explanatory of the functions of the cruisers, which has a very distinct bearing on the numbers that are required. A cruiser is required for two purposes. It is required first as the scouting line for the main Fleet, and secondly, for the protection of trade. Taking the scouting line for the main Fleet first, the duties are twofold — that is before the main Fleet comes into action. She has to work in advance of the Fleet, and when contact is made with the advance forces of the enemy's Fleet she forces her way through the enemy's scouting line to obtain all the information which is possible, information of position, disposition, strength, course and speed of the enemy's Commander-in-Chief and his main forces, and it may well be, and in fact it surely would be, that success in the ensuing battle will depend upon the accuracy of the information which our Commander-in-Chief will secure and obtain by the proper use of his scouting line of cruisers. And to enable him to be sure, to give him the best possible set of cirumstances, to achieve victory, it is surely recognisable that the cruisers in our scouting line should be more numerous and more powerful than those in the opposing enemy's scouting line.

The Chairman: You will say something about aircraft in that connection, won't you? I only want to have my mind balanced so that I can know what is coming.

Lord Beatty: Yes. The second function before the Fleet joins battle is the reverse, that is to say, he has to prevent the enemy from obtaining similar information regarding our Fleet, by bringing to action or driving off any vessels in his scouting line. After the main forces have joined battle, he has very important duties to perform. It is the duty of cruisers, which up to this time have formed scouting lines, to prevent the enemy's destroyers from delivering torpedo attacks on our battle Fleet. Massed attacks by destroyers which now carry long range and powerful torpedoes is a far greater menace to-day than it was in 1916. Also, should a favourable opportunity occur, our cruisers will themselves deliver torpedo attacks on the enemy's battle Fleet. As on the success or otherwise of a main Fleet action the whole of the safety of the Empire may depend, it is, in the Admiralty view, essential that on the day of battle we should have with the main fleet a number of cruisers at least equal, and superior if possible, to the number in the enemy's fleet. Therefore, the number of cruisers which are required for this purpose must depend on the number which is possessed by the enemy. In addition to the cruisers required for the main fleet in the Far East, in the event of a war with Japan, for instance, a small force of cruisers will be required to work with the small battleship forces which will remain in home waters. It is recognised by the Admiralty, and I do not suppose that anybody would disagree with it, that in the event of a war in the Far East the country would not attempt to remove all our units from European waters to the distant waters, and that the Admiralty would be obliged to maintain in European waters a certain force of battleships with their attendant craft. The ratio which exists with Japan is 5 to 3, which gives us, allowing for that retention in home waters, a bare equality with Japan, in the area of operations.

Mr. Churchill: Could we have the figures?

Lord Beatty: The figures 5 to 3.

Mr. Churchill: Could we have the actual figures? How many are to stay at home and how many are to be with the battle fleet?

Lord Beatty: Yes.

Mr. Churchill: You are coming to that later?

Lord Beatty: Yes. And it will give you rather a shock when you see how we shall be situated, *vis-à-vis*, for instance, France, about which we have had our flesh made to creep by the stories of what is going to happen in the air. It would be nothing to what is going to happen on the sea.

Mr. Churchill: You mean if you send all the fleet away to the other end of the world?

Lord Beatty: Exactly. For the protection of trade, which is the second function of the cruisers — we have dealt with the one of the fleet — and we have to deal with the second function, which is the question of the protection of trade. For this purpose cruisers and armed merchant vessels have to be stationed on the trade routes, and on all the trade routes, because it is not possible to determine where the attack will take place. Cruisers are necessary to support the armed merchant vessel as it, by itself, is of no value against enemy cruisers. Also, the armed merchant vessel will not be ready on the outbreak of war. It will take some considerable time to fit him out, to equip him, and certainly in the first months of war we shall be dependent upon our cruisers alone for the protection of our trade. The cruisers and the armed merchant vessels, in protecting our trade will, of course, at the same time perform an offensive service, in that they will be used for the destruction of enemy's trade, but what is more important, also for the interception of enemy trade in neutral bottoms. To illustrate the very large number of cruisers required to hunt down cruisers or raiders, i.e., enemy's cruisers or raiders, the experience that we have had, which, as I have said before, is our guide in these matters, may be quoted. In the late war the commitments were world-wide and had to be made simultaneously. In the Indian Ocean the *Emden* was responsible for a concentration of 23 vessels, either actively engaged in search of her or in convoying merchant ships on account of the menace of her presence in those waters. In addition to that, a hunting force of 8 more cruisers had been organised before she was finally destroyed. At the same time, or at the same date, and in the same Ocean, another force of a concentration of cruisers was hunting for the *Konigsberg*, and again in the same period, the same time, in the West Indies and South American waters, 18 ships in all were at one time or another detached to search areas for the *Karlsruhe*. Again in the Pacific and South Atlantic, at approximately the same time, no less than 22 ships, including the *Good Hope* and the *Monmouth*, were searching for or protecting trade against Von Spee's squadron. In the end, the destruction of this squadron was achieved by certain ships from the Grand Fleet, whence they could ill be spared at the time, and it was only accomplished just in time to prevent a very disastrous attack upon our more than valuable South American trade. Nearer home, i.e., in the protection of the Northern Atlantic, it absorbed many ships continuously from the outbreak of the war. Therefore, you can say that our experience in the late war is a very important and valuable guide, which should not be ignored. But one can even go further back into this question of experience. It is not unique, because I think it is a fact that during the war between the Northern and Southern States of America there were no less than 58 ships looking for the *Alabama* before they brought her to heel. If you put the trade into convoy you do not reduce the requirements in cruisers, because not only have the convoys themselves to be protected, convoys which are made up of slow ships, but the raiders have to be hunted down simultaneously to prevent them from interfering with the faster ships which continue to proceed out of convoy or independently. From the above it will be seen that the number of cruisers required for the protection of trade depends primarily on the length of our trade routes and only to a small extent on the number of cruisers possessed by an enemy Power. Now, you may take the factors requiring consideration before discussing the numbers and the types which are required. The factors which require consideration are the employment of British and Japanese cruisers in the event of a war between the two countries. We have to start with some basis.

The Chairman: Of course.

Lord Beatty: And, therefore, we will take the one that has the greatest cruiser strength, i.e., Japan. How these vessels are employed. We take the question of the development of airships, which you referred to, as affecting the number of cruisers, and we take the question of the relative fighting qualities of various existing and projected types of cruisers and its bearing on the full efficiency life of existing cruisers that we possess. Now, the employment of the British and Japanese cruisers in the event of a war between the two countries. If you take the British cruisers first, as I have said, the British Isles depend upon overseas supplies for their food and other essential commodities. The great ocean trade routes are of such distance from the area over which the British main fleet will exercise control, that detached forces must be employed for their protection. It is an important point that, as I will show, that as the area in which the British main fleet will exercise control is a long way from the areas which have to be protected by our cruisers in time of war, it is impossible to determine where the attack will fall, i.e., on what trade route, and, therefore, all your trade routes have to be protected. At the same time, the safety of the Empire depends upon the main fleet being victorious in battle. Therefore, cruisers, as I have already indicated, are an essential part of a fleet before battle and in battle. Therefore, it comes to this, that whether we like it or not we, this country, the British Empire, is definitely committed to divide up its cruiser forces. You go to the other picture. Take the Japanese problem, which is a very different one. The lines of communications which are vital to Japan, i.e., to China and Manchuria, are directly protected by their main battle fleet. They have no need to detach cruisers to protect their trade. They may detach them to attack ourselves, but it is not incumbent, it is not necessary, for them, as it is for us, to detach cruisers to protect their own trade. We, therefore, are placed in an unfortunate position of being forced to divide our cruisers between the main fleet on the one hand and the great ocean trade routes on the other, and must simultaneously be in a position to meet the full Japanese cruiser strength in a decisive battle and to protect our trade from a Japanese attack.

Mr. Churchill: You must add the home waters too.

Lord Beatty: Yes, the home waters — besides the home waters. The home waters ones will actually be employed in protecting the trade in home waters.

Mr. Churchill: I see.

Lord Beatty: Which, of course, might be a very vital place. It is a focal point. The development of airships as affecting the number of cruisers required. Up to the present time the protection of our trade routes has been carried out by cruisers and armed merchant vessels. An armed merchant ship cannot destroy an enemy cruiser, but he is essential for assisting the cruiser to find the raider, as well as for attacking the enemy's trade. The armed merchant cruisers cannot be on their stations until some weeks after the declaration of war, because they have to be converted and provided with guns, etc. During this period airships will be of great value from a reconnaissance point of view when working in co-operation with cruisers. Until, however, these airships have been fully tried out, it is not possible to say to what extent it will be possible to reduce the number of cruisers and the armed merchant cruisers required for the protection of, and attack on, trade; but there is a possible loophole of escape from some portion of the financial burden in that direction. If you deal, which is a very important factor, with the relative fighting qualities of the various existing and projected types of cruisers —

The Chairman: About the aircraft, I do not want to interrupt the First Sea Lord, but he would not like to leave out the value of the airship in the scouting screen as well as in the reconnaissance.

Lord Beatty: That, of course, comes into the picture when we deal with aircraft carriers.

The Chairman: Very well. That is quite true.

Lord Beatty: I am dealing with cruisers. But there is a factor which is one of considerable importance, and that is the relative fighting qualities of the various existing and projected types of cruisers and their bearing upon the full efficiency life of existing cruisers. The relative fighting qualities of cruisers mounting 8-inch, 7½-inch, 6-inch and 5½-inch guns respectively is a matter which has given us a great deal of consideration. I can produce a paper on that subject which I think will be of interest to the Committee as indicating the difficulties with which we have to contend. But the following conclusions are arrived at, that an 8-inch ship is in a position to crush a 7.5-inch ship without laying herself open to be crushed in return, and obviously equally so with the 6-inch ship or the 5.5-inch ship. The advent of the 8-inch gun ship has made not only the 6-inch ship, but also the 7½-inch ship out of date, and if you pit a 7½-inch gun ship against an 8-inch ship you are courting disaster, and you will be having further regrettable incidents which it is hoped could be avoided.

*   *   *   *

166.   *To his wife* [Baden-Baden]

[BTY/17/71/36–39]   Admiralty
                                                    Tuesday [7 Jul 1925]

. . . We have reached an impasse with the Government on the cruiser question [?] and I do not see the way out. We have made our proposals, as being the very lowest we can agree to, and they won't have them, with the result that somebody has got to give way completely, and Willie Bridgeman is as firm as a rock. Therefore the whole of the Admiralty is with him *en bloc* and I suppose we shall all have to go. There can be no other way out. I hope we shall get a definite decision in a few days, one way or the other. This uncertainty is very unsettling and difficult to deal with.

There is no doubt the Prime Minister is in a very unsettled

condition and does not know which way to turn, what with this crisis and the industrial depression and unrest. On the top of it all comes the China situation, which seems slowly going from bad to worse under Bolshevist influence and in every place becoming more threatening to the unfortunate foreigners, and the loss of trade amounting to 250 millions a year. And there are people who talk of peace all over the world.

*   *   *   *

167. *Hankey to Beatty*

[Holograph]

[BTY/8/8/1]   Office of the Cabinet
Personal   2 Whitehall Gardens
                                                      S W 1
                                                      10.7.25

I have been carefully considering your notes on policy[1] and I am rather attracted by the general idea, which would require very careful handling in execution.

If some policy of the kind is not adopted I am afraid of the following situation arising. We shall have a real 'bust-up' in China. Japan will have to rescue the legations and pull the chestnuts out of the fire for us all. Once at Pekin Japan will say '*j'y suis, j'y reste*'. We and America will make a hullabulloo [*sic*], and produce that very situation of antagonism which we all want to avoid. In fact Japan would then get alongside China against us.

If we adopt your policy we escape this. We say to Japan 'good luck to you. Do your best. We shall not oppose you as long as you let our commercial people alone. You will want them and their money to develop China. So leave it at that.'

To America we say, 'You and we are not prepared to take this country in hand. Better leave it to Japan. She may get the lion's share, but the general improvement of China under her guidance will also benefit our trade as compared with the present chaos.'

I wonder if you could next [?] as a personal suggestion, develop your ideas when the China Report comes before the CID.

[1]See Document 178 below.

168. *To his wife* [Baden-Baden]

[BTY/17/71/52–54] Admiralty
10.7.25

the situation is a little easier today and slightly more hopeful. The Prime Minister is more open to entertain the Admiralty views and I hope will be induced to settle the question in our favour by himself stating in Cabinet that for many reasons apart from those considered by the Committee it would be to the advantage of the country to accede to the Admiralty demands. — I am not sure as to the time table of possible events, but I gather that the Committee will report today or tomorrow and that it will if necessary come before the Cabinet on Monday, when a definite decision will be arrived at and we shall know where we are. But it is possible that the policy of procrastination will prevent this and we shall drag on over the next week, in which case it will be difficult to get away, but I think I could manage Friday or Saturday . . . It is not a question of not wanting to. I would like to come over to meet you there Friday morning; and get away from this atmosphere of intrigue and wrestling with these political gentlemen.

* * * *

169. *Churchill to Beatty*

[Copy]

[BTY/8/7/1] 10th August 1925

My dear Beatty,

I have never thought that there was the slightest justification for an increase in the emoluments of Naval Officers by granting them a marriage allowance, and I have endeavoured to express this view in repeated communications from the Treasury, largely drafted personally by myself. I formed this opinion from my knowledge of the three Services for one or more of which I have been Ministerially responsible for a good many years. My view of this matter has been endorsed by a careful enquiry undertaken by the Secretary for Scotland[1] who was quite impartial and by whose opinion I declared myself ready to abide. I hold most

[1]Sir John Gilmour (1876–1940): Unionist MP 1910–40; Secretary for Scotland 1924–9; Minister of Agriculture 1931; Home Secretary 1932–5; Minister of Shipping 1939–40.

strongly that without the marriage allowance the Naval conditions are on the whole not inferior, but indeed rather superior, to those prevailing rank for rank and age for age in the Army and the Air Force with their marriage allowances.

This being so, I thought it very wrong and unsuitable of the Admiralty to press for this advantage for Naval Officers at a time when other demands they were making on the taxpayer were so very great. Still more do I think it unseasonable at a period when practically every request of the lower deck has had to be refused, when we are about to publish reduced scales of pay for all new entrants to the fighting Services, and when in general reductions and retrenchments in salaries throughout the Public Service are so incessantly demanded.

I should have been very glad to have been able to meet your wishes (though I did not think them justifiable) to some extent, if that had been possible. I therefore wrote to the Prime Minister as early as June that, although I could not agree on the merits, I would be prepared to provide £100,000 for a reduced scheme to meet the hardest cases of married Naval Officers over a certain age and under a certain rate of pay, if the Admiralty cared to prepare one. I made it perfectly clear, however, that this offer was conditional on the First Lord being able to arrange with the Secretaries of State for War and Air that no consequential new demands were to be forwarded by them. I renewed this offer in writing to the Prime Minister a week after the Cabinet had reached its decision to submit to your demands about the cruisers. I understood from the Prime Minister that he had shown this communication to the First Lord. The Admiralty, however, did not seem to think that such a solution would be of any use; and quite apart from that, both the other Services were prepared to protest most strongly and to demand consequential increases. In these circumstances you have no grounds whatever for saying that I have gone back on any promise.

Lastly, it is not for me to settle these matters. The Cabinet is the sole and final authority. I do not believe that the Cabinet would in any circumstances have agreed to override the Gilmour report which was drawn up by four of their number. The feeling was most decisive and, except of course for the First Lord who is naturally the guardian of the special interests of the Navy, I think unanimous in its opinion. I am very sorry indeed that the decision should cause you pain, and I wish it had been within my power and within my duty as Chancellor of the Exchequer to meet you.

170. *Beatty to Churchill*

[Holograph Copy]

[BTY/8/7/1]

Grantully Castle
Aberfeldy
Perthshire
26.8.25

My dear Churchill

I am more sorry than I can say that you should have come to the conclusion that you have in the matter of Marriage Allowances for naval officers. I cannot believe that all the facts are known to you.

You say that you formed the opinion there was no justification for an increase in the emoluments of the naval officer, an opinion which was endorsed by the Secretary for Scotland and you hold most strongly that the naval conditions are on the whole rather superior to those in the Army & Air Force with their marriage allowances. These are not questions of opinion, they are questions of fact which cannot be got away from, which show conclusively that the naval officer is inferior to officers in the other services.

I enclose you a table prepared by the Secretary of the Admiralty & which you have presumably not seen. But, unless its accuracy is challenged, it seems to me decisive. It does not include the facts that married military officers get free passages for their wives etc when they go abroad, and the military officers receive free medical treatment for their wives and families, which naval officers do not get.

A similar table could be prepared showing a comparison for the Air & Naval Officer. On board an aircraft carrier it can be shown that air officers of the same rank etc are infinitely better paid than the naval officers &, living as they do, together, the difference is a sore subject among naval officers.

The Navy has always looked upon you as their friend & one [?] with a knowledge and experience of the Service, which made them feel happy in the thought that you would see that what is an injustice was rectified, & for that reason when they saw that the money had been put into the Naval Estimates, they thought that their case was at last understood. To have it turned down at the 11th hour has been a bitter blow & the Service is consequently very unhappy & disgruntled & they feel that they have no friend & every man's hand is against them.

It is making my task of maintaining an efficient navy, which depends upon contentment, very difficult & I cannot expect the same willing cooperation in making economies & reductions as I should [*sic*] have done.

Surely the question can be reduced to one which is governed by facts – and nothing but facts.

171. *Chiefs of Staff Committee*
Minutes of 23rd Meeting [Beatty in the Chair]

[Cab 53/1]   [Extract]   November 5 1925
SECRET

*   *   *   *

[Annual Review of Defence Policy]

Lord Beatty: said he wished to raise a question which was not on the Agenda. The Chiefs of Staff Sub-Committee had now been constituted for about two years, during which time a large amount of work had been undertaken in reviewing certain specific aspects of Defence policy. It seemed that it would now be desirable to prepare a general review of the Defence situation as a whole. In this connection it should be remembered that the Report on National and Imperial Defence[1] allocated to the Committee of Imperial Defence, assisted by the three Chiefs of Staff, the duty of keeping the Defence situation as a whole constantly under review. Before any actual steps in the matter were taken, it would however be desirable for the Secretary to ascertain the views of the Prime Minister.

[CIGS and CAS agreed to the Secretary seeking the Prime Minister's approval and if this were obtained, to preparing an outline of the scope of the Review.]

172. *Beatty: Speech at Lord Mayor's Banquet, 1925*

[Draft]

[BTY/11/8/22]   [9] November 1925

It is a great privilege to respond to the Toast of the Navy on this distinguished occasion.

In the process of recovering from a great war it is but natural

[1] Cmd. 2029 (1924–5): the report of the Salisbury Committee.

that demands should be made to reduce those National Forces on which the fate of the Country depended in time of danger.

We do not need to probe history to realise that this phase has occurred after all our great wars of the past, and that history is but repeating itself.

It may be well, therefore, to recall the facts which demand the existence of an adequate British Navy today. It exists for the preservation of peace in the world and for the security of the British Commonwealth of Nations.

In the words of the Articles of War, which date from Elizabethan times, 'it is the Navy whereon under the good Providence of God the wealth, safety, and strength of the Kingdom chiefly depend'.

It exists, therefore, as a great potential factor in the development of the British Empire and in furtherance of closer relationships between the British peoples.

By the Washington Treaty the strength of the Navies of the Great Powers was definitely laid down so far as Capital Ships and Aircraft were concerned. Therefore the policy of the Government as regards these ships is equality with the strongest Naval Power, the 'One Power Standard'.

It was agreed at Washington that our peculiar situation as a scattered Empire admitted of special treatment in the matter of Cruisers. Therefore the policy of the Government in this respect is to provide an adequate number of Cruisers for the protection of our territories over the seas and the sea communications of the Empire, on which the safety and existence of the various British peoples depend.

The Board of Admiralty are accordingly charged by the Government with responsibility for putting this policy into execution.

This duty necessitates tendering of advice to HM Ministers, which in present circumstances is unpalatable to the Country. It is sometimes said that the Admiralty are going beyond their duty and are attempting to assert an undue influence on the policy of the Country. This is a most profound misreading of the situation. Their duty is to *advise*, and the searching examination to which the latest Admiralty proposals have been subjected by the Government before receiving approval, should satisfy any reasonable man that they have been accepted only because they represent bare necessities.

If and when the Country adopts some other policy, the Admiralty will loyally advise in accordance with the new formula, whatever it may be.

That the present policy imposes a great strain on the finances of the country is undeniable, but what are the facts of the situation? The world wide trade routes upon which we are dependent for our food and for the raw materials of our industries, are no shorter or less complicated in their geographical disposition than they were in 1914. We are no less, in fact more, dependent upon their security. On the other hand our means of ensuring the safety of these supplies are now far less than in 1914.

It will be said, indeed has been said, that the conditions have changed; in 1914 we were faced with a powerful potential maritime enemy, that menace has disappeared, and to-day there is no sign of danger to the Empire. This is true, and has been taken fully into consideration and the Naval Policy has been formulated accordingly.

In 1914 we possessed 108 Cruisers.

To-day we have 59 afloat, under construction, and to be laid down this year.

In 1914 we possessed a very great advantage from our geographical position in being able to command the exits of enemy vessels destined for attack on our trade, yet still the number at our disposal was barely adequate. Such a favourable strategic position would not obtain in the unfortunate event of war with any other Power, and the demand for Cruisers and the protection they provide, will be far greater than in the Great War. Therefore the suggestion that this number (55) is unduly large, is one which I personally, and I venture to say any Board of Admiralty, can never support.

The task of the Admiralty in carrying out their great responsibilities is not made any easier by a campaign of ill-informed criticism. Many of the statements made are so wide of the truth, and so oblivious to the necessities of the Empire, that it can only be concluded that the object of the critics is political.

Fair criticism is always welcome, misrepresentation cannot be helpful.

The campaign is persistent and one-sided, in that the attacks are given prominence while the replies to the attacks are given obscurity, and the critic returns to the attack on the same ground.

I ask is this fair play? I ask — is it patriotic to attempt to stir up in this great Service dissatisfaction and want of confidence in administration for purely political or personal reasons?

The First Lord at Colwyn Bay, and the Parliamentary Secretary of the Admiralty at Harpenden, made very clear statements and replies to the allegations of reckless expenditure forced upon successive Governments, and have made plain the causes which have brought about increases in the cost of the Admiralty Office.

It is forgotten that 1914 was the end of a prolonged period of naval peace, which did not tend to the full development of the capabilities either of the personnel or of the material of the fleet.

It is not the fault of the Admiralty that the impetus of war has added vastly to the complexity of the technique of naval warfare; that new weapons have been evolved, and the scope of existing weapons expanded beyond imagination. They were but natural and inevitable processes of science and psychology [sic]. To cope with this development and to keep pace with further progress, the organisation of the Admiralty as it was in 1914 was totally inadequate. This phenomenon was not peculiar to the Admiralty; for instance, the Government found it necessary to create a new Ministry and Service to meet the extension of war into the air.

The formation of new Technical Departments and new Divisions of the Naval Staff to deal with strategical, tactical, and material aspects of old and new weapons and contrivances was imperative if we were not to lag behind other Countries in scientific attainment.

When it is remembered that the size and number of Capital Ships and the size of Cruisers and aircraft carriers is now limited by International Convention, it will be realised that now, less than at any time in the past can we afford not to utilise the fruits of progress to their fullest extent.

Apart from this side of the question, I ask if any industrial concern or business in the Country finds that it can conduct its affairs with the same overhead charges as it incurred in 1914.

The proposal of the Board of Admiralty to effect substantial economies by limiting the activities of Rosyth and Pembroke Dockyards in time of peace, has met, quite naturally, with a volume of opposition from the localities interested, and less reasonably from many people whose demands for economy are not the least clamorous.

As to whether these Yards are necessary for Naval purposes, the Admiralty is the only competent judge. As to whether they are necessary for political or social reasons, is for the Government to decide. The fact is that so far as the upkeep of the Fleet is concerned they are entirely redundant.

Is it suggested that the Admiralty should not have brought this fact to the attention of the Government? and is it intended that the Naval Estimates should include the expenditure of money for social purposes extraneous to the maintenance of the Fleet?

Earnest amateur strategists have been prolific in advice to the Admiralty, pointing out the strategic advantages of Rosyth and Pembroke Dockyards over the Southern Yards. In the first place the reduction of Rosyth and Pembroke to a state of Care and Maintenance does not render them any less available for use in emergency than their upkeep at their present standard. The suggestion that either of the Southern Yards should be closed and that Rosyth or Pembroke should take its place, is one which is altogether out of the question from the financial point of view, apart from other important considerations.

To render Rosyth or Pembroke capable of dealing with the work which can be undertaken by one of the Southern Yards would entail cost which is beyond contemplation under present circumstances. The alternative is, in short, to keep Rosyth and Pembroke going in their present state in addition to the other Yards, or to cease keeping them in active operation, as has been proposed.

A much more reasonable line of criticism is to the effect that the Admiralty having produced estimates this year for a sum which they considered to be the minimum necessary, have subsequently undertaken to produce further economies, and until the facts are examined there would seem to be reasonable grounds for criticism of this nature. The explanation is, however, perfectly plain and comprehensible.

The Admiralty have, during the past 4 or 5 years advocated continually the adoption of a steady programme of replacement for Naval Defence, but owing to the instability of the various Governments, who have never lasted more than a few months, no programme has been accepted, and therefore no programme adopted. Obviously it is far more economical to have a steady programme than to do as we have had to do in the last five years.

The present Government, with its prospects of stability, has been able to accept a definite programme, and so by stabilising expenditure on new construction it has enabled the Admiralty to exercise economies which would not have been possible under the previous circumstances. The effects are far reaching and include the demolition of many older ships now on the Active List, with a corresponding reduction of expenditure on repairs, maintenance and personnel.

A factor of still greater importance is that the Government, having taken into consideration the international outlook, have authorised some temporary relaxation of the immediate readiness of the Fleet for Active Service. This recent decision has opened up fields of economy hitherto closed to us, and the sacrifice of preparedness has already resulted in financial gain. To tamper with the traditional standard of the Fleet is a grave step which can only be justified by the most serious exigencies, and we know that the Government has reached its decision only after the most anxious consideration.

This step has rendered more important than ever the utmost efficiency in the Naval Staff.

Vigilance, foresight, and the study of problems in conjunction with the Military and Air Staffs become matters of even greater moment than before.

Such Naval disasters as occurred during the war were the direct result of the lack of a sufficient and efficient Staff, and it would be criminal to lapse once more into such a state.

We paid very dearly for the experience which led to its formation, and nothing should interfere with its development.

The task of the Sea Lords during the last few years has at periods been carried through with personal feelings of bitter regret. It has been their duty to reduce the Fleet from a magnificent and incomparable force to the modest dimensions at which it now stands, and concurrently to deprive of their professional livelihood thousands of zealous, highly efficient, and loyal Officers and Men.

It has indeed been a painful duty, but it has been made easier by the unquestioning loyalty and resignation with which the blow has been accepted by individuals. All honour is due to these Officers and Men for the example they have set of subjugating their personal claims to public interest.

173.   [CCC: *Bridgeman's Diary*]

[Extract]   [January] 1926

The dog-fight with the Chancellor for a building programme last year, which was the most exhausting struggle I have ever had in politics, has made it possible for us to make great economies. By the knowledge of a certain number of ships being added each year for some time, one can look ahead with some confidence, and scrap many obsolescent vessels, which otherwise one would have had to keep and repair.

When one lives from hand to mouth or year to year & does not know which ships the Govt. will sanction, if any, in the year ahead, one is bound to play for safety and keep a considerable reserve for contingencies. The peaceful outlook also justifies some retardation in the accumulation of reserves and we have saved a good deal by cutting down the annual addition of oil reserve by a considerable amount.

The Admiralty responded most splendidly to the call for economy, and as the Board (Beatty, Brand, Field, Chatfield, Dreyer,[1] Kelly,[2] Stanhope,[3] Davidson and Murray, Secretary) are a remarkably capable set of men, they produced economies much in excess of what I had ventured to hope for. Field, Chatfield and Dreyer did wonders. I think that Field is the ablest naval officer all round that I have met yet & could hold his own in any company, & on most subjects. The result was that we not only saved enough to pay for the new construction of the year provided for the decision of July last; *ie* about 3 million, but actually reduced the other expenses by over 2 million, over 5 million in all of savings. So we have done our share of saving for the year and ought not to be pressed for much more in future. Winston has shown much appreciation of our exertions.

[1] Admiral Sir Frederic Dreyer (1878–1956): entered RN 1891; became recognised as the most able gunnery officer of his time; Flag Captain to Jellicoe 1915; DNO 1916–19; Commodore and Chief of Staff on Jellicoe's Empire Mission 1919; Director of Gunnery Division Naval Staff 1920; Rear-Admiral 1923; ACNS 1924; Battle-Cruiser Squadron 1927; Vice-Admiral 1929; DCNS 1930; Admiral 1932; C-in-C China Station 1933–6; retired 1939. He is roughly treated in Anthony Pollen (1980), *The Great Gunnery Scandal: The Mystery of Jutland*. The relevant documents are in J.T. Sumida (ed.), 1984, *The Pollen Papers*: NRS.

[2] Admiral Sir John Kelly (1871–1936): entered RN 1884; gunnery specialist; Rear-Admiral 1921; Home Fleet 1922–3; 4th Sea Lord 1924; Vice-Admiral 1926; commanding 1st Battle Squadron and 2nd in command Mediterranean Fleet 1927–9; Admiral commanding Reserves 1930; C-in-C Home Fleet where restored discipline and morale after Invergordon mutiny, 1931–3; Portsmouth 1934–6; Admiral of the Fleet 1936.

[3] James, 7th Earl Stanhope (1880–1970): Civil Lord 1924–9; Parliamentary Secretary 1931; 1st Lord of Admiralty 1938–9; Chairman, Trustees of National Maritime Museum 1934–59; President of Navy Records Society 1948–58.

174. *Beatty: Minute on* Naval Review *Censorship*

[ADM 1/8708/226]   5.2.26

The matter of censorship of *The Naval Review* resolves itself into two main questions.

(a) Is the *Review* of value to the Service?

(b) Does the censorship adversely affect the *Review*?

The answer to (*a*) is emphatically in the affirmative. It is equally so as regards (*b*), for the following reasons.

(1) The *Review* is given a semi-official status.

(2) Official sanction is given to the opinions expressed in the articles, which gives them a weight they may not merit.

(3) It certainly deters officers from contributing articles. There are definite cases of Senior Officers, previously regular contributors, who have ceased to write under the censorship, as they object to its being done by an officer junior to themselves.

(4) The officer responsible for the censorship naturally has more regard to his own safety in the event of future trouble than to the well-being of the *Review*. He undoubtedly is liable to be over-cautious and to eliminate matter which is in itself innocuous.

The Secretary's suggestion at 'A' is objectionable in that the censorship would become a personal matter. For instance, if the 2nd Sea Lord objected to an article on Training, he would blame the individual officer who had allowed it to pass. The present impersonal arrangement is preferable.

If the censorship were relaxed and an article appeared containing objectionable confidential matter, or remarks critical of the Admiralty or individual senior officers, it could hardly cause a national disaster or do irretrievable harm, as appears to be anticipated. The censorship or suppression could be imposed immediately.

By the imposition of censorship and the use of the Admiralty's power of suppression, the *Review* has been taught a lesson which should prevent any further indiscretion. I am satisfied to leave the matter in the hands of Admiral Henderson,[1] whose discretion in such matters is not less than that of an officer in the NID.

In view of all the circumstances, I consider that the censorship

---

[1] Admiral W. H. Henderson, first Honorary Editor of *The Naval Review*.

should be lifted during the term of Admiral Henderson's Editorship and the matter reconsidered if a new Editor is appointed.

B 5.2.26

Minute by 1st Lord

[Holograph]

It seems to me open to question whether the 1st SL's proposal does not recommend a course at variance with K.R., in view of the ruling given by the present Sol. Gen.[1] and referred to in Secretary's minute at (B).

I think the Board should consider the matter.

W.C.B. [8.2]

Minute by Secretary   18.1.26

[Copy]

(B) Present Solicitor General when Acting Head of Naval Law has given his opinion that in law, publication in the N.R. was publication from point of view of K.R.

*   *   *   *

(A) I think that the proposal to abolish the censorship of the material proposed to be published in the *Review* ought not to be agreed to. I suggest that a method of going some way to meet Admiral Henderson would be to require him to include an Admiralty representative, say DNI, or his representative, in the Committee of Naval Officers; the representative to see all manuscripts and concur that they are suitable for publication.

[O.M.]

175.   *To his wife* [Freiburg]

[BTY/17/72/34–35]   Admiralty
                                        Monday [15 Feb 1926]

. . . I am sitting on the office stool endeavouring to reconcile the maintenance of a Navy with the ideas of economy which fills [*sic*] the minds of all men to the exclusion of everything else.

[1]Sir Thomas Inskip (1876–1947): lawyer and Conservative politician; served in Naval Intelligence 1914–18; MP from 1918; Solicitor-General 1924; Attorney-General 1927–8; Minister for Co-ordination of Defence; in 1937 recommended return of Fleet Air Arm to Admiralty control.

It seems like a madness which assails them; all precautions to be thrown to the winds, to completely trust the goodwill of every nation and give up everything, which will take years to reproduce, for the sake of saving a few millions to spend on making roads which will only benefit the road-hog millionaire and to pay out the Doles [sic] to people who don't want to work.

If we have to economise — which we do — then why not on things that the country can do without, have [sic] done without up to now. Then [?] the handling of the Coal Subsidy has cost us 20 millions & will cost much more, and in the end will end in a strike which will cost the country many more millions.[1] And so it goes on, although we have got the strongest and most staple [sic] government we have ever had.

Abroad, we pin-prick the French on every occasion & are inclined to do the same with Italy. Germany agrees to every suggestion but does not act up to it. Now they say she has an alliance with Austria which will shake the world, but as both are bankrupt and have no arms [?] etc., it seems difficult to understand how they can be a menace to anything. The one real danger, Russia, they ignore, although they are ceaseless in the spreading of their doctrines, and have actually penetrated into Japan. If that country adopted the doctrines of Bolshevism & allied themselves to Russia, then we should have some trouble, and the prophesies of the Pyramids would come true that the races of the North & East would join hands and sweep across Europe.

I do not know why I am enlarging on all these points, perhaps because I have been in close touch with them for so long they have made a deep impression on my mind.

*   *   *   *

176. Board Minute No. 2169

[ADM 167/73]   25 Feb. 1926

Naval Review Censorship
SECRET: for the infomation of board members only

The Board considered the question of the remission of the censorship at present exercised over the *Naval Review*, which has been

---

[1]Government had subsidised the coal industry by £10 million in 1921 and by £23 million in 1925, to maintain wage levels. Beatty's prophecy was fulfilled in the General Strike of May 1926, triggered off by the miners' grievances.

raised by Admiral W. H. Henderson. The history of the censorship had been described in a memorandum.

The Board concurred in the view expressed by the First Sea Lord, *viz*, that the printing of articles on naval interest in the *Review* was of considerable value to the Service, and afforded a convenient medium for the ventilation and discussion of subjects of naval importance, for which no other opportunity at present existed. It was understood that Admiral Henderson's responsibility for the *Review* was shared by a committee of naval officers, who, he thought, could be relied upon to see that nothing objectionable or confidential was issued.

It was accordingly agreed that Admiral Henderson should be asked to submit the names of the committee to the Admiralty, and, subject to the names meeting with the Board's approval, the present conditions for Admiralty censorship should be waived. Admiral Henderson should be further asked to submit to the Admiralty any proposed changes in the composition of the committee. In the event of Admiral Henderson ceasing to be responsible for the N.R., the question should be brought up again for the Board's consideration. Should it at any time be desired that articles from the *Review* should be printed in other periodicals the permission of the Admiralty should be obtained.

177. *To his wife* [Freiburg]

[BTY/17/72/75–77]   Admiralty
26.2.26

*   *   *   *

I saw Birkenhead yesterday at the meeting of the Committee of Imperial Defence. He looks an awful wreck physically, but mentally he is all there, and having a strong physique I presume he will now pull through and recover his normal capacity for the consumption of alcohol. But they say if he doesn't lead a more abstemious life it will kill him — still, threatened men live long.[1]

*   *   *   *

We have been very busy preparing our Estimates which come before Parliament on the 11th or 12th. They took the Air Estimates yesterday which, though showing an increase on Estimates of last year, passed without very much friction. So we hope that

[1]See note 1 on page 78.

as ours show a considerable diminution in expenditure we shall at long last receive some credit for our labours.

The situation in China is becoming more alarming and there is no doubt that the Bolshevist activities which have ceased in Europe are meeting with considerable success in the Far East. All of which goes to show that the prognostications outlined in that amazing book 'The Pyramids & their Divine Message' are on the way to be fulfilled.

Our friend Birkenhead has been interesting himself in the situation and was moved to make a most eloquent speech at the meeting yesterday, pointing out the real peril with which we were faced and which I called their attention to 6 months ago. It is good to know that a Minister of his calibre and force such as he should take such a serious view, and it is reassuring to know that this great problem is not being lost sight of. I feel in my bones that it is a very real peril, and unless we are careful will find us unprepared by thoughtful [?] preparation and we shall consequently suffer as we have never done before. In fact I believe we have very stormy times ahead of us, not at home, but in the great world, and before very long Europe will become once again an armed camp.

Bless you dear heart, I don't know why I should bore you with all this, but these problems are uppermost in my mind and are always in my thoughts.

I pray for you night and morning to have strength to recover your equilibrium & to help Martin to find & treat the causes of all our misery so that it will never happen again.

178. *Beatty to Prime Minister*

[BTY/8/8/3]   1 March 1926

Notes on Relations with China and Japan (made in July 1925)[1]

Hypothesis

1. That the present state of affairs in China is the result of Bolshevist exploitation of the anti-foreign feeling which is always latent among Chinamen.
2. That the Bolshevists have succeeded in focussing this ill-feeling upon the British, since they regard us as the most stable

[1]See Document 167 above.

of the Great Powers, and the most powerful enemy of Bolshevism.

3. That we possess no means of curbing Bolshevist activity in
    China or of stemming the tide of anti-British feeling: neither
    can we see any way of rendering our interests more secure.

4. That there is no effective Government in China.

Discussion of policy

Our commercial interests in China are of immense value to us.
Their security is based upon Treaties with former Chinese Governments, and the disappearance of effective Government necessitates our relying upon the goodwill of the Chinese people, except
in the few centres where protection can be given by armed force.

Speaking generally, it is upon the Navy that the main responsibility for armed protection normally falls.

China has always been a Naval responsibility, and the views of
the Admiralty upon the recent developments must therefore
receive attention.

The situation has already been considered by the Chiefs of Staff
of the Navy, Army and Air Force, and a report has been forwarded upon various measures which the CID had referred to
them for consideration.

If, however, it is correct to assume that the position is one of
great gravity, possibly involving ultimately an upheaval similar to
that which took place in Russia, then it seems inconceivable that
measures such as those discussed by the Chiefs of Staff can be of
any avail.

The despatch of a few Brigades of Soldiers, the bombing of a
Chinese city, the strengthening of the River Gunboat force,
cannot possibly bring into subjection 350 million Chinamen. Their
operations would probably serve only to consolidate the feeling
against us, and bring into play vast sections of the populace who
are now apathetic.

We should incur great expense, and the result could hardly be
anything but failure.

It is a problem which demands broad treatment; a very great
problem of Statesmanship.

In the time of the Boxer troubles there was a Government in
China with which it was possible to treat after dealing with its
armed forces.

To-day there is no such Government, and instead of having to exercise pressure upon a Government, we have to exercise pressure upon a whole people.

This can only be done by military operations upon a grand scale such as we in this country cannot contemplate.

If it is necessary for us to restore tranquillity in China, and we cannot do it ourselves, then who can do it?

Japan.

Japan is ambitious and is on the threshold of becoming a really great Power.

We have long been apprehensive as to the direction in which she will look for aggrandisement.

If her efforts were diverted to China we should feel less apprehensive for our own Eastern Possessions.

China would absorb her energies, and if she were given a more or less free hand there, she would be loth to antagonise the British Empire by encroaching upon our interests.

She would naturally do her utmost to exploit China commercially, and our merchants would experience much keener competition than at present; but commercial competition would surely be a less formidable problem than a hostile country in a state more chaotic than Russia.

If we were to hold aloof the Bolshevists would find it difficult to maintain their doctrine that Britain was the chief enemy of China, and we have the example of the USA in the late war to show how a Country can prosper by leaving others to pluck the chestnuts from the fire.

It would be a return to the policy which our Statesmen adopted in former European wars, with our Navy to 'keep the ring'.

It will be urged that the USA would resent bitterly any proposal to give Japan a free hand in China, but if we are not in a position (as we are not) to undertake the task ourselves, it would be for them to settle with Japan.

Our only interest in China would be to preserve our commercial status quo, and as war is an exhausting effort, we could hardly fail to find our own strength relatively enhanced if we held aloof from it.

179.   *Beatty to Baldwin*

[Holograph]

[Baldwin 2/306ff]   Admiralty
                                                           3.3.26

Dear Prime Minister,
   I enclose the paper on economies in connection with the Fleet
Air Arm which you asked me for on Monday.
   I hope it is clear and what you required.

Your sincerely,
BEATTY

ECONOMIES IN CONNECTION WITH THE FLEET AIR
ARM

[Typescript]   3 Mar. 1926

   In the 1925 Estimates the Admiralty effected a saving of
£275,500 by informing the Air Ministry (in a letter dated 6th Jan.
1925) that, in view of the urgent need for economy, they considered a reserve of 150 per cent of engines for the Fleet Air Arm
sufficient, instead of a reserve of 275 per cent of engines, which
had been proposed by the Air Ministry. Since that date, the
Commanders-in-Chief of the Atlantic and Mediterranean Fleets
have reported that they consider the 150 per cent of engine
reserves to be adequate.
   In the 1926 Estimates *the Admiralty effected a saving of £357,000*
by informing the Air Ministry (in a letter dated 25th Nov. 1925)
that they considered, as a result of the Government's view as to
the existing state of the political horizon (expressed in Cab. 24(25)
dated 5th May 1925) and also because of the urgent need in
economy in connection with the Fighting Services, that the peace-
time reserve of aircraft for the Fleet Air Arm should consist of
100 per cent instead of 200 per cent aircraft as hitherto provided.
The Air Ministry agreed to this for trial.
   The Admiralty agreed with the Air Ministry that, instead of
providing four of the flights required for the aircraft carrier *Cour-
ageous* at the end of the financial year 1926 they should be provided early in the financial year 1927. This made a further
reduction to the 1926 'Grant-in-Aid' of some £251,000. It is

realised by the Chancellor of the Exchequer and the Admiralty that this *is not a saving but only a deferral.*

It is easy to make irresponsible proposals for reducing expense.

Thus the Colwin Committee, who incidentally, also, had no responsibility as regards the efficiency of the Fleet, made the proposal that 70 per cent of officers of the Fleet Air Arm, other than Observers, should belong to the Royal Air Force, this number to include 'a suitable proportion of officers holding short-service commissions, to provide an adequate reserve on an economical basis'.

This recommendation could not have been made by anyone with a knowledge of sea requirements, or anyone with responsibility for the efficiency of the Navy.

No real economy is achieved by the simple means of employing landsmen, and short-service landsmen at that, to carry out naval work, and this is not in the best interests of the State.

In the navies of the United States and Japan, which are the most powerful after that of Great Britain, the Naval Air Arms are completely manned by sailors and completely administered by the Admiralties of these two countries.

It is anomalous that, in the Navy of Great Britain, the greatest maritime power the world has ever seen, the Fleet Air Arm has for the past eight years been partly manned by the landsmen of the Royal Air Force, and has suffered from the fundamental handicap of dual control by both Air Ministry and Admiralty.

Anyone with any real acquaintance with the sea and sailors will understand that sailors will never have any confidence in the work of landsmen over the sea. The effect of this lack of confidence upon efficiency, particularly in war, need not be laboured.

*   *   *   *

There are however directions in which *further economy can be effected in the Fleet Air Arm* without loss of, and indeed with an attendant increase of efficiency.

Some of these are dependent upon the adoption of the Admiralty's proposals for a Naval Air Arm comprising both the Fleet Air Arm and the Coastal Aircraft.

(A) Economies in personnel

(1) *Officers*

In the *headquarters* of carriers it is possible to effect a reduction of about 30 per cent by substituting Naval for RAF officers, owing to adopting a strictly naval organisation; *ie* omitting *inter alia* 'The Adjutant', 'The Staff Officer', 'The Signal Officer' etc, etc.

In the Fleet Air Arm and Coastal Flights a reduction of about 27 per cent would be made possible by introducing a proportion of Lower Deck Pilots instead of officers.

In the *Administrative Staffs* (outside the Admiralty and Air Ministry) a reduction of over 70 per cent would be possible since the bulk of the administration of the Naval Air Arm would be common to that of the Navy generally, if the Admiralty's proposals are adopted.

In the *aerodromes* it would not be proposed to make a reduction until experience had shown it to be possible, though there are good grounds for believing that this would be found to be the case. (The aerodromes referred to are those now allocated to the sole use of the Fleet Air Arm and Coastal Aircraft.)

(2) *Ratings*

Throughout the personnel of carrier headquarters, flights, and aerodromes, an overall reduction of about 15 per cent is proposed. This amounts to the fact that *the Admiralty propose to carry out the work now performed by 20 airmen, with 17 naval ratings.* The justification for the proposal rests upon actual observation of the working of the headquarters and flights, upon the fact that Naval technical personnel is more highly trained than corresponding men of the Royal Air Force, and upon the utilisation of dockyard resources adjacent to Naval Air Arm aerodromes.

In support of this proposal, two facts may be stated. Firstly, the introduction of naval ratings into the Fleet Air Arm to the limited extent now authorised *has already resulted in carrier complements being reduced by from 3.5 per cent to 11.5 per cent*; the reduction varying in different ships, as one of the governing factors is the siting of the guns. Secondly, the substitution of naval for RAF technical ratings in one instance, the upkeep of torpedo flights, has already resulted in a reduction of 4 men per flight, with an annual saving on nearly £500 per flight.

(3) *Economy Produced*

The result of the Admiralty proposals will be to produce *a saving on pay and allowances of £92,000 per annum.* This figure does not include Marriage Allowance to RAF officers, which is expected to produce a further saving of not less than £10,000 per annum.

(B) Economies other than in personnel

The foregoing amounts are calculable, but savings in other directions will be made whose size cannot be definitely stated.

(1) The employment of the more highly skilled Naval engineering personnel on the upkeep of engines will reduce the expense of repairs and replacement, and, possibly, the size of engine reserves.

(2) Use will be made of existing Naval storage and transport facilities to a degree which is impossible while the Naval Air Arm is under other than Admiralty administration.

(3) The facilities for manufacture of spare parts in the Dockyards will tend to keep Contractors' prices down.

(4) Expenses in married quarters at aerodromes etc will be obviated, since they are not provided for naval officers and ratings.

(C) The question of reserves

The system of short-service commissions for officers of the Naval Air Arm is recommended by the Colwin Committee as an economical method of producing a reserve. As has been stated elsewhere, this system is entirely unsatisfactory to the Admiralty on account of its lack of efficiency. *Furthermore the proposal involves more officers receiving marriage allowance on board HM ships, where this allowance is not paid to Naval officers.*

The Admiralty have in view a reserve of over 100 per cent of Pilots, consisting in part of those who were employed in General Service after air training, and in part, of officers of the Royal Naval Reserve and Volunteer Reserve.

If experience shows the reserves to be insufficient, the Admiralty can draw upon a vast amount of suitable material in the Lower Deck of the Navy, and, by the employment of long-service Lower Deck ratings, can produce a more efficient and more economical reserve than would be obtained by the use of short-service officers.

Summary

The Admiralty claim for their proposals as to personnel *an economy* of about £100,000 per annum, which may be enlarged to *twice that amount* by the savings in other directions mentioned above, whose size cannot be definitely stated.

Moreover, these savings will be accompanied by an increase in the efficiency of the Navy and the contentment and confidence of the Fleet.

180. Chiefs of Staff Committee
Minutes of 27th Meeting [Beatty in the Chair]
[Extracts]

[Cab. 53/1]   March 11 1926
SECRET

*   *   *   *
[Joint War Plans]

Lord Beatty: stated that the discussion in regard to the Annual Review led to a question which he wished to place before the Committee in regard to Joint War Plans. He explained that in 1923 the Chiefs of Staff had proposed that the question as to what each Service should do in the event of war with certain Powers should be investigated. In January 1924 the Chief of the Imperial General Staff[1] put forward certain objections to the drawing up of War Plans, as a result of which no further action had been taken. One of the reasons urged for the postponement by the Chief of the Imperial General Staff had been that, between the outbreak of hostilities and the ultimate expansion for war, conditions would have so changed as to stultify any plans which had been previously arranged, and that therefore it was not advisable to have any cut and dried plans, but that only principles should be laid down. Admittedly this was so in the case of the Army and Air Force. In a war in the Far East where probably six weeks at least would elapse before the conditions under which these two Services would be called upon to act could be realised. Such however was not the case in regard to the Navy, which would be called upon to take action at once, and also, by the nature of the war itself, to act alone in the first instance. The Admiralty had therefore prepared plans for the war which had now reached a point where no further progress could be made without the co-operation of the other Services. This co-operation would take the form roughly of the protection of the routes and bases to the Far East, such as the Suez Canal, Aden, Trincomoli etc. In order to check the plans which the Admiralty had prepared, it would now

[1]Lord Cavan

be very helpful if the three Services could work together on certain specific points in those plans and then proceed to an examination of the possible later phases of the war on certain definite assumptions. In the case of a war with France conditions were somewhat different, as activity by all three Services would be required from the very outset. It was essential however, that the objectives of each of the three Services should be clearly defined. The Admiralty had prepared certain plans in this connection and would like them to be examined by the Joint Staffs. He thought that this examination would be very valuable and would lead to a comprehensive view of the whole problems involved [sic]. Such joint actions by the three Services could, in his opinion, result in nothing but good.

Sir Hugh Trenchard: said that he was in agreement on this point. In regard to a war in the Far East he explained that as far as the Air Force was concerned, action was entirely dependent upon the Naval plans, and the Air plan would have to be built upon the base of the Naval plan. So far as France was concerned, he thought that the same procedure would be adopted, but suggested that a war with Japan should be considered in the first instance, and that a war with France should be considered at a later stage.

Sir George Milne: stated that he quite agreed with Lord Beatty's proposals. In the case of the War Office, any Army plans were dependent upon the Naval appreciation . . .

Lord Beatty: stated that a war with Japan would probably entail political reaction as well. There might, for example, be risings in India, and the War Office might find themselves embarrassed by the situation there. From the Naval point of view, the defence of Hong Kong and Singapore, and the defence of the trade routes and the bases on those trade routes, were the essential features. He suggested therefore that after an examination of the Naval appreciation, the other two Services might draw up their plans to be superimposed on the Naval plan. He drew attention however to the fact that the plans were very secret, and that for these reasons it would be better if the meetings of the Joint Staffs were held at the Admiralty.

Sir Hugh Trenchard: suggested that each of the Chiefs of Staff should send their Deputies to attend the meetings at the Admiralty. He urged that for the preparation of adequate plans, it would be essential that each of the Staffs should have a copy of the Naval plan to work on. He further suggested that at the first meeting Lord Beatty should himself preside and that the other two Chiefs of Staff should also attend, so as to secure a general idea of the plans which the Admiralty had in mind. After this meeting, further examination could be carried out by the Deputies of the Chiefs of Staff.

Sir George Milne: considered that it would be very helpful indeed if Lord Beatty were to preside at the first meeting and the other Chiefs of Staff could also attend.

[Agreement unanimous.]

*   *   *   *

[*Institution of a Joint Services Staff College*]

[The Secretary, Sir Maurice Hankey, informed the meeting that the Prime Minister had asked the CID to reconsider the matter. The CID had now approved it in principle and passed it to COS for detailed consideration.]

Lord Beatty: stated that he was in agreement with the proposals on which a Joint College should be instituted, except that the higher strategical problems should now be submitted to the Chiefs of Staff Committee and not to the Committee of Imperial Defence. The original recommendations on the subject had been framed before the Chiefs of Staff Committee had been brought into existence.

The Admiralty was favourably disposed towards the creation of a Joint College . . . The danger of a Joint College was the possible creation of a super-Staff. He was convinced that a super-Staff would prove unworkable.

In regard to questions of Naval Policy and Strategy, the Chief of the Naval Staff was the only adviser to the Government. He was served by a Staff who worked up the cases for him, a super-Staff was therefore unnecessary and, if created, it would not have the knowledge which was necessary for the full and proper examination of any particular problem. Questions of naval strategy were governed by factors, such as personnel, material and economics, full knowledge of which was only to be found in the Admiralty. Unless these factors were taken into account correct appreciations were impossible. If, however, officers trained at the Joint College were utilised to replace officers on the existing Staffs, he felt that the proposal would lead to very useful results.

*   *   *   *

[The Chiefs of Staff agreed to reconsider the institution of the College in principle.]

181. *To his wife* [Freiburg]

[BTY/17/73/30–33]   17 Grosvenor Square
                                                     Thursday [11 Mar 1926]

. . . Everything is now in train for the Naval Estimates which begin in the House of Commons today. I do not anticipate we shall have much trouble until they begin to shower us with questions, which will be next week . . .

They are going to renew the attack on the creation of a Minister of Defence which is gathering strength in the House of Commons. But I do not think we shall have much trouble in defeating that idea, although I personally am all for a Minister of Defence in certain conditions. Only, I am afraid they would never accept my conditions, which are to do away with the First Lord, Secretary for War and Secretary for Air, and let the one Minister do the lot, with the Naval, Military & Air officers chiefs in their own departments without another civilian over them. Then one might get a real working machine, and certainly economy. As soon as I start that idea it will no doubt put a stop to the whole thing. But some of these young Members of Parliament have very small knowledge, and take themselves *very* seriously.

*   *   *   *

182. *Chiefs of Staff Committee*
Minutes of 28th Meeting [Beatty in the Chair]

[Extract]

[Cab. 53/1]   April 22 1926
SECRET

[*Foundation of the Imperial Defence College*]

Lord Beatty: stated that the Committee of Imperial Defence at its 211th Meeting held on March 29 1926 had agreed that:–

The Chiefs of Staff should be requested to formulate recommendations in regard to the number of students, revised syllabus and other details, and to report to the Committee of Imperial Defence.

Since that date he had had the question of a Joint College examined by officers at the Admiralty, as a result of which a Memorandum had been drawn up, which he would circulate to members of the Committee. The proposals contained in the Memorandum were briefly as follows:–

Name of the proposed College

He was in favour of the name 'Imperial Defence College', as that name would not be provocative. He had, however, no strong feelings on the matter, and was willing to fall in with any suggestions which might be made.

Functions

He considered the primary function of the College should be to produce a body of officers and officials from all Departments concerned, who had been trained to look at Imperial Defence problems as a whole. The secondary object was to investigate problems of Imperial Strategy referred to the College by the Chiefs of Staff Committee.

Composition

His proposals in regard to the number of students differed from those contained in the report of the Wood Committee in that he advocated the inclusion of graduates from various Government Departments, in addition to those from the three Fighting Services . . . In addition, the Self-Governing Dominions and India might be invited to send two students each, while such Departments as the Foreign Office, Board of Trade, Treasury, Home Office and the Colonial Office, might be requested to detail one graduate each . . . He thought that this suggestion would be in the nature of a *beau geste* on the part of the Fighting Services and would show that Imperial Strategy was not confined only to the exercise of the powers of the Fighting Services, but necessitated the co-operation of all National and Imperial resources in order to produce the maximum pressures on the enemy. It followed therefore that a College, the primary function of which was the study of Imperial Strategy, should include among its graduates both Service officers and civilian officials. This suggestion, if adopted, would have this further advantage, that it would obviate any possibility of the graduates of the new College entering as a body into the sphere of the planning of actual operations, and would confine their activities to the plane of Imperial Strategy. From a financial point of view also, assistance would be secured by the inclusion of officials from other Departments.

Cost

In his view it was most undesirable that the creation of the new College should result in a reduction of the funds allocated to the existing Staff Colleges, which were at the present time most economically run, and were also absolutely indispensable.

Syllabus

He considered that the syllabus should be laid down on broad and general lines, and should consist of lectures on such subjects as Political History, Naval and Military History and Strategy, Economics, i.e. Social, Industrial and Financial Resources of the British Empire and their effect in co-ordinating National efforts in war, Trade, including the resources of Foreign Powers whose policy might conflict with ours, and the means of bringing economic pressure to bear upon them, with due regard to the requirements of neutrals. Lectures on these subjects would, of course, be followed by discussions . . . In addition, concrete problems could be referred to the College, which would involve investigation into problems of Imperial Strategy, as might from time to time be decided by the Chiefs of Staff Committee.

*   *   *   *

183.   *Hankey to Beatty*

[Copy]

[BTY/8/1/13]   May 26, 1926
SECRET

I think it is possible that, as Chairman of the Chiefs of Staff Committee, you may like to have some preliminary observations on the Papers which are to be considered at the Meeting tomorrow.

On reading the whole of the Papers again, the point which impresses me most is one to which I alluded briefly once before, namely, that the review of the situation cannot be based solely on our commitments as set forth in the Papers by the Foreign Office, Dominions Office, Colonial Office and India Office. (N.B. We have not received the Home Office Paper yet, but I sent a 'hastener' last week.) The commitments as revealed by these Papers have to be tested and amplified from a study of Defence Policy as a whole.

I can well illustrate my point by a reference to the Navy itself. We are always told that war with America is not to be thought of. The Cabinet decided less than a year ago that 'aggressive action against the British Empire on the part of Japan within the next ten years is not a contingency seriously to be apprehended'. The Foreign Office, in their new Memorandum, tells us that the likelihood of war with Japan is exceedingly remote. We are also told that war with France during the next decade is among contingencies 'so improbable that they may legitimately be dismissed in any survey of the immediate future'.

If these statements are accepted at their face value and without consideration from a wider point of view, the logical conclusion would be that for the next ten years we only require a very small Navy.

But the Chiefs of Staff have to take a much wider view. They have to bear in mind that a Navy takes years and years to build up, both as regards material, constructive skill, and, above all, *personnel*. Once these fall below a certain level they can only be built up again very gradually. But they have to look further than this. Surely they have to consider also the importance of the objects to be defended. The risk of attack may be very remote, but the value of the object to be defended may be so great that you simply cannot take risks. I suppose that is why a military guard is still kept at the Bank of England. Broadly speaking, the Navy has to defend our territory against attack, as well as our trade routes on which we depend for the essentials of existence. Hence it would be absurd to trust, in such a vital matter, only to political security. In the words of the Cabinet Committee on the Air Force (words suggested by Sir Austen Chamberlain himself), 'In addition to political security some measure of practical security is required'.

It seems to me *the task of the Chiefs of Staff is to advise the Government as to the cases in which material security is required, and the extent to which it should be provided, having regard to all relevant circumstances.*

The Chief of the Air Staff maintains that the provision of a Home Defence Air Force falls within this category. He has behind him the support of a Cabinet decision, taken within the last few months, but, just as the Cabinet Committee postponed the date for completion of the Air Force scheme, so the Chief of the Air Staff seems to indicate a slowing down of the ancillary measures, such as the provision of anti-aircraft defence. The CIGS appears at first sight to go rather further in suggesting 'The need for concentration on provision for Home Defence against either attack by sea, *or attack by air*, becomes less urgent; and it would seem more profitable to adopt . . . an air policy of giving priority to the requirements of co-operation with the Navy and Army rather than to the needs of schemes of defence against air invasion'. But I do not think he and the Chief of the Air Staff are really very far apart in this.

Singapore obviously falls into the same kind of position, except that, as you have always insisted, the provision of the nucleus of the expanded scheme cannot be postponed unduly without risk.

As regards Locarno,[1] both the CIGS and the Chief of the Air Staff seem to contemplate that we cannot provide special forces for the fulfilment of our obligations, and, even if we tried, financial considerations would prevent us from providing a sufficiency. All that we can do is to organise such forces as we have in such a way that they can be used for this purpose, but, even so, they will be an earnest of our intention to mobilise our full strength rather than a force in any way adequate to the needs of the situation. The existence of this commitment, however, seems to justify the whole of the arrangements which we have been working out in the CID for expanding our man-power and munitions in case of necessity, and I should hope the Chiefs of Staff would bring this point out in their Report.

The order of priority of the above would seem to be the major issues at the moment. I do not propose in this letter to follow the other commitments, important though some of them are. If the main points are settled, these will fall into place later on.

I should, however, like to give one more illustration of the point with which I began, namely, that the Departmental Memoranda do not cover the whole of the ground. The case to which I refer is that of the Persian oilfields. I do not think it is mentioned anywhere in the Foreign Office Memorandum, either under Persia

[1]The Treaty of Locarno, 1925: a non-aggression pact between France, Germany and Belgium, with Britain and Italy acting as 'guarantors'.

or Iraq, nor is it mentioned in the Colonial Office Memorandum. Yet, when the needs of the Navy and Mercantile Marine for oil fuel are considered, the protection of these oilfields becomes, from an Imperial Defence point of view, almost a major consideration. I think all recent Governments have aspired to get quit of our responsibilities in Iraq. If we succeed in this, the position in the Persian oilfields will be much less secure than it is now, since the British forces in Iraq will no longer be available to delay and harass a Turkish advance which will be confronted (at first, at any rate) by nothing more serious than the forces of Iraq itself, and the oilfields will be dependent exclusively upon the despatch of forces from India.

I have not sent a copy of this letter to anyone else.

184. *Chiefs of Staff Committee Minutes of 30th Meeting* [Beatty in the Chair]

[Extract]

[Cab 53/1]   May 27 1926

Secretary's Full Notes Circulated to Chiefs only

[*Discussion on Annual Review of Defence Policy*]

Lord Beatty: . . . With regard to the One-Power Standard he pointed out that there was really no such thing and the title was a misnomer. The One-Power Standard applied only to capital ships and aircraft carriers, while the standard for other vessels was determined solely by the necessity of insuring freedom of sea passage on a world wide basis. As pointed out by the Chief of the General Staff [*sic*] in his Memorandum, unless freedom and security of sea passage throughout the Empire was assured, the whole system of Imperial Defence broke down. It was on this basis that the building programme for the Navy had been drawn up last year. Under that programme we should be weaker than the United States of America, Japan and France in regard to submarines, and the United States of America in regard to destroyers, but we should be the strongest Power in the world in regard to cruisers. He considered that it would be advisable for the Chiefs of Staff to confirm in their Report the necessity for maintaining the One-Power Standard *in regard to capital ships and aircraft carriers as determined at Washington*, and the maintenance of such other vessels as might be necessary to secure British territory and freedom of sea passage throughout the world.

[After contributions by CIGS and CAS on their own Services Beatty resumed.]

Lord Beatty: suggested that in order to cover these points, the Committee might confirm the necessity of maintaining:–

(*a*)   The One-Power Standard in regard to capital ships and aircraft carriers *as determined at Washington*.

(*b*)   Such other ships as might be necessary to ensure the freedom and security of sea passage throughout the world.

(*c*)   Properly defended bases *en route* to the Far East, culminating in Singapore; and that air developments should be continuously watched with a view to ensuring that full opportunity would be taken of utilising Air Power in contributing towards the maintenance of the freedom of sea passage throughout the world.

[This was agreed.]

With regard to Singapore *Lord Beatty* considered that a differentiation should be drawn between (a) the defences at Singapore and (b) the Naval Base on the Johore Strait. In regard to the defences at Singapore, the Foreign Office Memorandum definitely stated, 'all that it seems necessary to do is to make our strategic position in the Far East defensively as safe as our resources allow. A strong position at Singapore and the power to defend it, seem to give us all that we require in the Far East. We do not want to attack Japan, but we must be strong enough to deter her from attacking us.' (Paragraph 128). It was for this reason that the Naval Staff has constantly pressed that the defences at Singapore should be provided on such a scale as would be sufficient to deter Japan from making any attack upon it. Should Singapore by any chance be lost, it would be almost impossible to retrieve the situation in the Far East, and until Singapore was adequately defended, its very weakness might act as an incentive to attack it. He considered therefore that the Committee should endorse the Foreign Office view and should recommend that Singapore should be placed in such a condition as to act as an absolute deterrent to any attack on the part of Japan.

[Beatty's proposal was accepted, but CAS added the proviso that the method by which Hong Kong was to be defended was a separate matter which had yet to be decided.]

185. *A Review of Imperial Defence by the Chiefs of Staff Sub-Committee, 1926*

[Extracts]

[Cab. 4/15]   June 22 1926

The Problem

1. The problems of Imperial Defence arise out of the unique conditions of the British Empire. Scattered over the globe in every continent . . . they are dependent on the sea communications which unite them. If these communications are closed, they become liable to defeat in detail . . . The maintenance of these sea communications therefore is the first principle of our system of Imperial Defence. The whole fabric is built upon the assumption of the command of the sea. Unless freedom and security of sea passage throughout are assured, the system breaks down.

*   *   *   *

Order of urgency

*   *   *   *

31. The Foreign Office Memorandum (Printed in CID Paper No 700–B) indicates that our relations with France, the nation which is geographically best sited to damage us, are such that war with France during the next decade is among those contingencies which are, 'so improbable that they may legitimately be dismissed in any survey of the immediate future. Indeed, it is unlikely that Franco-German relations will ever be of such a kind as to make it possible for France to contemplate an armed conflict with Great Britain.'

32. The position as regards Japan is not quite so satisfactory. It is true that in the opinion of the Foreign Office there is no substantial cause 'to regard Japan as a potential enemy'. But, referring to the Four Power Treaty, the Memorandum describes Japan as the least dependable of the signatories, and, while affirming that Japan is not at present in a bellicose mood, the Memorandum warns us that 'no consideration of political probability in the Far East should therefore disregard the possibility of a reversion at a favourable moment to a policy of conquest and

of a recrudescence of the war spirit. There is however no immediate prospect of such a reversion.' Finally, . . . the Memorandum emphasises the necessity 'to make our strategic position in the Far East as safe as our resources allow', and affirms the desirability of establishing a strong position at Singapore.

33. It is impossible to foresee how the international situation affecting our position in the Far East may develop in future years, but at the present time we think it safe to ignore possible combinations of Powers, whether friendly or hostile to ourselves. We recommend therefore that Japan only should be taken as the Naval Power by which, for purposes of calculation, we measure our defence arrangements in the Far East.

34. Applying these considerations to the order of urgency, we think that the guiding principle should be the maintenance of our sea communications, the importance of which was emphasised at the outset of this Memorandum. The only Naval Powers which bear any comparison to the British Empire are the United States and Japan. Successive Governments have ruled the United States out of consideration in their defensive preparations. Having regard to the strong views of the Foreign Office already referred to, and without striking any alarmist note, we think that, as a general principle, the order of urgency at the present time should be governed by the desirability of securing our position in the Far East, and, above all, as already indicated, in providing the naval base and the necessary defences at Singapore, which we place first.

35. In accordance with the same principle, we think that second in order of urgency should come the defence of the trade routes, including air defence of these routes, and the revision of coast and anti-aircraft defences of the ports on the line of communication between Great Britain and Singapore.

* * * *

37. In the third category of urgency we place the arrangements for the security of the position at home, i.e. the coast and anti-aircraft defences of naval bases and other defended ports, and coastal defences of all kinds. In present conditions, as already explained, the dangers to Great Britain are not imminent, but the importance of home defences cannot be ignored, for the reason that a secure position at home is a prerequisite of the despatch of the forces necessary to protect our interests in the Far East and elsewhere.

* * * *

40.   As a governing principle however, we recommend that the programme of the Service Departments, including the provision of accommodation, should aim at the completion of the Singapore base and defences by the year 1935.

(Signed) BEATTY

G.F. MILNE

H. TRENCHARD

186.   *Beatty to Keyes* [HMS *Warspite*]

[Holograph]

[Keyes MSS S6/5]   *S.Y. Sheelah*

31.8.26

Thank you very much for your letter and for all that you say in it. I quite realise that there are a number of people, Political, Press and Naval, who would like to see the last of me in my present position.

As regards my relations with the 1st Lord, they have always been of the most friendly and happy character, and the only conversation I have ever had with him on the subject of the length of tenure of my office, was soon after he took over the 1st Lordship, when he asked me not to think of going (he having heard rumours that I was contemplating leaving) until he was firmly fixed. I replied that I would remain as long as he wished, but that I would like some notice of it, if it ever came he thought he would like a change, to which he replied that he hoped I would remain there as long as he did.

There is a clause on the Admiralty Instructions which says that the appointment should not be held for more than 7 years unless the emergencies of the Service demand otherwise. The AFO you refer to I have heard nothing of & I assume that it is a very recent one, and was issued with the object of paving the way for my departure.

Personally, I should like to go, and I think the time is very favourable, except for the new idea of pooling the Estimates, which will take some tackling and will be very hard on the new man. But I shall have achieved my object in getting the Singapore scheme definitely settled, which will be clinched at the Imperial Conference in October next, and that in itself marks an opportune moment in which to resign.

Unless there is a very definite expression of a wish for me to remain in view of the AFO you refer to, I should not think of remaining, and I am not sure that I should even then.

Under the circumstances I think it would do no harm, in fact it would do nothing but good, if you write to Bridgeman on the lines of your suggestions *re* the pooling of the Estimates, but I should *not* refer to the fact that I should be normally leaving on 1st Nov. in accordance with the established custom. You could say that I spoke to you about giving up, but, that in view of the new methods about to be established of dealing with the Estimates, you thought it would be a great pity to lose me at this juncture, and hoped that he (Bridgeman) would persuade me to remain, anyway until they were dealt with. A letter to Winston would also be of use, because I know that, although we have had many bitter battles, in which I have generally won, he bears [?] no malice, and I believe he thinks that I can establish more in the economy line than anybody else. A letter to him on the lines we spoke of & similar also to what you write to Bridgeman, would do nothing but good.

Even so, and all was satisfactory [*sic*], I am not binding myself to remain. I am getting fed up with the constant struggling, intriguing and underhand methods which are employed against me. My little lady's health is not good & causes me a great deal of anxiety. I can enjoy [*sic*] a season's hunting & a life free from the cursed office work for which one gets no thanks whatever. Moreover I think that I can be of considerable use to the Service when I have left the Admiralty and can voice views and opinions more freely outside than I can when in harness.

I know, my dear Roger, that you are moved [?] by your loyal spirit to write as you did, and I appreciate it very much indeed, and you know that I value your good opinion and your loyalty far more than I can express in a letter like this. You know, as few can do, the difficulties I have had to contend with in the last 7 years, and how heart-breaking it has been to reduce the great machine [?] both [?] in material and personnel, to its present moderate condition, and at the same time to preserve the spirit and retain the efficiency which we attained during the war. It has been done successfully, thanks to the loyalty of the whole Service, and without which it could not have been done.

I should love to carry out the programme you suggest of visiting the combined Fleets' exercises, and cruising with you to Malta, but the possibility of doing that is in the lap of the Gods.

I am afraid that I shall not be able to get back to the Aegean.

I shall have to be home by the 24th and in view of possible moves [?] to get rid of me, it is more important than ever it was. I must find out about this AFO & who started it and why it was necessary. Somebody should receive a severe shake . . .

I shall leave here tonight or Thursday morning and the *Witch* will leave here Thursday morning to rejoin you with this.

We all enjoyed our visit to the Fleet and wish it could have been longer.

187. *Keyes to Bridgeman*

[Holograph Photocopy]

[BGMN/1]   HMS *Warspite*
Mediterranean Fleet
8th September '26

The *Sheelah* spent two days with us in Gavrion Bay in the Doro Channel last week. Beatty looked very well and was in very good form. I got him to allow my Doctor, and the best [—] man in the [—] to overhaul him, and they found him quite sound and normal, but they impressed on him that he must go slow for some weeks. I think he had been rather overdoing it playing tennis at Therapia, and Lady Beatty was rather anxious — but quite happy after I gave her the Drs' report. Please don't mention this to them. Lady Beatty was better than I have seen her for years — and I thought him wonderfully well and cheery. He told me all about your battles of the last year or so since I left England. He talked about going soon, but I do hope you will persuade him to stay over these next Estimates. It would be very hard for a new 1st Sea Lord to go into the arena with Trenchard and the CIGS in the Chiefs of Staff meetings. I can't help feeling the pooling arrangement might be a very good one. If the three Services would stick together and play the game they would be bad to beat, but I must confess I can't quite see one or two of the people concerned playing the strictest cricket.

Just before I came out you told me you meant to ask Madden to relieve Beatty if he went — I hope you are still of the same mind because I am sure it would be a most popular appointment in the Service. I think I told you he once said to me in one of the many crises, 'Thank God Beatty is there, I couldn't compete with this sort of thing'. But if Beatty could only be persuaded to stay on long enough to tackle his dear colleagues on this pooling arrangement, it would give his successor a fair start.

*   *   *   *

188.   *To his wife* [Baden-Baden]

[BTY/17/74/2–7]   17 Grosvenor Square
                                                  Sunday [26 Sep 1926]

. . . I also got your wire that you had arrived safely . . . My Dear you must not talk or think because we have got on each other's nerves that it is the end of all things. The great thing is to realize it and then take steps to correct it, which can be done if we make up our minds to do so. And there is no question of your going away for 6 months or of your staying away for ever. We are both human beings with the faults that human beings are heir to, and so long as we recognise that and do not expect too much from each other, and really give and take, I cannot see why we should not be able to live happily together for the rest of our lives.

My dear heart there is no use being down & miserable about everything. I feel that out of evil cometh good and I believe that out of all the misery we have been through in the last 6 years we are going to arrive at a more staple [*sic*] understanding, suitable to our more advanced ages. There is one thing that is inevitable and nothing in the world can alter, and that is that we get older and as we get older, our ideas of life, our desires and our wants, alter, which necessitates a reshuffling of one's ideas and a recutting-out & planning of one's life. They say that all ages have their compensations, but we have to adapt ourselves and our outlook to them. You keep on harping on the fact that I want to enjoy life. Of course I do, of course everybody does, but I do not want to do so at the sacrifice of somebody else, least of all you. You do not think that is unreasonable do you? And I do not see why we cannot enjoy life together if there is a real & proper understanding between us and a real give and take in the conduct of our lives.

Now Tata dear you really must recognise that I am ready to meet you in any way possible and to help so that there shall be no more misunderstandings. Give me a little time to think things out and consider what our future is going to be.

For instance I cannot & will not stop on at the Admiralty for much longer and I have to think of what is going to happen after I leave, and the kind of life that is before us. All of which has to be considered in the scheme of things before arriving at a decision even of a temporary nature. But you must trust me a little more in the future and remember, that whatever my faults, I have always been loyal and true to you . . .

189.   *To his wife* [Baden-Baden]

[BTY/17/74/12–19]   17 Grosvenor Square
Thursday [30 Sep 1926]

*   *   *   *

I *never* said you were spoiling my life by saying what half of England said about W.C. & you have no right to say that I did. What I did say was that by saying what half England said about W.C. — your words not mine — you made my task & work at the Admiralty much more difficult.

I have to work with the man & when it gets to his ears, as it has done, that my wife continually describes him as a Danger to the State, he very naturally describes that opinion as coming from me.

How could for instance the Prime Minister work in harmony with W.C. his Chancellor of the Exchequer if Mrs Baldwin went about proclaiming loudly that he was a danger to the State?

*   *   *   *

190.   *To his wife* [Baden-Baden]

[BTY/17/74/99–102]   17 Grosvenor Square
19.10.26

*   *   *   *

We had our first meeting with the Prime Ministers today, and a self satisfied lot they looked.[1] I doubt — looking at them — if we get much out of them. They are all on the make, ready to receive but not to give . . .

The strike news is not so good. The weekend speeches of Mr Cook have had the effect of reducing the number of miners that have gone back to work, and they will never do any good so long as that rascal is allowed to remain at large, preaching sedition as he does. Why they don't lay him by the heels I cannot think. They could do so over and over again, and in no other country

[1]Gathered for the Imperial Conference, 19 October–23 November 1926.

would he be allowed so much licence. — But that is our way of living up to the democratic idea of Free Speech.

Midnight.
I have returned from a colossal banquet at Lancaster House to greet the Prime Ministers, followed by the usual reception after. You never saw such a collection of real stodgy people in your life. One wonders where they all come from, just real [?] middle class Conservatives. But on the other hand I did a certain amount of good by talking to the Colonial gentlemen and getting their heads set in the right direction . . .

191. *To his wife* [Baden-Baden]

[BTY/17/74/105–110] 17 Grosvenor Square
Thursday [21 Oct 1926]

*   *   *   *

We have been busy all day with the Conference, which as you can imagine is a very long winded affair; and much time is wasted with long speeches, which on the whole mean nothing, and is only lip service. But I hope with private conversations to get through a good deal, my principal object being to get support from the Colonies for the Admiralty policy to convince our own politicians. This I think I have been fairly successful with at present, and they all say they trust me and my advice more than that of anybody else, which, gratifying as it may sound, is of real value if they will voice these sentiments at the big meetings, and I think they will.

*   *   *   *

Friday night
The Dominion people are awful and they themselves told me they arc full up with engagements and never have a moment to themselves. I am dining with the 1st Lord tonight to meet the men, but not their wives. I will think of your suggestion and let you know. We could have a reception for them of sailors & their wives at the Mall House . . .

I have been dining tonight with the Royal Naval Reserve, a terrific banquet & interminable speeches. They got the Prince of Wales to come & were awfully pleased. It was the biggest dinner they had ever had and I had to make a speech about them, which was very tiresome, but they liked it as I laid on the butter very thick . . .

192. *Imperial Conference 1926*

[Cab 32/46]   Oct 26 1926

STATEMENT BY THE FIRST SEA LORD, ON BEHALF OF THE CHIEFS OF STAFF COMMITTEE

Lord Beatty: As the Prime Minister has already informed the Conference, as Senior Officer of the Chiefs of Staff Committee, I will deal with the strategical aspect of Imperial Defence.

It it obvious that measures of Imperial defence in their strategical aspects must be founded upon, and in a large measure dependent upon, the considered views of the Foreign Office and other Government Departments in regard to the political outlook in various parts of the world, and must take into particular account any commitments which have been entered upon by the Governments of the Empire.

The Secretary of State for Foreign Affairs has dealt with these aspects of the problem, and it only remains for me to give you a short review of the defensive situation that arises from them. I will, therefore, state the problem as it presents itself to the Chiefs of the Staffs.

Problems of Imperial Defence

The problems of Imperial defence arise out of the unique conditions of the British Empire. Scattered as it is over the globe in every Continent and sea, peopled by different races and in widely differing stages of progress, the component parts of the Empire have this much in common from the point of view of defence, that, with occasional and insignificant exceptions, they are able to maintain order with their own resources, supplemented, in some cases, by Imperial garrisons maintained for strategical reasons. But for any larger emergency requiring mutual support or co-operation they are dependent on the sea communications which unite them. If these communications are closed, they become liable to defeat in detail. Moreover, the Mother Country, the central arsenal and reserve for the whole Empire, is dependent for the essentials of life on the maintenance of a network of sea communications, extending not only to the territories of the Empire, but to every part of the world. The maintenance of these sea communications, therefore, is the first principle of our system of Imperial defence. The whole fabric is built up on the assumption of the command of the sea. Unless the freedom and security of sea passage throughout are assured, the system breaks down.

The communications of the British Empire are open to attack throughout their length by the sea, and the main responsibility for their protection and for denying them to any enemy must, therefore, rest with the Navy. In some zones, however, more especially in the narrow seas where they approach the land, these communications are also liable to attack from the air, and the Air Force are required to assist in their protection. As the range of aircraft increases, these zones will become extended, and air development should be continually watched with a view to ensuring that every opportunity is taken of utilising air power in contributing towards the maintenance of the freedom of sea passage throughout the world. In the Suez Canal the sea communications narrow to such an extent that they are open to attack from the land, and can only be secured by the co-operation of military forces. So exposed are some of our normal communications under modern conditions that plans have been made for the diversion, if necessary, of shipping in certain contingencies to safer routes.

If the responsibility of protecting sea communications of the Empire, for denying them to our enemies, and for deterring or intercepting sea-borne attack on British territory rests primarily with the Navy, the local protection of the terminal points (so far as these lie in British territory), of the bases and the fuelling stations on which the Fleet and Mercantile Marine depend for their mobility, is primarily the responsibility of the Army and the Air Force, subject to the important exception of the Dominions and India, which undertake full responsibility for their own local defence.

The capital of the Empire, and certainly the southern half of Great Britain, have within the last few years become potentially liable to a new form of attack from the air launched from the Continent. Politically, the chances of such an attack have been reduced to a minimum by diplomatic means. Materially, the main responsibility for countering this form of attack, if it should ever mature, rests with the Air Force, with the co-operation of the Army from the ground. The Air Force have the further duty of augmenting the striking power and reach of the Navy and Army.

Apart from co-operation with the other Services as already indicated, the Army is specially charged with making provision, firstly, for the land defence of the Empire generally, subject to the exception of the Dominions and India, that is, for Border defence and internal security, and, secondly, for external commitments incidental to our foreign policy.

The problem, as I have enunciated it, governs the policy of the Admiralty, the War Office, and the Air Ministry, and I will now deal briefly and separately with the policy of the three Services.

Naval Policy

Naval policy is chiefly concerned with the provision and maintenance of a fleet capable of shouldering the immense responsibilities devolving on the Navy, but without mobility the Fleet, however strong, would be of no avail.

Naval policy, therefore, falls under two main headings, the strength of the Fleet, and, secondly, the provision of naval bases and fuelling stations to enable the Fleet to be used effectively.

The standard of naval strength is determined by the principle set forth in the Report of the Imperial Conference of 1923, that is to say equality with the strongest foreign Naval Power in accordance with the Washington Treaty.

We have thought it necessary to emphasise that the One-Power standard, which is so frequently referred to, applies only to capital ships and large aircraft carriers, as was settled at Washington. In regard to cruisers, the standard of strength is necessarily determined by the requirements to ensure freedom and security of sea passage throughout the world. It is this principle that has determined the present programme of new construction of this type of vessel in this country.

We do not attempt to equalise the United States, Japan, or France in the number of submarines to be maintained, nor to gauge our destroyer requirements by the numbers maintained by the United States; on the other hand, the programme aims at making the British Empire sufficiently strong in cruisers to safeguard the sea communications of the Empire.

This is a reflection of our needs, particularly of our total dependence on overseas communications for our existence as an Empire, the extent of which may be gauged by the fact that 35 per cent. of the world's total mercantile tonnage is owned by the British Empire, and that, on any one day of the year, 3,500 ships of the Imperial Mercantile Marine will be found scattered over the trade routes engaged in the Empire's trade.

The principle may be summarised as follows:–

(a) The maintenance of the One-Power standard in regard to capital ships and aircraft carrier tonnage as determined at the Washington Conference.

(b) The maintenance of other types of vessels at such strength as will provide, firstly, the necessary component parts of a main fleet, and, secondly, the forces which, under cover of the general strategical support of the main fleet, are designated for the protection of British territory and the sea routes to and from all parts of the British Empire, this being the foundation of our system of Imperial Defence without which all other measures of defence are of little avail.

Naval Bases and Fuelling Stations

The provision of naval bases and fuelling stations at convenient points on our Imperial sea communications is essential to the mobility of the fleet and of the mercantile marine, and these require to be equipped with defences.

The principles governing the system of coast defence have been settled and considerable progress has been made in planning the revision of the defences of particular ports in accordance with these principles both at home and overseas. In particular, the plans for bringing up to date the defences of Imperial defended ports east of Suez, as well as an order of urgency for these ports *inter se*, have been approved by the Committee of Imperial Defence.

In this connection the Chiefs of Staff Committee have strongly urged that the development of Singapore as a naval repair and fuelling base should be placed first in order of urgency of our defence requirements, and that, moreover, the defences of that port should be on a scale unmistakably sufficient to deter attack, and this has been approved in principle by His Majesty's Government.

Singapore is a key position whose occupation by a hostile fleet would expose our lines of communication with all parts of the Empire in the Pacific and the Bay of Bengal to interruption, with incalculable consequences to the Dominions of Australia and New Zealand, and to our position in India. To deny this possibility by the provision of defences on a scale sufficient to deter attack and to provide a naval base at Singapore for our own use is the surest way of reducing an enemy's power to inflict permanent damage on us and is therefore a measure calculated to prevent war and to ensure peace.

Military Policy

Dealing with the military policy, the self-governing Dominions have accepted the responsibility for their own military defence until such time as reinforcements can reach them from the other parts of the Empire. India, with the help of a British garrison, has accepted a similar responsibility.

The size of the British Regular Army is based on the requirements for the immediate defence of our overseas garrisons and is governed by a system which demands an approximate equilibrium between the number of units maintained overseas and at home. The Expeditionary Force being organised from those units at home is therefore a by-product of this system, and as regards size has no relation to that of foreign armies.

Financial stringency has led to the reduction of our overseas garrisons to such a point that they are barely sufficient for the rôle they may be called upon to play. A small Imperial reserve would be most valuable east of Suez, but our overseas garrisons are insufficient to provide this. The British Expeditionary Force, therefore, represents our only immediate reserve, and it is of the first importance that it should be highly efficient and capable of transportation to any threatened point.

Whereas prior to 1914 the centre of gravity was unmistakably in Europe, this centre has now shifted eastwards, although at the same time we have treaty commitments in Europe. The same organisation for a war in the East would not necessarily best suit a war in the West, and financial considerations prevent us from developing fully an efficient organisation for both theatres.

This shows some of the problems with which the Army is confronted. Our policy is to modernise our striking force and so equip and train it that it may be more efficient than any enemy which it may be called upon to meet. At the same time it is necessary to ensure its transportation to any threatened point, and with this in view we are completing, to commence with, the defences of such ports on the Far Eastern route as are required by the Navy.

At the outset of any war, we are likely to be at a disadvantage as regards numbers until the Territorial Army can be got ready and the Dominions provide such contingents as they may see fit. We propose that the organisation of the Territorial Army shall be based on that of the Regular Army, and we hope that the Forces of the Dominions will assume a similar organisation, as the homogeneity of an Empire Army is one of the essential provisos for success in a war demanding an Empire effort.

Air Policy

Now turning to the air and air policy, it is the policy of the Government steadily to expand the Home Defence Air Force to a strength of fifty-two squadrons. Until recently the aim was to complete this measure of expansion by 1928, but in view of the improved international situation in Europe, coupled with the need for strict economy, the date of completion has been postponed until 1935.

This force of fifty-two squadrons, although called the Home Defence Air Force, is also the main reserve for action in the air both at home and overseas, corresponding in this respect to the Army Expeditionary Force, and for this reason no further slowing up in the rate of expansion is considered justifiable by the Chiefs of Staff Committee.

Our vital sea communications pass through zones which will increasingly be exposed to air attack, and even now, did our resources permit, we should be glad to increase the number of aircraft available at shore bases for co-operation with naval forces and to supplement the military defences.

Undue dispersion would, however, be detrimental to the fullest development of the air service, and at present, when much research and experiment is required, it is desirable to maintain the bulk of the Royal Air Force at home. Any additional squadrons required in an emergency for co-operation either with the Army or with the Navy would have to be drawn from existing resources. The development of air routes and air bases would enable movements by air to be carried out more freely, and would thus increase our ability to move units rapidly by air to such areas as circumstances or emergencies may demand.

The activities of Russia in Asia make it important that the Air Force in India should be strengthened.

After reviewing our requirements as a whole, and giving due weight to the circumstances that affect the growth and development of this comparatively new factor in Imperial defence, we have recommended that the policy of the Royal Air Force should be developed, broadly speaking, with a view, first, to research and experiment, leading to further development; secondly, to meeting the requirements at home and for Imperial Defence; thirdly, to meeting Admiralty requirements for the Fleet Air Arm and shore based units at selected naval ports; fourthly, to providing squadrons for co-operation with the Army and bombing and fighter squadrons to accompany the Expeditionary Force; and, fifthly, to improving air communications by the development of air bases on strategic routes.

Order of Urgency for Development

Having stated the problem and dealt very briefly with the main outlines of our defence policy, I think it is necessary to add a few words in regard to the order of urgency in which particular developments should be undertaken. This depends to a considerable extent upon the state of our relations with foreign Powers, and that is a consideration which the Chiefs of the Staffs have to take fully into account.

Taking this into consideration, and in default of any clear threat to the Empire such as existed prior to 1914, we consider that the guiding principle in determining an order of urgency for development should be the maintenance of our sea communications, the importance of which I have already emphasised.

We therefore recommend that, as a general principle, the order of urgency at the present time should be governed by the desirability of securing our position in that part of the world where there are Dominions, territories, and an enormous volume of shipping without adequate protection — that is to say, east of Suez. For this, as already stated, the first requirement would be the provision of a defended naval base at Singapore. The situation of this base marks it out as a corner-stone of Imperial Defensive Strategy.

In accordance with the same principle, we place second in order of urgency the defence of the trade routes, including air defence of those routes, and the revision of coast and anti-aircraft defences of the ports on the lines of communication between Great Britain and Singapore, while in the third category of urgency we place the arrangements for the security of the position in Great Britain with due regard in particular to the defence of London.

Under present conditions, as already indicated, the dangers to Great Britain are not imminent, but the importance of home defence cannot be ignored, for the reason that a secure position at home is the pre-requisite of the despatch of the Forces, Naval, Military, and Air, that might be required to protect the overseas interests of the Empire as a whole or those of any one of the Dominions comprising the British Empire.

Finally, account has to be taken of those political dangers to which the possession of great land frontiers exposes us, notably on the frontier of India. To these questions no order of urgency can be assigned. They are always with us, calling for a degree of consideration and vigilance according to whether other nations are pursuing an aggressive policy or not.

193. *To his wife* [St Moritz]

[BTY/17/75/15–17]   Admiralty
                                                    Monday [17 Jan 1927]

*   *   *   *

I had to come up over the China trouble which is getting worse instead of better and the Cabinet are going to have another meeting this evening to which I have to go.[1] I have a squadron of cruisers all ready to leave Malta and am collecting 1,000 Marines which I can send off by Friday. The Soldiers are so slow, but they will have to despatch a brigade from India, if not more, before they have done, and the sooner the better unless we intend to lose all our prestige in China.

I have just returned from a stormy Cabinet meeting at which I succeeded in getting my way, and they have agreed to send a brigade from India and get another one ready to follow as soon as possible. But it will take them 5 weeks to get them there, and that may be too late. We have been humming and hawing over this for 3 weeks & at last they recognise that they have got to do what they should have done in the first instance . . .

---

[1]From 1920 civil war and near anarchy in China had increasingly threatened the European Concessions. The situation in January 1927 caused Britain to send three brigades as reinforcements to protect life and property in Shanghai.

194. *Hankey to Beatty*

[BTY/14/7/5]   Office of the Cabinet
2 Whitehall Gardens
S W 1
30 iv 27

I am very sorry to see that you have decided to go. I can guess that your motives are generous and that you feel you must give others a chance. I dare say also that you will be glad to get out of the ties of office life.

Still, you will be very much missed. You are the only First Sea Lord I have known in my 26 years who could really talk on even terms to the highest cabinet ministers and stand up to them in argument. Fisher is an exception, but Fisher was a crank, and even he didn't really state a case clearly.

This has meant everything in starting the COS Committee. Without a really first class chairman we might have failed, and that would have been disastrous. It might have brought a Ministry of Defence even.

You have tremendous achievements to your name, but your successful pilotage of the COS Committee through its early days will, I believe, be one of your great contributions to the Empire's welfare.

I am glad to think how well I have always worked with you.

195. *To his wife* [Baden-Baden]

[BTY/17/77/67–72]   Admiralty
Tuesday [14 June 1927]

*   *   *   *

You said in one of your letters you hoped I was dining out and enjoying myself. That I simply cannot do while you are away and I should hate to do. There would be no pleasure in it and I much prefer a quiet life and am happier under the existing circumstances when I am alone, and I certainly am not good company for anybody.

The World is in a very serious state of unrest and consequently am [sic] very fully employed. China, Egypt, the Balkans, Yugoslavia versus Albania, Roumania, Russia & Poland, Iraq, the Red Sea and the Flag question in South Africa, are all cases which might develop into something serious. And, on the top of it all we have the Disarmament Conference[1] which commences next week, and is a source of providing an enormous amount of work and will have to be handled with a considerable amount of care and delicacy. The First Lord is getting fussed about it and wishes now that he was not going and that I was in his place. I think however that the questions which require immediate decisions & the providing of important technical advice require me here, and the Prime Minister said that he could not spare me to go to Geneva with all these very real troubles in hand, and he keeps bombarding me with questions all day long. However we are getting along and I do not think they are getting any worse now, and hope that in the near future they will get very much better.

*   *   *   *

196.   *To his wife* [Baden-Baden]

[BTY/17/77/108–111] Admiralty
Tuesday [21 June 1927]

*   *   *   *

I spent an hour with the Prime Minister this morning discussing Naval Policy in the absence of the First Lord. He really is very ignorant on the first needs of the Empire, but seems to be imbued with a total distrust of the United States and yet hasn't the courage to agree to a very definite line on our part.

As a first disclosure of the proposals of the USA and Japan at the Conference, it would appear that we are a very long way apart, and a lot will have to be bridged before we can even [?] dream of coming together. Mercifully I have tied our naval representatives up so that they cannot give very much away without referring to me, and I think that all will accordingly be well. But the actual proposals of the other two powers does [sic] not mean much in the way of economy, in fact it would mean a greater expenditure, whereas our proposals definitely indicate a means of achieving very large savings amounting to many millions. How-

---

[1]The Geneva Conference opened on 20 June 1927. Its failure to continue the naval reductions of Washington, particularly in cruisers, is summarised in Roskill, *Naval Policy I*, p. 516 and described as the nadir of Anglo-American naval relations.

ever, this is only the first day and there is a lot of water to be covered before they can reach any agreement . . .

The disappointment will be great here if they cannot get them to agree to something much clearer than they are thinking about at present . . .

197. *Beatty to Bridgeman*

[Holograph Photocopy]

[BGMN/1]   23.6.27

My Dear First Lord,

Thank you for your letter of first impressions.

From them I gather that the situation at Geneva created by the first broadsides was not altogether too bad, and that our proposals evidently took them by surprise as going considerably further than they ever thought we should go, & for that reason have taken a great deal of wind out of their sails, and the 'beau geste' which the Americans thought they were making has fallen very flat . . .

I think that the statement made by Gibson[1] in his opening address that 'Navies should be reduced to the minimum strength compatible with National Security', should be seized upon by us and never let go of. It will be difficult for the US to make a case for a large number of cruisers if that is one of the governing principles . . .

I saw the PM on the subject of the reconstruction [?] of the great [?] building firms, more especially Vickers and Armstrongs, and he is to circulate a memorandum to us on this very vital question. We have all the information from the Admiralty point of view readily available, and I think we will be able to provide data which will enable him to come to a decision.

*   *   *   *

I am glad that you find Field and Egerton[2] a great assistance. They send me a daily telegram which keeps us *au fait* with all that is going on, which is valuable in keeping us up to date.

Good Luck to you with your endeavours. I am sure we will

[1]Hugh Gibson (1883–1954): American Ambassador at Brussels, leader of US Geneva delegation. Roskill depicts him as ignorant of naval affairs and very much under the influence of his naval adviser, Admiral Hilary P. Jones (1863–1938) who was strongly anti-British.

[2]Captain W. A. Egerton, Director of Plans Division, Naval Staff.

come out all right and I am happy that you should be there and not let Cecil[1] too free a hand with the Locarno spirit.

Yours ever

BEATTY

198. *To Eugénie Godfrey-Faussett*

[SLGF 15/6/11]   Admiralty
                                                          12.7.27

. . . It will be a wrench to sever my connection with the Service I have spent my life in. I have never admitted it to anybody, hardly to myself. The great days of the past were and are unforgettable. The latter days since 1919 at times appear like a nightmare but they had their compensations. However the everlasting struggle is over and my task is done.

*   *   *   *

199. *Beatty to Bridgeman*

[Holograph Photocopy]

[BGMN/1]   29 July 1927

My Dear First Lord,

On this, my last day in the office of 1st Sea Lord I must write to say how much I regret leaving the Admiralty and all the work which has occupied me during the past 8 years, less 3 months.

Also to thank you for your trust in me and for the support you have always given to the many recommendations I have put forward, and for the consideration you have given to the Naval point of view.

I think you were probably right in suggesting having fresh blood and a new outlook on the many Naval problems, and I shall not be sorry to have a holiday. We certainly have had a most tempestuous time in the Admiralty since I have been here, and the last few weeks have been a good sample.

[1]Robert Cecil, later Viscount Cecil of Chelwood (1864–1958): 3rd son of 3rd Marquis of Salisbury; Conservative MP 1906–10, 1911–23 when created Viscount; Parliamentary Secretary for Foreign Affairs 1915–18; Minister of Blockade 1916–18; Assistant Secretary of State for Foreign Affairs 1918–19; leading influence in founding of League of Nations; Lord Privy Seal in charge of League affairs 1923; continued in Baldwin's 2nd administration 1924; delegate to Geneva Conference 1927 and resigned when Cabinet refused to accept Cruiser parity with the USA.

I sincerely trust that the results of the Conference will be in accordance with the needs of the Empire and you will return after successful achievement [*sic*]. We have gone as far as is possible to go; further would jeopardise the fate of the Empire and it would be better [— — —] the Conference than do that.

The latest reports of Field[1] are hopeful, but I do not imagine that he will be able to return to the Admiralty for a considerable time; the longer leave he has the better for his usefulness to the Navy, and it may be that it were better he should remain free from work & worry until he relieves Keyes, in which case his place at the Admiralty could best be filled by moving up 4th Sea Lord,[2] as I suggested to you some time ago. Madden may ask for Fuller[3] who was his Chief of Staff in Atlantic Fleet. I personally do not think Fuller would make a satisfactory DCNS. We had experience of him when Controller, and although he has many good qualities, he is not a tactful or judicious person to deal with the committee work outside the Admiralty where he has to meet [?] many conflicting personalities.

I understand that you agree with this, but, as I shall not be here, I am only putting forward for your benefit my advice [*sic*]. I do think Fisher has the necessary qualifications and would get on well both in the Admiralty and outside it.

Before leaving the Admiralty I should like to bring to your notice the eminent services of the PAS(S) to the Naval Staff during my tenure of office. Mr Flint has been indefatigable in co-operating with the various Directors of the Staff Divisions and his tact and professional knowledge have been invaluable. Possibly you may deem it desirable [?] to submit his name in due course for an Honour.[4]

Well, First Lord, I must shut up & say my Farewell to our official relations, but trust we shall see something of you and Dame Caroline[5] in a private capacity very frequently,

Yours very sincerely,
BEATTY

---

[1]Sir Frederick Field remained DCNS until May 1928, when he was relieved by Vice-Admiral Sir W. W. Fisher. Field then relieved Keyes as C-in-C Mediterranean in June 1928 and became 1st Sea Lord in June 1930.

[2]The 4th Sea Lord was W. W. Fisher.

[3]Admiral Sir Cyril Fuller had been 3rd Sea Lord and Controller 1923–5 and became 2nd Sea Lord in 1930.

[4]A. Flint, CB, a Principal Assistant Secretary, duly received a CMG.

[5]Bridgeman's wife.

200. *Bridgeman to Beatty*

[Holograph]

[BTY/13/3]   Geneva
July 29, 1927

My Dear Lord Beatty,

I am sorry to be away on the last day of your time at the Admiralty in one sense, but glad in another because it would have been a very painful thing to me to bid you an official goodbye after the three years of companionship in the work at the Admiralty.

By word of mouth it would have been difficult to express my gratitude to you for all your help, support and instruction, — and even by letter I can hardly say what I feel. I have had now a good many years experience in various Government Offices — but never have I come across a colleague with whom I could work as easily as with you, in calm as well as in troubled times.

You have never bothered me with unimportant affairs and you have never let me run up against serious difficulties without pointing them out to me — and never have I had an adviser who was able to put a case more plainly or more concisely before me.

More than that you have always been able to see the political trials of my position, though it is often held that the Royal Navy can see nothing outside their own Service. That is not my experience of those [*sic*] principal members of the Admiralty Staff.

You have never spared yourself in time or trouble when we were pressed, and never lost your equanimity even under the very trying circumstances which you and I have had to go through together occasionally.

So, I thank you with all my heart for the splendid work you have done at the Admiralty and greatly regret its termination — I shall always remember our association as one of the most agreeable chapters of my political life and I hope you will sometimes be able to look back on the time we have spent together with satisfaction.

And, in conclusion, I must wish you every happiness and an agreeable scope for your great success and ability in whatever direction you may seek it.

Yours v. sincerely
W. C. BRIDGEMAN

201. *Beatty to Bridgeman*

[Holograph Photocopy]

[BGMN/1]   17 Grosvenor Square
[London] W. 1
6.8.27

I must write and thank you for the very charming letter which I greatly appreciate.

I am glad to know that the Conference has come to an end without the Americans having achieved what they undoubtedly set out to do: *i.e.* to achieve command of the sea at no cost.

Every nation in the history of the world has only obtained Sea Power as the result of great achievements and the price of many lives and much money. The D— — — —D Yanks thought they could get it for nothing!! I wish the true story of their ridiculous attitude under the guise of economy and disarmament could be made plain to the World. It would flatten the Big Navy party in the United States for all time.

I thank Le Bon Dieu that you were head of our delegates. No one else would have had the patience and clear headedness to have weathered the storm, and I expect you were tried beyond endurance.

Now I assume we shall continue [?] with our programme somewhat [?] delayed, as if there had been no Conference. But I am sure you will have a rough passage with the next Estimates, as the Chancellor will find in what has happened cogent reasons for reconsidering it [*sic*] . . .

PART IV

THE SINGAPORE BASE
1921–1926

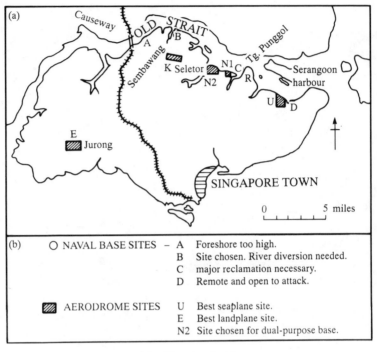

(a)

(b)
    ○ NAVAL BASE SITES – A   Foreshore too high.
                                         B   Site chosen. River diversion needed.
                                         C   major reclamation necessary.
                                         D   Remote and open to attack.

    ▨ AERODROME SITES   U   Best seaplane site.
                                         E   Best landplane site.
                                       N2 Site chosen for dual-purpose base.

(a)   *Choosing the site*

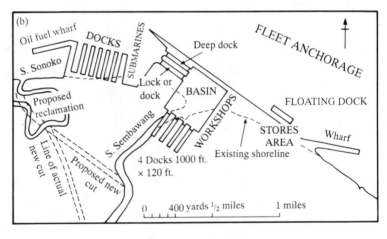

(b)   *The first proposals (1922) including an enclosed dock basin*
The Singapore Base 1920–1922

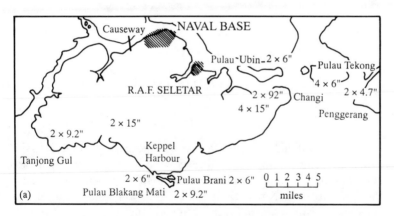

(a)   *The first coastal artillery proposals (1923). In 1926 the central battery of 15-inch guns was changed to Blakang Mati; three were authorised in 1926, only to be suspended in 1928*

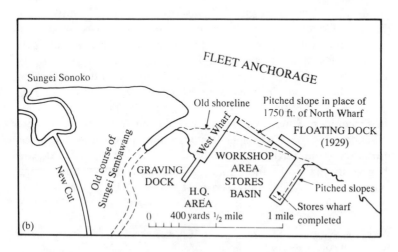

(b)   *The truncated scheme (1926), which was completed with half the walls unbuilt at first*
The Singapore Base 1923–1926

359

INTRODUCTION[1]

By the second half of 1919 a growing perception that a major threat to Britain's imperial interests would come from Japan was revealed both in Jellicoe's Reports on his Empire Mission[2] and in the work of the Naval Staff. The Staff were sceptical of any substantial American help and built up the argument that only a superior fleet operating in the Pacific could deter Japanese expansionism and that such a fleet could not function effectively without a secure base at Singapore. When Beatty took office in November 1919 he had found the scene already set for what was to be one of his most difficult struggles with successive governments. By 1921 Lloyd George's coalition government was committed to the scheme but, in announcing this to the Imperial Conference which opened in June, Balfour, the Chairman of the Standing Sub-Committee of the Committee of Imperial Defence, which had recommended the decision to the Cabinet, also stated that the financial situation did not permit the allocation of the necessary funds for work to begin. On this occasion and at subsequent Imperial Conferences in 1923 and 1926 one of the British government's aims was to persuade the colonies and India to contribute to the costs of establishing the base from which the security of their territory and trade would benefit. At the Washington Conference, which began in November 1921, and the Four Power Pact between the United States, Britain, France and Japan, signed in December, which was seen as replacing the Anglo-Japanese alliance, Singapore was specifically excluded from the restriction forbidding the fortification of islands in the Pacific. Work was begun, but halted by the Labour government of 1924, and recommenced, but without any sense of urgency, after the Baldwin government succeeded it in November of that year.

[1]The background to this section is in Roskill, *Naval Policy I*, Chapters VII–XIII; W. David McIntyre (1979), *The Rise and Fall of the Singapore Naval Base 1919–1942*, London, with its diagrams of the development of the general design and defences is particularly informative.
[2]*Jellicoe Papers II*, Part III.

The government made defence, particularly in the Far East, the central theme of the 1921 Imperial Conference and put up Beatty to explain the strategic issues involved. He seized the opportunity for a full proclamation of his naval doctrine.[1] The Far Eastern Empire and its trade could only be assured by a decisive defeat of Japan's main weapon against them, her fleet. He accepted that the navy's role in a major war was the defence of sea communications, but attacked opinions which suggested that this could be achieved before the enemy's main strength had been destroyed. Although he did not mention his name, he was obviously tilting at those influenced by Sir Julian Corbett, who was held to underestimate the importance of the decisive battle in naval warfare. It will be remembered that when Corbett's third volume of his official history of the Great War at sea, *Naval Operations*, appeared in 1923, the Admiralty was to insist on inserting the disclaimer which reiterated Beatty's views:

> Their Lordships find that some of the principles advocated in this book, especially the tendency to minimise the importance of seeking battle and forcing it to a conclusion, are directly in conflict with their views.

To Beatty, Singapore was a base for offensive action but had to be able to defend itself during the six weeks or so it would take for a major fleet – on this occasion detailed as consisting of at least 8 capital ships and 16 cruisers – to reach it from European waters. The size of the force was to vary in future plans, but the principles of Britain's Far Eastern strategy were to remain constant throughout Beatty's term of office, as was his pressure on governments to provide the resources to implement them. He was ready to compromise on details if minor economies would enable the main design to go forward, but never shifted from his central position, that the base should be adequate to fuel and maintain a fleet strong enough to defeat its enemy counterpart and must be secure against the strongest force that could be launched against it, until the fleet arrived [202–4, 206].

Beatty's toughest struggle was with the Clynes Committee set up by Ramsay MacDonald to investigate the Admiralty's linked proposals for a long term construction programme and the establishment of the Singapore base, against the background of the Labour government's strong desire to reduce defence expenditure.

[1]See Document 87a above.

Although Beatty largely succeeded in his proposals for cruiser construction, he failed on Singapore.[1] This was not because of any refutal of his strategic arguments, or even mainly on economic grounds, but because the government, and Ramsay MacDonald in particular, saw the build-up of the base as opposed to his great ambition of bringing about a new international atmosphere favourable to general disarmament and the peaceful settlement of disputes. The documents show in detail how strongly Beatty put his case in committee, not hesitating to confront the Prime Minister himself [207–9]. There is strong evidence that he was constantly supported at Cabinet level by Chelmsford.[2] Their efforts continued after the Cabinet's decision not to proceed with the work, in which Beatty, true to his belief in the offensive, challenged the government to demonstrate real progress in its diplomatic and disarmament negotiations as an alternative means of national and imperial security. He considered that only the scrapping of Japan's entire battle fleet would be an adequate response to the abandonment of the Singapore base, a sacrifice he knew Japan would never make [211–12].

Beatty had another battle to fight over Singapore, not with the politicians but with his two professional colleagues in the Chiefs of Staff Committee, which he himself now chaired. The main clash was with Trenchard and centred on the defence of the base before the Fleet arrived in eastern waters to challenge its Japanese counterpart. The specific issue was whether, as Beatty asserted, the only effective weapons were heavy fixed guns to keep the enemy fleet out of bombardment range, or torpedo aircraft which Trenchard argued would be at least equally effective and more economical. Trenchard had to acknowledge that suitable planes were not immediately available but would become so during the ten year period of peace upon which all government defence planning was based. Beatty based his case on the need to produce a deterrent against attack as quickly as possible, and challenged Trenchard's claim for economy on the grounds that he was proposing far too small an air force, especially in the provision of fighters to protect the torpedo bombers from Japanese carrier-borne attack aircraft. Their positions were so far apart that the Chiefs of Staff had to report that agreement was impossible [204–5, 213–16].

[1] See Document 147 above.
[2] An example is his argument with Snowden the Chancellor in the Clynes Committee, 11 April 1924 (BTY/8/5/17).

202.   *Notes on Singapore by Naval members of Overseas Defence Committee*[1]

[Copy]

[BTY/8/5/2]   Naval Staff
                                                              5th May 1921

1. The principal reasons for the Admiralty desire that Singapore should be developed as a naval stronghold is that at the present time there is no secure fleet base in the East in a good strategic position.

2. Hong-Kong occupies a more favourable strategic situation than Singapore, but by reason of its advanced position the War Office have expressed their inability to guarantee its security from the land side without the employment of such large military forces as to be out of the question.

3. It must not be inferred from the foregoing paragraph that the Admiralty would view the fall of Hong-Kong with equanimity. Far from this being the case, its loss would be a tremendous set-back both to our prestige and our strategical policy. It is hoped that the arrangements proposed to speed up its relief by the fleet will prevent this happening. It is obvious, however, that no plans could be matured that depended upon such a doubtful factor as the retention of Hong-Kong in the face of strong Japanese attack. It is also well known that Japanese ambitions extend southward, and this tends to leave Hong-Kong more and more exposed.

4. The first requisite for the fleet in the East is a secure base, and as Hong-Kong cannot be relied upon for this purpose a base further south must be provided.

5. Singapore stands at the western gateway to the Pacific covering the eastern approaches to India and our other Asiatic possessions, and flanking the route from Eastern Asia to Australia and New Zealand.

6. It occupies the corresponding position to the British Empire in the East that Gibraltar does in the West and its development has become a necessity in any sound Empire Naval Policy. This

[1] Presumably used by Beatty in preparation of his address to the Imperial Conference in July 1921. Document 87a above.

development would undoubtedly have been effected at an earlier date had it not been for our preoccupation in Home Waters and the comparative weakness of the Japanese Fleet.

7. The principal requirements of the near future at Singapore are the establishment of Defences and the provision of fuel reserves. Docking and Repair facilities can be gradually developed to meet fleet requirements.

8. In the opinion of the Naval Staff Singapore should be rendered secure and self-contained against the maximum scale of naval attack, without fleet support, for a period of six weeks. This will necessitate a thorough revision of the Defence scheme. The present scale of defence is intended to deter a powerful squadron of armoured cruisers with a raiding force of about 2,000 men from making an attack, and to provide protection for the large volume of trade which passes through the Straits covered by the defences.

9. The main point for decision before a revision of the Defence Scheme can be undertaken is the selection of the fleet anchorage. This question has been under consideration at the Admiralty for some time. The choice lies between:–

(a) The water area enclosed by the Islands to the south west of Singapore Island, i.e. Selat Sinki.

(b) The Old Strait (including the entrance to the Johore River) to the north of Singapore Island.

(a) Selat Sinki is not considered practicable from a naval point of view owing to the difficulty of providing efficient seaward defence against torpedo attack by submarine and light surface craft and the prohibitive cost of obstructions.

(b) The Old Strait is suggested as likely to meet naval requirements but its selection involves important military defence questions which are now being investigated by the War Office.

10. On the assumption, however, that the Old Strait is to be the fleet anchorage, it is possible to give some indication of the naval requirements so far as the defence of Keppel Harbour and the Old Strait are concerned.

11. There will be two distinct phases in the future defence of Singapore.

(a) The period before the arrival of the main fleet.

(b) The period after its arrival.

It is during phase (a) that an enemy, having local sea supremacy, might undertake a combined attack with a view to rendering useless the resources of the port or possibly with a view to occupation, but sea attack would probably be confined to bombardment at long and moderate range of vulnerable objectives; blocking the entrance to the naval anchorage and minelaying in the approaches.

Provision must therefore be made

(*i*)   To protect Keppel Harbour, its docks, wharves, repairing and commercial facilities and fuel.

(*ii*)   To protect the Old Strait and the entrance to the Johore River against blocking attack and mine-laying especially during the precautionary period; to preserve such docks, naval works, magazines, oil fuel as may be established in the vicinity and to provide a secure anchorage for such naval forces as may be on the station awaiting reinforcement.

During phase (*b*) adequate protection for the fleet will also be required, particularly against torpedo attack, by light surface craft and submarines. It is improbable that any combined naval and military operation on a large scale would be undertaken or continued after the arrival of the fleet in the main theatre.

12.   In so far, therefore, as naval requirements are concerned it will be necessary to establish, in peace, permanent seafront and seaward defences, at both entrances to Keppel Harbour and Johore River capable of withstanding those forms of sea attack which, as indicated above, may be anticipated during phase (*a*), for it is not considered that any defences, which could be improvised during the period of strained relations could be adequate for this purpose.

13.   It will also be necessary to provide for the establishment during phase (*a*), of such additional seaward defences as will be required to guarantee a safe anchorage for the fleet against those forms of attack which may be expected on and after its arrival.

14.   As regards the military question of the preservation of the land front, which arises more particularly during phase (*a*), it is considered that it will be possible to minimise the risk of hostile landing by the provision of local Defence Flotillas of submarines of [*sic*] light surface craft. Such forces, in addition to the provision of heavy long range guns on shore would also constitute a deterrent to bombardment from the sea.

15.   The possibility of attack by land will be better able to be estimated after the report of the combined naval and military

reconnaissance of the south east coast of the Malay Peninsula has been received.

203. *Memorandum by Secretary of Committee of Imperial Defence*

[Extract]

[Cab 24/159 (C.P.118(23))]   Feb 19th 1923

At the 26th meeting of the Standing Defence Sub-committee on November 13th 1922, Lord Beatty made an important statement which is recorded as follows:–

The First Sea Lord stated that as this was the first meeting of the Committee which he had attended since it had been re-established under the new Government he wished to place on record a warning as regards the naval situation in the Pacific.[1] He wished it to be clearly understood that since the Washington Conference, the situation from the Naval point of view had altered in the Pacific. The United States was now incapable of Naval action in the Western Pacific, thus leaving the British Empire the sole force to counter with naval force any aggressive tendencies on the part of Japan. We exist in the Far East on sufferance [*sic*] of another Power. This had already been pointed out to the Committee of Imperial Defence, and a decision had been taken that the naval base at Singapore should be proceeded with. Without Singapore we should be swept out of the Western Pacific and have no means of countering a naval offensive by Japan. There was reason to believe that if the war had taken a definite turn against us, Japan would have thrown over the Allies and associated herself with Germany, and that, even during the war, Japanese agents were in touch with Indian agitators. Japan might fall to a similar temptation in the future . . .

[M. Hankey]

[1] During the war the work of the CID and its standing sub-committees had been taken over by the War Cabinet and several *ad hoc* bodies. From February 1921 it began to resume its pre-war functions but the Standing Sub-Committee was not activated until after the fall of the Lloyd George coalition government in October 1922. Normally the Sub-Committee was chaired by one of the most senior Ministers, such as the Lord President of the Council.

204.   *Notes of Sea Lords' Meeting*[1]

[Copy]

[BTY/8/5/21]   28 January 1924

The Sea Lords had under discussion the amount of money to be expended on the Singapore Base.

The 1st Sea Lord pointed out that the House of Commons and the Country had been informed that the total cost of the naval base would be approximately £11,000,000.

One of the principal criticisms always directed against the scheme was that it would cost nearer £30,000,000, and that estimates in this connexion were invariably falsified.

It now appeared from the plans before them that £11,000,000 in reality did not cover even the naval expenditure proposed on Singapore.

When defence expenditure was taken into consideration the total cost would certainly be £21,000,000.

The 1st Sea Lord pointed out the weak position in which the Board of Admiralty would be placed if the expenditure on Singapore could not be limited to that which had been announced. He urged therefore the further consideration of what were the minimum requirements.

He outlined these as the construction of a base where in 1931 at the conclusion of the Washington Treaty the Fleet could take refuge and be fuelled, munitioned, docked and repaired etc.

He asked if to meet these requirements some modification of the supply arrangements could not be entertained. Whether many of the buildings could not be economised on, and whether as regards other expenditure consideration could not be given to postponing completion until after 1931.

In the discussion which arose the 4th Sea Lord[2] stated that he considered if the fleet were to be supplied, then the expenditure of the 4½ million on the wall and supply basin must be faced.

He saw no method of curtailing this. If, however, the Board agreed, the date 1931, on which the completion of the supply basin was now intended, could be extended. The early expenditure on construction would thus be diminished.

On the basin scheme as it now stood depended the supply of the fleet in war.

[1] See Document 138 above.
[2] Rear-Admiral the Hon Algernon Boyle.

Other points came under discussion, such as the necessity for the armament supply base, local defence base, and certain buildings.

Finally the 1st Sea Lord asked the 2nd Sea Lord and ACNS[1] to go into the question of the Singapore Base, on the lines that a total of £11,000,000 was available to be expended and that the base in 1931 should be a base from which the British Fleet could operate.

In regard to the land and air defence of the base, the 1st Sea Lord requested that the Committee should consider this being provided and worked entirely by the Admiralty on the same lines as the Invergordon Base.

204a.   *Minute by 2nd Sea Lord and ACNS on Singapore Defences*

[BTY 8/5/30]   30 Jan 1924

THE DEFENCE OF SINGAPORE BASE

To understand why the expense of providing Military defences is so heavy, it is necessary to consider the ownership of the territory each side of the Eastern approach to Singapore.

Without regard to territorial rights the obvious way to keep a hostile fleet as far as possible from Singapore Naval Base would be to defend the Strait to the Eastward, only ten miles wide, and to site guns and howitzers North and South of the Strait, which could smother ships with direct and indirect fire at easy ranges.

Unfortunately Johore and Dutch Territory lie on each side of the Eastern approach, and Singapore Island is the only British land available on which to place gun defences to command the approaches which are available for a Fleet.

The heavy guns of the defences must be large because, in order to keep a hostile fleet outside the distance at which it can damage the Naval Base, they have to engage the Fleet at very long ranges and make very accurate shooting at these long ranges.

The necessity for very accurate shooting at long range rules out the possibility of escaping the expense of permanent sites with solid foundations for the guns; railway mountings or the portable steel platforms used for the heavy Naval guns in Belgium could

_____
[1]Admiral Sir Henry Oliver; Rear-Admiral A. K. Waistell.

not be depended on for the necessary accuracy, and they besides were only capable of a very limited arc of training, and would be unsuitable for use at moving objects.

The necessity for fixed sites for the heavy guns causes a corresponding increase in the provision of Anti Air-Craft guns, as the position of the guns is certain to be known beforehand to the Enemy.

The D of GD[1] has gone into the defence questions with the War Office and his report is enclosed. It will be seen that, short of detailed examination by Military experts on the spot, no real estimate of the *total* cost of the Military defences can be arrived at. It would probably be round about three millions.

The important point about the defences is that, without adequate defence, the money spent on the Naval Base will be wasted, as the Enemy will take it before the Fleet arrives there.

Another point is that, apart from the Naval Base scheme a very large provision has already been made for Singapore as a fuelling station. If the Naval Base is dropped, some considerable addition will be necessary to the existing Singapore defences to protect the oil fuel storage, so that all the cost of improved defences should not be credited to the Naval Base scheme.

[Initialled] H. F. O.
A. K. W.

205. *Director Gunnery Division Naval Staff*

[Secret Memorandum]

[BTY/8/5/31]   31.1.24

Singapore Gun Defences (Revised)

1.   The gun defences provisionally proposed for Singapore by the Admiralty are as follows, but it is probable that the War Office will desire to reduce the number of 15″ guns:–

8 — 15 inch guns	£160,000
8 — 15 inch 45° mountings	360,000
4 — 9.2 inch guns (available)	–

[1]The Director of the Gunnery Division of the Naval Staff was Captain St G. Collard (1876–1962). As a Rear-Admiral in 1928 he, along with Captain K. G. B. Dewar, figured ignominiously in the *Royal Oak* affair, and was ordered to strike his flag. Dewar and his Executive Officer, Commander H. M. Daniel, were dismissed their ship.

6 — 9.2 inch 45° mountings	96,000
6 — 9.2 inch shields	16,500
8 — 6 inch VII guns (available)	–
4 — 6 inch 15° mountings (available)	–
4 — 6 inch 45° mountings	22,000
4 — 6 inch shields	14,000
2 — 4.7 Q.F. guns (available)	–
2 — 4.7 20° mountings (available)	–
18 — 2 pdr guns and mountings	45,000
24 — 4.7 AA equipments	112,000
Total cost of guns and mountings	£825,500

If 15 inch guns are supplied by the Admiralty and they are available, the total can be reduced by	£160,000
Total, less cost of 15 inch guns	£665,500

The above is only an approximate estimate of the total cost and is derived from such sources as are available at the moment.
(N.B. No reserve 15″ guns or mountings have been allowed for, and it is considered that 2 guns should be provided.)
2. The following *guesswork estimate* for mounting the above guns is put forward:–

There is nothing to go upon, and it is doubtful if the War Office could give even an approximate figure until the localities have been accurately surveyed and an estimate worked out by military engineering experts.

Engineer Works

Four — 15 inch Batteries (2 guns each) including barrack accommodation @ £110,000 each	£440,000
Railway for above, say	120,000
Two — 9.2 inch Batteries as above @ £54,000 each	108,000
Converting 2 existing 9.2 inch guns to 45° mounting	20,000
Four — 6 inch Batteries as above @ £44,000	176,000
One — 4.7 inch Battery as above	30,000
Four — Anti C.M.B. Batteries as above @ £12,500 each	50,000
Ten — Electric Lights including barrack accommodation for R.E. @ £8,000 each	80,000
Main communications, roads, cables, telephone, etc., say	110,000

Piers, jetties, gantries, etc., say   46,000
AA defences, say   126,000

Total   £1,306,000

3.   If the estimates are accepted as approximately correct, the total cost of the gun defences proposed for Singapore is somewhere about £2,131,500 if 15 inch guns are not supplied by the Admiralty or £1,971,500 if the Admiralty supply the 15″ guns.

4.   These figures include nothing for personnel, ammunition, cost of land, etc., and it is considered impossible to give any figures which could be accurate in any way until a detailed estimate has been prepared by military experts, but it is suggested that £2,800,000 would be somewhere nearer the total amount required, perhaps more.

5.   D of GD knows of no other way of adequately defending Singapore against attack from the sea except (a) by fixed defences of heavy guns and (b) by guns mounted in ships afloat. Heavy guns may have been mounted on mobile carriages on shore during the 1914–18 war, but these guns were not required to fire against moving targets like ships. D of GD has no detailed knowledge of such mobile carriages but considers it impossible to obtain the accuracy from such carriages, which is required to fire against moving ships at extreme ranges.

6.   Considering first 5(b) − guns mounted in ships afloat. We have 3 monitors with 15 inch guns, total 6 guns. If these are used for the defence in place of the 8 − 15 inch guns in fixed emplacements, the total rough estimate would be reduced from £1,971,500* to £1,000,000*.

Against this reduced figure must be added the cost of bringing and keeping these three vessels up to date, of steaming the *Erebus* and *Terror* and of towing *Marshal Soult* out to Singapore, of providing additional personnel to man them, of making the ships suitable for a hot climate, etc., etc., for which no estimate can be given.

7.   Even then, the defence by these ships would not be comparable in efficiency to the proposed fixed emplacement and ships are very much more vulnerable to hostile gun attack and to attack by hostile aircraft. They would probably suffer the fate of the Monitor *Raglan* in Eastern Mediterranean.

8.   Considering 5(a) − fixed defences of heavy guns. In D of

---

* Assuming guns were given free by the Admiralty.

GD's opinion this is the only sure method of making Singapore reasonably safe against attack and capture by hostile naval forces and in his opinion the armament should be the last item to be reduced. Singapore inadequately defended would be tempting bait for the Japanese, whereas if the defences made the place reasonably impregnable, it is probable that hostile attack would never be attempted. Adequate defences are an insurance against attack and indirectly against war in the Far East.

9. But if money *must* be saved on the defences, then it is considered that it would be preferable to reduce the fixed defences from 8 − 15 inch guns to 6 − 15 inch guns. The saving would be roughly £255,000* and the estimate reduced from £1,971,500* to £1,716,500*.

10. It is considered that the whole question is one for the War Office in consultation with the Naval Staff and that it cannot and ought not to be considered only by the Admiralty.

[Signed] ST. G. Collard

206. *Chiefs of Staff Committee Minutes of 7th Meeting*
[Viscount Haldane, Lord Chancellor, in the Chair]
[Extract]

[Cab. 53/1]   January 31 1924
SECRET

[The Singapore Base]

Some discussion of a preliminary nature took place in regard to the reasons for the proposed base at Singapore.

The First Sea Lord pointed out that until there was a properly equipped base East of Suez the British Fleet could not proceed to the East, and our Imperial interests in the Indian Ocean and the Pacific could exist only by sufferance of another Power. Unless provision were made by fuelling stations at proper intervals for the Fleet to proceed to the East, and at Singapore for its maintenance, there were no means by which command of the sea in those waters could be maintained. Unless such provision were made, and unless Singapore was adequately defended, a Far Eastern Power could occupy Singapore without much difficulty, and use it as a base from which to dominate the Indian Ocean with its naval forces. It would hardly be possible to eject an enemy from

---

* Assuming guns were given free by the Admiralty.

Singapore once it had been occupied. The provisions of the Washington Conference had made it impossible for an American Fleet to proceed and maintain itself in the East by means of American resources . . . These considerations had been repeatedly urged by the Admiralty on successive governments. Although decisions had been taken to establish a base at Singapore, practically nothing had as yet been done. The Admiralty recognised the financial difficulties, but were bound to warn the government against the dangers of postponing the decision too long. It would take eight or ten years to complete the base at Singapore. 1931 had always been regarded as the latest date by which the work ought to be completed, that being the year in which the Washington Quadruple Treaty relating to insular possessions and insular Dominions in the Pacific Ocean might be determined. Should the whole position in the Pacific be reconsidered in that year, our diplomatic position would be much stronger if we had a base at Singapore capable of maintaining the Fleet.

Lord Haldane . . . asked that in view of the fact the naval base at Singapore could not be completed for many years, the First Sea Lord should consider what could be done in the event of an enemy arising in the interval.

207. *Clynes Committee*
Minutes of Meeting

[BTY/8/5/15]   27th February 1924

CABINET

FINAL COPY
COMMITTEE ON REPLACEMENT OF FLEET UNITS
OTHER THAN CAPITAL SHIPS AND SINGAPORE

MINUTES of a Meeting of the above Committee held
in the Board Room, Treasury Chambers, S.W.1, on
Wednesday, February 27th, 1924, at 12 Noon.

PRESENT:–
The Right Hon J.R. Clynes, MP,
Lord Privy Seal. (In the Chair)

The Right Hon Philip   The Right Hon J. H. Thomas,
Snowden, MP, Chancellor of   MP, Secretary of State for the
the Exchequer.   Colonies.

The Right Hon Stephen Walsh, MP, Secretary of State for War.

Brigadier-General The Right Hon Lord Thomson, CBE, DSO,[2] Secretary of State for Air.

The Right Hon Lord Olivier,[1] KCMG, CB, Secretary of State for India.

The Right Hon Viscount Chelmsford, GCSI, GCMG, GCIE, GBE, First Lord of the Admiralty.

Mr V. A. A. H. Wellesley, CB,[3] (representing the Secretary of State for Foreign Affairs).

THE FOLLOWING WERE ALSO PRESENT:–

Admiral of the Fleet Earl Beatty, GCB, OM, GCVO, DSO, First Sea Lord and Chief of the Naval Staff.

Captain A. D. R. Pound, CB, RN,[4] Director of Plans Division; Admiralty.

Lt Col Sir M. P. A Hankey, GCB. .... Secretary

Commander H. R. Moore, DSO, RN.......... Assistant Secretary

Mr Thomas suggested that it would be advisable if the Committee divided their enquiry into two separate parts — (*1*) The Question of Singapore and (*2*) The Replacement of Fleet Units. He enquired whether this met the views of the Admiralty.

[1]Sydney Haldane Olivier, 1st Baron (1859–1943) civil servant and politician: one of the founders of the Fabian Society of which he was Secretary 1886–9; contributed to its most influential publication *Fabian Essays* (1889); served in Colonial Office and West Indies 1882–1913; Permanent Secretary Board of Agriculture 1913; Treasury as Asst. Comptroller of Exchequer 1917; retired 1920; Peerage and Secretary of State, India in 1st Labour Government 1924.

[2]Christopher Thomson, later 1st Baron Thomson of Cardington (1875–1930): served in Royal Engineers from 1894; retired as Brigadier-General 1919; failed to win three elections as Labour MP; Secretary for Air and peerage, 1924; Secretary for Air, 1929; killed in crash of airship R101, 1930.

[3]The future Sir Victor Wellesley (1876–1954): joined Diplomatic Service 1899; Asst. Under-Secretary 1924–5; Deputy Under-Secretary 1925, responsible for Far Eastern affairs; retired 1936. Ramsay MacDonald was Foreign Secretary and Wellesley sat as a member of the Committee in his absence; otherwise he was in attendance as an official, as was Beatty.

[4]The future Admiral of the Fleet Sir Dudley Pound (1877–1943): entered RN 1891; captain of *Colossus* at Jutland; Director of Plans Division of Naval Staff 1922; COS Mediterranean 1925; Rear-Admiral and ACNS 1926; Battle-Cruiser Squadron 1929; 2nd Sea Lord 1932; C-in-C Mediterranean 1936; 1st Sea Lord 1939; retired on ill-health September 1943 and died in October.

LORD CHELMSFORD stated that he was very anxious to keep the two enquiries quite separate.

The Committee agreed –
that the first part of their enquiry should
be into the question of Singapore.

THE CHAIRMAN considered that the best way of commencing the enquiry on Singapore would be for Lord Beatty to explain the strategical aspect of the question first.

LORD BEATTY stated that our traditional Naval policy in the past had been to maintain sufficient naval Forces to protect our commitments and interests in all parts of the world, having regard to the naval strength maintained by other Powers in those waters, the main British Fleet being based in the best strategic position. In accordance with this policy we had maintained in the Pacific a Fleet consisting of battleships and cruisers, based on Hong Kong where docks and repair facilities were available, with Singapore as a secondary base.

At the beginning of this century our Fleet in the East was our second most powerful Fleet, but in 1905, this policy was departed from and the battleships were moved into Home Waters to meet the menace nearer home. Early in 1914 it had been recognised, however, that this departure from our traditional policy was a mistake and steps were being taken to reinforce our Eastern Fleet by battle cruisers, when war broke out. The result of this mistake had been to enable the German Pacific Squadron to dominate the Pacific for several months and inflict considerable damage and loss of prestige on the British Empire. The existence of the Anglo-Japanese Alliance had, no doubt, been an important factor in the decision that was taken in 1905 to leave our possessions in the East, which were of such magnitude and importance, to small and inadequate naval protection. After the war it was proposed to return to our well tried policy of protecting, as far as possible, our possessions. The position from the Naval point of view, however, had been completely altered by the Washington Conference; Hongkong could no longer fulfil the requirements of our principal Naval base in the Far East. No alterations or additions could now be made to the facilities there in order to make them adequate for a modern fleet. The necessity for a base suitable for a modern fleet in the East was first considered in October 1919, first of all by Committees and then by the Committee of Imperial Defence; finally it was considered and accepted by the Cabinet in June 1921. The decision to proceed with a base at Singapore was endorsed in

1921 by the Imperial Conference before the Washington Conference. Our delegates at the Washington Conference knowing of the decision to proceed with Singapore and that Hongkong was no longer suitable for a base were able to concur in the *status quo* being maintained in the Pacific so long as Singapore was outside the area. The policy agreed to was, in fact, one of replacement — Singapore for Hongkong.

As a result of the Washington Conference the balance of power in the Pacific had altered; the United States of America were no longer capable of action in the Western Pacific, consequently the British Empire was left as the sole Naval Power besides Japan in these waters. At the present moment, our existence in the Western Pacific rests on the sufferance and goodwill of another Power. This important and serious fact had already been pointed out to three Cabinets and two Imperial Conferences, all of which had accepted and confirmed the decision to proceed with a base at Singapore.

MR SNOWDEN enquired why it had been decided to abandon Hong Kong in preference to Singapore before the Washington Conference.

LORD BEATTY explained that to develop Hong Kong would cost more than the proposed base at Singapore. Hong Kong Harbour although of sufficient size for a pre-war fleet would not provide sufficient room for the size and number of ships in a modern fleet. It would also be difficult to find sufficient accommodation for the increased dockyard facilities required. Another important reason for preferring Singapore to Hong Kong was brought out at a discussion in May 1921 on the Defence of Hong Kong, when the War Office expressed their inability to guarantee its security from the land side without the employment of such large military forces as to be out of the question. Singapore was also preferable strategically and might be described as the 'Gateway of the Pacific', just as Gibraltar was the gateway of the Mediterranean.

In reply to Lord Thomson, LORD BEATTY stated that Lord Balfour, before proceeding to Washington, had been instructed by the Cabinet to keep Singapore clear of any restrictions as regards defence or development. The Japanese and Americans had been fully aware of our intention to develop Singapore.

In reply to Lord Olivier, LORD BEATTY stated that when Singapore was sufficiently developed, it was proposed to strengthen our forces in the Far East. These reinforcements would be drawn from the Naval sources at present in Home and Mediterranean Waters.

LORD BEATTY explained that he thought it would be easier for him to explain the strategical aspect of the Far East by means of Questions and Answers —

Q. What would happen if Japan forced war upon us at the present time?
The Japanese would be able to seize Singapore and destroy our Oil Fuel reserves at Colombo, Trincomali, Madras and Rangoon. In fact, Japan could exercise control of sea communications in the Indian and Pacific Oceans — for forty-two days in the case of the Indian Ocean and a year, at least, in the case of the Pacific.

Q. What would be the effect of Japan exercising control of the Sea communications in the Indian Ocean for 42 days?
All British trade in the Indian Ocean would cease. The Trade Division at the Admiralty had enquired very fully into this problem. He did not wish to confuse the Committee with a mass of figures, but might point out that in the area of the Indian Ocean and Western Pacific, the yearly value of the Oversea trade of the British Empire was £890 millions, all of which would be liable to capture.

The loss we should sustain would depend on the time that our sea communications were in the hands of Japan, but to this must be added the indirect losses following on the dislocation of our trade. We should cease to get direct importation of many essential commodities such as wool, rubber, tea, jute, manganese, tin and zinc ore and also a large proportion of our food supplies, such as wheat, meat, cheese, etc; the number of ships captured or destroyed would also, probably be very great. The *Emden* working alone in the face of superior forces, in little over one month, captured 20 ships of which she sank 16, with a consequent loss of hull and cargo of over £2¼ millions. Japanese cruisers backed up by heavier forces and with only weak British forces acting against them, would be able to cause us enormous losses. He pointed out to the Committee that in any one day in the area under consideration there were at risk 742 ships of 3,000 tons gross of a value equal to £180 millions. The proposed expenditure at Singapore was a very small sum for insurance in view of these figures, and taking the total yearly value of the trade at £890 millions it worked out to 2/- per £100 for the nine years estimated as necessary to complete the base.

The coast of India would also be open to attack, and if this coincided with risings organised by the Japanese on the cry of

'Asia for the Asiatics' a very serious situation would arise, which could probably only be met by sending reinforcements to India; but with the control of the Indian Ocean in the hands of the Japanese, it would not be possible to send these reinforcements until we had re-gained [sic] control in that area.

Q. What might happen if the Japanese controlled the sea communications of the Western Pacific for one year?
We should lose Hongkong. The loss of Hongkong which acts as the door to the Far Eastern markets would be a serious blow to our prestige and also from a financial point of view. In 1922 the value of the imports into Hongkong was £61 millions. Hongkong is the largest port we have, judged by the standard of the volume of tonnage entered and cleared; in 1922 700,000 vessels with a total tonnage of 46 million tons entered and cleared.

We should lose the Malay States. The value of trade with the Malay States is £107 millions and 70% of our Rubber and 57% of our Tin is drawn from this area.

We should lose British North Borneo, in which case the Japanese would obtain control of oil supplies which are vital to them.

Australia and New Zealand could be threatened and possibly invaded if the Japanese were so foolish. He considered that an attempt by the Japanese of the invasion of Australia and New Zealand would, sooner or later, end in disaster, but the damage done to the British Empire would be terrific.

Q. If the United States of America decided to intervene could they take action in the Western Pacific?
The United States were unable to take effective action in the Western Pacific unless they could gain control of the sea communications in that region. To do this it would be necessary for them to send at least equivalent naval forces to the Japanese and this would be a tremendous effort. The United States Fleet could reach the Western Pacific via the Atlantic and Mediterranean using sea-borne supplies of fuel, but on arrival their Fleet would be immobilised for want of fuel and would, therefore, be almost useless. The distance from New York to Singapore, east or west about, was practically equal but the only practicable way would be for the American Fleet to come via the Atlantic and Mediterranean as, if the Japanese had any information that the United States Fleet was crossing the Pacific they would immediately seize

the Philippines and the American Fleet would have no secure anchorage or base.

LORD THOMSON enquired whether the United States of America had erected defences in the Philippines.

LORD BEATTY replied that the Philippines were practically undefended and any increase in their defence was now precluded by the Washington Conference.

MR SNOWDEN enquired why the United States of America had agreed at Washington to a Treaty which, in effect, practically immobilised them in the Western Pacific.

LORD BEATTY stated that many people in the United States of America had thought, and some still thought, that a war between Japan and America was the most probable future war. The American Authorities, however, had now awakened to the fact that a war of this nature was a practicable impossibility. If these two countries declared war on each other the Japanese could capture the Philippines, beyond that they could only exert a small economic pressure on the United States of America by cutting off their comparatively small trade in the Pacific. On the other hand, the United States of America could only exert a small economic pressure on Japan by cutting off the trade between Canadian ports and Japan. Neither of these two effects would be sufficient to bring about a decision.

Q. What steps are necessary to remove the present state of impotence of the British Fleet to safeguard our Eastern possessions?
The British Fleet exists to secure the sea communications to our Empire. To control the sea communications we would have to send a force of at least equivalent strength to the Japanese Fleet in eastern waters. When the Fleet reached the eastern area it was necessary that it should have mobility on arrival. This could only be secured if —

(1)   There are adequate supplies of fuel.
(2)   These supplies are safe, e.g. if the storage of oil fuel is adequately defended.

The Fleet must be safe from enemy action in harbour, hence a defended anchorage must be provided. The same defences could be used for protecting the oil supplies and the Fleet anchorage.

In order that the strength and efficiency of the Fleet shall be maintained it is necessary that repair facilities for damaged ships are near at hand so that ships may be re-fitted periodically and docked in order to maintain their speed and endurance. One slow ship reduces the speed of the whole Fleet, and the ship that has lost part of its endurance, and in twelve months a ship can lose as much as 40%, may necessitate the return of the Fleet to harbour or serious weakening at a critical moment.

It might be asked why cannot the repair and docking facilities at Malta and England be used. There were two reasons why this was not possible. If there was no Dock in the Far East a ship damaged in action might quite possibly be lost altogether. Ships would have to be sent a great distance to Malta or England and the length of time thus taken up would seriously reduce the strength of the Fleet.

To keep the Fleet efficient it was necessary that victuals, stores and ammunition should be provided and that the arrangements should be such that these could be embarked with great rapidity in order that the Fleet might be ready to proceed to sea again without loss of time. Reserves of stores, victuals and ammunition should, therefore, be held in store at the Base. In order that wastage of ships might not reduce the Fleet below the danger line it was necessary to either have a great superiority in numbers or docking and repair facilities close to the scene of operations. Superiority in numbers had been ruled out by the Washington Agreement and consequently the docking and repair facilities were necessary if the Fleet was to be able to function in Pacific waters. The Washington Treaty allowed us equality with the American Fleet and five-thirds of the Japanese Fleet. In the event of war with Japan it would be false strategically not to send to Singapore some measure of superiority of ships over the Japanese. He did not suppose any British Cabinet would agree to denude the British Islands of naval defence altogether and consequently our margin was very small indeed.

Q. Why was Singapore selected for the Base?
Singapore was selected on account of the following governing factors. The Base in the east must cover our trade routes in the Indian Ocean. It could only cover them if it was in advance of them, hence the Base must be on the east side of the Indian Ocean. The Base must be on the flank of the lines of communication between Japan and Australia. Singapore was well placed to intercept raids by the Japanese on Australia and New Zealand. If the Base was to be on the east side of the Indian Ocean it could not be to the north-east as this was prohibited by the *status quo*

agreement. It could not be to the south-east as this would leave the gate open into the Indian Ocean and, therefore, the Singapore site was the only one left which would fulfil the requirements. It had been described as the finest strategical position in the whole world. Singapore fulfilled all requirements. It was as near Hong Kong as we could get; it provided a safe anchorage for the Fleet.

Q. The claim that the Base should be in Australia
It had been recommended in the Press on several occasions that a Base in Australia should be selected in lieu of Singapore.

MR BRUCE, the Prime Minister of Australia, had never made that claim and at a meeting held in the Admiralty during the last Imperial Conference Mr Bruce had stated that he was satisfied that a Base in Australia would not meet the requirements and that Singapore would do so. The reasons why a Base in Australia would not meet requirements were as follows:–

On the outbreak of War the Fleet would have to proceed to Australia and would require to fuel at Colombo and Singapore. It was probable that these places being practically undefended would no longer exist as British Possessions and consequently the Fleet would never get to Australia. The Fleet having arrived in Australia our trade routes in the Indian Ocean would be open to attack. Hong Kong, Malay Straits and Borneo would also be open to attack. The British Fleet would have to return to Singapore in order to control the sea communications in these areas.

LORD OLIVIER stated that he was convinced that a Base at Singapore was better placed strategically than one in Australia. The question before the Committee, however, was whether it was necessary to construct a Base in the Far East at all.

MR SNOWDEN enquired why the Fleet, if it reached Singapore, should go on to Australia. Why should it not remain at Singapore and operate from there, sending ships as necessary to be docked in Australia?

LORD CHELMSFORD pointed out that it would take a damaged ship twelve days to reach Sydney and another twelve to return, consequently an absence of twenty-four days over and above that required to repair a ship would have to be allowed for.

Q. Is Singapore a menace to Japan?
LORD BEATTY stated that this was primarily a question for the

Foreign Office. He did not think that any responsible Japanese Statesman had stated that Singapore was a menace to his country.

MR WELLESLEY stated that the Japanese Minister of Foreign Affairs had told our Ambassador that the Japanese fully realised that Singapore was purposely kept outside the *status quo* area in the Washington Treaty. They had no objection to our constructing a Base there, their only objection was to suggestions in our Press of the possibility of a war between Japan and the British Empire.

MR THOMAS stated that it would be necessary for the Committee to take into consideration the evident lack of desire by the Japanese to attack us; also the effect of the recent earthquake should be weighed and it would be necessary for the Committee to decide whether any circumstance remained which warranted our constructing a Base in the Far East.

Q. Whether Singapore is an infraction of the Washington Agreement?

LORD BEATTY stated that as Singapore was to the west of the boundary 110° east of the *status quo* area it was clearly not contrary to the terms of the Treaty. Any idea that the British Government had acted against the spirit of the Treaty or had not been perfectly open on the question was disproved by the telegrams which passed between Lord Balfour and the Government during the Washington Conference which were quoted in the summary prepared by the Secretary, R.S.(24)2.

Q. Site of the Base at Singapore

The old Strait is the only anchorage in this part of the world which will accommodate a modern Fleet. The question had arisen as to where the Base which includes docks, repair and store facilities should be placed. Three positions had been considered. The first, an extension of the commercial facilities at Keppel Harbour; the second, a new site on the south side of the island to the west of Keppel Harbour; third, the site in the old Strait. The Admiralty Committee had investigated these sites on the spot and had ruled out any idea of an extension of the commercial docks as there was no ground available. The site to the westward of Keppel Harbour would have necessitated the construction of a breakwater estimated to cost £20,000,000 over and above the cost of the Base; also any site on the south of the Island was open to attack from seaward and from the Dutch Islands which lie to the southward.

Q. The use which it is proposed to make in war time of the existing facilities at Keppel Harbour

Full use of the commercial dry docks would be made for all unbulged ships. It had also been suggested that use might be made of the sheds in Keppel Harbour for unloading and housing the stores of the Fleet. This possibility had been fully examined but it had been found quite impracticable and it would stop all trade. The task of the Navy was to keep the British trade open. Even in England, where we had many Ports, the interference by war of the working of a commercial port was bad, but in the case of Singapore where there was only one port, the result would be disastrous. Singapore was one of the greatest transit ports in the world. It was the great distributing and collecting port for the Malay Straits, Straits Settlements and to a large extent for the Dutch East Indies.

Q. The reasons why work on Singapore Base should be commenced

The estimated time for the completion of the Base was two years for the preliminary work and seven years for the contract work, i.e. even if it was commenced at once the Base could not be completed until 1933. Owing to the nature of the work it would not be possible to expedite the estimate of seven years for the contract work. The completion of the Base at Singapore would right the strategical situation to a considerable extent because it would enable us to revert to our traditional naval policy and increase our Naval Forces in the Far East to a strength commensurate with our interests and commerce in that part of the world. It was proposed to strengthen our eastern forces by battle cruisers. The oil at Singapore would be safeguarded if the defences are adequate and the presence of our battle cruisers in the far east would safeguard the oil supplies at Rangoon, Trincomali and Colombo. The necessity for Singapore was confirmed by the Imperial Conference in 1923 and the Government of New Zealand had already promised £100,000 towards its cost. The feeling in New Zealand and Australia was very strong on the necessity of Singapore. The site for the Base had been presented by the Straits Settlements. If the construction of the Base at Singapore was not proceeded with, it would necessitate additional expenditure on the defences at Trincomali, Colombo and Rangoon as the present scheme of defences at these Ports was based on the supposition that we should station a battle cruiser force in the Far East.

Lord Thomson enquired whether the site in the old Straits was not open to shell fire from the Johore Mainland.

Lord Beatty replied that the Mainland consisted of swampy ground over which it would be very difficult for a Force to advance.

Lord Chelmsford stated that he understood the Military Authorities had agreed that an advance over this country would be impracticable from the Military point of view.

Lord Beatty summarised his statement as follows:–

We are spending large sums annually on a Fleet which, without a Base in the east, was unable to carry out its task of safeguarding the commerce of the Empire. The British Dominions, Colonies and Trade in the east at present existed on the sufferance and goodwill of another power. The Base at Singapore was purely a defensive measure and was in replacement of Hong Kong. The requirements of the Base had been reduced to a minimum.

The premium of £11,000,000 spread over nine years was small when it is remembered that the value of the trade for which it acts as an insurance is £890,000,000 annually. The value of the possessions for which it was also an insurance could not be reckoned in money values. When His Majesty's Government agreed to the *status quo* Agreement at Washington, the development of a Base at Singapore had been approved. He doubted whether that Agreement would have been come to if it had not been intended to complete the Base at Singapore.

The acceptance of the one-power standard had made Singapore increasingly necessary and any further limitation of Fleets would make it still more so. The provision of a Base at Singapore was realised by Australia and New Zealand to be necessary for their safety. Abandonment or delay in the commencement would have a most unfortunate effect at a time when there was every reason to believe that these Dominions would not only increase their naval effort but contribute substantially towards the cost of the Base.

This concluded the statement by Lord Beatty. The Committee agreed:–

That their next Meeting should be held at 11 a.m. on Monday, 3rd March, at which the Representative of the Foreign Office would make a statement on the foreign policy aspect of the question, and Members of the Committee would have an opportunity of putting questions to the Chief of the Naval Staff.

208. *To his wife* [Nice]

[BTY/17/65/108–109]   Admiralty
                                           Wednesday [27 Feb. 1924]

I know how furious you will be at my not turning up on Thursday, but it cannot be helped. The attacks have been very severe and are not over yet, and the result may well be the break-up of the Admiralty.

However I don't care a damn now & have told 1st Lord [*sic*] I am leaving on Saturday & the question must be settled by then, and it will. I've seen the Prime Minister three times and am waiting to go and see him again now. It's all about the Singapore question and the Government intend to turn it down, but I say they must in consequence release the Admiralty of the responsibility of protecting the Empire and the trade, and then we shall be satisfied, but otherwise we shall not.

Of course there is the usual difference of opinion over the phraseology of the Memorandum they propose to issue to Parliament, and we don't find what they propose at all satisfactory and are endeavouring to find a wording that will suit everybody. I've no doubt we shall succeed. If we don't, we can reserve our action in the matter until I return. It's most unfortunate that it should have come at this time, but then it always comes at the most inconvenient moment. Of course the Sea Lords are very anxious for me to remain, but I've definitely refused, and that's all there is to it, and we cannot see what the result will be later on.

Bless you my dear, I am just off to see the P.M. Forgive me, it is not my fault & I am much harassed.

209. *Clynes Committee: Minutes of Meeting*

[BTY/8/5/16]   3rd March 1924

Mr CLYNES requested the members of the Committee to ask Lord Beatty any questions they might wish on his statement made at the last meeting.

Mr WALSH enquired what were the actual conditions imposed by the Washington Treaty, with regard to Replacements and Improvements in the defence and dockyard facilities at Hong Kong.

LORD BEATTY stated that by the Washington Treaty we were

prohibited from making any improvements in the dockyard facilities or defences. We were allowed to make replacements when necessary, but not to increase the standard of the defences. The British Delegates representing the British Empire at Washington had been able to concur with this arbitrary condition lightheartedly owing to the understanding that a base would be constructed at Singapore. The Cabinet instructions given to the Delegation had been very explicit on the point of keeping Singapore outside any restricted area. All the other parties to the Washington Treaty had understood that Singapore was reserved.

In reply to Mr. Thomas LORD BEATTY stated that Mr. Hughes at the Imperial Conference in 1921 had given strong support to the Singapore proposals.

MR. SNOWDEN enquired what use could be made of Hong Kong at present.

LORD BEATTY replied that Hong Kong acted at the present time as a base for a Squadron of Light Cruisers. The facilities at Hong Kong were only capable of dealing with ships of the light cruiser and smaller classes.

MR. SNOWDEN asked whether any other sites in the vicinity of Singapore had been considered instead of or in place of the proposed base in the Johore Straits?

LORD BEATTY stated that Keppel Harbour had also been considered, but had proved unsuitable, owing to lack of space. A further site to the westward of Keppel Harbour had also been considered, but the cost of this would be prohibitive. An initial expense of £20 millions would be required to build a breakwater for this site. He explained that the most dangerous form of attack to which a base, or fleets at anchor in a base, were exposed was by submarine. A breakwater would be necessary to adequately defend this alternative site from submarine attack. If money was no object, this site would have been preferable. He stated that the site chosen in the Johore Strait was naturally the most admirable anchorage in the whole world; it provided suitable depth of water, accommodation for the fleet and in general suitability could not be bettered.

MR. THOMAS said that in his opinion Lord Beatty had made out a most admirable case for a base at Singapore from a strategical point of view and he considered nothing more need be said in that direction. He suggested that the Committee should now go into the question from the other points of view.

MR. SNOWDEN said that he hoped, before the end of the

enquiry, the Committee would hear evidence from the financial point of view, treating this aspect in its widest sense.

At this point Mr. Ramsay MacDonald joined the Committee.

MR. RAMSAY MACDONALD said that on Saturday he had read a Memorandum giving an expression of the Foreign Office views on the question of Singapore, with a view to it being circulated to the Committee. He was not in agreement with the Memorandum. The major argument was that it would be useful to have a fleet based in the Pacific in view of the political difficulties which might arise in the future, as regards Japan and China. With this argument he profoundly disagreed. He did not think it would help us and in fact he considered it would increase the difficulties of the problems to be faced. He was ready, however, for the Foreign Office point of view to be expressed to the Committee. He said that the gist of the Memorandum was as follows:–

> It was important that the British Empire should not be powerless in the Pacific;
> The question of a base at Singapore was not a question of going to war with Japan;
> We did not want to make it plain to the whole world that the British Empire was unable to interfere in Pacific troubles;
> Our prestige was involved;
> We ought to be in a position to show clearly that if threatened we had the strength to uphold our rights;
> Our command of sea-power must be general and not local;

The Memorandum also raised the more general political point of whether if we had not at least a beginning of a base in the Pacific our general political position was being weakened and the Foreign Office would be hampered in their negotiations. He took the opposite view, viz. that if we start on the expansion of the military situation in the East at the present moment (not necessarily in a year hence) it would hamper us rather than help us. We were at present in a position after a great war when we were able to hold our hand. Later, when the world had settled down and the balance of power became more settled, it might then be folly to hold our hand. It would be wise policy and strategy to take the opportunity now presented of attempting to reach agreement on the problem of limitation of armaments. Once a start was made in building bases and work of that kind, although our intentions might be limited, the consequences passed beyond our own power. Speaking purely as a non-party Secretary of State for Foreign Affairs his view was that it would be a mistake to go on with the scheme. He did not say a base at Singapore should never be made, but not at the present moment. The scheme should be prepared but pigeon-holed.

LORD BEATTY stated that he understood the question raised by Mr. Ramsay MacDonald was as follows:–

Supposing it was right to build a base at Singapore, is this the time to commence it? He pointed out that, as regards our naval forces the responsibility for looking ahead rested on the Admiralty. As the Prime Minister had said in the House of Commons when speaking of the Light Cruiser Programme, it was necessary to work on a scheme. Nothing was more wasteful than a hand-to-mouth policy in matters of this sort. Unless we had a base in the Pacific it seemed of little use to maintain a large Fleet which was unable to protect our Dominions and positions East of Aden. A base at Singapore would enable our Fleet to fulfil its duty of protecting our Dominions. He pointed out that by a previous Cabinet decision all question of the possibility of war with the United States of America had been ruled out. If a base was not provided at Singapore the possibility of successfully carrying on a war with Japan in the Pacific was also out of the question. Consequently there remained only the possibility of a war with Mediterranean powers. If the two former conditions were accepted our present naval forces could be very largely reduced and yet be equal to the French and Italian fleets. He considered it was of no use keeping a great fleet in being which was unable to exercise its function. He pointed out that we had already made a start with the base at Singapore. Money had been spent on it. The Dominions were in agreement with the scheme and were subscribing towards its cost. Japan and the United States of America were both aware of our intentions to build a base at Singapore. If His Majesty's Government would agree to the principle that Singapore should be developed in order that the Navy could protect the Eastern half of the Empire and would confirm the decision already taken by three Cabinets and two Imperial Conferences, then the Admiralty wished for the provision of only a very small sum during the next 12 months. This would be expended on preliminary work, borings, etc. which were necessary before the main work could start. No work would be done during the next twelve months that could in any way be alarming from the Foreign Office point of view. He pointed out that the factor of time was very important. The base could not be commenced until the borings etc. had been completed and every twelve months delay in commencing these borings put off the date on which the British Empire would no longer be dependent on the good-will of other powers in the Pacific.

MR. THOMAS enquired whether the earthquake in Japan, which was not in the minds of previous Cabinets when their decision was taken, would not justify a delay of twelve months.

LORD BEATTY stated that the earthquake had caused no material handicap to the Japanese Navy. A few small ships had been damaged also an aircraft carrier but she had been replaced by another battleship due to be scrapped under the Washington Agreement. One dock at Yokosuka had been damaged and they had lost some 80,000 tons of oil. He considered that in 8 years time from the Japanese naval point of view the effects of the earthquake would have ceased to operate. He agreed that owing to its financial effect on Japan the earthquake had bettered our position in the Pacific which before the earthquake was one of extreme danger to this country. The completion of our base at Singapore had originally been intended by 1931. It was now put back two years to 1933.

LORD OLIVIER said he understood the Foreign Office view was that it was necessary for us to be able to speak with authority at Tokio and Pekin.

LORD BEATTY said that we could not do this at present. We were powerless in the Pacific at the present moment.

MR. SNOWDEN enquired in what way the situation differed from 1913.

LORD BEATTY stated that in 1913 the Japanese fleet had been much smaller, and also the Anglo-Japanese Alliance was in existence which had really covered the situation. It was a sound doctrine to either be strong or to make alliances. Also in 1913 the Fleet was coal-burning and was consequently mobile. Our naval strength in 1913 could have been capable of leaving sufficient forces to be a match for the German fleet and at the same time to have sent a British fleet to Eastern waters equal to that of the Japanese. We had at that time a two-power standard with a small margin.

LORD THOMSON enquired as to the state of completion of Singapore in five years time.

LORD BEATTY stated that we could have battle cruisers based on Singapore in about 4 years time, making use of a floating dock.

The graving Dock would be of no use until fully completed. Our aim was to be able to maintain a Fleet, not of the size of our war fleet, but consisting of battle cruisers and smaller ships so that if the blow did fall our trade in the Far East would not be defenceless. If there was no base at Singapore there would be no armoured ships in the Far East equal to the protection of our trade, or of our bases and reserves of oil fuel which would be necessary for our fleet when we attempted to re-assert our position in Eastern waters. If there were no heavy ships stationed in the Far East the money required for defences of Ports such as Trincomali, Madras, Rangoon, Bombay, etc. would be far greater, as a heavier scale of defence would be necessary than that at present recommended which was based on the presence of battle-cruisers in the Far East.

LORD OLIVIER stated that from the view expressed in the Foreign Office Memorandum it would appear that they considered it would be hopeless to pull the world out of the present mess it was in. This might not be possible but he considered the Government should take the other line and make the attempt. One or two years remained in which this attempt might be made, and of which he considered full advantage should be taken. This policy might not be possible of fulfillment [sic] and we might be driven back to our old foolish policy of building up armament against armament. But in the meantime he was strongly of the opinion that we must drop all gestures in the direction of armaments and whole-heartedly attempt to reach agreement on better lines.

LORD BEATTY stated that there was nothing in the Admiralty request which was contradictory to the views held by Lord Olivier. They were not asking for the quick development of the base but if the Millenium did not arrive and we had to revert to our old method of armed forces we would then have the preliminary work on the base completed. He stated that the Admiralty asked for £150,000 for the next twelve months and part of this sum would be subscribed by the Dominions.

MR THOMAS stated that he understood the promised contribution by New Zealand and Australia was only promised on condition that we decided to complete the base at Singapore. If there was any doubt as to whether the completion of the base was intended it would not be fair to the Dominion Governments to accept their contributions.

LORD BEATTY agreed that, if there was any doubt about going

on with the construction of the base, the financial burden should be shouldered completely by his country. If the Government's decision was against the policy of a base at Singapore he considered that it would be better to carry out that policy *in toto* and scrap at least half the British Navy and relieve the taxpayers of the cost of up-keep.

MR. RAMSAY MACDONALD said he understood that Lord Beatty was not suggesting that the Navy should be used in any immediate way to enforce our policy in the Far East.

LORD BEATTY replied that he did not think any Officers in the Fighting Services who had taken part in great battles would be in favour of ever unnecessarily exposing this country to war again.

MR. RAMSAY MACDONALD agreed. He pointed out that it was not a question of scrapping the Navy and if we failed to improve the world-conditions and reach an agreement on armaments then it would be necessary to go on with the base. If we commenced Singapore now he considered that it would make any chances of success on the lines of limitation of armaments very remote. Once Singapore was commenced circumstances would inevitably continue to build up a military situation in the East until we reached a state similar to that in the North Sea in 1914. If we found we were unable to reach agreement to limit armaments he considered that the case for Singapore had been made out and it was the most suitable position for a naval base.

LORD BEATTY stated that when it was considerd what we had at stake — the British Empire, millions of money — the cost of building a base at Singapore did not seem a large insurance. He urged that the work should be commenced at once in order to reduce the length of time during which this country was in the position of having to exist in the Pacific on sufferance of another Power.

MR. RAMSAY MACDONALD said that the word 'sufferance' was only comparative. On paper it might be argued that we had at stake the British Empire and the millions of trade involved; in practice he did not consider that this was so.

MR. WALSH enquired if war broke out in the East in the next twelve months what could we do?

LORD BEATTY replied that the whole of our Eastern trade East of Aden would go. India would be open to attack and our Ports of Trincomali, Colombo, Rangoon, etc. would fall.

MR. SNOWDEN enquired how would the Japanese be able to hold all these captures?

LORD BEATTY replied that they would not hold them but would destroy them. Once these Ports and the Oil reserves accumulated there had been destroyed we would be unable to use them and unable to re-assert ourselves in those waters. He agreed that £150,000 spent during the next twelve months would not actually alter the state of affairs during that time but it would shorten the length of time before a base was completed in Eastern Waters. He assured the Committee that the great responsibility which rested on him whilst our fleet was powerless to act in Eastern Waters was very heavy indeed. He would do anything in his power to shorten the period during which our fleet could not be considered capable of carrying out its traditional duties in the Pacific. All he asked the Government to do was to agree in principle that a base was necessary in the Pacific, and that Singapore was the right place for such a base, and to allow the Admiralty to include a small sum of £150,000 in the estimates for 1924–5 for expenditure on preliminary work.

(At this point all present except the Members and the Secretary withdrew, in order that Ministers might confer among themselves.)

210. *To his wife* [Nice]

[BTY/17/66/9–11]   Admiralty
                                    Monday night [3 March 1924]

*   *   *   *

I spent the whole morning at the Cabinet, talking Singapore and had a serious wrangle with them. I am afraid they will turn it down because they are afraid their own party will not support them, and, with the aid of the Liberals, they would be defeated. Once again it is a question of loyalty to party taking precedence over loyalty to country. They are to let me have a decision tomorrow and it depends upon the wording of the statement as to what the Admiralty will do. But I hope to get it fixed tomorrow, so can leave on Wednesday morning.

*   *   *   *

I am quite exhausted tonight as we had two more meetings this afternoon of Committee of Imperial Defence, to get rid of some of the questions to be settled before I leave . . .

211.   *Consequences of Suspending Work at Singapore*

[Copy]

[BTY/8/5/22]   28.4.24

NOTES BY THE NAVAL STAFF

The decision of HM Government to suspend work upon the Naval Base at Singapore creates a new situation from the point of view of Naval Defence. Until the system which is to take the place of Naval Force is brought into being, the British possessions and British commerce in Far Eastern Waters remain exposed to invasion and attack.

The Admiralty is therefore anxious to emphasise the great importance of pressing on with the attempt to obtain the International Agreement foreshadowed by the Government, in order that we may not be left in the perilous position of having jettisoned our former means of defence and having nothing in being to replace it.

In order to appreciate the urgency of the problem it is perhaps necessary to point out that our acceptance of the 5–3 ratio of Capital Ships at Washington, was based upon the assumption that Singapore would be developed according to plan.

Taking into consideration the distance from our Home Bases and the fact that we could not denude Home Waters of ships, the 5–3 ratio, with Singapore, would have placed us roughly on a footing of equality with the Japanese in Far Eastern Waters.

The suspension of Singapore means therefore that we are in a position of inferiority, and incapable of providing for our defence.

A situation has in fact been created in which we are unable to utilise Capital Ships in the Far East, and it will therefore be apparent that any agreement with Japan, to give us security, *must stipulate the scrapping of all Japanese Capital Ships, and the abandonment by that Country of any Capital Ship building programme*. So long as we are unable to employ Capital Ships, it is essential to prevent our potential enemies from doing so.

Limitation in numbers of other craft will affect the situation only in a minor degree.

Our Light Cruiser strength, for instance, is determined much more by the length of our trade routes than by the Light Cruiser strength of other Countries.

We cannot afford to gamble with the safety of the British Empire, and ipso facto we cannot agree to surrender any part of our naval preparedness unless our possible enemies agree to do something in return which makes such preparedness unnecessary. It is not sufficient that they should engage by treaty to respect our possessions or interests, because such an engagement may be broken at short notice, whereas the Naval preparations which we would have foregone on their word could not be built up equally quickly.

Any agreement for reduction of armaments must embrace all Naval Powers and cannot be confined to Japan alone or even Japan and America.

Should any Power, such as Russia, which at present possesses comparatively weak naval forces, become a great or even a secondary naval power, similar to France or Italy, the present ratios would need revision.

Effect of the balance of Naval strength in maintaining the peace of the World

Japan
Consider the position in the Far East.

The wealth and importance of this part of the British Empire and its trade, which is enormous.

Japan, an Island Empire well aware of the value of sea power.

A large part of the British Empire bordering the Western Pacific and much nearer Japan than the British Isles.

The population of Japan increasing at the rate of 700,000 persons yearly, unless the birth rate is to be controlled, which the Japanese Ambassador in this Country has specifically denied.

This increased population must be absorbed in one of four ways —

(*a*)   On the land.
(*b*)   By industrial expansion.
(*c*)   By emigration.
(*d*)   By Japan acquiring new oversea possessions.

Taking the whole of Japan as suitable for habitation, the density of the population is 339 per square mile.

Owing to the mountainous nature of the country, however, only one-sixth is suitable for cultivation, which means that the populations of the available area is in the neighbourhood of 2034 per square mile.

The possibility of absorbing the surplus population on the land appears to be out of the question.

When the attitude of the British Empire and America to Japanese entering their territories is considered, it does not appear that emigration is likely to solve the problem.

Thus we have left only Industrial development or territorial expansion.

Japan is dependent for her industrial existence to a very large extent on raw materials imported from abroad and as her industrial development proceeds she will become increasingly dependent on her imports.

Will Japan be content to rely on foreign imports, or will she desire to control the source of these raw supplies, which in the case of coal, iron and manganese ore come from China.

Whether Japan will look to territorial expansion or industrial development, followed possibly by the control of the areas producing some of the vital raw materials to solve the problem of disposing of her surplus population, is impossible to say. The one factor which will tend to influence Japanese policy is the power of the British Fleet, and this power will have no effect in the Far East when the Fleet has no mobility owing to the lack of a base.

The most disturbing element in the situation is the strength of the Japanese Fleet at the present time and its projected development.

This strength is not justified by her degree of dependence upon imports, and still less by the measure of danger to her Trade Routes.

Why does she want this Fleet?

The behaviour of Japan during the late war should not be forgotten.

Seeing us in the throes of a great struggle, she did not scruple to attempt to stir up trouble in India.

The extent to which we can rely on her good-will or trust her solemn undertakings, must be reckoned in the light of this recent experience.

It must not be forgotten that at one of the original sittings of the League of Nations Commission, Japan put forward a draft article of the Covenant abolishing racial discrimination between the subjects of states members of the League. This was agreed to by all members of the Commission except the British Empire and the United States, and was only rejected by the Chairman, President Wilson, on the grounds that in a matter of this importance unanimous consent was necessary. As the United States is no longer a Member of the League, the British Empire now stands alone.

For the time being, Japan has dropped this claim; if she brings it forward again, a divergency of policy will exist which the League of Nations may not be able to reconcile.

As has already been stated, any agreement for reduction of armaments must embrace all Powers. Therefore it is desirable to review the situation vis-a-vis USA, France and Italy.

USA

War between the British Empire and America is put down as 'unthinkable', and from our point of view it is.

The Arbitration Treaty with America lessens the chances of war, but in gauging whether war is possible, the vital question is whether the advantages which may accrue or the disadvantages which may result are so great as to cause a nation either to go to war or to refrain from doing so.

It is not claimed that America has any intention or desire to go to war with the British Empire, but it is abundantly clear that she stands to gain a great deal more than she stands to lose by so doing. Whatever the point at issue which caused the war, it must fade into insignificance in comparison to the question of Canada.

Should America go to war with this country, she would either invade Canada or demand that Canada declares her independence and break away from the Empire.

America would temporarily lose many of her oversea markets and her export trade would suffer, but this would be offset to a certain extent by the additional imports into Canada, the latter being unable to obtain imports from Europe.

Whether America desires war with this country is extremely doubtful, but should this ever be the case, the one thing that might deter her from doing so is the British Fleet.

Neither the Army nor the Air Force could materially affect the situation.

The authority with which a country speaks in the councils of the world depends primarily on her naval strength, and unless we are prepared to play second fiddle to America, it is essential, apart from other reasons, to be her equal in this respect.

France
In the event of war with France, the latter knows that—

(*a*) Her trade could be swept from the seas.
(*b*) Her Colonial possessions, with the exception of those in North Africa, would soon be captured by military expeditions from some portion of the British Empire. In the case of the French North African possessions, it is doubtful whether we should launch a military expedition against them, but even if this were not done, they would probably be lost to France, as the French white forces in the country could not hold it against the risings which would probably occur.
(*c*) In the event of her being attacked on her Eastern frontier, she would be unable to get the reinforcements from her North African possessions on which she places such great reliance.

At the present time, it is the British Fleet alone which would deter France, with her overwhelming Air Force, from going to war with us.

Later, when the British Air Force is commensurate in strength with that of France there would appear to be little chance of France seeking war with this country, owing to her knowledge of what sea power can achieve against her.

Italy
It is sufficient to say that Italy, with her dependence on imports and her exposed coastline, is never likely to seek war with this country.

From the foregoing discussions it is clear that a strong British Fleet plays a great part in maintaining the peace of the World.

[Initialled] B.

212. *Draft Naval Staff Memorandum with alterations by Beatty*[1]

[BTY/8/5/24]   5.5.24

(My Lords regret that They are unable to express Their concurrence) *The Naval Staff cannot concur* in the draft telegram which in their opinion could not fail to convey to H.M. Ambassador at Tokyo, and through him to the Japanese Government, the impression that the non-development of Singapore could be offset by a further International 'Limitation of Armaments'.

2.   Any vague suggestions made to the Japanese for a further International 'Limitation of Armaments' would undoubtedly be understood by them as meaning a reduction which would maintain the 5:5:3 ratio.

The 5:5:3 ratio was agreed to by our Delegates at Washington and confirmed by the Government of the day on the definite understanding that a well equipped strategic base would be established at Singapore.

The further the Limitation of Naval Armaments is carried, the greater becomes the necessity for well equipped bases to enable ships to be repaired or refitted on the spot.

3.   As explained in Par: 6 of the Enclosure to A.L.M.0702/24 of 30th April, the only quid pro quo which the Japanese can offer for the non-development of Singapore is the elimination of the Capital ship from their Fleet. There would be no corresponding elimination of this Class from the British Fleet, since the abandonment of Singapore would automatically prevent our stationing such ships in Far Eastern Waters. Should H.M. Government not make this clear to the Japanese Government when they approach the latter, the Japanese Government may agree to take part in a Conference on a false understanding.

4.   In the opinion of (My Lords) *the Naval Staff* the quid pro quo which the Japanese must offer for the non-development of Singapore, and the further International 'Limitation of Armaments' are questions which must be treated separately unless we are prepared to put the Japanese into a false position or get into such a position ourselves. In the following remarks these two questions will be dealt with separately:–

5.   The question of what the Japanese must offer in return for the abandonment of Singapore is a matter of great urgency and

---

[1]Beatty's excisions are bracketed ( ); his alterations are italicised.

one in which it is realised that H.M. Government must take the initiative.

6. *Quid Pro Quo on the part of Japan for the non-development of Singapore.*

In the opinion of (My Lords) *the Naval Staff* there is no alternative method of dealing with this question than to intimate to the Japanese Government that if they do not want Singapore developed as a Naval Dockyard, they must scrap their Capital ships and agree not to build any in future.

Even then we must be free to erect such defences as are necessary for the protection of the Naval Anchorage in the Old Strait and the Oil Reserves.

In the unlikely event of the Japanese agreeing to this, they would almost certainly require that the USA should not develop a base in the Hawaiian Islands and the agreement would become a tripartite one.

7. *Conference for further International Limitation of Naval Armaments.* This question is one which, in the opinion of (My Lords) *the Naval Staff* can only be considered after the question of the Japanese quid pro quo for the non-development of Singapore has been settled.

(My Lords have studied most carefully) *T*he question of a further International Limitation of Naval Armament *has been most carefully considered* and (have definitely arrived at) the following conclusions *have been definitely reached*:–

(*a*)   Any such agreement must embrace all Naval Powers, if possible, but in any case the following Powers:–
        USA, JAPAN, FRANCE and ITALY.
(*b*)   Any agreement for the further Limitation of Armaments must be confined to Auxiliary Craft (Light Cruisers, T.B.D's, Submarines) except in the very exceptional circumstance of the Japanese agreeing to abolish their Capital ships as a quid pro quo for the non-development of Singapore.

        A further strong objection to any extension of the limitations regarding Capital ships, the special circumstance mentioned above excepted, is that any such steps would mean upsetting and interfering with the existing Washington Treaty. That Treaty is now ratified and generally in force and represents a definite achievement towards the limitation of armaments.

        The effect of proposing to modify it so soon after it has been concluded could not fail to introduce a feeling of instability and might quite possibly result in the scrapping of the Washington Treaty in favour of some other Treaty that might never gain general acceptance. It has to be remembered that the circumstances at Washington were quite exceptional.

(c)   It is distinctly to the disadvantage of the British Empire which, owing to its dependence on seaborne supplies must have a larger number of auxiliary craft than any other Nation, that HM Government should initiate or convene such a Conference, though there is no reason why the British Empire should not agree to take part in a Conference initiated by another Power.

At Washington the American proposal for a limitation of Auxiliary Craft broke down for the following reasons:–

Light Cruisers

The question of a limitation in Light Cruisers was specifically avoided *by the British Delegates* for the reason that the number required by the British Empire was so disproportionate to those required by USA and Japan that it was considered that it was of little use discussing the question with any possibility of reaching an agreement.

Destroyers

The proposal of the British Delegates that submarines should be abolished not finding favour with the other Powers and notably France, the British Delegates were unable to accept any limitation regarding Destroyers, the type of vessel on which we mainly rely to counter the submarine.

Submarines

The extravagant French demands regarding the total submarine tonnage they should be allowed prevented, in conjunction with the difficulties regarding Light Cruisers and Destroyers, any agreement being reached regarding a limitation of Auxiliary Craft.

It will thus be seen that the question of the Limitation of Auxiliary Craft bristles with difficulties which arise largely from the reluctance of other Powers to make allowance for the dependence of the British Isles on seaborne supplies of food.

Should we initiate proposals for a conference on the Limitation of Auxiliary Craft we should not be in such a favourable position for making sacrifices to prevent the failure of the Conference as would the USA, which does not depend on sea power for its security.

8.   In conclusion; (My Lords would) suggest*ed* that any instructions sent to HM Ambassador at Tokyo should be comprehensive so as to avoid any misunderstanding.

213.   *Chiefs of Staff Committee*
Minutes of 16th Meeting [Beatty in the Chair]

[Extract][1]

[Cab. 53/1]   February 24 1925
SECRET

[*Defence of Singapore*]

*   *   *   *

With regard to the local seaward defences he [Beatty] pointed out that the Admiralty proposals had already been approved by the Oversea Defence Committee, and there appeared to be no outstanding question with regard to this point. As regards the military seafront defences, agreement had already been reached between the Admiralty and the War Office, with the exception that the number of 15″ guns to be provided still remained outstanding. He called attention to the fact that the Oversea Defence Committee had recommended that a technical sub-committee should be appointed to enquire into the question of the effect of naval bombardment against fixed defences under modern conditions, and that the Oversea Defence Committee had expressed themselves as unable to make a final recommendation with regard to the scale of heavy armament until the Technical Sub-Committee had furnished a report. He understood that the Technical Sub-Committee, owing to the fact that certain gunnery trials had not yet been completed, was unable to complete its investigations at present.

LORD CAVAN [CIGS] expressed the opinion that there was no immediate necessity to arrive at a decision with regard to the number of 15″ guns to be provided, since it would take fully three years to establish even six 15″ guns . . .

LORD BEATTY then called attention to the examination of deterrents as alternatives to heavy guns against attacks by capital ships. From paragraph 18 of CID Paper No 237–C, it appeared that the Air Staff did not consider that heavy gun defences were necessary, and he presumed that they would submit their alternative pro-

---

[1]Bracketed comments [ ] in this and following documents are the Editor's.

posals. Turning to naval alternative measures of defence he explained that these consisted of submarines and mine-fields, but he pointed out that neither of these alternative methods were recommended by the Admiralty, since their provision was very expensive and not as efficacious as heavy gun defences. The provision of submarines for the purpose would cost in the neighbourhood of three million pounds, which would be more expensive than the provision of heavy gun defences. Moreover, it was doubtful if they could be relied upon to do sufficient damage to a hostile bombarding fleet. With regard to the minefields, these must be employed with other forms of defence. Their provision was also expensive. A minefield between Johore and the Dutch islands would cost £280,000 to install and it would also be necessary to provide large stores of mines and two mine-layers. Their efficacy was doubtful, since channels could be swept through the fields.

[Sir Hugh Trenchard CAS followed this with an argument that aircraft could fulfil the task less expensively by destroying the Japanese Fleet on its passage from Japan to Singapore, and doubted if Japan would ever risk such an expedition.]

LORD BEATTY stated that although we possessed additional repairing facilities at Malta, Colombo, etc, the Japanese repairing facilities were infinitely closer to Singapore than our own. He explained that with regard to the question of risks, this was answered by a proper understanding of what a fortress and a base were intended for. The main principle from a naval point of view was that before any naval force could undertake operations it must have a secure base on which it could rely with absolute certainty. A base must contain all the ingredients to enable a fleet to carry out operations . . . A Commander-in-Chief must be perfectly satisfied that the base would continue to remain a base in the absence of the main fleet; that it should be absolutely safe, not only from capture, but also from attack. To afford such protection there were at present certain recognised methods of defence, mainly by gun-fire, the volume of which was based on the scale of the probable attack. The Admiralty had already laid down the scale of an attack on Singapore, and the War Office had drawn up a scale of defence to meet such an attack. It was evident that the Chief of the Air Staff did not agree with those proposals. He [Lord Beatty] pointed out that at present the Air Staff had put forward no concrete proposals as alternative methods of defence. He suggested that, before the question could be further discussed, the Chief of the Air Staff should prepare a paper showing his proposals. He pointed out that at the present moment Singapore was practically unprotected, and that the Japanese could today seize Singapore with no risk whatsoever. If they were successful, they would thus obtain command of the China Sea and the Indian Ocean. In his opinion it was unquestionable they would take the gravest risks to obtain a result of such immeasurable value. By such a course they would achieve more than they could possibly hope to achieve by a successful fleet action. In his opinion, the defences of Singapore should be so strong as to act as a serious deterrent to any such attempt on the part of Japan.

[Lord Cavan followed, supporting Beatty.]

*   *   *   *

[*Conclusion*: CAS to prepare a paper embodying his proposals.]

214.   *Chiefs of Staff Committee*
Minutes of 18th Meeting [Beatty in the Chair]

[Extracts]

[Cab. 53/1]   May 5 1925
SECRET

[*Defence of Singapore: Trenchard's Alternative Plan (COS Paper
No 14)*]

LORD BEATTY: pointed out that the Admiralty, which was the department responsible for formulating the strategical naval plans and the tactical plans for the handling of naval units, had given these questions the closest consideration. He was not prepared to agree with certain assumptions which had been made by the Chief of the Air Staff and considered that they were based on a misconception of the situation. For instance, it was stated in the Memorandum that the British main fleet, which would be dispatched to Far Eastern waters in the event of a war with Japan, would be in a proportion of 5:3 over the Japanese fleet. This statement was inaccurate since the Admiralty in formulating their plans had always taken into consideration the necessity of retaining a proportion of the fleet in European waters. In fact, it was only proposed to send 14 capital ships to Singapore. The true proportion therefore was more in the neighbourhood of 7 to 5. It was necessary to retain a proportion of our capital ships in European waters to protect the country against potential enemies in Europe, or elsewhere, who might range themselves on the side of Japan. The latter, on the other hand, was not faced with the possibility of contending with any other hostile Power in their home waters, and could therefore afford to use the whole weight of their fleet in an attempt to capture Singapore. Again, the Memorandum called attention to the risk of damage to the Japanese battleships, but, he pointed out that the risk in reality was very slight if the fixed defences of Singapore remained as they were at present, since the Japanese could bombard Singapore outside the range of the existing defences. The Chief of the Air Staff had suggested that even should the Japanese succeed in damaging our oil supply and docks at Singapore, nevertheless on the arrival of the main battle fleet we should be in time to be able to repair the loss of oil at Singapore far more quickly than Japan could repair the damage to her fleet. In this connection however, he would point out that the destruction of the oil fuel reserve at Singapore would render our main fleet completely immobile when it arrived in those waters, and operations would become imposs- ible. It would take many years to re-establish a sufficient oil supply at Singapore. The Japanese would not be faced with the same difficulty in regard to supplies of oil since their fleet consisted, for [sic] a considerable part, of coal burning ships.

He himself had repeatedly stated that under existing conditions and with the defences of Singapore in their present state, the Japanese would have complete command of the seas, not only to the East of Singapore, but also to the West. In 1928/29, when the defences of Singapore had been completed, and the Far Eastern peace [sic] fleet, augmented by battle-cruisers, the situation would have changed, and we should possess a sufficient measure of command of the waters to the West of Singapore to justify sending military reinforcements from India. He did not think that the Japanese would risk sending their inferior battle-cruisers West of Singapore in face of the superiority of our own battle-cruisers of the Far Eastern Fleet. Even if the Japanese battle-cruisers reached the neighbourhood of Singapore before the arrival of our military reinforcements, the latter could land at Penang and proceed to Singapore by rail.

*   *   *   *

LORD BEATTY: referred to the suggestion made by the Chief of the Air Staff that the Admiralty would be able to provide some portion of the Far Eastern Fleet to harass the main Japanese fleet, and pointed out that the Admiralty were of the opinion, and always had been of the opinion, that the oil fuel reserves at Singapore should be protected by fixed defences and not by naval mobile forces. If Singapore were adequately defended, it would enable the Far Eastern Fleet to perform the essential functions of guarding the oil fuel installations to the West of Singapore, the safety of which was necessary to enable the main fleet to get to Singapore at all.

He did not agree with the estimate given in paragraph 5 of the Memorandum as to the size of the Japanese fleet, nor to the probable number of transports which would accompany it. The Admiralty estimate was that the Japanese fleet would consist of 117 vessels and the transports would number 18.

SIR HUGH TRENCHARD: called attention to a statement contained in an Admiralty letter written in 1923 when a discussion was taking place with regard to the site for an oil fuel installation on the South of Singapore Island to the effect that the Admiralty considered that when the future Far Eastern peace Fleet had been increased, the risk of bombardment from the mainland would be reduced. It appeared logical to conclude, therefore, that the Admiralty had contemplated at that time using the Far Eastern Fleet to hamper the movements of the main Japanese fleet.

LORD BEATTY: explained that the statement referred to had been made at a time when a landing by a Japanese force on the mainland of Johore, some 100 miles to the North of Singapore Island had been considered feasible. Subsequently, such a possibility had been ruled out, partly owing to the difficulty of carrying out a landing on the coast in the face of a hostile fleet, and partly owing to the evidence which had been obtained as to the difficulties of the country in the Johore State which would have to be traversed even should a landing be successful. He did not consider that it was practical for a fleet to operate in the narrow waters in the vicinity of Singapore, since these waters gave more assistance to the attackers than to the defenders.

In spite of the criticism which the Chief of the Air Staff had directed against the two main assumptions on which the scale of defence, as recommended by CID Paper No 237–C was based, the Naval Staff remained unshaken in their views, both with regard to the main Japanese objective and to the employment of the Far Eastern peace Fleet. The question of the safety of Singapore was of vital importance to the Navy. If it were lost, its recovery would entail an operation of the greatest magnitude, and therefore no risks should be taken. The Admiralty considered that the provision of the heavy fixed defences were of vital importance to the safety of Singapore. If they were installed, it was considered they would provide a complete deterrent and that Singapore would be absolutely safe. He called attention to the fact that in the late war we had not dared to undertake an attack on Heligoland. Similarly, he considered that the Japanese would not dare to attack Singapore if it were provided with adequate defences in the shape of heavy guns.

[At this point Beatty was supported by Cavan.]

* * * *

SIR HUGH TRENCHARD: then called attention to the suggestion contained in paragraph 7 of his Memorandum, to the effect that aircraft capable of offensive action would give equally effective protection and at less cost to that provided by the installation of 15″ guns at Singapore.

LORD BEATTY: expressed the opinion that the first question to be taken into consideration was the maintenance of our air superiority The Chief of the Air Staff proposed: one squadron of fighters, two squadrons of torpedo-bombers, and one flight of seaplanes. The Chief of the Imperial General Staff had suggested one squadron of spotters and three squadrons of fighters. It was evident that Japan would attempt to establish air superiority, more especially if they knew that aircraft constituted our main line of defence. The Admiralty estimated that the Japanese would employ four squadrons from their carriers, which would give them superiority over the one squadron of fighters as proposed by the Chief of the Air Staff. Superiority in the air having been obtained, the Japanese would be able to destroy our medium armament. On the other hand he considered that the proposals put forward by the Chief of the Imperial General Staff would enable us to maintain air superiority.

SIR HUGH TRENCHARD: maintained that his proposals were sufficient. He pointed out that the number of carriers which the Japanese could possess was limited by the Washington treaty and that Japan at present had no skill in flying aeroplanes off carriers and showed no signs of achieving a higher standard of aviation. Moreover the carriers themselves would provide a most valuable target. He undertook that in 6 years he would be able to provide the three squadrons which he had proposed, in the event of hostilities breaking out.

A considerable discussion then took place with regard to the relative effect of bombs and torpedoes fired from aeroplanes, as against the effect of long range heavy gunfire, in the course of which reference was made to the experimental attacks on the *Agamemnon* and *Monarch*. As a result it appeared that the Committee were in agreement that the scale of defences as recommended in C.I.D. Paper No 237–C, omitting the provision of 15" guns, was inadequate. The First Sea Lord and the Chief of the Imperial General Staff were agreed that in order to make the defences adequate the provision of 15" guns was essential. The Chief of the Air Staff on the other hand maintained that his proposals for the provision of bombing and torpedo aircraft would prove equally efficient.

LORD CAVAN: expressed the opinion that it was essential to defend Singapore in depth. The provision of 15" guns was essential, but he would welcome the addition of torpedo and bombing aircraft as an additional measure, as by this means the depth of the defences would be further increased.

After some further discussion, the Committee agreed: that the Secretary should be instructed to prepare a draft report for consideration, bringing out the measure of agreement which had been reached, and the points of difference which still existed between the First Sea Lord and the Chief of the Imperial General Staff on the one hand and the Chief of the Air Staff on the other.

215. Chiefs of Staff Committee
Minutes of 21st Meeting [Beatty in the Chair]

[Extracts]

[Cab. 53/1]   July 3 1925
SECRET

[*Defence of Singapore*]

*   *   *   *

LORD BEATTY: expressed the view that the Sub-Committee must deal with the situation as it existed at present. He personally was much alarmed at the position existing at present throughout the world. He was in fact so disturbed that he could not agree to the postponement for even one hour of the commencement of the work necessary to ensure the safety of Singapore. He called attention to the present situation in China. He was disturbed, not so much at the existing position of affairs as to what might happen afterwards. There were people who believed that China was an unhomogeneous mass incapable of taking action as a whole, and that Japan was of a pacific disposition, and entirely desirous of retaining friendship with this country. He was not inclined to agree with either of these ideas. The Japanese were a race who considered themselves to possess a mission in the world, and were a military race from beginning to end. In a comparatively short space of time Japan had brought three wars to a successful conclusion. Their population was increasing, and they must in due course look for an outlet. He considered that the menace from Japan was most serious, and that to believe that there was no possibility of war during the next ten years, was, in reality, living in a fool's paradise. It was true that Japanese statesmen were calm and suave in their dealings with us, and appeared to be desirous of maintaining friendly relations, but on the other hand, judging from the Japanese Press, and reports which had been received, there was in Japan a considerable amount of opinion hostile to this country. If it could be laid down as an absolute certainty that there was no possibility of war within the next three or four years it might conceivably be possible to await future aerial development, but he personally could never agree that war within that period was an impossibility. We were steadily increasing our reserves at Singapore day by day, but at the moment we were powerless to give any protection whatsoever, either to Singapore itself or to that portion of the world to which Singapore was the key. If the Japanese took the bit between their teeth and attempted to dictate their will to this country, we were totally incapable of taking any action whatsoever, and should merely have to submit to their demands. In fact we were actually at the present moment existing on the good will of another Power, and would continue to do so, until Singapore had been made secure. Thus the British Empire was in a situation which had never existed previously in the course of its history. In his opinion this was deplorable and must be rectified immediately. He did not consider it beyond the bounds of possibility that we should be at war by 1928.

[Trenchard's response was that Japan would not risk a war in the next 10 years, during which time the development of air power would produce a better and cheaper defence for Singapore than the 15″ guns advocated by Beatty and the Chief of the Imperial General Staff.]

*   *   *   *

[*The Situation in China*]

LORD BEATTY: referring to the existing situation in China drew attention to the British interests involved, which were greater than those of any other Power, totalling in monetary value something like £300,000,000 a year. All had been built up by British commercial enterprise and in the past had been safeguarded by the good relations which existed between the government of China and the government of Great Britain, and by the fact that Chinese merchants generally recognised the advantage of trading with British merchants. It now appeared that China was coming under Bolshevik influence, the first object of which would be to destroy British commercial interests. Great Britain was, in present circumstances, powerless to protect her own interests in China, in fact the only Power which could protect British and other interests in that country was Japan. He suggested that it might be advisable to ask Japan to undertake such a duty, for he visualised the situation as follows:– If Japan did not undertake to protect British interests, then it appeared that all those interests would be destroyed and there would be a complete loss. If Japan did undertake to protect British interests there would probably be a partial loss, in that there would be a certain amount of interference with British trade, and British traders would meet with greater competition, but they had been used to that sort of situation in the past; they had been successful then, and there was no reason why they should not be so again in the future. Certainly, any question such as this was mainly a Foreign Office matter, but naval interests were considerably involved. The trade in the Far East had been built up largely under naval protection and he accordingly considered that the Admiralty had a responsibility for the protection of that trade.

[Trenchard's reply stated that the argument that Japan was bound to become predominant in China and that to encourage her was no better than China's falling under Bolshevik influence.]

215a. *Beatty: Minute to Civil Lord[1] on Cost of Singapore Base*

[ADM 116/2416]   3.6.26

Civil Lord

I think it will be better if I set down here the exact situation in regard to Singapore:—

1.   £1,250,000 has already been authorised by the Cabinet for defences exclusive of 15" guns, although the money has not been voted. £750,000 has also been authorised by the Cabinet for a Floating Dock and its appurtenances.

2.   This means that £2,000,000 of the total of £11,000,000 has already been authorised.

3.   This leaves £9,000,000 of which £2,000,000 should be earmarked for 15" gun defences.

4.   £7,000,000 therefore remains to be allocated for the development of the Naval Base, in conformity with the principles laid down in my minute of the 28th April 1926.

5.   For your guidance, I consider that the term 'a number of years' quoted in recommendation (1) should be taken as meaning three years or more; and that 'a comparatively short period' referred to in recommendation (2) should be taken as meaning less than three years.

[Initialled] B.

216.   *Chiefs of Staff Committee*
Minutes of 34th Meeting [Beatty in the Chair]

[Extract]

[Cab. 53/1]   June 22 1926

SECRET

[*Defence of Singapore Base: Discussion of CAS's
Memorandum (COS PAPER 40)*]

*   *   *   *

LORD BEATTY (continuing) said that it might be advisable to restate briefly certain facts which had such an important bearing on the subject of the defences of Singapore. The Review had been based on their own knowledge and views on strategy and on a Foreign Office Memorandum which definitely stated that a properly defended base at Singapore would act as a deterrent and reduce

---

[1]Earl Stanhope was Civil Lord 1924–29.

the possibility of a war in the Far East. The question now was how to make Singapore a deterrent? The Chief of the Naval Staff and the Chief of the Imperial General Staff had argued repeatedly that adequate security could not be obtained, nor could a deterrent be provided, without installing permanent defences at Singapore. The Chief of the Air Staff admitted that 15″ guns would constitute a deterrent . . . The Chief of the Air Staff only differed from the other Chiefs of Staff in so far as he urged that torpedo bombing machines could replace guns as a deterrent. He would ask the Chief of the Air Staff to consider this matter most carefully from all points of view. The Chiefs of Staff Committee had met frequently to consider various problems, some of a simple nature, some more obstruse [sic]. Their recommendations had always hitherto been unanimous, and for this reason, the Sub-Committee had, so to speak, grown in strength and importance. The Chief of the Air Staff had put forward not an alternative scheme of defence, but a scheme for air reinforcements, which was by no means the same thing. Whatever faith they had in the Air Force, however strong their belief in future developments, the question of the defences at Singapore, as they had emphasised in their Review, was one of imperative and immediate necessity. Allowing everything that was claimed by the Chief of the Air Staff to be justified, and even that in five or six years, his ideas would become practicable working propositions, this should not prevent us from taking steps to safeguard a part of the Empire which was at present at the mercy of another Power.

The actual cost of the scheme for installing 15″ guns was roughly £1½ millions. If all the plans of the Chief of Air Staff were justified, and his scheme was finally put into effect, we should, at the worst, have spent £1½ millions on defence, which might have been saved, but under the Chief of the Air Staff's scheme for reinforcements, the defences would not be there. If they were there on the outbreak of war, and all the world, including Japan, knew they were there, he did not think they would act as a deterrent to attack and therefore would not prevent Japan from going to war with us. He did not think that any Admiral would be deterred from attacking Singapore by the fact that bombing aircraft were known to be stationed there, but he was convinced that no Admiral of any nationality would be deterred from attacking Singapore in the face of 15″ guns. Under the Chief of the Air Staff's scheme aircraft would not be at Singapore when war broke out. On the other hand if his scheme was modified and aircraft were stationed at Singapore in peace-time, the cost of these arrangements would approximate very closely to the cost of the 15″ guns scheme.

SIR HUGH TRENCHARD: remarked that it must not be overlooked that aircraft could move forward to where they were next required while 15″ guns would remain locked up at Singapore.

LORD BEATTY: said that the chief advantage claimed for the Air Scheme would disappear unless it could be shown that it was very much cheaper than the gun scheme. The initial cost of the former was about £250,000 less than the latter. Even then, the cost of the upkeep in the former case, provided that aircraft were to be stationed at Singapore in peace-time, would be greater. If aircraft were not to be stationed at Singapore in peace, he was even more definitely opposed to the scheme, because it was quite possible that within 24 hours of the declaration of war, if not before, Singapore would be attacked by the Japanese fleet with possibly calamitous results. He would go so far as to assert that, unless it was defended in such strength, and by such means as could be accepted by *all* as a sufficient deterrent, it was no use having a base there at all. He would ask the Chief of the Air Staff to consider the matter from that point of view.

The Air scheme might be possible in years to come, but it could not be the immediate solution. The Japanese could produce a large number of aircraft and carriers. Battleships could stand a great deal of bombing and a few hours bombardment could destroy all our valuable resources at Singapore. He hoped there would be no further delay in settling the question, which was one of the first importance. It would take some time, say 5 years, to install the gun defences. Were we to do nothing except hope that developments in the air would solve the questions for us during this time, when at worst, if we started the gun defences at once, a cost of £1½ millions would be involved?

[After further discussion]

LORD BEATTY: remarked that he did not assert that the scheme of the Chief of Air Staff was a visionary one and he agreed that developments in the air might take place as predicted by him, but their immediate need was to begin on something which they could all agree was a deterrent. He enquired whether Sir Hugh Trenchard thought that the force indicated on page 4 of COS 40, namely two torpedo-bomber squadrons, one fighter squadron and one reconnaissance flight, would make Singapore safe and act as a deterrent.

SIR HUGH TRENCHARD: assented.

LORD BEATTY: remarked that the Japanese could produce an equal number of aircraft and, supposing an attack on Singapore was made during which two squadrons of torpedo-bombers were sent out to attack the ships, the Japanese could put up two squadrons of fighters to attack them.

SIR HUGH TRENCHARD: observed that the first object of shore-based aircraft would be to sink the aircraft carriers.

[The discussion continued without agreement being reached, CIGS supporting Beatty. In conclusion the Chiefs reported that, while they agreed on the need for adequate defences for Singapore, they could not agree on the methods to be used.]

PART V

THE JUTLAND CONTROVERSY
1916–1927

INTRODUCTION[1]

After the war, with the inevitable post-mortem, the controversy reached its height, because the bird's-eye view depicted on diagrams could not always be identified with the situation as seen by those in command when they made their decisions. Owing to low visibility, no two commanders got the same view of the action, and although 250 ships took part, there were never more than three or four enemy capital ships in sight at the same time from any point in the British line.

(W. S. Chalmers: *The Life and Letters of David, Earl Beatty*,
p. 265)

Beatty's first biographer thus firmly established why controversy about Jutland was inevitable. That it was so bitter and prolonged, and so divisive, was due to the public and personal emotions aroused by the Royal Navy's failure to inflict a visible and decisive defeat on its German enemy. As has clearly emerged in the documents printed in this volume and its predecessor,[2] Beatty shared in this emotion to such a degree that the events of 31 May and 1 June 1916 became increasingly painful for him to recall. Believing firmly as he did that the destruction of the High Seas Fleet had been the only acceptable outcome of the war at sea, he became also convinced that this could have been achieved at Jutland. This conviction hardened and narrowed into an assertive belief that his own conduct and the performance of the battle-cruisers were entirely blameless and that responsibility for the failure lay entirely on others, particularly on his Commander-in-Chief,

---

[1]The background to this section is in Marder, *From the Dreadnought*, III. Roskill, *Beatty* analyses Beatty's conduct critically and sensitively. The *Jellicoe Papers* II give the point of view of Jellicoe and Harper. Donald M. Schurman (1981), *Julian S. Corbett 1854–1922: Historian of British Maritime Policy from Drake to Jellicoe*, London: Royal Historical Society, records Beatty's attempts to influence Corbett's official history of naval operations.

[2]The *Beatty Papers* I, parts V and VI.

417

Jellicoe and Rear-Admiral Hugh Evan-Thomas,[1] commanding the 5th Battle Squadron, as well as in defects of British projectiles, for which he, unlike Jellicoe, had no responsibility.

It was this unshakeable certainty of his blamelessness for the failure at Jutland which governed Beatty's attitude to all the post-war arguments and publications concerned with the battle, and which led to the interventions which his position as First Sea Lord made possible, to ensure that they reinforced his version of what had happened and who was responsible for failure. Sir Julian Corbett,[2] the author of the official history of naval operations during the war, and, more directly and fiercely, Captain J. E. T. Harper,[3] appointed by the Admiralty to produce a factual record of Jutland, felt the strength of his feelings, as did Jellicoe and Evan-Thomas. Corbett's death in September 1922 removed him from the conflict, but the admirals, as the documents demonstrate, carried the mental scars of the dispute to the end of their lives. Nor was the damage confined to individuals. The popular press used the controversy for political ends. The Navy itself was divided, and some of their supporters took up far more extreme positions than either Beatty or Jellicoe themselves. Although time may have modified the intensity of feeling, the controversy was long lived. Efforts to learn the lessons of Jutland figured in the syllabuses of both Tactical and Staff courses until the eve of

---

[1]Later Admiral Sir Hugh Evan-Thomas (1862–1928): entered RN 1876; Rear-Admiral and 2nd in command 1st Battle Squadron 1912; commanding 5th Battle Squadron 1915–18; Vice-Admiral 1917; C-in-C Nore and Admiral 1920; retired 1924.

[2]Sir Julian Corbett (1854–1922): Schurman (see note 1 on page 417) analyses his many publications, including five volumes for the NRS. In 1902 he was appointed Lecturer in Naval History at the RN War College which resulted in the publication of his classic *Some Principles of Maritime Strategy* in 1911. In 1910 he was invited by the Admiralty to write a history of *Maritime Operations in the Russo-Japanese War 1904–5* (1913), an officially restricted publication. There is a copy in the Library of the Ministry of Defence (Naval). It is worthy of open publication. In 1914 he began his work on what was to become the official naval history of the Great War, of which he completed the first three volumes before his death in 1922. The remaining two were produced by Sir Henry Newbolt (see note 2 on page 466).

[3]Captain, later Vice-Admiral J. E. T. Harper (1874–1949): in 1919, as Director of Navigation, was selected, before Beatty came to the Admiralty, to produce a *Record* of the battle. Although made Rear-Admiral in 1924 he was not given active employment and retired in 1927. Roskill concludes that Chatfield was responsible for this. See Roskill, *Beatty*, ch. V; *Jellicoe Papers* II, Part IV, which includes Harper's detailed account of the controversy; and Marder, *From the Dreadnought*, III, 76n, 86n, 148–9, 246–8.

the Second World War.[1] Those who still find Beatty's conduct unattractive must, if they are to understand as well as condemn, keep in mind the intensity of personal emotion and damage to professional pride which lay behind it, as well as the pressures of the public debate.

Another dimension which puts the controversy into perspective and helps understanding, is consideration of the disputes which lay behind the compilation and publication of Julian Corbett's official history, especially volume III dealing with Jutland, published posthumously in 1923. In addition to the inevitable differences of fact, the opinion and judgements which he expressed antagonised some naval officers by the mere fact that here was a civilian presuming to assess their conduct in circumstances he had never experienced. However distinguished he might be, whatever his literary skills, it was insupportable that he should pass judgements which would affect how they were to be remembered in history. This attitude in turn was an example of the gulf between the 'Frocks' and the 'Brass' during the war itself, and of later attempts at self-exculpation from its errors and disasters when the magnitude of its human and material cost began to haunt the nation. In particular, the self-justifying memoirs of Lloyd George[2] with their strong criticisms of service leaders, and, of more direct relevance to Jutland, those of Winston Churchill[3] with their partisan judgements, created an atmosphere in the Navy which encouraged disagreement and self-justification. The Jutland controversy must not be judged in isolation and even less as a personal confrontation between Beatty and Jellicoe. It can only be understood as a part of the total experience of Britain during the Great War, and the subsequent revulsion against it.

It is illuminating to examine this atmosphere of controversy, self-justification and the attempts of those in authority to impose their interpretations on history, in more detail. Corbett's difficulties over the compilation of his official history began when Churchill was too burdened with political office to produce his own version of events quickly. The former First Lord, as jealous of his reputation as any admiral, argued at Cabinet level that Corbett's work should not be published without the parallel issue

[1]On 29 July 1938, a month before he retired as 1st Sea Lord, Chatfield was given a revised presentation on Jutland, replacing the one compiled in 1935 (Chatfield Papers 8/2, National Maritime Museum).

[2]David Lloyd George (1936), *War Memoirs*, 6 vols, London.

[3]Winston Churchill (1927), *The World Crisis*, London, especially vol III, subsequently cited as Churchill, *World Crisis*.

of a full and fair selection of the official documents, so that readers should not be misled into giving undue credence to the judgements of an 'official' historian. By this and other arguments he held up publication for nearly a year, until the Cabinet decided against him. Within the higher ranks of the Navy Corbett had support and advice from Wemyss and Jellicoe, but was heavily criticised by the Second Sea Lord, M. E. Browning:

> I notice many personal opinions and judgements which I consider out of place . . . I think it should be fully revised by a flag officer.[1]

Even when all objections had been answered or overcome, the Board, with Beatty now installed as First Sea Lord, insisted on the inclusion of a disclaimer in Corbett's first volume:

> The Lords Commissioners of the Admiralty have given the author access to official documents in the preparation of this work, but they are in no way responsible for his reading or interpretation of the facts as stated.

Inevitably there was more controversy over the volume on Jutland, and a strengthened disclaimer was inserted. The Admiralty's concern was increased by the knowledge that Corbett and Jellicoe were on close terms and it was therefore probable that Jellicoe had advised him and commented on his drafts.

> It is wonderful how you have seen into my mind in your account of the action and how accurately you have diagnosed my intentions merely from a study of the reports. Please accept my warmest congratulations on the clear and interesting analysis of the action. The notes are of course for such use as you think fit, and for disregarding if you so decide.[2]

Beatty, knowing of the Corbett–Jellicoe relationship, was bound to feel that such an official history would not do him justice and that any Admiralty publication must correct the imbalance. As Donald Schurman wisely comments:

> This sense of injustice and a real desire that the men in his ships should feel no reason for shame, made him react. It is regrettable that this situation led him to contemplate manipu-

[1] Schurman, *Julian Corbett*, p. 182.
[2] Jellicoe to Corbett, 12.9.22 (Corbett Papers, Box 7, National Maritime Museum).

lation that under other circumstances he would have scorned.[1]
[236a, 243]

Winston Churchill's volume dealing with Jutland did not appear
until 1927 when Beatty's active career was drawing to a close.
Although it did imply some shortcomings by Beatty, its main
thrust was a sustained criticism of Jellicoe. This was directed at
his tactical caution and rigidity of command organisation and his
excessive fear of underwater weapons, which together had led to
the inconclusive result. The style was not fiercely condemnatory
of the Commander-in-Chief and took into account British weaknesses in *matériel*, which had contributed to the indecisiveness of
the battle, and the vagaries of weather over the area which had
added to his difficulties. Nevertheless Churchill's considered verdict is that a more positive and aggressive commander could have
overcome these obstacles. Yet even here there is the wise comment:

> There are profound differences between a battle where both
> sides wish for a full trial of strength and skill, and a battle where
> one side had no intention of fighting to a finish, and seeks only
> to retire without disadvantage and dishonour from an unequal
> and undesired conflict.

Churchill makes no criticism of Beatty's battle-cruiser force's
weaknesses in reporting and signalling but does permit himself a
mild rebuke on the handling of the Fifth Battle Squadron, which
figures largely in the following documents [217, 239, 241–2,
244–7].

> It would however no doubt have been better if the original
> formation of the battle-cruisers and the 5th Battle Squadron
> had been more compact.

But in general, and not surprisingly since he had closely consulted
K. G. B. Dewar[2] during the writing of his account, he constantly
contrasts what he saw as Jellicoe's unnecessary caution with
Beatty's dashing and gallant leadership of the battle-cruisers
despite his heavy losses:[3]

> [Jellicoe's] praiseworthy caution had induced a defensive habit
> of mind and scheme of tactics which hampered the Grand Fleet,

---

[1]Schurman, *Julian Corbett*, p. 187.
[2]Captain K. G. B. Dewar, one of the founders of *The Naval Review*.
[3]Churchill, *World Crisis*, III chapters V and VI.

even when the special conditions enjoining caution did not exist.

A rhetorical flourish shows where Churchill's sympathy really lay. If the Royal Navy were to identify personalities who brought to the Great War 'the audacious and conquering tradition of the past' it must look towards Beatty and the battle-cruisers, Keyes of Zeebrugge and Tyrwhitt of the Harwich Striking Force, and it will be to them 'that the eyes of rising generations will turn'.[1] What light have the perspective of time and the advantages conferred by the mass of scholarly research which has emerged enabled the two most distinguished historians of the Royal Navy of our age, Arthur Marder and Stephen Roskill, to throw on the controversy? Marder, whose revised study on Jutland in volume III of *From the Dreadnought to Scapa Flow* is most valuable for his balanced and dispassionate critique of Beatty's and Jellicoe's conduct of the battle. He is rightly critical of Beatty's weaknesses, including the failure to concentrate his force at the beginning of the battle-cruiser action, but is unqualified in his praise of his handling of 'the run North' and his 'staunchness and skill in leadership' which 'left nothing to be desired'. He dismisses the common allegation that the gunnery training of the battle-cruisers had been neglected, and blames their failure to secure more effective hits upon poor visibility and defective projectiles. His most provocative conclusion is that, if Beatty had been in overall command in the actual circumstances of Jutland as distinct from what he thought after the event, the battle would not have ended any differently, 'for I do not believe that Beatty would have tried anything sensational'. As for Jellicoe, he 'has been most unfairly blamed for not doing miracles at Jutland. He was as brave and enterprising as the best of them, and did the best that was possible'.[2]

As for the controversy, Marder points out that it broke out as soon as the reports of the battle had been received and began with attacks on Jellicoe by senior officers. Prominent among them was Admiral of the Fleet Sir Hedworth Meux[3] who in August 1916 wrote to the influential Lord Stamfordham, the King's Private Secretary:

If Jellicoe had grasped the opportunity which Providence,

[1] See note 3 on page 421.
[2] Marder, *From the Dreadnought*, III, p. 232.
[3] Sir Hedworth Meux (1856–1919): C-in-C Portsmouth 1912–16.

assisted by Beatty, placed in his way, and destroyed the German Fleet, he ought to have been made an Earl — but instead of following the German fleet he let his van division (Jerram's) wander aimlessly away and they hardly fired a shot — and the others followed. Jellicoe's despatch stating his battle fleet was engaged for two hours is most disingenious [*sic*] and has naturally created a false impression in the country. Practically the whole of the fighting was done by the battle-cruisers and our own battle fleet only fired very few rounds — hardly any of them were touched, and probably did a similar amount of damage to the enemy![1]

Opinions such as this, echoed at lower levels in the service, and in society, lay behind the significant rise in bad feeling which arose between the Grand Fleet and the Battle Fleet and were influential in hastening Jellicoe's publication in 1919 of *The Grand Fleet, 1914–1916*, stating his case. This was followed by more journalistic tirades and the publication, or non-publication, of official accounts which made up the core of the Jutland Controversy on which Marder prudently writes: 'The details of this unsavoury affair, including the rights and wrongs, I gladly leave to others.'[2] If Marder had Stephen Roskill in mind, he had recommended the task to capable hands.

In his 1981 biography Roskill committed himself to writing a fair and balanced treatment of Beatty's career, including of course his part in the Jutland battle and the ensuing controversy. Like his predecessor Chalmers thirty years earlier, he stresses that any valid assessment must be based on the nature of the battle itself and the circumstances in which it was fought. These made controversy inevitable, especially as:

Many perfectly genuine uncertainties existed regarding the movements of ships and what the combatants saw — or thought they saw. By modern standards the plotting of ships' movements was then archaic . . . and on 31st May 1916 weather conditions were such that few, if any, opportunities existed for navigating officers to establish observed positions from celestial bodies . . . Thus when it came to drawing maps of the various phases of the battle, historians had inevitably to rely chiefly on the deck and signal logs of ships and on the diaries kept on their bridges or at their plots. It was therefore by no means unreasonable

[1]Marder, *From the Dreadnought*, III, p. 245.
[2]Ibid, III, p. 248.

that wide disagreements should have existed between those charged with analysing events for historical purposes and those who had been present on that fateful day.[1]

In these circumstances it was inevitable that those who had figured prominently in the battle should try to ensure that the ambiguities and uncertainties were resolved in ways which cast the most favourable light on their own decisions and actions. Roskill firmly establishes that Beatty was heavily involved in such a process. He was convinced that both Harper and Corbett were treating him unfairly and used his position as First Sea Lord to try to amend their work so as to present a more favourable view of his own performance and that of the battle-cruisers. In addition he initiated the preparation by the brothers Dewar of the Naval Staff Appreciation which, with its severe criticisms of Jellicoe, strengthened the tendency to personalise the controversy. From these facts and Beatty's subsequent conduct Roskill demolishes what he terms 'the Legend' that Beatty had not personally partici-pated in the controversy but had unwisely involved himself 'in the production of the historical accounts of Jutland — especially when he was First Sea Lord'. Although he continues by stating that if Beatty had not intervened, the accounts of Jutland produced in the 1920s would have been considerably weighted in Jellicoe's favour, he sums up with the trenchant but fair judgement:

> Thus, although Beatty must stand convicted of highly inju-dicious, even reprehensible interference in the preparation of the various accounts of the battle, a generous verdict would be to acquit him of the most damaging charges made against him by Harper, Frewen and others in the opposite camp.[2]

How violent these charges became under the stress of controversy is very clear from the documents which follow.

It is helpful to recall the titles and fates of the official compi-lations which lay at the root of the Jutland controversy during Beatty's term as First Sea Lord.

Battle of Jutland, 30th May to 1st June 1916. Official Despatches with Appendices
Published 1920 as Cmd 1068.

[1] Roskill, *Beatty*, pp. 322–3.
[2] Ibid, *Beatty*, p. 339.

The Official Record of the Battle of Jutland, 31st May to 1st June 1916
Although 'Published by HMSO, 1920' appears on the cover, Harper's *Record* was withdrawn before publication, after Board decisions in September 1920 in which the First Lord, Walter Long, decided that the differences between Beatty and Jellicoe were irreconcilable. The material was sent to Julian Corbett for inclusion in his Official History. Beatty's copy, marked CNS, is in BTY/22/8.

Naval Staff Appreciation of Jutland
Compiled by the brothers Dewar in 1922 as an Admiralty Confidential Book (CB0938). It was not distributed as it was thought to be too controversial and was ordered to be destroyed by Madden after he succeeded Beatty as First Sea Lord. One of the few surviving copies is in BTY/22/9 and is signed by him.[1]

Sir Julian Corbett, *History of the Great War, Naval Operations*, vol III
Published 1923; revised edition 1940, London: Longmans.

Narrative of the Battle of Jutland
Essentially the Naval Staff Appreciation without the judgements and criticisms. Published in 1924 by HMSO.

Reproduction of the Record of the Battle of Jutland
Written by Captain J. E. T. Harper and others. Substantially the withdrawn Record of 1920, but without the diagrams. Published in 1927 as Cmd 2870.

The documents which follow deal almost entirely with Beatty's direct interventions in the controversy. With rare exceptions they do not include papers already printed in earlier volumes published by the Navy Records Society. Chief amongst these is

The Jellicoe Papers, volume II, 1916–1935, edited by A. Temple-Patterson (1968)
Part IV deals with the Jutland controversy, and a substantial

---

[1] A note in the Chatfield Papers by a civil servant in the 1st Lord's private office during the controversy contains further information on the fate of some of the official Jutland documents. It states that in 1927 Beatty ordered the destruction of Harper's charts, but that two sets were sent to the Secretary's office, which had not been subsequently found. In 1930 all copies of the Naval Staff Appreciation, except for three, had been destroyed. Frederic Dreyer (DCNS 1930–33) had handed the relevant papers to the Secretary, Oswyn Murray, but no trace of these had since been found. (Chatfield Papers, 8/2 8 March 1938). See also note 1 on page 419.

Appendix contains the Harper Papers which detail Beatty's interventions as they were experienced by Harper.

The Keyes Papers, volume II, 1919–1938, edited by Paul G. Halpern (1979)
Keyes was a close friend and supporter of Beatty, and became DCNS in 1921. Along with Chatfield, the ACNS, he headed the Naval Staff who prepared much of the material which Beatty used.

The Beatty Papers, volume I, 1902–1918, edited by B. McL Ranft (1989)
Part V deals with the battle and early reactions to it. Part VI includes its impact on Beatty emotionally and on his policies as Commander-in-Chief Grand Fleet until the end of the war.

All three of these volumes form an essential background to this selection.

The two early appreciative letters from Beatty are highly ironical in view of what was to follow in his intensive criticisms of Jellicoe and Evan-Thomas as he sought to find reasons for the failure to destroy the German fleet and reacted sharply against any suggestion that he himself was in any way responsible, either in detail or in the general handling of his force. It was this attitude which was at the root of his sustained pressure on Harper during the preparation of the Admiralty *Record*. Particularly significant among the detailed points was Beatty's rejection, against all the evidence, of the view that he had ordered *Lion* to make a 360 degree turn during the pursuit of the retiring High Seas Fleet, presumably because it suggested that he was not pressing on relentlessly. The documents [219–22], as well as Chalmers, Marder and Roskill, all support the view that such a turn was in fact made.[1] A more important element of the controversy was whether Beatty had erred in not ensuring the concentration of the Fifth Battle Squadron and the battle-cruisers before engaging Hipper, or if Evan-Thomas had failed to show adequate initiative by not anticipating Beatty's intentions. This widened the dispute into contrasting the differences between the operational practices of

[1] In discussion with the Directing Staff of the RN Tactical School which followed the updated presentation on Jutland on 29 July 1938 (see note 1 on pages 419 and 425) Chatfield was asked about the controversial 360 degree turn, supposedly caused by gyro failure, 'CNS could give him no information as he was between decks seeing the wounded, and had turned over the ship to Captain Bentinck the Chief of Staff' (CHT/8/2).

the Grand Fleet and the battle-cruisers and thus between the different temperaments of Jellicoe and Beatty. Evan-Thomas's contributions to the conflict also show how bitterness and sense of grievance sharpened with the passing of time [239, 241, 244–7].

When Professor Temple-Patterson's second volume of *The Jellicoe Papers* appeared in 1968, with its Appendix of *The Harper Papers*, it was natural to presume that the publication of Beatty's papers would enable readers to gain a more balanced view of what appeared to be a very unattractive episode in his career. The documents certainly demonstrate the extent and nature of his pressures on Harper to correct errors of fact and remove comments detrimental to his own reputation, and also contain Harper's reactions and replies to them. As the years passed, Harper (like Evan-Thomas and their supporter Oswald Frewen) became more vehement and extreme in his condemnation of Beatty, and all their assertions and charges must be assessed accordingly [223–9, 234, 247–9]. If Leopold Amery's recollections of his talks with Beatty in 1923 are accurate, Beatty's condemnations of Jellicoe similarly hardened. It would also appear that even such firm supporters as Keyes and Chatfield, and other senior members of the Naval Staff, did not agree with Beatty's satisfaction with the *Naval Staff Appreciation* and its sweeping attacks on Jellicoe [235–6, 238, 240].

By 1923 the hardening of Beatty's position produced a similar reaction by Jellicoe. In response to Beatty's recent pressures on Corbett and his support of a proposed publication of the *Staff Appreciation*, he threatened to resign as Governor-General of New Zealand, return to Britain and publish a refutation of all the charges and criticisms levelled at him. This he did not do, but it was presumably after finishing his term and returning to Britain in 1924 that he began to produce drafts of a full defence of his conduct at Jutland. These are remarkable not so much for their strong restatement of all his earlier arguments in support of his conduct and in refutation of the Admiralty's attacks upon it, but in their attempt to analyse how the whole controversy had originated. He argues that the fact that the post war Naval Staff was headed by and largely drawn from the battle-cruiser force, and therefore had so limited a view of the battle as to have no comprehension of the problems facing the Commander-in-Chief, and hence had been led to make unfounded criticisms of his actions and decisions. It is a remarkably charitable judgement and an illuminating one [244].

It supports the proposition that rather than considering the controversy over the battle of Jutland as a clash between two admirals concerned mainly with their own reputations, it should be seen as arising from the nature of the battle itself. There were very real difficulties in establishing what actually happened, difficulties experienced both by participants and by those who sought to record the events for posterity. In addition, those who had most opportunity to influence the historical record after the war were those who had had the most limited view of the battle as a whole. It needed only the emotions of professional pride and self-esteem, and the factionalism which has been so strong in the history of the Royal Navy, to turn this hitherto unrecognised combination of complex causes into the distasteful personalised affair that it became.

There is however a compensation. A blazing row is always more interesting than a smouldering debate, and it may well be that this continuing interest in the clash of personalities and factions will encourage historians to go on looking for a final solution to the riddles of Jutland.

217. *Beatty to Rear-Admiral Sir Hugh Evan-Thomas*

[Holograph]

[Add 52504]   *Lion*
                                                        4.6.16

My Dear Evan-Thomas,

Just a line to thank you from the bottom of my heart for your gallant and effective support on Wednesday. It was fine to see your fine Squadron sail down as it did. I hope your good ships are not too much knocked about.

Warspite will not be long; nothing serious.

Your coming down in support and poor Hood's magnificent handling of his Squadron will remain in my mind for ever.

The old spirit is still alive & as bright as ever.

I make out the enemy must have lost much more heavily than we are given credit for.

                          yours ever
                    [Signed] DAVID BEATTY

[PS] My most hearty and sincere congratulations on the CB. It ought to be more after the 31st, but that will come.

218. *Beatty to Jellicoe*

[Holograph]

[Add 49008]   *Lion*
                                                      [Rosyth]
                                                        9.6.16

My Dear Commander-in-Chief,

My letter by Forbes[1] was very hurried, he was here such a short time, and there were forty thousand things going on, that I had little time to write you but the scantiest information.

---

[1] Jellicoe's Staff Flag Commander, later Admiral of the Fleet Sir Charles Forbes (1880–1960): entered RN 1894; gunnery specialist; Rear-Admiral 1928; commanded Mediterranean Destroyer Flotillas 1930–31; 3rd Sea Lord 1931–4; Vice-Admiral 1933; 1st Battle Squadron and 2nd in Command Mediterranean; Admiral 1936; C-in-C Home Fleet 1938–40; Admiral of the Fleet 1940; C-in-C Plymouth 1940–43.

First, I want to offer you my deepest sympathy in being baulked of your great victory, which I felt was assured when you hove in sight.

I can well understand your feeling, and that of the Battle Fleet, to be so near, and miss, is worse than anything. The cursed weather defeats us every time. It must have been tantalising in the extreme. I've no doubt that my smoke spoilt your view to some extent, but I could not get ahead of you faster. I was going top speed and hotly engaged. Poor Robert Arbuthnot put me out of my stride for a moment, but not to matter very greatly. Every time, the weather conditions beat us: 16th December; 24th January (too clear) and now, this time.[1]

It is heart breaking for the fine fellows to have waited so patiently, so cheerfully, for so long. And indeed I can well understand your feelings. It was unfortunate that my position did not tally sufficiently accurately, but that was a small matter if the weather had remained clear.

Your sweep South was splendid, and I made certain that we should have them at daylight. I cannot believe now that they got in to NE[d] of you and feel they must have tried the SW. It was perhaps unfortunate that those who sighted the enemy to the Northward did not make reports. Perhaps they did, but I did not get them, but then our wireless was not very good. It was shot away three times.

* * * *

I had already started committees on the subject of learning all we can from the action when I got your wire. It ought to be very productive. I have learnt a great deal.[2]

I do hope you are able to come here in the *Iron Duke* soon. It would do us from top to bottom a great honour to know that we have earned your approbation.

We were sick to death when we returned, and found that we had been defeated, as *per* Press. I enclose you an ode to the Press on the subject. [not with MS] We are all rather sore, so if you can see your way to coming here, it would do us *all* no end of good and would be greatly appreciated. We are part of the Grand Fleet and would like to see our Commander-in-Chief.

I am afraid the Report of Proceedings is delayed somewhat. I

[1] 16 December 1914, Hipper's raid on Scarborough; 24 January 1915, Dogger Bank Battle.
[2] *Beatty Papers* I, Documents 159, 168, 169, 172, 173, 176.

cannot get all the Reports and without them all it is difficult to construct the correct story.

It seems hard, terribly hard, that after all this weary wait, after losing so many of our best friends after a veritable nightmare of an afternoon, we have been baulked. My heart aches with thinking about it, and that our magnificent Battle Fleet should have been deprived at the 11th hour of their reward. So please come and see us and tell us that we retain your confidence.

yours ever

[Signed] DAVID BEATTY

[PS] The Commodore, Bruce is splendid.[1]

[Note by Jellicoe on a typed copy of above letter]

[Holograph]   [Undated]

It will be seen from the following letter from Sir David Beatty that he too considered that the High Sea Fleet would try to regain their ports by passing to the SW of the Grand Fleet. His signal to me at 3.50 am on June 1st asking permission 'to sweep SW to locate enemy' is confirmatory of the fact.

219. K. Creighton[2] to Captain J. E. T. Harper

[Copy]

[Add 54477]   HM Yacht *Victoria & Albert*
                              12.11.19

That question of the 32 point turn has been argued ever since the action. A week after Jutland Captain Strutt, who was then Navigator of the *Lion* came to see me and asked me whether I had made it a 32 point turn, as he had done so, but the Admiral would not allow it, and made Chalmers his assistant (N) alter it on *Lion's* track. Both Strutt and Chalmers[3] agreed with me that it was 32 points, but the Admiral has consistently refused to allow this.

---

[1]Commodore (2nd Class) Henry Bruce, in charge of Rosyth Dockyard.
[2]Commander K. Creighton had been Navigator of *New Zealand* at Jutland.
[3]Beatty's future biographer, W. S. Chalmers.

220.   *Commander Ralph Seymour to Captain J. E. Harper*

[BTY/9/2/11]   [Admiralty]
                                                    December 18th 1919

Dear Captain Harper,
    The First Sea Lord has sent out your suggested order for the concurrence of the Second Sea Lord and ACNS.[1] You do not mention the record of signals but the First Sea Lord concurs in its being published simultaneously as an appendix. I presume that you will arrange this, as well as what signals should be omitted by direction of the DNI.
    With regard to the controversial turn made by the *Lion*, the First Sea Lord says he will not concur in the turn being through 360°, and that the track of the *Lion* must be shown as a turn to starboard followed by a turn to port.
    So long as the two established positions of the *Lion* at 6.50 pm and 7.5 pm remain relatively fixed, he is of the opinion that no established fact is in dispute.
    He has no objection to there being a note to the effect that evidence is conflicting as to exactly what the *Lion* did between these times, but he will not consent to her movements being shown as a circle through 360° as he states that such a turn would have been senseless and did not, in fact, occur.
    The First Sea Lord is of the opinion that the details of salvoes fired by the *Iron Duke* and other battleships on page 34 *et sequitur* are unnecessary and should be omitted. They would now be duplicated in Lord Jellicoe's despatch.
                                        Yours sincerely,
                                        [Signed] R. F. SEYMOUR

---

[1]2nd Sea Lord was Admiral Sir Montague Browning; ACNS Rear-Admiral James A. Fergusson.

221. *Captain J. E. T. Harper to ACNS*

[Copy]

[BTY/9/2/72–6]   20 December 1919

ACNS
Submitted.

Commander Seymour, Naval Assistant to the First Sea Lord[1] has informed me that the First Sea Lord says he will not concur in the 32 point turn shown in the *Lion's* track in the charts included in the Official Record of the Battle of Jutland, and that the track of the *Lion* must be shown as a turn to starboard followed by a turn to port.

The evidence on which the track was plotted is given below and it is submitted that it be forwarded to the First Sea Lord for his information.

If this evidence which is all that has been found in Admiralty records is considered insufficient to justify the track of the First & 2nd Battle Cruiser Squadron as now plotted, it is submitted that I may be authorised to obtain and make use of further evidence to assist in deciding on exactly what track to plot. My previous verbal order being not to obtain oral evidence but to adhere strictly to Admiralty records.

Evidence obtained from the Admiralty Records

There are three tracings signed by the Commander-in-Chief, Grand Fleet, the first one dated 18th June shows the *Lion's* track as marked in black on attached copy of tracing. The note about *Lion's* gyro compass being out of action being inserted in pencil.

The second tracing, undated, gives a similar track but a different geographical position. The geographical position not being in question, this track is not shown.

The third tracing dated 19th June which superseded the former two shows *Lion's* track as marked in blue. In this tracing the distance run between 6.50 and 7.5 is only 3 miles, whereas *Lion's* speed was 24 knots until 6.53 p.m. when it was reduced to 18

---

[1]Ralph Seymour (1886–1922) had been Beatty's Flag Lieutenant throughout the war. Roskill, *Beatty*, p. 102, makes him responsible for four significant errors in signalling, including one at Jutland; retired in 1921 after nervous breakdown; committed suicide in October 1922 (p. 316). (See note 1 on page 476.)

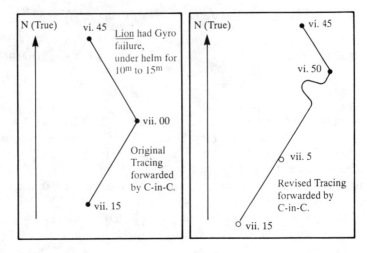

Track of HMS Lion: *first tracing*   *Track of HMS* Lion: *third tracing*

knots to keep station in Battle Fleet. The subsequent track of *Lion* to about 7.15 p.m. on this tracing also differs from the *Lion's* tracing and from the courses given in the despatch signed by the Vice-Admiral, Battle Cruiser Fleet and the report from *Lion* which are as follows:–

> *From Vice-Admiral, Battle Cruiser Fleet*: 'Between 7 and 7.12 we hauled round gradually to SW by S to regain touch with enemy.'

> *From Lion*:– '7.3 altered course to SSE, 7.6 to S, 7.9 to SSW, 7.11 to SW by W.'

It was obvious therefore that the final tracing forwarded by Commander in Chief could not be accepted as strictly correct.

The tracing forwarded from *Lion* and signed by Vice Admiral, Battle Cruiser Fleet (copy attached, the scale being increased to the same scale as the other tracks) indicates that *Lion* turned through a circle of 360°, and *Lion's* report also implies that *Princess Royal*, *Tiger* and *New Zealand* were on station astern of *Lion* and it has been asumed that they followed in *Lion's* wake.

Princess Royal's track chart (enlarged copy attached) shows no turn, (but this tracing is on a very small scale and gives little detail.)

Tiger forwarded no tracing.

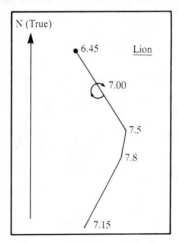

Track of HMS Lion: *signed tracing*

New Zealand's track chart (copy attached, enlarged to same scale as the other tracks) clearly shows a turn of 360°. The report from *New Zealand* states '6.59 p.m. gradually circled round to starboard': the *New Zealand's* log states '6.57 course SW. Turning gradually to starboard to SW through a circle of 360°.' In *New*

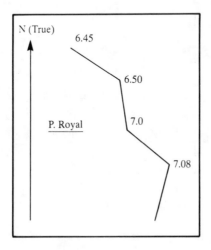

Track of HMS Princess Royal

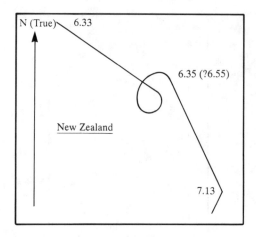

Track of HMS New Zealand

Zealand's tracing the time 6.35 p.m. should obviously read 6.55 p.m.

The Lion's track as plotted on the Jutland charts is attached.

It is submitted that, if this paper was handed to the present DCNS; Naval Secretary; & 4th Sea Lord for their remarks, the

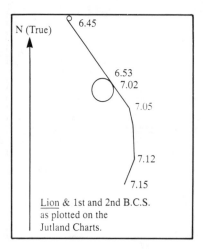

Track of HMS Lion *plotted on Jutland charts*

evidence obtained would be of great value in deciding what track to substitute for the 32 point turn.

[Sgd] J. E. T. Harper
Captain

222.   *Minute by Beatty*

[Holograph]

[BTY/9/2/71]   22.12.19

All the evidence in the world will not alter the _fact_ that we did not turn 32 points to Starboard.

We did turn to Starboard about 16 points and then back 16 points back to Port.

The object was to turn 8 points to see what the Battle Fleet was doing, but owing to Gyro failure we turned more before it was noticed. We could not have turned 32 points without colliding with the rear ships.

[Beatty]

223.   *Jellicoe to Oswald Frewen*[1]

[Holograph]

[Add 53738]   St Lawrence Hall
Ventnor
Isle of Wight
12/2/20

My Dear Frewen,

Many thanks for your letter.

It was kind of you to write. I went to the Admiralty yesterday to pay my official call & knocked up against Captain Harper in the passage, very angry with the *Daily Mail* for an attack on him. I have not seen the article, as that is a paper I do not read. I fancy the First Lord is taking up the matter in the House.

I mentioned to him the delay in publication and am seeing him again next week, when I intend to go into the question of alterations in the report. I shall not of course say where I heard of

---

[1]Oswald Frewen, a Navigation specialist, retired as Lieut. Commander in September 1919; had assisted Harper in preparing the *Record*; he was a first cousin of Winston Churchill and friendly with Jellicoe, of whom he became an increasingly strong supporter. (See Document 247 below.)

them, but many people have spoken to me on the subject. I may ask to see the original report. Captain Harper told me that the erasures were only thinly ruled through and I could easily see what was said in the original. I understand that von Scheer's report is to be published.

What a mine of wealth this publication will be to those so-called naval experts to write articles for money!! . . .

yours sincerely,
[Signed] JELLICOE

224. *Harper: Minute to ACNS*

[BTY/9/2/19]   20.2.20

Submitted

The Official Record of the Battle of Jutland is now completed and is submitted for final approval before printing.

2. In accordance with orders received the following alterations have been made since the Record was handed to you on 2nd October, 1919.

3. *Appendices added*:–

The Commander-in-Chief's Despatch contained in M.05697–16 with covering letter, omitting references to telegrams which it is undesirable to publish.

Admiral Scheer's first and preliminary report with accompanying charts and plans.

Record of Messages prepared by the Communications Division.

4. Eight additional diagramathical [*sic*] plans have been added. The total number of charts and diagrams including the German charts is 28.

5. Certain telegrams and messages have been deleted as undesirable to publish and certain minor alterations have been made in the text.

Certain extracts from Commander-in-Chief's Despatch formerly included in the text have been deleted, this Despatch being now published in full.

The appendix, giving a full list of Wireless Telegraph messages dealing with the position of the enemy, has been deleted as all these messages are contained in the Record of messages, now included.

6. The track of the Battle Cruisers at about 7 p.m. 31st May has been altered as the evidence on this point contained in Admir-

alty Records is conflicting — a note to this effect has been added to the charts affected.

7.   Permission is requested for me to pass the accompanying Record to Keeper of Stationery and Printing.

The charts and diagrams are being produced.

225.   *Seymour to Beatty*

[Holograph]

[BTY/9/1/3]   20.2.20

I suggest that a foreword on the lines of the attached draft should be published with the official history of the Battle of Jutland.[1]

It is time that the truth should be told completely and if it is disagreeable in any quarter, that is preferable to further controversy.

If the substance of this is approved by you the question arises, who is to issue such a pronouncement?

It would be better from the 1st Lord than from the whole Board, but I doubt whether he would consent to stand alone in this matter.

DRAFT FOREWORD [Typed]

The accompanying narrative of the Battle of Jutland and its appendices contains the whole of the facts known to the Admiralty concerning this battle. From this material a history of the Battle can be written and just conclusions may be drawn, but the Lords Commissioners of the Admiralty expressly refrain from formulating a judgment concerning the tactics employed or the lessons which have been learned.

The reasons for this decision are that the Naval Members of the Board themselves took part in the action in various capacities, and it would therefore be unseemly for them to give an opinion either of the actions of the Officers under whose orders they then were, their own actions, or the actions of their opponents.

Moreover, it is considered that the event is too recent and too bound up with the Naval controversies of the preceding years to be seen in its true perspective.

At no time has the policy of the Admiralty been to conceal the

[1]The final printed but unpublished *Record* contains nothing of this highly biased, or any other, Foreword.

facts of this battle from the British Public. Such information as has been with-held hitherto has been with-held either because it was undesirable to publish it to the enemy, or because the evidence was too conflicting or insufficient to establish the facts beyond the region of doubt. Definite evidence of the movements of the enemy fleet during the operations was only obtained so recently as last July; and only then was it made clear beyond a doubt what hitherto had been controversial.

The manner in which the battle was originally reported gave the universal impression to those who were not present that there had been an engagement between the British and German main Fleets. There was no such engagement.

From the evidence of Admiral von Scheer's report it is established that the German Battle Fleet never saw the British Main Fleet, and fired neither their guns nor their torpedoes at it. From the evidence of the British Main Fleet it is established that a small number of rounds were fired from the main armament of certain ships, at what were then thought to be ships of the enemy's battle fleet.

It is established from the now known position of the enemy, that the majority of these rounds were actually fired at enemy Light Cruisers. The British Main Battle Fleet fired no torpedoes. One ship only of the British Main Battle Fleet, the *Colossus*, was hit by a heavy shell. This shell was apparently an 'over' aimed at another vessel not belonging to the Battle Fleet.

The action off Jutland was a reconnaissance by the opposing Advanced Forces, during which the British located and maintained contact with the enemy's main fleet.

Whilst maintaining contact the action of the British advanced forces, according to the testimony of the German Commander-in-Chief, was such as to render those vessels of the enemy with which they were engaged incapable of further fighting, and to produce such an impression throughout the remainder of the enemy's fleet, that the reported presence of the British Main Fleet was sufficient to cause the second strongest fleet in the world to give up all further thought of fighting, and for its Commander-in-Chief to issue an order for it to return at all costs to its fortified harbours by the shortest and quickest route.

In carrying out these orders the enemy's Battle fleet steamed during the night through a part of the British Destroyers. These Destroyers were keeping station on our Battle Fleet and were not making an attack upon the enemy. Such as found themselves in the presence of the enemy fired their torpedoes at them. Never at any time during the whole of the operations was there any question that a decision might be obtained against the British Fleet.

Those who after a study of the facts may wish to offer constructive criticism which will be of value to the Navy, or who may wish to assure themselves that the Navy will be unlikely to repeat mistakes, which in their judgment may have been made, will best achieve their object by scrutinising and criticising the future developments of Admiralty policy with regard to the organisation, training and research work of the Navy rather than by attempting to ascribe either praise or blame to individuals.

226. *Harper: Minute to ACNS*

[BTY/9/2/25]   12 March 1920

With reference to my submission dated 20th February 1920 (on which approval was given for publication) enumerating the alterations made since the Official Record of the Battle of Jutland was handed in by me on the 2nd October 1919, the following further report is made as some of the passages formerly altered have now reverted to their original form.

The Record has been passed to the Stationery Office for printing.

ADDITIONS

Appendix 8: Record of British Messages bearing on the operation
Certain messages have been omitted and in place of some of them paraphrases have been substituted in the narrative: this is in accordance with the First Lord's approval on N.I.D. 020 of 10th March 1920.

Appendix 9: Despatch from the Commander-in-Chief
with covering letter contained in M.05697/16.
The following words 'contained in Their Lordships' telegram number 434 of 30th May code time 1740' and again 'Admiralty telegram 1740' have been deleted as they refer to a telegram which is not to be published. These deletions in no way affect the sense of the despatch.

Appendix 10: Report by the Commander-in-Chief of the German High Sea Fleet

Added in accordance with Board minute dated 28th January 1920. Figure 11 from the second report mentioned in the above minute has not been published on account of verbal orders received from the First Sea Lord on 13th February, it having been explained to him that this figure was contradictory to a figure already included in the first report.

8 Diagramatical [*sic*] Plans, added in accordance with the orders received from the First Sea Lord on 11th February 1920.

DELETIONS

Certain messages as stated under Appendix 8 above.

A few extracts from Commander in Chief's despatch which are not now required in the text as they are included in Appendix 9.

ALTERATIONS

Certain messages paraphrased (see Appendix 8 above).

The track of the battle cruisers between 6.53 p.m. and 7.25 p.m. 31st May has been altered in accordance with instructions from the First Sea Lord dated 22nd December 1919. The evidence on this point contained in Admiralty records is conflicting and a note to this effect has been added to the narrative and also placed on the charts affected.

In the Record of Messages the words 'Received by C-in-C at . . .' which are inserted in those cases where any appreciable time elapsed between the 'Time of Origin' and the 'Time of Receipt' have been altered to read 'Received in *Iron Duke* at . . .'. The reason for this alteration is that the public might assume that the Commander in Chief himself handled the message at the time quoted whereas it has been ascertained from the DOCD that the time quoted is that of receipt by the operator, there is of course no evidence available as to the actual time taken to decypher each message and pass it to the Commander in Chief after its receipt in *Iron Duke*.

227. *Notes by 1st Sea Lord on the Harper Record*

[Copy: noted as not comprehensive]

[ADM 116/2067]   15 May 1920

pp. 32–3   Wording implies that C-in-C was badly served (A)
            and that many errors were made which pre-
            vented him from receiving such information as
            he could reasonably have expected.
            This was not the case.
            It is stated that errors in dead reckoning were (B)
            unavoidable, also that there were errors by
            cipherers and operators, which, by inference,
            were avoidable, which is unjust.
            The sentence, 'the first definite information of (C)
            enemy Battle-Fleet . . .' implies that indefinite
            information has been received by C-in-C pre-
            viously, and that definite information might
            have reached him earlier, whereas in fact, it was
            the first information received by anybody that
            the enemy's Battle-Fleet was present. Further,
            it is not considered that any other but the light
            cruisers could have located them sooner.
            The mutilation of *Lion's* message, as referred (D)
            to, is unfairly represented. The essential facts
            were correctly received, except the enemy's
            course. There were, however, sufficient other
            reports to make their course clear to the C-
            in-C.
            The *Princess Royal* was heavily engaged at the (E)
            time. Why its incomplete reception was 'unfor-
            tunate' is not understood, as this signal had no
            unfortunate result.
            I am of the opinion that 'Reports on the pro- (F)
            gress of the Action' might well be omitted, as
            they come in the category of criticisms which
            serve no useful purpose.
p. 39   The title is misleading in its inference that there (G)
            was a General Fleet Action, whereas it is admit-
            ted that the Battle-Fleet was, at the most, but
            intermittently engaged.
            The real course of events can be ascertained by

study of the text, and it ill becomes the Admiralty to holster [*sic*] up what is already a shattered illusion. The necessity for including all details of salvoes falling near ships is not understood. It appears to serve no particular purpose and to have no bearing on the battle.

Evidence from enemy sources shews [*sic*] that (H) *Hercules* and *Agincourt* were not sighted by them. Such details expose the ships named to ridicule.

p. 41   Cannot concur that at 6.30 pm the action was (J) general. Our battleships were firing only intermittently at an indistinct enemy, who did not, as their evidence discloses, realise the presence of our Battle Fleet, or return their fire.

pp. 42–3   It is not clear what useful purpose is served by (K) the Table of targets, times and ranges, which are not corroborated by the diagrams. Its futility is admitted in the paragraph which follows it.

p. 44   Report from *Revenge* as to supposed submarine (L) appears to serve no useful purpose. It is merely an expression of opinion, which later evidence has not corroborated.

p. 47   The disparaging remark as to the lack of dash (M) in the attack made by three German destroyers is unsuitable for inclusion, being unworthy of the British Admiralty.

p. 51   The title requires alteration; *vide* my remarks at (N) p. 39. The Battle Fleet action cannot be said to have ceased at any particular moment.

pp. 303–4   It seems unnecessary to publish the last three (O) telegrams which have no bearing on the record of the battle.

p. 339   The 'Translator's Preface' should be omitted as (P) tending to discount the value of what is really a very important contribution to the records of the battle.

Original Despatches are liable to contain matter which subsequently proves inaccurate, although compiled in good faith.

228.   *Memorandum: Harper to Naval Secretary;*[1] *for 1st Lord*

[ADM 116/2067]   Admiralty
                                                      27th May 1920

Submitted

Observations on the remarks made by the 1st Sea Lord are attached.[2]

In making these observations I have endeavoured to state accurately the reason why the various passages or words were originally inserted, without including any expression of opinion as to the desirability, or otherwise, of altering them.

Paragraphs in the 1st Sea Lord's remarks have been lettered, the same letters being used to denote each paragraph of my explanation.

REPORTS ON THE PROGRESS OF THE ACTION
Pages 32–33

A and F   This portion was rewritten by orders of the 1st Sea Lord received on 11.2.20: the altered wording being concurred in by him. A copy of this wording is attached hereto.

It reverted to its original form owing to orders received subsequently from Naval Secretary, at which time the 1st Sea Lord also issued an order that his previous orders were cancelled.

The wording is meant to show clearly without criticism the nature of the difficulties which the Commander-in-Chief must have experienced in estimating accurately the relative position of the enemy to the *Iron Duke*.

B   The insertion of this paragraph was intended to anticipate adverse criticism which might be made by anyone carefully analysing the W/T messages given in detail in Appendix VIII.

The analysis of these messages clearly showed that the positions of the enemy as received by the Commander-in-Chief did not agree, and it appeared impossible to ascertain whether the errors were introduced before the message left the sending ship or after the message reached the receiving ship.

The word 'unavoidable' was used as errors in dead reckoning are, in all probability, unavoidable. The accuracy of the dead

---

[1]Rear-Admiral Rudolph Bentinck, who had been Beatty's Chief of Staff at Jutland.
[2]See Document 227.

reckoning being dependent on a correct estimate of tides and currents etc., whereas cyphering and *de-cyphering* errors are not dependent on estimate but follow fixed rules.

C Information had been sent from Admiralty to Commander-in-Chief on 30th May (see page 12, line 2) which when taken into consideration together with the reports of enemy vessels sighted by the Light Cruisers before 4.38 pm would lead the Commander-in-Chief to suppose that the enemy Battle Fleet might be met with.

The *Southampton's* message (1438) was, however, the first definite information on this point received by the Commander-in-Chief, or in fact by anybody.

It was not intended to imply that the enemy Battle Fleet could have been located sooner.

D The wording of this message as sent and as received is given in List of Signals (see p. 174). The remarks explaining the fact of mutilation and unavoidable delay owing to *Lion's* W/T being out of action were inserted to emphasise the many difficulties which were encountered in getting through reliable reports to the Commander-in-Chief without any delay.

It was considered necessary to refer to this signal (1645) when comparing the position of the enemy as transmitted from Admiralty, with that transmitted from our ships.

E The word 'unfortunate' was used because the mutilation of any message containing valuable information was considered unfortunate, more especially in the case of a message from the Vice-Admiral Battle Cruiser Fleet on which the Commander-in-Chief would probably place more reliance than on a message from a Light Cruiser, in the event, that is, of the information being at variance.

The sense of the paragraph would be in no way altered if the word 'unfortunate' was deleted.

Page 39

G The title 'General Fleet Action' was used as during the time (6.15 pm to 7.25 pm) dealt with under this heading every squadron was taking a more or less active part in engaging the enemy, (with the exception of the Armoured Cruisers and this is referred to on page 46, line 26).

This was the only period during 31st May that all squadrons were engaged.

H This reference to *Hercules* and *Agincourt* was included as it appeared a matter of ordinary interest and showed that our Battle Fleet was within range of the enemy's guns at the moment of deployment.

Note This paragraph was deleted by order of the 1st Sea Lord on 11.2.20 and was re-inserted owing to a subsequent order from the Naval Secretary at which time the 1st Sea Lord cancelled his former orders.

Page 41

J The wording states that 'at 6.30 pm firing at the enemy capital ships became *more* general': as far as the Battle Fleet was concerned it was confined to a few Battle Ships only, as stated, before this time.

Pages 42 and 43

K It was considered that the times and ranges, at which each ship opened fire was a matter of interest. These tables were inserted to simplify the text, and for ready reference to obviate the necessity of searching through the text to obtain the information.

The Table of Ranges reported to have been taken confirms, when compared with the charts, the remarks on weather conditions (page 36, line 20).

Page 44

L It was an established fact that the *Revenge* hauled out of line. Her report of ramming a submarine is given in Commander-in-Chief's despatch as '*CERTAIN*'. (see Page 337). It was therefore considered advisable to refer to the incident in detail as the report must have been incorrect.

Page 47

M This sentence is a quotation and was included as it was considered that an opinion, formed at the time by a responsible Flag Officer, was of interest. (See Note to H. The same applies to this paragraph.)

Page 51

N See G. No Battle Ship fired at any enemy capital ship after 7.30 p.m. (see page 51, line 7).

Pages 303–304

O These were included as they were included in the List of Signals prepared by the Communications Division of the Naval Staff, and this publication was ordered to be included as an appendix.

Page 339

P This was included as received from ID. The first sentence was deleted by verbal orders of 1st Sea Lord. It is considered that the Note dealing with German time should be retained.

229. *Naval Secretary to 1st Lord*

[Holograph Memorandum]

[ADM 116/2067]   Admiralty
                                                                  29.v.20

First Lord

Attached are Captain Harper's reply [*sic*] to the ISL's criticisms. The situation now appears to be that:–

(*a*)   The Sea Lords should be each provided with proof copies of the Report.

(*b*)   They should be asked to forward to you in writing, their proposals for alterations, additions˙ and [?] deletions. (These can then be forwarded to Captain Harper for his remarks.)

(*c*)   When Captain Harper has prepared his answers, that the Sea Lords meet in your office & consider the Report.

(*d*)   The final Report should then be approved by the Board.

                                                                  R.W.B.
                                                                  29.v.20

                                                                  I approve
                                                                  W.H.L.
                                                                  30.v.20

230. *Remarks made by ACNS[1] on Official Record of the Battle of Jutland*

[Extract]

[ADM 116/2067]   2.6.20

I have not much criticism to offer as regards the official history, as in the absence of a plan it is not possible to check the narrative.

The main fault in it, in my opinion, is that it lacks the note and tone of victory, and reads rather, as a record of disasters and misfortunes. The principal reason for this is that the most vivid

[1]Chatfield became ACNS 15 March 1920.

passages are those that describe the damage done to our own ships.

2.   In a naval action very little indication of the enemy's troubles can be obtained until a culminating point is reached; *eg*, a ship heels, or sinks, or catches fire; on the other hand your own troubles are very apparent.

If therefore, an accurate account is given *by one side*, of the action, as it appeared to those who were fighting, while similar information is not furnished in regard to the other side, a very misleading narrative is given to the public. This is what the history effects.

3.   A fair history can only be written by a historian who has full access to both sides of the case.

For instance, the *Record* describes on p. 21 *et seq* the effect of enemy shell-fire on our ships, and, although it is known from subsequent evidence that much similar damage was received by the enemy, it cannot be expressed in the *Narrative*. This particularly occurs all through the narrative of the actual fighting.

*   *   *   *

E.C.

2.6.20

231.   *Remarks made by DCNS on Official Record of the Battle of Jutland*

[Holograph]

[ADM 116/2067]   14.6.20

I dislike this report; much for the same reason as Dr Fell was disliked.[1]

It is impartial, and to a great extent, impersonal, but it *does* convey to me the impression that not only was a great battle

---

[1] Dr John Fell (1625–86): Dean of Christ Church Oxford had aroused the dislike of Tom Brown (1663–1704), an undergraduate of the House, who had written the following quatrain:

I do not love thee Doctor Fell,
The reason why I cannot tell
But this alone I know full. well
I do not love thee, Doctor Fell.

Fell was an extremely active reforming Royalist and Anglican who was Vice-Chancellor 1666–9 and Bishop of Oxford 1675–86. He also did much to improve the printing at the University Press.

fought between the British and the German fleets, but that it was one in which we got the worst of it.

Neither of these impressions is correct; a great battle was not fought, the opposing battle fleets never really came into action, and far from getting the worst of it, the direct result of the day's fighting was to drive the German fleet ignominiously into its ports. I realise, however, that in order to get the right atmosphere, a finished man of letters must tell the story, and if we are bound to issue an official account, this account, with a few excisions, must be published, but I feel that it will do the Navy no good. It is a thousand pities that the promise in the House was given.

The book will have to be issued under the aegis of the Board, and it is for consideration whether any notice to the effect that no members of the Board are personally responsible for any of its contents, should be attached.

On the whole, I think it is best to say *Nothing*.

* * * *

[Initialled] O. de B.

232. *Extract from Board Minutes*

[Copy]

[BTY/9/2/65] Friday, 6th August 1920

Official Narrative of the Battle of Jutland

1251. The First Lord stated that he was anxious to come to a definite conclusion about the publication of the Official Narrative of the Battle of Jutland. It appeared that one of the most important plans appended to the Narrative was incorrect and would have to be altered, and that this alteration might involve some other plans. Moreover, some of the Members of the Board were not satisfied with the general tone of the Narrative, which necessarily proceeded on the information available on the British side at the time, and therefore left an impression on the reader quite different from that which, from information subsequently obtained from Germany, was known to have existed on the German side both during and after the action.

It was agreed that the Naval Staff should be asked to settle with Captain Harper the re-drafting of the plans, and that Sir Julian Corbett, who has already received a copy of the draft Narrative, should be asked to write a 'foreword' which would supply the necessary corrective to the impression that would be derived from reading the Narrative as it stood, and which should be shown to Lord Jellicoe, if possible, before he left England for New Zealand.

233. *Report from Admiral Hipper to Admiral Scheer 4 July 1916*

[Extract]

[Add 54477]   N.I.D. 12556

21.9.20

OBSERVATION ON ENEMY ARTILLERY FIRE

. . . The fire of the English battle-cruisers has not caused to our battle-cruisers damage of considerable gravity. Since the fall of shot was rarely in proximity to our own ships it is not possible to judge very accurately as to the 'spread' of the shot.

On the other hand the fire of the *Malaya* battleships (5ᵗʰ BS) and equally later on, that of the bulk of the enemy, produced an excellent impression.

The salvoes arrived absolutely dense (with no spread).

The fall in elevation and direction covered almost the same spot.

The firing constituted a proof of the care with which the British have eliminated in their guns all influences which increase the 'spread', and of the most remarkable manner in which English fire control arrangements have been produced, both elevation and direction. [*sic*]

If the English did not attain greater results, it is on account of the bad quality of their shell, particularly with reference to the insufficient efficiency of their exploders . . .

233a.   *Daily Mail Leading Article*

[Press cutting]

THE JUTLAND HUSH-UP[1]

[Corbett Papers Box 7]   28 October 1920

The Admiralty is still trying to hide the truth about the Battle of Jutland. The Navy and the nation have long wanted to know why Lord Jellicoe, with an overwhelming British battle-fleet, turned away from a beaten German fleet of half his strength and allowed it to escape, when it had been placed in his hands by the gallant fighting of Lord Beatty. He thereby prolonged the war by two years and rendered the deadly submarine campaign possible.

Again and again during the past eighteen months the Admiralty has promised to publish an official account of the battle, with all the vital documents, as soon as that account was completed. The account is made up and has been in print for four months. But yesterday the Admiralty representative in the House of Commons repudiated all the past promises and calmly announced that the account was not to be published at all. It is to be handed over to Sir Julian Corbett, who is writing an official history of the naval war. There is no assurance that all the vital documents will be printed by him. There is no security that they will not be censored, and when questioned on that point, the Admiralty representative was unable to give an immediate answer. There is no security that Sir Julian's volume will appear at an early date. The country is being put off with a fresh crop of vague official promises.

Why should this hocus-pocus be practised on the nation? The excuses given yesterday were ridiculous. It is alleged that further information had appeared in Germany which invalidates much of the Admiralty's account. But, if that account is to be held back until fresh information ceases to appear, it will not be published for a century. Meanwhile grave injustice is being done to the officers and men of Earl Beatty's ships. They suffered thousands of casualties, while among the 30,000 officers and men of Lord Jellicoe's battle-fleet, as Commander Bellairs MP pointed out in the interview which we published yesterday, the casualties were

[1]There was a similar leader in *The Times* of the same day and its Parliamentary Report recorded that the Parliamentary Secretary to the Admiralty, in reply to a Member's question, had replied that there was no truth in the rumour that the *Record's* publication had been delayed due to differences between Beatty and Jellicoe. Both had seen the report and had acquiesced in its going to Julian Corbett.

exactly four. Yet 'the captains of Lord Jellicoe's ships received honours equally with those under Earl Beatty's command'.

The country wants the official account to be published completely and at once, *because the nation wants progress*. Progress in naval affairs cannot be achieved if the truth is not known to the public. Experience of authority in the past shows that only through publicity and public pressure can officialdom be induced to act on facts. Today the nation is completely in the dark as to the exact value of a battle-fleet. The British people must know what happened at Jutland if it is to decide *what is the factor that is going to give our country the command of the sea in the twentieth century*. So long as it is kept in ignorance, the command of the sea is in danger, even though the German Fleet lies under the water.

234.   *Beatty to Shane Leslie*[1]

[Holograph Note]

[SLGF 6/4]   [1922]

Harper completed his Report from the logs of the ships engaged.

The logs, kept up under conditions of action were very inaccurate and did not agree, indeed it was difficult to reconcile the statements they contained, & consequently Harper had perforce to arrive [?] at a happy mean to produce plans etc, as nearly accurate as possible. These plans & diagrams when received by those who were present, were found in some instances to be entirely inaccurate and not in accordance with the facts as known to them, & subsequently were discarded, which caused Harper to be disgruntled.

Further later information received from sources which were not available to Harper showed that in many cases the deductions drawn by Harper were inaccurate & misleading, & consequently it was considered premature to issue an Official Record until all the detailed [?] information was available.

---

[1]Sir John R. Shane Leslie (1885–1971): 3rd Baronet; man of letters and Irish nationalist; worked in British Embassy in Washington 1916–17 supporting the Ambassador Cecil Spring-Rice's efforts to reduce Irish-American hostility and to persuade America to enter the war. His papers at Churchill College Cambridge, include a projected life of Beatty, and a verse, *Jutland: A Fragment of Epic* (1930). Roskill highly valued his work on Beatty.

235.   *Director of Training and Staff Duties to DCNS & 1st SL*

[Memorandum]

[BTY/9/5/2]   [26.7.22]

It was approved verbally that an abridged edition of the 'Naval Staff Appreciation of the Battle of Jutland' should be prepared for issue to the Fleet, on the ground [*sic*] that many valuable lessons from the action ought to be placed at the disposal of those who it is necessary should profit by them.

The circulation of the 'Appreciation' itself has been suppressed but an edition which confines itself to statement of fact is in preparation for public issue.[1]

The abridgement has proved a matter of considerable difficulty. The mental attitude of the writer was rather that of a counsel for the prosecution than of an impartial appraiser of facts, and obvious bias animates his statements throughout the book, leading to satirical observations and a certain amount of misrepresentation.

Moreover the writer vigorously condemns the use of the single line in a manner which would be more profitable if a practical method of employment of divisional tactics were indicated.

To criticise on such lines a system, which for all its faults has not yet been superseded, would be out of place in a Staff production intended for the general instruction of officers.

We cannot at this early stage criticise the strategy and tactics employed in so destructive a manner as will be possible ten years hence. The Battle Orders operative at the time of the battle were known to the Admiralty and they remained materially the same until the end of the war. It is doubtful if they would even now be departed from if war were declared in similar circumstances.

It has therefore been necessary to make large alterations in the text at the risk of emasculating the book. I have gone through the 'Appreciation' with Lieut. Commandr. Pollen[2] who having been associated with all the historical work in connection with the battle, is familiar with all its aspects, and have made tentative

---

[1]This was to be *The Narrative of the Battle of Jutland* (HMSO 1924). Jellicoe was critical of it from 1922 and an Appendix containing his objections was added, as was the Admiralty's response to his criticisms. (See *Jellicoe Papers* II, pp. 401–2, and Document 244 below.

[2]Lieut Commander J. F. H. Pollen, nephew of the civilian gunnery expert, A. H. Pollen; worked in the Historical Section of the CID and had helped Corbett with the writing of his Jutland volume. (See Document 247 below).

alterations with a view to adapting it for publication as a Fleet Issue.

The reasons for various deletions, modifications and additions are detailed on the attached sheet.[1]

Submitted for approval for revision to be completed on the lines indicated.

                          sgd V. S. HAGGARD
[Minute by A. Flint   28.7.22
Principal Asst. Secretary]

When the 'Appreciation' is issued to the Fleet it is for consideration whether officers should be warned to be discreet in conversation about the activities of Room 40 as revealed in the book.

[Minute by R. Keyes DCNS]   [Undated]

Approved, but Lord Jellicoe's reply must be awaited before this revision is sent to the printers.[2]

236. *Memorandum by Keyes DCNS and Chatfield ACNS on the Naval Staff Appreciation*

[BTY/9/5/2]   14.8.22

1st. Sea Lord
The following opinion on the difficult question of the issue of this book is put forward for your consideration.

2.   While not approving the tone in which this book is written, which is not suitable for what should be an expression of unbiassed technical opinion, nor in all respects with the criticism of the tactical ideas of the Commander-in-Chief, (eg; the criticism of the single line) we are in entire agreement with the main conclusions of the writer, both as regards;

(1)   The failure of Lord Jellicoe to seize the great opportunity before him on the 31st May, and,

(2)   His failure to make any disposition or give any instructions that would bring the enemy to action at dawn on the 1st June.

3.   It is not considered however that any sufficient cause exists at the moment to justify the issue to the Fleet of a book that

---

[1]They can be found in BTY/9/5/3.
[2]Keyes's minute has been covered over at some time.

would rend the Service to its foundations. To issue the book as expurgated by DTSD would be equally unsatisfactory, as it would not be the true opinion of the present Naval Staff. To issue a half-hearted and obviously incomplete appreciation would be merely to mislead those serving, and would therefore fail in its main object. Further, however carefully it was worded, the composition of the present Naval Staff would cause it to be received with hostility and suspicion in certain quarters. Discussion in the Service and elsewhere would ensue, and we might then be compelled to defend an incomplete and half-hearted book which did not adequately express our personal convictions.

4. Nevertheless, although it is true that no vital need exists at the moment for drawing the unfortunate lessons learned from the action, we do not consider that the matter can be abandoned indefinitely. The Naval Staff have a duty to see that the causes of failure are analysed and not lost to posterity.

5. For the moment, war is not on the horizon, the Admiralty is in safe hands and those in command are likely to command our fleets in the near future, have their own war experience to guide them. But this will not always be so.

6. We therefore advise:–

(*a*) That no expurgated edition should be printed.

(*b*) That the book as written should not be issued at present; that all proofs should be recalled; that, say 6, copies be retained in the possession of the 1st Sea Lord's office, and the remainder destroyed.

(*c*) That steps be taken to see that the printers break up the type and do not retain any copies.

(*d*) That on your vacating the position of 1st Sea Lord, you should place the book in the hands of the CID with a recommendation as to action according to the general situation at the time.

236a.   *Holograph Comments by Beatty and his Staff on
second galley proofs of Corbett's Volume III of Naval
Operations Chapters XVII–XVIII*

[Extracts]

[BTY/9/4/1–3]   21 December 1922

As printed in proofs	Comments by Beatty in green ink & by his staff (probably Spickernell) in pencil	As printed in 1923 edition Chapter XVII
The First Phase [Beatty's turn SSE at 2.32 to get between Hipper and his base, not seen by Evan-Thomas] 'It was thus not till seven minutes later that the 5th Battle Squadron began to follow his lead.'	'Not True' [*Beatty*]	p. 331 [No change made]
[Beatty's signal to turn NW at 4.40] 'Admiral Evan-Thomas had to pass before he could obey the signal.'	'Not correct' [*Staff*]	p. 340 [Changed to] 'Admiral Evan-Thomas had passed before he could carry out the order.'
[Beatty's turn North after sighting of High Seas Fleet] 'At 5.10 he reduced to 24 knots and under the lee of the 5th Battle Squadron made his way northward to join the main fleet.'	'Unpleasantly worded' [*Staff*] 'Not correct' [*Beatty*]	p. 343 'Under the lee of the 5th Battle Squadron' [omitted]

As printed in proofs	*Comments by Beatty in green ink & by his staff (probably Spickernell) in pencil*	*As printed in 1923 edition Chapter XVII*
The Second Phase First contact of the battle fleets [Jellicoe's decision on Grand Fleet deployment, 6.00–6.15] 'Across his front Admiral Beatty was steaming at 25 knots and shutting out all beyond in an impenetrable pall of funnel smoke . . . and in this blind distraction Jellicoe had to make the decision on which the fortunes of his country hung.'	'Not Correct' [*Beatty*]	[Changed to] p. 361 'battle-cruisers, cruisers and destroyers were hurrying to their battle stations, and the vessels steaming across his front were shutting out all beyond in an unpenetrable pall of funnel smoke.' [Added footnote] 'In addition to the battle-cruisers, several light cruisers (the *Duke of Edinburgh* in particular) & destroyers were pouring forth a dense volume of smoke, while the burning *Wiesbaden* contributed to the general smother.'
[Jellicoe's final decision not to deploy on the starboard wing] 'it would mean that Admiral Burney		

As printed in proofs	Comments by Beatty in green ink & by his staff (probably Spickernell) in pencil	As printed in 1923 edition Chapter XVII
whose squadron was the oldest and least powerful in the fleet would receive the concentrated fire of the enemy's best ships.'	[Substitute] 'strongest' for 'least powerful' [*Beatty*]	p. 361 [Substitution not made]
6.20–6.30 'Jellicoe had just settled down on the deployment course, but as Admiral Beatty was leading to cross, he had to reduce speed to allow the battle-cruisers to clear.'	'Cross what?' [*Beatty*]	p. 365 [No change made]
6.20–6.30 'Thus the passage across the battle front to which Admiral Beatty was committed in his keenness to keep his grip on his own particular adversary split a promising opening to the action. When the rear of the battleships was nearest the enemy he had masked them and when the van was nearest he was	[Sideline and] 'Not true' [*Beatty*]	[changed to] p. 365 'Thus the enforced passage of Admiral Beatty across the battle front, due to the sudden appearance at the moment of contact of the enemy battle fleet on an unexpected bearing, which necessitated deployment on the port wing, spoiled a promising

As printed in proofs	*Comments by Beatty in green ink & by his staff (probably Spickernell) in pencil*	*As printed in 1923 edition Chapter XVII*
preventing them from firing a shot.'		opening to that action.' [Added comment on role of battle-cruisers in Grand Fleet Orders: to destroy enemy battle-cruisers and to take post at the head of the line to frustrate enemy attacks by battle-cruisers on our van by long range torpedoes] 'In the circumstances Admiral Beatty's movement was inevitable.'

237. *Jellicoe to Frewen*

[Holograph]

[Add 53738]   Wellington
New Zealand
February 12th 1923

. . . You mention in your letter the fact of the *Princess Royal* having given the *Lion* the Challenge & Reply after dark in response to a request from VABCF. Yes, I had noticed this in the Jutland despatches (I did not know of it before) & I did not know of the Germans repeating it to Scheer. Corbett does not seem to have mentioned it in his story. At least, I can't find any mention of it. What you now tell me accounts for the rapid opening of fire on the 4th Flotilla when *Tipperary* challenged. Commodore Hawksley in his report (Jutland Papers) mentions the incident & states his opinion that the fact perhaps accounts for the ship being challenged by the Germans with part of our challenge.[1]

It was of course idiotic of the *Lion* to have taken this action. If Corbett's account is emasculated too much by the Admiralty & if the Admiralty insists on publishing the [?] Appreciation without my corrections & remarks, I may resign from New Zealand and return to England:–

(*a*)   to publish my comments on the Appreciation

(*b*)   to publish a correct account of Jutland, giving chapter and verse.

I should under these conditions not conceal from the public any longer the results that came about from the VABCF not having:–

(*a*)   let the RA 5th BS know his alteration of course by S/L or W/T after sighting the enemy, early pm on 31/5/16, thus causing the 5th BS to be 10 miles astern of him when he opened fire on the 1st Scouting Group instead of in close support.

(*b*)   and in this position the result of the VABCF not having turned the 5th BS to the Northward whilst the 5th BS was still to the North of the BCF at 4.48 pm.

Had either of these courses been taken the 1st Scouting Squadron would have disappeared as a fighting force long before it came North and our own 5th BS would not have come under the fire of the German Battle Fleet.

However, I hope the Admiralty will be wise as I don't want to wash dirty linen in public. But there is a limit to my patience.

*   *   *   *

238.   L. S. Amery: Diary

[Extract]

[Amery]   25 June 1923

Up by an early train and spent the morning at the office. Had some talk with Beatty both about the joint staff question[2] and

---

[1]Commodore J. Hawksley had commanded the 11th Destroyer Flotilla at Jutland.

[2]The Chiefs of Staff were to hold their first formal meeting as a CID Sub-Committee on 17 July 1923 (see Document 125 above). There were parallel discussions on the formation of a Joint Staff to serve it and the foundation of a Joint Staff College (see also Roskill, *Naval Policy* I, pp. 338–9).

about Jutland. He told me that two days after Jutland Jellicoe broke down in his cabin regarding himself as a man who had wrecked his career and the chances of victory, and that it was only gradually that he had come to think of himself as having done the best possible. B. undoubtedly feels — and I dare say it has vexed him ever since — that the whole German Navy might have been sunk and that there would be no criticism of the value of the Navy such as there is to-day. On the staff side, I think I got him to see my point as to the desirability of joint plans being built up from a common point of view from the very bottom and not merely combined at the top.

239.   H. G. Adams[1] to Evan-Thomas

[Holograph]

[Add 52504]   Camrose
                                                    Goring-on-Thames
                                                    July 22nd [1923]

As far as I can remember, the reckoning of the 5th Battle Squadron was adjusted to the noon position of the *Lion* & thereafter by distances & bearings of the *Lion*, or generally, individual ships of the Battle-Cruiser Squadron, while visibility permitted. Probably our own reckoning was entirely used after 2 pm. I cannot account for the discrepancy between the *Valiant's* time of turning and our own, but if the Signal Logs of the Squadron are available, I should say the time could be checked.

It seems unbelievable that your action in this matter can be adversely criticised; & on the contrary, an unfettered Staff might with more truth point out, that if on a misty day, such as the 31st was, our squadron had been stationed closer to the BCS, secondly, had the BCS method of zig-zagging been imparted to us, so that we could have followed suit, &, thirdly, if the BCS had the communications between the Squadrons better organised, there would have been less to guess [?] at by your Staff.

Having retired, I might add that any opinions are biassed as long as the present CNS is at the head of affairs, though you may say this presumptious [*sic*] of me . . .

---

[1] Adams had been Navigator of *Barham*, Evan-Thomas's Flagship at Jutland.

240.   *L. S. Amery: Diary*

[Extract]

[Amery]   3 August 1923

. . . I brought Beatty along to discuss with him one or two points outstanding on the battle of Jutland before settling the Narrative.

He assured me that all Jellicoe's arguments as to his not knowing during the night which way the German fleet was going are pretty moonshine, and that two days after the battle Jellicoe told him that he knew quite well, and never suggested anything else, but that he was not prepared to run the risks of a night engagement. Beatty's whole view in fact is that Jellicoe from start to finish funked an engagement, both in the afternoon and during the night, and that it is owing to him that the German Fleet was not sunk there and then, and the war not shortened by a couple of years; for if we had sunk the fleet we could have pressed our blockade home, prevented the subs coming out and induced Germany to throw up the sponge before the Russian revolution started.

241.   *Evan-Thomas to Haggard*

[Copy]

[Add 52504]   Admiralty House
                                                        Chatham
                                              14th August 1923

Thank you for sending the proposed account of parts of the battle of Jutland.

I do not consider page 20 to be a correct account of what occurred and there is still a tone given to the account which implies blame. Lord Jellicoe's objection has not been met.

The point is that in the visibility as it was, together with the intense smoke made by battle cruisers bringing fires forward, it was impossible to see what *Lion* was doing until most of the Squadron had turned. *Barham* was zig-zagging at the time, which caused delay, but as *Lion* had been signalling to *Barham* with a searchlight previously to the turn, and had made all alterations of course by that method, there was no reason why a signal should not have been made for *Barham* to turn with *Lion*, by searchlight, if not by wireless, had he wished her to do so.

*   *   *   *

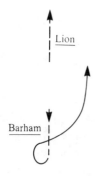

Page 37: Fifth Battle Squadron were definitely ordered to turn to Starboard. The signal was 'Compass 16' which was not hauled down some time after *Lion* had passed; so it should be stated. As it is at present written it would appear that it was open to *Barham* to turn which way she liked: the fact of turning to Starboard did make a considerable difference, because it made a further turn to Starboard necessary in order to get on the enemy side of *Lion*.

Again, according to plan and according to my recollection, the statement that she passed about two miles off on the Port hand is considerably over-stated. It was in my opinion about one mile — If anything a little less.

242. *Admiral Sir Charles Madden to Evan-Thomas*

[Holograph]

[Add 52504]

Lanfine
Newmilns
Ayrshire
Sunday 19th [August 1923]

Your letter followed me here where I have no papers to refer to. My remarks are therefore based on *unrefreshed recollections*.

I think your view of the case is moderate, the facts are more strongly favourable to you. Some minutes elapsed (how many?) between the time of the light cruiser's report of enemy in sight & the *Lion's* turn at 2.38. It might be expected that VABCF would have stationed 5th BS for action, or at least ordered it to close, which before 2.45 could have been rapidly effected. But the battle-cruisers & 5th BS were not manoeuvred as a unit and the late arrival of 5th BS in action is mainly attributed to this departure from Fleet custom. At least in favour to you the account should state that neither previous to sighting the enemy, or during the battle-cruiser action, did you receive instructions stationing your Squadron in action, & the heavy smoke rendered the prompt following of *Lion's* motions difficult. This & the fact that flag signals could not be read in *Barham*, & that they were not repeated by searchlight or the W/T guardship, introduced a lag in

5ᵗʰ BS's movements which materially reduced the support that Squadron should have been able to afford the battle-cruisers.

I know that the C-in-C gave 5ᵗʰ BS to VABC so that in Hood's absence he should be so superior to von Hipper, that the result of a meeting should not be in doubt. This needed keeping 5ᵗʰ BS close at hand on account of its lower speed; it might be argued that had the action opened with 10 British capital ships to 5 German, we should not have lost the *Q. Mary* & *Indefat* [*sic*] and the Germans might have been severely punished or crippled & the whole course of the battle changed.

I have not expressed these views to anyone, not even Jellicoe, so I hope you will treat them as *between us only*, as I have no wish to revive the controversy which is so harmful to the Service.

P. 37 [?] is less important but if VABCF desired you to turn earlier, a searchlight or W/T signal from guardship should have been made, & the fact that you were astern after the turn was easily remedied by a reduction in *Lion's* speed, but it was increased & the B-Crs ran out of action, at about 5.30, I think. It is so very important to get the facts firmly stated in the official account that I hope you will urge your views on the Admiralty, & I trust, will succeed . . .

PS I think that I am correct ·in stating that had the GF Signal Procedure been practised at PZ's by BCF as was done in the Battle Fleet, the signals in question would, as a matter of routine, have been passed to *Barham* by searchlight and W/T guardship.

242a.   *Beatty to Captain K. G. B. Dewar*

[Holograph]

[DEW/3]   Admiralty
                                                        23.4.25

Mr Dear Dewar,

Thank you very much for sending me your review on 'The Scandal of Jutland' [*sic*],[1] which I think a clear concise exposition of the fallacies with which it abounds &, I am afraid, I can say no more, the book being as it is, a personal attack on myself. But it does make clear that the material school had taken no thought of [*sic*] the strategical and tactical side of the problems of war.

---

[1] The 2nd edition of Admiral Sir Reginald Bacon's *The Jutland Scandal* was published in 1925.

There was one point which I think would be better left unsaid, and that is the reference to the 'Staff Appreciation' which for [?] many reasons, has not been issued, & therefore so far as the world in general is concerned, does not exist. To leave out the reference would in no way spoil the article if 'Admiralty Narrative' were substituted for 'Staff Appreciation', & would save much controversy.

Yours sincerely,

BEATTY

243. *Lieutenant Commander W. F. Clarke RNVR[1] and Beatty's views on Sir Julian Corbett's chapters on Jutland*

[Copy]

[BTY/9/9/12]   [Undated; probably 1924]

The attached document is of curious historical interest.

When the proofs of Sir Julian Corbett's chapters on the Battle of Jutland were submitted to the Admiralty I had to go through them for censorship purposes. The account was not approved of by the then Board with Admiral Beatty at its head and they desired it should be radically altered. One excuse for this would be Room 40's objections to the inclusion of its special information. As the account seemed a fair one to me I was very anxious that it should not be altered and ultimately persuaded the DNI to let a great deal of this special intelligence remain in, as the excision of it all might have necessitated rewriting.

I had several conversations with Sir Henry Newbolt[2] (who had succeeded Sir Julian Corbett) and Colonel Daniel[3] and the latter told me that Beatty had told him he had not had time to read the proofs and that it did not concern him. Two days later the proofs were returned to me for further remarks and this time the copy which had been sent to First Sea Lord and his immediate circle was the one I received. Looking through it I found a typewritten

[1]Clarke was present in Room 40 at the Admiralty during the battle of Jutland; his papers on the battle are in the Roskill MSS, Churchill College Cambridge. Marder, *From the Dreadnought III*, p. 76, n. 50, attributes these 'Remarks' to Chatfield rather than Beatty. Quite contrary to Clarke's view, Para 'Z' can only have come from Chatfield (see note 1 on page 426).

[2]Sir Henry John Newbolt (1862–1938): poet and man of letters; served in Admiralty and Foreign Office during war; accepted request of CID to complete Vols IV and V of *Naval Operations*; once described as a 'nautical Kipling'.

[3]Colonel E. Y. Daniel RM, Secretary of Historical Section of the CID.

document of which the attached is a copy. It was not signed but the language in paragraph Z makes it quite clear that Admiral Beatty is the author.

[Signed] W. F. CLARKE

Some remarks on certain paragraphs in the various chapters

A   We did not open fire as soon as we might have done, but *X* is a slight mathematical error as 15,000 metres = 16,400 yards. If it was a mistake on our part to open fire at such a short range as (say) 16,000 yards, were we not wise to gradually open the range to make use of our larger guns? He cannot have it both ways against the BCF.

B   This statement that the GERMAN Battle Cruisers hardly suffered at all gives an incorrect impression. It is probably taken partly from Von Hase who in *Derfflinger* was unfired at for 10 minutes (see *B*, p. 97) and was also made after the action and was therefore made *relative* to the more crushing damage subsequently inflicted on them.

On neither side were 'many hits' made in this phase, the salvo which sank *Queen Mary* was the first hit she had and was half an hour after the action started. *Lion* had 4 or 5 hits on her in this period, only one of which was serious. *Lion* was firing at *Lutzow* continuously the whole of this phase and there is (to say the worst) no evidence to show she was not badly damaged during this period. An officer does not know always in action when his ship is hit and certainly Von Hase could not know anything except about his own ship. The truth is that if it had not been for the blowing up of the *Indefatigible* and *Queen Mary* which was due to the superior German *shell*, <u>not</u> shooting, the first phase would have ended very differently. The British seamen cannot be blamed for bad fighting when the cause was not in his power to remedy. Yet no mention is made of this vital fact except as an explanation of why the 5th BS did not 'sink the lot', and the reason given here is not correct, it was *not* the fuzes, but the 'burster' and 'the bad quality of the shell'.

C   If this is correct it shows that she was hit almost immediately fire was opened on her which is not inaccurate shooting.

D   This is hardly correct, the danger did not actually arise until half an hour later.

E This reads as if *Lion* made off! The actual facts are that when you are steaming 25 knots and both yourself and enemy are altering course even a few degrees you are very apt to get out of range. We had no means of knowing Hipper's course and could only find out if we were opening or closing by the gun range indicators which fluctuated rapidly with the spotting. Hipper no doubt made similar errors. It was accidental, not intentional (as suggested), that we had to cease fire for five minutes.

F While we all admit the efficiency and gallantry of the 5th BS it is neither fair, nor politic, to so obviously contrast their shooting with that of BCF. It would at once be said by the officers of 5th BS – we *may* have shot better but we had better light, were unfired at, had an easier target and more modern material.

G This is a direct allegation that Hipper was able to reopen fire, as if he was anxious to and we were not. The next lines about the fire smothering *Lion* is incomprehensible, does it refer to the fire on board the ship or to the enemy's fire? In either case it is *pure imagination* and untrue. *Lion* was of course close to *Princess Royal*, and as visible to *Lutzow* (*Lion*'s target) as *Princess Royal* was to *Derfflinger*; most of the subsequent lines are pure gush and quite unnecessary.

H (p. 100) I was not personally aware that we turned to the 'shortest possible course'. We turned 16 points because it was the natural thing to do.

I This again can be interpreted to mean that Admiral Beatty alone 'made off' while ET gallantly kept his teeth in the enemy – a most vile suggestion.

J Is equally objectionable and untrue, in fact an absolute wilful travesty of the facts.

K This might well have been written by a German. The BCF turn was neither a 'retreat' nor 'premature'.

L (p. 101) This is again absolute nonsense.

M Is entirely incorrect. *Lion* had no serious hit after the 16 point turn. The fire that broke out at this moment in Q turret was caused by the shift of wind after the turn, causing the smouldering turret cordite (or other material) to burst into flame and so ignite the full charges left in the ammunition hoists. It had *nothing whatsoever* to do with the enemy's fire.

N Is a further suggestion that Goodenough did what Admiral Beatty failed to do.

O Appears to imply that Admiral Beatty had deserted Admiral ET.

P The first admission that the Battle Cruisers had been able to accomplish anything.

Q (p. 104) It is almost amusing to see that he has erased eight words which imply that the fault in not getting *this* signal earlier was due to the *Iron Duke*.

R He entirely omits to explain that with the then low visibility it was not possible to remain in touch or in sight of the enemy Battle Fleet without being under a concentrated fire.

S (p. 107) All the little difficulties here mentioned in defence of the C-in-C are conveniently omitted in criticizing Admiral Beatty and cannot be reconciled unfortunately!

T *Warspite* had had little damage by this time (if any) the jambing [*sic*] of her helm had of course *nothing* to do with the gunfire of the enemy.

U No doubt, but who [*sic*] is it *only* the 5th BS who comes in for this well deserved praise.

V It might have been added that by this time the GERMAN Battle Cruisers were all in a bad way, in spite of the inefficiency of our fleeing Battle Cruisers.

W This statement *appears* to be rubbish.

X Another gratuitous insult to the Admiral commanding BCF. How could we know that as soon as he had brought the GERMAN BF to the C-in-C the latter had lost it again. It was no longer the main duty of BCF to alone keep in touch with the BF of the enemy when C-in-C avoided doing so by retreating.

Y This is all very pathetic. Why did he not go and look for them? It sounds like Little Bo Peep!

Z The question of this 32 pt turn is one I have always been uncertain about, but I went below for five minutes about this time to see the damage, etc, with COS looking out for me on the bridge.

AA (p. 129) This is misleading and probably also incorrect. The charts as also the statement at 'Z' are based on the rejected Harper plans. If Admiral Beatty was further to Eastward it had nothing to do with his Compass; he had correctly stationed his squadron ahead of the BF when they were steering Easterly and could not therefore help being to the 'East of the BF'.

BB (p. 132) This statement is pure conjecture and untrue. It also cannot be reconciled with BB 2 and BB 3 pp. 132–133.

CC (p. 132) Surely this is too thin, Admiral Jerram could have speedily found the BCF if he had tried to. I shall never forget our agony of mind seeing him three or four miles astern of us leading his division 4 points too much to the Eastward while we were in touch with the enemy.

DD (p. 135a) Is this correct I wonder?

244. *Jellicoe's Defence of his Conduct at Jutland*[1]

[Typed Draft – Extracts]

[Add 49041]   [Undated]

Before it is possible for anyone to realise the difficulties which confronted me as Commander-in-Chief of the Grand Fleet at the Battle of Jutland it is essential for a clear idea to be formed and continually kept in view of the two main factors to which those difficulties were entirely due.

These two factors were:–

1. The absence of even approximately correct information from the Battle Cruiser Fleet and its attendant light cruisers regarding the position, formation and strength of the High Sea Fleet.
2. The lack of visibility when the Battle Fleet came in sight of a portion of the High Sea Fleet, due largely to mist, and partly to smoke from our own battle-cruisers and other vessels.

None of my critics, nor those responsible for the compilation of the Admiralty Narrative of the battle, nor the Naval Staff which attempted to reply to my observations on that Narrative, appear to have realised to the least degree the extent to which the factors mentioned above affected my handling of the Fleet during the two hours that followed the meeting of the Grand Fleet and High Sea Fleet.

[1]This material is not included in Temple-Patterson's *Jellicoe Papers* II. It is difficult to establish its precise date and provenance. On p. 106 a note by Dreyer states 'Dictated by Jellicoe and corrected in his handwriting', and 'written before Mr Churchill's last two volumes had appeared', i.e. before 1927. It could have been part of the material which Jellicoe compiled from 1922 to be used in a revised edition of his *The Grand Fleet*, which was never published, and for the Appendix which was subsequently added to the 1924 edition of what had been *The Naval Staff Appreciation*; an Appendix which was countered by the Admiralty's counter blast, 'wherever the Appendix differs from the *Admiralty Narrative*, Their Lordships are satisfied that the *Narrative* is more in accordance with the evidence available'.

There is some excuse for civilian critics whose ignorance of naval tactics would lead to a failure on their part to recognise the necessity for information, and failing that, the necessity of a clear view of the enemy's fleet so that the Commander-in-Chief could by his own observation make up for the failure of his cruisers, to whatever cause that failure was due. There is no excuse for Naval officers of experience in fleet work. The Narrative, as is well known was drawn up by two officers, one a retired Lieutenant of little sea experience,[1] but a constant writer on naval subjects, the other a recently promoted Post Captain who however had never handled a ship at sea. Excuse may be found for these officers, perhaps by their lack of experience.

The only reason I can give for similar failure on the part of the Naval Staff of the Admiralty is that it was almost entirely composed at the time in question of officers who were serving in the Battle-Cruiser Fleet at Jutland. These officers had been in sight of the German Fleet, or a large part of it, for some two hours before the Battle Fleets met, and, of course, were fully aware of all the information which I lacked. They too, from their position well ahead of the British Battle Fleet after deployment, did not have their view of the enemy fleet obstructed, as did those in the British Battle Fleet by the smoke of the battle-cruisers, light cruisers and destroyers ahead of the Battle Fleet. Their range of vision was limited only by the misty weather, and the conditions were nothing like so difficult in the way of visibility as were those confronting me as Commander-in-Chief in the centre of the Battle Fleet. The result may well be that these officers could not get out of their minds their own experience during the battle, and, when replying to my observations, they still looked at the conditions as they saw them, and failed to grasp the great difference in those conditions which made the situation so difficult for me.

It is undoubtedly no easy matter to divorce from one's mind when considering the handling of the Grand Fleet before and during the Battle of Jutland, as well as during the night following the battle, the information which has come to light since May 31st, both from the British and German side, and there must be a tendency to forget the all-important fact that none of this information was in the hands of the Commander-in-Chief at the time.

---

[1]A. C. Dewar had retired as a Lieutenant in 1910; re-employed as a Commander in 1916 he retired after the Armistice. (See Roskill, *Beatty*, p. 332).

The Admiralty Narrative of the Battle of Jutland

A perusal of this history indicates that the main idea of the then 1st Sea Lord (Lord Beatty) and some other members of the Naval Staff, who were in the Battle of Jutland, was to glorify the work of the battle-cruisers (to which I take no exception whatever) but at the same time to belittle the work of the Grand Fleet, to which I have the strongest objection, knowing as I do, the far greater extent to which the battleships made use of the fewer opportunities presented to them than did the battle-cruisers earlier in the day. Incidentally too, the obvious object was to compare unfavourably the handling of the Battle Fleet with that of the battle-cruisers.

The compilers of the Admiralty Narrative appear to have set themselves to mislead the reader as to the deductions which could be drawn by the Commander-in-Chief from the reports he received and that there was an entire disregard of the fact that the Vice-Admiral Battle-cruiser Fleet should have made it his principal duty to keep his Commander-in-Chief informed of the enemy's position. The Commander-in-Chief's Battle Orders laid the strongest emphasis on this duty.

The Admiralty comments on my remarks[1] are an exceedingly ungenerous attempt to throw blame upon Sir Hugh Evan-Thomas for an occurrence for which Sir David Beatty was entirely to blame, and which resulted, not only in the loss of 2 of our battle-cruisers, but also the escape of the enemy's battle-cruisers from almost certain destruction. The signals made by the *Galatea* at 2.39 pm and 2.51 pm (Signals 1435 and 1445 J.P.) by the *Nottingham* at 3.24 pm (Signal 1522 J.P.) and by the *Galatea* at 3.25 pm (Signal 1515 J.P.) unquestionably gave Sir David Beatty ample warning that there were other enemy vessels in his vicinity besides the light cruisers and destroyers first sighted, and his proper course was to concentrate his heavy ships. Had he done so, the overwhelming and always accurate fire of the 5th Battle Squadron, combined with the fire of his battle-cruisers, must have resulted in the practical annihilation of the German battle-cruisers before the High Sea Fleet battleships could have come to their assistance. Had I foreseen the attitude which Sir David Beatty subsequently adopted in regard to this incident I should have certainly pointed out in my original despatch the error of which he had been guilty.

*   *   *   *

[1]See *Jellicoe II*, Document 143, Jellicoe to Admiralty, 27 Nov 1922.

245. *Evan-Thomas to Jellicoe*

[Holograph]

[Add 49037]   Cople House,
                                                            Bedford
                                                            June 30 1926

My Dear Commander-in-Chief,

. . . I have never complained and have never even read what the Admiralty said about me (advised to leave it all alone by my doctors). I, as C-in-C The Nore, just before I had my stroke, or partial stroke, went up to see the First Lord (Amery) about the 1st Admiralty [—] of Jutland. I spoke to him for some three or four minutes, I think less, when he was informed that he *must* see the *First Sea Lord* — so I was shown out.

And was so worried at the way things were going on that I was knocked over.[1]

I have never been given a chance of correcting the things that those acting under the First Sea Lord had been writing. Nowhere is it mentioned that no signal had been made to me to turn (at that time only a destroyer had been sighted) and we all thought that we were intended to go on & that a signal would be made to us directly how to steer to cut something off, was our idea. He made a signal to me to turn 16 points to Starboard later, and because I obeyed and went over a bit to get a little between his badly damaged squadron and the enemy, he suggests that I shouldn't have got behind, without one word to me of any kind [*sic*].

I don't know that I ever had known a case before in the Navy where a man who was in command and made a bad mistake, not seeing that his forces were concentrated (more or less) for battle, is able to use his position to shelter himself and throw blame on others who were mad keen to do anything possible to obey his slightest wish.

The Admiral in command must be to blame if a signal is not made. It was made when *Tiger* asked. It was quite out of the question for us to see flags. The smoke was black and previous signals had been made by searchlight. A great mistake was made by the Admiral commanding (Admiral, of course including his Staff) but he must be responsible. No attempt seems to have been made by him to concentrate his force — well, I will say no more.

[1] Not literally.

* * * *

I apologise for inflicting this long story on you,
Every good wish
yours sincerely,
HUGH EVAN-THOMAS

246. *Evan-Thomas to the Editor of The Times*

[Press Cutting 16 Feb 1927]

[Add 52506]   Charlton House
Shaftesbury
Feb 13 1927

The Battle of Jutland

In your issue of February 9th is a portion of an account of the
Battle of Jutland. This account is written by Mr Winston Churchill, who holds one of the most important positions in the Government, and therefore his writings are read by a very large number
of people, quite apart from the fact that he is such an able writer.

As that first part of the battle of Jutland concerns me, and as
no remarks from me have ever been asked for, by either the Chief
of the Naval Staff or those under him, who I presume have written
the so-called official account, it appears necessary for another and
more detailed account to be given of the time when German light
craft had just been sighted by *Galatea*. The signal for 'Steam for
full speed' had been made and all the battle-cruisers were drawing
their coal fires forward and making a tremendous smoke, which
made it impossible to distinguish flag signals from the Fifth Battle
Squadron, stationed five miles off, except possibly on very rare
occasions. Had signals been made by searchlight, as they had been
on other occasions on the same day, they would have been seen
immediately.

So far as the Rear-Admiral commanding Fifth Battle Squadron
was concerned he knew that two enemy light cruisers had been
reported, and that the battle-cruisers were turning, but to what
course it was impossible to see; and they rushed off into space
without his having received a signal from the Vice-Admiral in
command, neither searchlight nor wireless having been used by
Lion.

The only way I could account for no signals having been
received by me was that the Vice-Admiral was going to signal
another course to Fifth Battle Squadron — possibly to get the

enemy light cruisers between us. Anyway, if he wished us to turn, the searchlight would have done it in a moment. It was not until *Tiger* asked *Lion* by wireless whether the signal to turn was to be made to *Barham*, that the Vice-Admiral seemed to realise the situation. But those lost minutes turned out afterwards to be a most serious matter. After all, isn't it one of the fundamental principles of naval tactics that an admiral makes sure that his orders are understood by distant parts of his fleet before rushing into space, covered by a smoke screen? Also, if, as I believe, he knew that German heavy ships were at sea, should he not have seen that his most important ships were at hand?

With regard to the remarks of Mr Churchill about the later stages of the Battle of Jutland, I would submit, as one of the Flag Officers who were [*sic*] there, that they are a mixture of armchair criticism, want of vision from a sailor's point of view, and utter disregard of the effects of smoke, gun fire and fog, added to a terribly partisan account.

247.   *Lieutenant Cdr O. Frewen to Evan-Thomas*

[Holograph]

[Add 52504]   94 Mount Street,
                                                    London W1
                                                    Feb 22 1927

Very many thanks for your most interesting letter which forms a grim pendant to the Harper Report. I retired in September 1919 & went over to Canada. I returned in December, and desiring a personal copy, called on my old chief, Capt Harper, then at the Hydrographic Dept, and asked him what about it. He told me this: that the proofs, on their return from the printers, were circulated, *pro forma*, to the members of the Board & were passed by them. Lord Wester Wemyss noted his copy for publication, but, as he was on the point of being relieved by Beatty as First Sea Lord, left him the copy as being of immediate interest. Beatty immediately revoked the passing for publication, blue-pencilled extensively, & sent it back to Harper with directions to make the changes indicated.

As these were in many instances entirely at variance with the logs, track-charts & signal logs, Harper meekly replied that he would be pleased to do so upon the written and signed authority of the First Sea Lord! Ensued months of wrangles, at one stage of which, Beatty's Signal Commander, who was a go-between, did shoot himself![1] At the end of it, Harper, unyielding to the end, retired to Devonshire with a nervous breakdown. Lord Jellicoe, whom I had met in Ottawa, warned the First Lord (Long) that if the Harper Report was published with any amendments or corrections, not sanctioned by Captain Harper himself, he would have questions asked in Parliament. (Lord Jellicoe wrote me this himself.) Accordingly, the Harper Report, since it could not be garbled, was suppressed.

The Dewar brothers were then turned on to write a Staff précis of the battle on the lines desired. They sailed in gaily but got bogged down in a month among the masses of battle-cruisers' signals and reports. They obviously couldn't go to Harper to get disentangled. *I* was known as a 'hostile witness', so they went to young Pollen,[2] nephew of A. H. Pollen, the scribe, who was the only person who knew the battle inside out at that time, and was helping Sir Julian Corbett in his 'Naval Operations' with our Harper Report track-charts. I called on Pollen soon after, who told me the story & he said, 'I disentangled them all right and got them back to the bare bones of fact, and of course when you cut out the cackle and get down to the bare bones, you are left with — The Harper Report'. So that particular essay missed fire too.

Then, much later, after the Corbett narrative in fact, came the eventual Staff History, which neither you nor I have troubled to read. In the last resort, I think Beatty has been forced merely to stifle information until the public has lost interest in the whole thing, but there is sufficient information available to render it possible for a serious student to get at the facts (with great labour) & the public never will be able to grasp the lessons of the battle from any ten-minutes dissertation. Future reputations will rest on intellectual analyses of the tactics employed, by unprejudiced students, and within the [sic] hundred years History will see the rehabilitation of Jellicoe in even greater measure than the early XX century saw the rehabilitation of Lord Barham's reputation. Even now I think, the impression of 'the man in the street' is that the Press & politicians applaud Beatty but that the Navy itself is 'pro-Jellicoe'. And a letter like yours adds to that impression.

You yourself, of course, are on a top pinnacle. Your Senior

[1]Seymour had in fact thrown himself from a cliff near Brighton (see Roskill, *Admiral of the Fleet*, p. 316 and n).
[2]Lieut Commander J. F. H. Pollen, see note 2 on page 454.

Officer, meeting the enemy with 10 ships to 5, ignored your presence, put his 4 most powerful ships out of action & then, due to inefficiency of pre-concentration arrangements (surely the Admiral's fault) suffered the enemy to put two more of his ships out of action, and he then turned North again, which enabled you to come into action while he went out of it. And, I note with amusement, that it was at *this* stage that even Winston claims that most of the damage was done to the enemy! You then got into the hottest corner of the lot at deployment.

There is not the least doubt that as a squadron, the 5th BS were the heroes of the day, but they sailed in company with the battle-cruisers, and, through the absolute silence they have maintained ever since, they might well have been supposed to share the battle-cruisers' opinion, had not your letter proved dramatically the very opposite; that is why I welcomed it as infinitely valuable. We all understand your silence — especially remembering the little good that came of Lord Charles Beresford's reprimand to Sir Percy Scott[1] — but, when the gentlemen are silent with a self-seeker loudly advertising himself in their midst, the ignorant public are apt to be deceived & suppose that judgement has gone by default. And that is the pity of it . . .

. . . I took the liberty of writing to you because I am in a way, a link in the chain of knowledge of the secret history of Jutland, However acutely I suffer from 'juniority'! . . .

248. *Beatty: Minute on the Publication of the Harper Record*

[ADM.1/8722/290/27]   10.5.27

To clear up the supposed mystery the best form of publication would be a copy of the original typescript submitted by Captain Harper on October 2nd 1919, but it is understood that no copy is available in the Admiralty.

Since it is not available, it is considered that the next best course is to publish Proof Copy No 3 in its original and *uncorrected* form, without any corrections whatever, not even printers' corrections.

---

[1]In 1907 Beresford, as C-in-C Channel, had publicly reprimanded Scott, then Rear-Admiral commanding 1st Cruiser Squadron, for sending what he regarded as an insulting signal. This added to the Beresford-Fisher feud which was then splitting the Navy. Geoffrey Bennett (1968), *Charlie B: A Biography of Admiral Lord Beresford*, London, Chapter 10 gives the whole story.

Copy No 3 is selected out of those available because it has been subjected to fewer corrections than the others: it would seem that the corrections that do appear, in red ink or typed slips, comprise the criticisms on the text which had been made by the Sea Lords up to the date (May 1920).

A contemporary précis of these exists in First Sea Lord's office.

With regard to the diagrams: it would entail a large expense, and would add greatly to the cost of the book to reprint the diagrams in colour, and it is suggested that they should not be published, but could be on view to accredited Press representatives by written application to the Secretary of the Admiralty.

B

Further Minute

[Holograph]

Secretary

I concur in the draft Preface as amended by you.

Now that publication has been decided upon, I consider the matter should be pressed forward with the least possible delay.

I should be glad if you would inform me the earliest date by which it can be published.

B. 10/5

[Noted] Ready for publication to Parliament Tuesday 31 May.

249. *Harper to Frewen*

[Holograph Copy]

[Rosk 3/11]   [Extract]   11 am
Hawkhurst, Kent
23.12.1944

*   *   *   *

It is amusing to think of you working under A. C. Dewar; — an opportunist he was [*sic*]. There is nothing he can tell me, but a deal I could tell him about his so-called 'History of Jutland'. I will tell you briefly, *for your own information*. This 'History' was officially styled a 'Staff Appreciation'. The Staff (!) was A. C. and K. Dewar who wrote what Beatty told them to do. At first, 12 numbered copies were issued to Board of Admiralty etc, and immediately it was issued, the Board suppressed it, because it was flagrantly inaccurate. This was long before Madden went to Admiralty. All copies were then recalled and all were returned, except that issued to Beatty, who up to 1932 had refused, in spite of 3 applications, to return his. He left Admiralty in 1927.

I have documentary evidence (reported by me to DNI) that in August 1932 Beatty invited Langhorne Gibson (USA),[1] who was collaborating with me in writing 'The Riddle of Jutland', to stay a week-end. He told him to believe nothing I said, etc, etc. He then lent him this *Secret* Book to read. Luckily he did not realise that it was a Secret Book, and he asked me to 'buy him a copy from Admiralty Library'!! I explained why this could not be done. Gibson then said, 'If I had only known, I would have sat up all night; copied the whole thing and published it in a New York paper.' At the time I hesitated to believe that Gibson had actually seen CB.0938, and Jellicoe refused to believe it either; but subsequent events proved it to be absolutely true, and Jellicoe proved this after I had provided evidence for DNI.

In regard to 'Battle Orders', Dewar has not had a chance to study Jellicoe's papers. The 'Battle Orders', said by Bros Dewar to cancel Jellicoe's useless ones, were drawn up by Jellicoe's staff on [— —] marginal notes made by J. and then sent for printing. The 'issue' was not actually made until B. took command. B. took all credit, J. actually produced them.

*   *   *   *

---

[1]The American historian Langhorne Gibson, joint author with Harper of *The Riddle of Jutland: an Authentic History* (London, 1924); Marder, *From the Dreadnought* V, p. 376, describes it as 'not free from bias'.

LIST OF DOCUMENTS AND SOURCES

Collections used

Add: *Additional Manuscripts, the British Library*
  Jellicoe Papers: 49008, 49014, 49037, 53838
  Evan-Thomas Papers: 52504–6
  Harper Papers: 5477–9
  Long Papers: 624–6
ADM: *Admiralty Papers, The Public Record Office*
  ADM 1 Secretary's Letters
  ADM 116 Cases
  ADM 167 Board Minutes
AIR: *Air Ministry Papers, The Public Record Office*
  AIR 8/17 CAS Archives
Amery: Papers of L. S. Amery; in the possession of the Rt Hon Lord Amery of Lustleigh
Baldwin: Papers of Stanley Baldwin; University of Cambridge Library
BGMN: Papers of William, 1st Viscount Bridgeman; Churchill College Cambridge
BL: Papers of A Bonar Law; House of Lords Record Office
BTY: Papers of Admiral of the Fleet Earl Beatty; National Maritime Museum
Cab.: Cabinet Papers, The Public Record Office
Cab. 53/1: Chiefs of Staff Committee Papers, The Public Record Office
DEW: Papers of Vice-Admiral K. G. B. Dewar, National Maritime Museum
DEY: Papers of Sir Eustace Tennyson d'Eyncourt, National Maritime Museum
Keyes: Papers of Admiral of the Fleet Lord Keyes, The British Library
Lee: *A Good Innings: The Private Papers of Viscount Lee of Fareham*; ed. Alan Clark (1974)

480

Ll.G: Papers of David Lloyd George, House of Lords Record Office

RA Geo V: Royal Archives Windsor Castle

ROSK: Papers of Captain S. W. Roskill, Churchill College Cambridge

SLGF: Papers of Sir Shane Leslie and Captain Sir Bryan Godfrey-Faussett, Churchill College Cambridge

PART I

1.	Beatty: Notes on Armistice terms	21 Oct 1918	BTY/7/11/2
2.	Wemyss to Beatty	10 Nov 1918	BTY/13/14/20
3.	Wemyss to Beatty	12/13 Nov 1918	BTY/13/14/22
4.	Beatty to Admiralty on Command Structure	Dec 1918	BTY/7/10/15
5.	Beatty to Admiralty on post-war naval strength	Dec 1918	BTY/7/10/16
6.	Phillimore to Beatty	25 Jan 1919	BTY/13/30/2
7.	Long to Beatty	25 Feb 1919	BTY/13/28/11
8.	Wemyss to Beatty	28 Feb 1919	BTY/13/40/29
9.	Beatty to Wemyss	1 Mar 1919	BTY/13/40/30
10.	Long to Beatty	13 Mar 1919	BTY/13/28/3
11.	Beatty to Long	15 Mar 1919	BTY/13/28/4
12.	Long to Beatty	21 Mar 1919	BTY/13/28/6
13.	Beatty to Long	25 Mar 1919	BTY/13/28/7
14.	Beatty to Admiralty on disposal of German Fleet	4 Apr 1919	BTY/13/29/17
15.	Beatty to Grand Fleet	5 Apr 1919	BTY/7/10/20
16.	Admiralty to Beatty	5 Apr 1919	BY/7/10/22
17.	Beatty to Eugénie Godfrey-Faussett	19 Apr 1919	SLGF/14/1/B
18.	Churchill to Lloyd George	1 May 1919	Ll.G/F/8/3/46
19.	Long to Lloyd George	5 May 1919	Ll.G/F/33/2/54
20.	Beatty to Eugénie Godfrey-Faussett	22 May 1919	SLGF/15/2
21.	Naval Staff Memorandum on lessons of War	10 June 1919	BTY/8/1/9
22.	Long to Stamfordham	14 June 1919	RA Geo VO1474/3
23.	Long to Lloyd George	15 June 1919	Ll.G/F/33/2/54
24.	Henry Wilson to Lloyd George	16 July 1919	Ll.G/F/47/8/27

PART II

46a.	d'Eyncourt to Beatty on shipbuilding problems	3 Dec 1920	BTY/8/2/27
47.	Beatty to Long	9 Dec 1920	BTY/12/28/29
48.	Long to Beatty	10 Dec 1920	BTY/13/28/31
49.	Beatty: Memorandum for Cabinet on capital ship building	10 Dec 1920	ADM 116/1176/275
50.	Long to Lloyd George	13 Dec 1920	BTY/13/28/36
51.	Beatty to Long	13 Dec 1920	BTY/13/28/35
52.	N. J. S. Barnes to Long	13 Dec 1920	BTY/13/28/39
53.	Lloyd George to Long	14 Dec 1920	Add: 62425
54.	Beatty: Memorandum rejecting capital ship obsolescence	14 Dec 1920	BTY/8/2/18
55.	Beatty: Memorandum to Cabinet on Naval Construction	14–15 Dec 1920	ADM 116/1175
56.	Beatty: Memorandum for CID on armour plate production	15 Dec 1920	ADM 116/1175
57.	Beatty to Long: Report on CID meeting, 14 Dec 1920	15 Dec 1920	BTY/13/28/41
58.	Churchill to Beatty	17 Dec 1920	BTY/8/2/2
59.	Chatfield to Beatty	20 Dec 1920	BTY/8/2/2
60.	Beatty to Churchill	22 Dec 1920	BTY/8/2/2
61.	S. H. Wilson to Beatty: List of witnesses at Bonar Law committee	1 Jan 1921	BTY/8/2/4–5
62.	Questions for DCNS at Bonar Law committee	Jan 1921	BTY/8/2/9
63.	Beatty: Notes for Bonar Law committee	Jan 1921	BTY/8/2/10
64.	Questionnaire for Rear-Admiral Hall at Bonar Law committee	Jan 1921	BTY/8/3/19
65.	Beatty to his wife	3 Jan 1921	BTY/17/54/2
66.	Beatty to Long	3 Jan 1921	BTY/13/28/49
67.	Plans Division: Paper on war with USA and Japan	4 Jan 1921	BTY/8/1/7–8

68.	Roger Bellairs to Beatty: Progress of Bonar Law committee	8 Jan 1921	BTY/8/3/16
69.	Naval Staff Memorandum for Bonar Law committee	13 Jan 1921	BTY/8/3/22
70.	Beatty to his wife	23 Jan 1921	BTY/17/54/27–30
71.	Beatty: Notes on technical evidence at Bonar Law committee	Jan 1921	BTY/8/3/1
72.	Beatty: Concluding remarks at Bonar Law committee	27 Jan 1921	Cab. 16/37/555–9
73.	Beatty to Eugénie Godfrey-Faussett	2 Feb 1921	SLGF 15/4/3
74.	Long to Beatty	12 Feb 1921	BTY/13/28/52
75.	Churchill: rejection of draft report of Bonar Law committee	13 Feb 1921	BTY/8/4/14
76.	Beatty's secretary's comments on draft report	14 Feb 1921	BTY/8/4/17
77.	Beatty to his wife	15 Feb 1921	BTY/17/55/9–10
78.	Beatty to his wife	16 Feb 1921	BTY/17/55/13–14
79.	Beatty to his wife	18 Feb 1921	BTY/17/55/20–22
80.	Beatty to his wife	23 Feb 1921	BTY/17/55/37–38
81.	Admiralty Memorandum to CID on Auxiliary Services of Fleet (Cruisers, Destroyers, etc)	23 Feb 1921	BTY/8/2/13
82.	Beatty to Long on draft report	1 Mar 1921	BTY/8/4/10
83.	Lady Lee of Fareham's Diary	Mar–Apr 1921	Alan Clark (ed.) (1974), *The Private Papers of Lord Lee of Fareham*, London
84.	Admiralty Remarks on draft report	Mar 1921	BTY/8/4/3
85.	Beatty: Memorandum on draft report	10 Mar 1921	BTY/8/4/16
86.	Beatty to Long	16 Mar 1921	Add: 62426
87.	Lord Lee: Paper on Naval Staff Organisation	1921	Parl. Papers Cmd. 1343

87a.	Beatty's Address to Imperial Conference	4 July 1921	Cab. 32/2
88.	Beatty to Eugénie Godfrey-Faussett	July 1921	SLGF/15/4/8
89.	Beatty to 1st Lord: On naval air requirements	21 Sep 1921	ADM 1/8611/155
90.	Beatty to his wife	27–28 Sep 1921	BTY/17/57/13–14
91.	Beatty: Note to CID on RN/RAF relationship	7 Oct 1921	ADM 1/8511
92.	Beatty at Conference on Naval Defence of Ireland	13 Oct 1921	Ll.G/F/25/2/32
93.	Beatty to King George V	12 Nov 1921	RA Geo V.O 1735/741
94.	Balfour to Lloyd George (Washington Conference)	13 Nov 1921	ADM 1/8630
95.	Beatty to Admiralty	15 Nov 1921	ADM 116/3445/93
96.	Balfour to Cabinet and CID	17 Nov 1921	ADM 116/3445
97.	Beatty to DCNS	18 Nov 1921	ADM 116/3445/104
98.	Beatty to Controller	19 Nov 1921	ADM 116/3445/105
99.	Lloyd George to Balfour	1 Dec 1921	ADM 116/3445/73–4
100.	Beatty to Cabinet	10 Dec 1921	ADM 116/1776
101.	Beatty to his wife	20 Jan 1922	BTY/17/58/19–21
102.	Beatty to his wife	27 Jan 1922	BTY/17/58/40–41
103.	Beatty: Memorandum on reduction of Naval Staff	28 Jan 1922	ADM 116/2105
104.	Beatty to his wife	31 Jan 1922	BTY/17/58/55–56
105.	Beatty to his wife	1 Feb 1922	BTY/17/59/1–3
106.	Admiralty Memorandum to CID on RN/RAF relations	6 Feb 1922	Cab. 21/225
107.	Beatty to his wife	6 Feb 1922	BTY/17/59/15–16
107a.	Beatty to his wife	19 Feb 1922	BTY/17/59/23–24
108.	Beatty to his wife	20 Feb 1922	BTY/17/59/29–32
109.	Beatty to his wife	22 Feb 1922	BTY/17/59/36–37
110.	Beatty to his wife	1 Mar 1922	BTY/17/60/1–3
110a.	Beatty to his wife	11 Mar 1922	BTY/17/60/21–24
111.	Beatty–Churchill notes on RN–RAF relations	17 Mar 1922	Cab. 16/48

PART III

130.	Sea Lords' Memorandum on Balfour Report	9 Nov 1923	Cab. 21/267B
131.	Beatty: Speech at Lord Mayor's Banquet	9 Nov 1923	BTY/11/8/23
132.	Admiralty Minute to Air Ministry	13 Nov 1923	ADM 116/2236
133.	Beatty to his wife	23 Jan 1924	BTY/17/64/4–7
134.	Beatty to his wife	25 Jan 1924	BTY/17/64/9–10
135.	Alan Lascelles to Owen Morshead	3 June 1952	RA Geo V K.1918/184A
136.	Beatty to his wife	26 Jan 1924	BTY/17/64/11–14
137.	Beatty to his wife	undated	BTY/17/64/35–42
138.	Notes of Sea Lords' Meeting on Cruiser Programme	28 Jan 1924	BTY/8/5/21
139.	Beatty to his wife	31 Jan 1924	BTY/17/64/29–34
140.	Beatty to his wife	1 Feb 1924	BTY/17/65/2–3
141.	Beatty to his wife	2 Feb 1924	BTY/17/65/4–11
142.	Beatty to his wife	4 Feb 1924	BTY/17/65/18–21
143.	Beatty to his wife	6 Feb 1924	BTY/17/65/23–24
144.	Beatty to his wife	8 Feb 1924	BTY/17/65/35–38
145.	Beatty to his wife	15 Feb 1924	BTY/17/65/58–59
146.	Beatty to his wife	21 Feb 1924	BTY/17/65/78–79
147.	Beatty to his wife	23 Feb 1924	BTY/17/65/88–91
148.	Beatty: Minute on Arms Limitation	23 Apr 1924	ADM 1/8683/131
149.	Beatty to his wife	9 Jan 1925	BTY/17/69/18–21
150.	Beatty to his wife	22 Jan 1925	BTY/17/69/76–79
151.	Beatty to his wife	26 Jan 1925	BTY/17/69/98–99
152.	Beatty to Bridgeman	27 Jan 1925	BTY/8/7/2
153.	Beatty to his wife	28 Jan 1925	BTY/17/69/102–4
154.	Beatty to his wife	29 Jan 1925	BTY/17/69/107–12
155.	Beatty to his wife	30 Jan 1925	BTY/17/69/115–20
156.	Beatty to his wife	31 Jan 1925	BTY/17/69/123–26
157.	Beatty to his wife	2 Feb 1925	BTY/17/70/3–5
158.	Beatty to his wife	5 Feb 1925	BTY/17/70/12–13
159.	Beatty to Bridgeman	8 Feb 1925	BGMN/3
160.	Beatty to Bridgeman	8 [Feb 1925]	BGMN/3
161.	Beatty to his wife	14 Feb 1925	BTY/17/70/40–43
162.	Beatty to his wife	20 Feb 1925	BTY/17/70/65–66
163.	Beatty to his wife	27 Feb 1925	BTY/17/70/94–95
164.	Beatty to Eugénie Godfrey-Faussett	Apr 1925	SLGF/15/6/2

165.	Birkenhead Committee, 8th Meeting	30 June 1925	Cab. 27/273
166.	Beatty to his wife	7 July 1925	BTY/17/71/36–39
167.	Hankey to Beatty	10 July 1925	BTY/8/8/1
168.	Beatty to his wife	10 July 1925	BTY/17/71/52–54
169.	Churchill to Beatty	10 Aug 1925	BTY/8/7/1
170.	Beatty to Churchill	26 Aug 1925	BTY/8/7/1
171.	Chiefs of Staff Committee, 23rd Meeting	5 Nov 1925	Cab. 53/1
172.	Beatty: Speech at Lord Mayor's Banquet	9 Nov 1925	BTY/11/8/22
173.	Bridgeman Diary Extracts	Jan 1926	Bridgeman Papers
174.	Beatty: Minute on *Naval Review* Censorship	5 Feb 1926	ADM 1/8708/226
175.	Beatty to his wife	15 Feb 1926	BTY/17/72/34–35
176.	Admiralty Board Minute on *Naval Review* Censorship	25 Feb 1926	ADM 167/73
177.	Beatty to his wife	26 Feb 1926	BTY/17/72/75–77
178.	Beatty to Baldwin: Notes on China and Japan	1 Mar 1926	BTY/8/8/3
179.	Beatty to Baldwin: on Fleet Air Arm	3 Mar 1926	Baldwin 2/306ff
180.	COS: 27th Meeting	11 Mar 1926	Cab. 53/1
181.	Beatty to his wife	11 Mar 1926	BTY/17/73/30–33
182.	COS: 28th Meeting	22 Apr 1926	Cab. 53/1
183.	Hankey to Beatty: On role of COS Committee	26 May 1926	BTY/8/1/3
184.	COS: 30th Meeting	27 May 1926	Cab. 53/1
185.	COS: Review of Imperial Defence	22 June 1926	Cab. 4/15
186.	Beatty to Keyes: possibility of his retirement	31 Aug 1926	Keyes MSS S6/5
187.	Keyes to Bridgeman	8 Sep 1926	BGMN/1
188.	Beatty to his wife	26 Sep 1926	BTY/17/74/2–7
189.	Beatty to his wife	30 Sep 1926	BTY/17/74/12–19
190.	Beatty to his wife	19 Oct 1926	BTY/17/74/99–102
191.	Beatty to his wife	21 Oct 1926	BTY/17/74/105–110

PART IV

235.	Haggard (DTSD) to Beatty	26 July 1922	BTY/9/5/2
236.	Keyes (DCNS) & Chatfield (ACNS): Minutes on *Naval Staff Appreciation*	14 Aug 1922	BTY/9/5/2
236a.	Beatty: comments on Corbett's Vol III	21 Dec 1922	BTY/9/4/1–3
237.	Jellicoe to Frewen	12 Feb 1923	Add: 53738
238.	Amery Diary	25 June 1923	Amery Papers
239.	H. G. Adams to Evan-Thomas	22 July 1923	Add: 52504
240.	Amery Diary	3 Aug 1923	Amery Papers
241.	Evan-Thomas to Haggard	14 Aug 1923	Add: 52504
242.	Madden to Evan-Thomas	19 Aug 1923	Add: 52504
242a.	Beatty to K. G. B. Dewar	23 Apr 1925	DEW/3
243.	W. F. Clarke: Comments on Beatty's views on Corbett's Jutland chapters	Undated	BTY/9/9/12
244.	Jellicoe: Defence of his conduct at Jutland	Undated	Add: 49041
245.	Evan-Thomas to Jellicoe	30 June 1926	Add: 49037
246.	Evan-Thomas to *The Times*	13 Feb 1927	Add: 52506
247.	Frewen to Evan-Thomas	22 Feb 1927	Add: 52504
248.	Beatty: Minute on publication of Harper *Record*	10 May 1927	ADM 1/8722/290/27
249.	Harper to Frewen	23 Dec 1944	ROSK/3/11

INDEX

[Ranks are those then held. Distinguished careers are outlined in the footnotes.]

Navy Records Society
(Founded 1893)

The Navy Records Society was established for the purpose of printing unpublished manuscripts and rare works of naval interest. Membership of the Society is open to all who are interested in naval history, and any person wishing to become a member should apply to the Hon. Secretary, c/o Barclays Bank Plc, Chatsworth House, 66/70 St. Mary Axe, London EC3A 8BD, United Kingdom. The annual subscription is £15, which entitles the member to receive one free copy of each work issued by the Society in that year, and to buy earlier issues at reduced prices.

A list of works in print, available to members only, is shown below; very few copies are left of those marked with an asterisk. Prices for works in print are available on application to Mrs. Annette Gould, 5, Goodwood Close, Midhurst, West Sussex GU29 9JG, United Kingdom, to whom all enquiries concerning works in print should be sent. Those marked 'TS' and 'SP' are published for the Society by Temple Smith and Scolar Press, and are available to non-members from the Ashgate Publishing Group, Gower House, Croft Road, Aldershot, Hampshire GU11 3HR. Those marked 'A & U' are published by George Allen & Unwin, and are available to non-members only through bookshops.

Vols. 1 and 2. *State Papers relating to the Defeat of the Spanish Armada, Anno 1588* Vols I & II, ed, Professor J. K. Laughton. TS.

Vol. 11. *Papers relating to the Spanish War, 1585–87*, ed. Julian S. Corbett. TS.

Vol. 16. *Logs of the Great Sea Fights, 1794–1805*, Vol. I, ed. Vice-Admiral Sir T. Sturges Jackson.

Vol. 18. *Logs of the Great Sea Fights, 1794–1805*, Vol. II, ed. Vice-Admiral Sir T. Sturges Jackson.

Vol. 20. *The Naval Miscellany*, Vol. I, ed. Professor J. K. Laughton.

Vol. 31. *The Recollections of Commander James Anthony Gardner, 1775–1814*, ed. Admiral Sir R. Vesey Hamilton and Professor J. K. Laughton.

Vol. 32. *Letters and Papers of Charles, Lord Barham, 1758–1813*, Vol. I. ed. Sir J. K. Laughton.

Vol. 38. *Letters and Papers of Charles, Lord Barham, 1758–1813*, Vol. II, ed. Sir J. K. Laughton.

Vol. 39. *Letters and Papers of Charles, Lord Barham, 1758–1813*, Vol. III, ed. Sir J. K. Laughton.

Vol. 40. *The Naval Miscellany*, Vol. II, ed. Sir J. K. Laughton.

Vol. 41. *Papers relating to the First Dutch War, 1652–54*, Vol. V, ed. C. T. Atkinson.

Vol. 42. *Papers relating to the Loss of Minorca in 1756*, ed. Captain H. W. Richmond.

Vol. 43. *The Naval Tracts of Sir William Monson*, Vol. III, ed. M. Oppenheim.

Vol. 45. *The Naval Tracts of Sir William Monson*, Vol. IV, ed. M. Oppenheim.

*Vol. 46. *The Private Papers of George, Second Earl Spencer*, Vol. I, ed. Julian S. Corbett.

Vol. 47. *The Naval Tracts of Sir William Monson*, Vol. V, ed. M. Oppenheim.

Vol. 49. *Documents relating to Law and Custom of the Sea*, Vol. I, ed. R. G. Marsden.

Vol. 50. *Documents relating to Law and Custom of the Sea*, Vol. II, ed. R. G. Marsden.

Vol. 52. *The Life of Admiral Sir John Leake*, Vol. I, ed. G. A. R. Callender.

Vol. 53. *The Life of Admiral Sir John Leake*, Vol. II, ed. G. A. R. Callender.

Vol. 54. *The Life and Works of Sir Henry Mainwaring*, Vol. I, ed. G. E. Manwaring.

Vol. 60. *Samuel Pepys's Naval Minutes*, ed. Dr. J. R. Tanner.

Vol. 65. *Boteler's Dialogues*, ed. W. G. Perrin.

Vol. 66. *Papers relating to the First Dutch War, 1652–54*, Vol. VI, ed. C. T. Atkinson.

Vol. 67. *The Byng Papers*, Vol. I, ed. W. C. B. Tunstall.

Vol. 68. *The Byng Papers*, Vol. II, ed. W. C. B. Tunstall.

Corrigenda to *Papers relating to the First Dutch War, 1652–54*, ed. Captain A. C. Dewar.

Vol. 70. *The Byng Papers*, Vol. III, ed. W. C. B. Tunstall.

*Vol. 71. *The Private Papers of John, Earl of Sandwich*, Vol. II, ed. G. R. Barnes and Lt Cdr J. H. Owen.

Vol. 73. *The Tangier Papers of Samuel Pepys*, ed. Edwin Chappell.

Vol. 74. *The Tomlinson Papers*, ed. J. G. Bullocke.

Vol. 77. *Letters and Papers of Admiral The Hon. Samuel Barrington*, Vol. I, ed. D. Bonner-Smith.

Vol. 79. *The Journals of Sir Thomas Allin, 1660–1678*, Vol. I, ed. R. C. Anderson.

Vol. 80. *The Journals of Sir Thomas Allin, 1660–1678*, Vol. II, ed. R. C. Anderson.

Vol. 89. *The Sergison Papers, 1688–1702*, ed. Cdr R. D. Merriman.

Vol. 104. *The Navy and South America, 1807–1823*, ed. Professor G. S. Graham and Professor R. A. Humphreys.

Vol. 107. *The Health of Seamen*, ed. Professor C. C. Lloyd.

Vol. 108. *The Jellicoe Papers*, Vol. I, ed. A. Temple Patterson.

*Vol. 109. *Documents relating to Anson's Voyage round the World, 1740–1744*, ed. Dr. Glyndwr Williams.

Vol. 111. *The Jellicoe Papers*, Vol. II, ed. A. Temple Patterson.

Vol. 112. *The Rupert and Monck Letterbook, 1666*, ed. Rev. J. R. Powell and E. K. Timings.

Vol. 113. *Documents relating to the Royal Naval Air Service*, Vol. I, ed. Captain S. W. Roskill.

Vol. 114. *The Siege and Capture of Havana, 1762*, ed. Professor David Syrett.

*Vol. 115. *Policy and Operations in the Mediterranean, 1912–14*, ed. E. W. R. Lumby.

Vol. 116. *The Jacobean Commissions of Enquiry, 1608 & 1618*, ed. Dr. A. P. McGowan.

Vol. 117. *The Keyes Papers*, Vol. I, ed. Dr Paul G. Halpern.

Vol. 119. *The Manning of the Royal Navy: Selected Public Pamphlets 1693–1873*, ed. Professor J. S. Bromley.

Vol. 120. *Naval Administration, 1715–1750*, ed. Professor D. A. Baugh.

Vol. 121. *The Keyes Papers*, Vol. II, ed. Dr Paul G. Halpern.

Vol. 122. *The Keyes Papers*, Vol. III, ed. Dr Paul G. Halpern.

Vol. 123. *The Navy of the Lancastrian Kings: Accounts and Inventories of William Soper, Keeper of the King's Ships 1422–1427*, ed. Dr Susan Rose.

Vol. 124. *The Pollen Papers: The Privately Circulated Printed Works of Arthur Hungerford Pollen, 1901–1916*, ed. Dr Jon. T. Sumida. A & U.

Vol. 125. *The Naval Miscellany*, Vol. V, ed. N. A. M. Rodger. A & U.

Vol. 126. *The Royal Navy in the Mediterranean, 1915–1918*, ed. Professor Paul G. Halpern. TS.

Vol. 127. *The Expedition of Sir John Norris and Sir Francis Drake to Spain and Portugal, 1589*, ed. Professor R. B. Wernham. TS.

Vol. 128. *The Beatty Papers*, Vol. I, 1902–1918, ed. Professor B. McL. Ranft. SP.

Vol. 129. *The Hawke Papers: A Selection: 1743–1771*, ed. Dr. Ruddock F. Mackay. SP.

Vol. 130. *Anglo-American Naval Relations 1917–1919*, ed. Dr Michael Simpson. SP.

Vol. 131. *British Naval Documents 1204–1960*, ed. John B. Hattendorf, R. J. B. Knight, A. W. H. Pearsall, N. A. M. Rodger and Geoffrey Till. *SP.*